ALSO BY THOMAS HEALY

The Great Dissent: How Oliver Wendell Holmes Changed His Mind—and Changed the History of Free Speech in America

SOUL CITY

SOUL CITY

· · · · · · · · · · ·

RACE, EQUALITY, AND
THE LOST DREAM OF
AN AMERICAN UTOPIA

· · · · · · · · · · ·

Thomas Healy

METROPOLITAN BOOKS
HENRY HOLT AND COMPANY   NEW YORK

Metropolitan Books
Henry Holt and Company
Publishers since 1866
120 Broadway
New York, New York 10271
www.henryholt.com

Metropolitan Books® and 🅜® are registered trademarks of
Macmillan Publishing Group, LLC.

Library of Congress Cataloging-in-Publication Data

Names: Healy, Thomas, author.
Title: Soul City : race, equality, and the lost dream of an American utopia/
Thomas Healy.
Other titles: Race, equality, and the lost dream of an American utopia
Description: First edition. | New York : Metropolitan Books, Henry Holt and
Company, 2021. | Includes bibliographical references and index.
Identifiers: LCCN 2020034252 (print) | LCCN 2020034253 (ebook) | ISBN
9781627798624 (hardcover) | ISBN 9781627798617 (ebook)
Subjects: LCSH: Soul City (N.C.)—History. | McKissick, Floyd B. (Floyd
Bixler), 1922–1991. | Planned communities—North Carolina—History—20th
century. | African Americans—Civil rights—North
Carolina—History—20th century. | North Carolina—Race
relations—History—20th century. | City planning—United
States—History—20th century. | Civil rights workers—North
Carolina—Biography. | Warren County (N.C.)—Biography.
Classification: LCC F264.S685 H43 2021 (print) | LCC F264.S685 (ebook) |
DDC 975.6/52—dc23
LC record available at https://lccn.loc.gov/2020034252
LC ebook record available at https://lccn.loc.gov/2020034253

Our books may be purchased in bulk for promotional, educational, or business use. Please
contact your local bookseller or the Macmillan Corporate and Premium Sales Department at
(800) 221-7945, extension 5442, or by e-mail at MacmillanSpecialMarkets@macmillan.com.

First Edition 2021

Designed by Kelly S. Too

Printed in the United States of America

1 3 5 7 9 10 8 6 4 2

In memory of Margaret L. Healy

CONTENTS

SOUL CITY

"Comes the Colored Hour"

On a sweltering summer day in 1972, Floyd McKissick led a reporter for the *New York Times* across the green fields and red clay roads of an old plantation in his home state of North Carolina. Once a thriving tobacco farm worked by a hundred enslaved people, the estate had fallen on hard times in recent decades as tobacco prices sagged and the economy of the agrarian South collapsed. Tumbledown sheds and shacks now marred the landscape, while cattle from nearby ranches grazed the fallow pastures. But there were still signs of earlier prosperity, including a white eighteenth-century mansion resting on a small hill among a stand of cedars. Strolling in the shade of these ancient trees, McKissick looked up at the house, then turned to his guest and laughed.

"I can just see 'ole massa' now," he said. "Up there on the veranda, fanning himself and watching us black folks slaving in the field—and I can't help but wonder what he might say now."

What "ole massa" might have *said* is anybody's guess, but he would certainly have been stunned by the transformation taking place around him. Where Black men and women once toiled in bondage and despair, they were now engaged in an ambitious project to complete their emancipation: the building of a new city where Black people would have a majority share of power, capital, and opportunity. Named Soul City, the project was designed to be a model of Black economic empowerment, bringing money and jobs to a region that had been left behind by the twin forces of industrialization and urbanization. In the process, its supporters hoped, it would reverse the exodus of poor Blacks from the rural South and ease the overcrowding of the northern slums.

Launched by McKissick three years earlier, Soul City had at first seemed little more than a quixotic dream, another in a long line of Black separatist fantasies. McKissick, a lawyer by profession, had risen to prominence as head of the Congress of Racial Equality, one of the foremost civil rights groups of the 1960s. He was a fiery speaker, a tenacious litigator, and a visionary civil rights leader, one of the few remaining after the assassination of Martin Luther King Jr. and the self-exile of Stokely Carmichael to Africa. But McKissick had no experience building a city and nowhere near the resources to do so. And the site he had chosen was an unlikely location for an urban utopia: five thousand acres of tapped-out farmland in Warren County, North Carolina, one of the poorest areas of the country, where 40 percent of homes lacked indoor toilets and seven out of ten adults lacked a high school diploma. One-third the size of Manhattan, the site had none of the infrastructure a viable city needs—no water or sewer systems, no paved roads, no electrical grid. And it was desolate: an hour from the nearest existing city, it lay in the middle of what one roadside billboard boldly proclaimed "Klan Country."

Perhaps the biggest obstacle was the idea itself. Although Soul City was intended to be an integrated community open to all races, McKissick made clear that his primary goal was to help Black people, especially those who were poor or unemployed. For that reason—and because of its name—Soul City was quickly branded an experiment in Black Nationalism, a sort of domestic Liberia. This played well among advocates of Black Power, whose ranks and influence had grown sharply in recent years. But to many who had fought for integration, or at least come to accept it, Soul City seemed like a step backward, not forward. As one southern newspaper put it when McKissick announced his plans, in January 1969, "How terribly tragic it would be should all civil rights roads cut in the past twenty years lead to Soul City—a Camelot built on racism."

In reality, McKissick's dream was about economic equality, not separatism. It is true that he had emerged as one of the leading spokesmen for Black Power and that his rhetoric was often divisive and inflammatory. "If white America does not respond to peaceful protest," he wrote in his 1969 book *Three-Fifths of a Man,* "Black People will be forced to work for their liberation through violent revolution." But he had also spent his entire life breaking down racial barriers—first for himself, then for his children, then for the Black community at large. It was McKissick who integrated the University of North Carolina Law School in 1951. It was McKissick whose children integrated the Durham public schools in 1958. And it was McKissick who led nonviolent protests against segregated buses, lunch counters, dime stores, ice cream parlors, swimming pools, bathrooms, water fountains, and amusement parks for two decades, enduring taunts, beatings, arrests, and humiliations, all in the name of integration. Over the years, however, he had become frustrated by the failure of the civil rights movement to bring about sustained, meaningful change. Like many Black leaders, he had come to realize that marches and demonstrations, lawsuits and legislation, could only achieve so much. For Black Americans to be truly free, he believed, they needed power—economic power, to be precise. "If a Black man has no bread in his pocket, the solution to his problem is not integration," McKissick liked to say. "It's to go get some bread." That's why, although McKissick had no desire to exclude whites, his dream was to build a city where Blacks would call the shots, where a race of people who had once been bought and sold to enrich others would finally control its own economic destiny.

And despite the obstacles he faced, that dream was no longer fantastical. Just weeks earlier, the Nixon administration had awarded Soul City a $14 million loan guarantee (the equivalent of about $87 million today) to prepare the land for development. The loan was part of a fledgling program created by Congress to finance the building of new towns across the country, and Soul City was not the only project to receive support. So far, the Department of Housing and Urban Development had approved the building of eleven new communities, from a futuristic high-rise complex near downtown Minneapolis to an eco-friendly exurb outside Houston. But Soul City was the only project located in a rural area, far from a major metropolis, and the only one led by a Black developer. And federal support had not come cheaply. In return for the loan guarantee, McKissick had changed his party affiliation from Democrat to Republican and endorsed Richard Nixon's 1972 reelection campaign. He would soon become the president's chief Black spokesman, traveling the country giving stump speeches and raising money from Black voters.

It was a bizarre political union: Nixon, the "law and order" president whose "southern strategy" had exploited racism to win white votes, and McKissick, the militant Black leader who was under surveillance by the FBI. And it raised more than a few eyebrows, with conservatives questioning Nixon's judgment and prominent Black leaders accusing McKissick of selling out. But like most political unions, it offered benefits to both sides. For Nixon, Soul City was a chance to improve his image among Black voters without risking his support among whites. Instead of embracing civil rights and an expansive welfare state, he could portray Soul City as a capitalistic solution to the problems of race and poverty. McKissick, meanwhile, desperately needed federal backing to get Soul City off the ground. Although he had secured private loans to purchase the land, investors were not exactly lining up to bankroll a speculative new town. If becoming a Republican meant he could get the money he needed for his dream—and show that Black people were capable of achieving something truly monumental—he was prepared to take whatever heat came his way.

Already the alliance was paying dividends. In June, McKissick had given the keynote address at a Black fundraiser for Nixon at the Washington Hilton. Speaking to a crowd of 2,500, he declared that it was time for Black voters to stop "sucking the sugar tit" of the Democratic Party. The event was a roaring success, bringing in a quarter million dollars and emboldening Nixon's campaign to predict that he would receive 25 percent of the Black vote in the fall election, double his share from 1968.

News of the loan guarantee had also given Soul City a jolt of momentum and credibility. Major corporations such as General Motors had begun to take the project seriously, the governor of North Carolina had offered his state's full support, and the national press had weighed in enthusiastically. An editorial in the *Washington Post* praised Soul City as "the most vital experiment yet in this country's halting struggle against the cancer of hectic urbanization," while the *New York Times* called it "a sane and practical as well as imaginative concept." Even local skeptics had come around, with one official saying Soul City was "the best thing that has happened to Warren County in the last hundred years."

Now McKissick was living with his wife and youngest daughter in a trailer on the edge of a cornfield, a far cry from the Harlem brownstone they had occupied for the past five years. They were joined by a half dozen other families, mostly Black but a few white, some with babies still in diapers. They had come from different places—New York, Boston, Washington, DC—but all for the same reason: to pursue the dream of building a new city. And after three years of planning, negotiations, and frustrating delays, they were eager to get started. The night before, they had celebrated the first annual Soul City Founders Day with a banquet at the old armory in Warrenton, the county seat. Seven hundred supporters had packed inside the unair-conditioned building, where the temperature soared above 100 degrees. But the heat did not faze those in attendance, who were there to contemplate the future, not complain about the present. They listened in rapt attention to a speech by Robert J. Brown, a Black Nixon aide and longtime friend of McKissick who had played a key role in obtaining federal backing for the project. Praising McKissick for his vision and Nixon for his willingness "to put money where mouths and promises had been before," Brown assured the crowd that, together, they were "about to transform a nineteenth-century slave plantation into a booming American city."

So as McKissick led the *Times* reporter across the grounds on that scorching July day, he had every reason to feel optimistic, even playful. His dream was finally coming to fruition. Soon construction crews and bulldozers would arrive to clear trees, pave roads, and build houses, shopping centers, schools, churches, and factories. There would be hospitals, hotels, parks, art galleries, theaters, golf courses, and a college. There was even talk of building light-rail and an airport, connecting Soul City directly with the major commercial centers of the country. And if projections held true, within three short decades a city of fifty thousand people would populate this once forsaken land.

"Yes sir," McKissick said once more, smiling to himself as much as to his guest. "I wonder what 'ole massa' would have to say now."

THIS IS THE story of a *lost* dream, so it should come as no surprise that Soul City does not have a population of fifty thousand today, that there are no hospitals or schools, golf courses or hotels. There is certainly no light-rail or airport, which means it is not especially easy to get to Soul City these days. In fact, without planning and a little effort, it can be hard to find at all.

I first made the trip in the summer of 2014, on a day nearly as hot as the one on which the *Times* reporter visited four decades earlier. As was the case then, the closest city is still Durham, an hour away, so I landed at the Raleigh-Durham airport and headed north on Interstate 85. As I left the city behind, the highway narrowed from ten lanes to four and the landscape changed quickly, with car dealerships and budget hotels giving way to the dense woods of the Carolina piedmont. About eight miles south of the Virginia border, where at one time a large green sign marked the exit for Soul City, I took the off-ramp and followed a country road past an abandoned service station and an old farmhouse. Coming to an intersection with a tin-roofed shack and another shuttered gas station, I turned left, then veered right over a single set of railroad tracks.

The area had not yet been mapped by Google, so without realizing it I followed a back route, past soybean fields and mobile homes. As I approached Soul City the first thing I saw was a squat brick-and-concrete building, brown on the bottom, tan on top. The sign read "HealthCo Medical and Dental," but I knew from my research that it had closed years earlier and was now empty inside, vandals having stripped it of copper and anything else of value. Next door stood an assisted living center, also vacant and vandalized, so I kept driving and turned onto Liberation Road, once intended to be a major thoroughfare but now just another rural highway. I passed the First Baptist Church of Soul City, a small white structure with a peaked roof, and a cluster of one-story apartment buildings before I found what I was looking for: the entrance to Green Duke Village, the first and only completed neighborhood in Soul City. It could have been the entrance to any subdivision in America: a two-lane road divided by a wide, grassy median with a wooden marker planted in the middle. But out here, amid pastures and pine groves, it looked out of place, like the set of a movie that had been left behind. And there was something else that marked it as unusual. Beyond the first sign loomed another, a concrete monolith twenty feet high with the words "Soul City" engraved beneath a large, swooping S cast in red iron and repeated three times, one above the next. Originally erected several miles away, at the entrance to the city itself, the monolith had been moved to its present location in the 2000s, years after the building of Soul City had abruptly ceased. The iron had long since rusted, leaving brown streaks on the gray concrete, while inside the O of Soul City were two pockmarks that appeared to have been made by bullets.

Just inside the entrance to Green Duke Village stood the old mansion, still shaded by the same stand of cedars, its white paint chipped and peeling, its burgundy shutters in need of repair. I turned right and followed a loop road with short cul-de-sacs radiating off both sides. There was Turner Circle, Brown Circle, Scott Circle—seemingly

The entrance to Green Duke Village, the first of eight planned residential neighborhoods in Soul City.

generic names until one remembered that this was Soul City and these roads were named for Nat Turner, John Brown, and Dred Scott. The houses were modest but pleasant, a mix of split-level and ranch styles, some with carports or garages, a few with front porches or porticoes. Dogwoods and red maples that had been planted almost forty years ago were now full-grown, giving the neighborhood a lush, tranquil feel. But the roads, which had not been repaved in decades, were badly cracked, with long strips of grass and weeds pushing up through the sun-bleached asphalt. And although there were cars in the driveways, the streets were empty, and no signs of life could be seen outside the houses.

Halfway around the loop, I came to the Magnolia Ernest Recreation Complex, a pool and sports center named for McKissick's parents, Magnolia and Ernest McKissick. The nets on the tennis courts were in good shape, and the water in the pool was crystal blue, but the gate was locked, and a "Keep Out" sign was posted on the chain-link fence. Parking the car in an empty lot, I walked down to a small lake and picnic area just beyond the pool. Named after McKissick's mother-in-law, Daisy B. Williams, the lake had been formed by damming a nearby creek and was one of many natural spaces included in the Soul City master plan. Bordered by a tall thicket of pines and oaks, it had the makings of a pretty scene, but the brush was so overgrown and the shoreline so littered with bottles and trash that it felt forlorn instead.

Back in the car, I completed the loop and left Green Duke Village. Turning onto Liberation Road again, I found the entrance to Pleasant Hills, a subdivision that had been laid out with roads and lots but never developed. If Green Duke felt neglected and lonely, Pleasant Hills was positively eerie. The roads here were in even worse shape, the cracks and fissures forming an endless maze across the pavement, the woods creeping in from both sides. On some streets, it was nearly impossible to get through, and I could hear weeds and fallen branches scraping against the bottom of the car. As I drove deeper into the woods, I began to lose my bearings and worried I might not find my way out. At one point, I came to a dead end that had been turned into a makeshift dump. The ground was strewn with used tires, car seats, garbage bags, clothing, furniture, and a broken TV. Leaving the engine on, I stepped out of the car briefly to snap a few pictures, then got back inside and made my way quickly to the main road.

Over the next few hours, I explored the rest of what remains of Soul City—a boarded-up shopping center, a volunteer fire department, a barely used cemetery. Eventually, I found the other landmark I had been looking for: Soul Tech I, a seventy-two-thousand-square-foot manufacturing plant that had been built in 1975 in the hopes of attracting industry. It was located near the main entrance to the city, which I had missed earlier. Discovering it now, I turned onto Soul City Boulevard, a winding, tree-lined avenue that looked like the approach to any of the hundreds of industrial and office parks that had sprouted up across the South over the past half century. As I crossed the railroad tracks again, I saw Soul Tech I on my left. It was a long, low building made of concrete and glass that had probably seemed state-of-the-art in 1975 but that looked rather ordinary today—with one exception. It was surrounded by two twenty-foot-high fences, each topped by coils of barbed wire. The fences were not designed to keep criminals out; they were designed to keep them in. In 1997, eighteen years after the federal government pulled the plug on Soul City, the state built a medium-security prison down the road from Soul Tech I. A few years later, prison officials converted the abandoned plant into a soap factory. It is now the Correction Enterprises Janitorial Products Plant, a $6.5 million-a-year business staffed by inmates earning about fifteen cents an hour.

The irony was not hard to grasp. A building designed to promote Black economic freedom had become a prison. There was only one consolation, I thought to myself: at least Floyd McKissick didn't live to see this.

SOUL CITY WAS not the first utopian venture to fall tragically short of its goals. It is the very nature of utopia that it can never be fully realized, and American history is littered with utopian experiments that began with giddy promise and ended in depressing failure, from the Shakers and other millenarian movements of the nineteenth century to the hippie communes and religious cults of the twentieth. America itself was once cast in utopian terms. It was there, the German philosopher Georg Hegel said, that "the burden of world history shall reveal itself," while the Puritan lawyer John Winthrop described the Massachusetts Bay Colony as "a City upon a Hill," with the eyes of all the world watching.

Nor was Soul City the first attempt to build a predominantly Black town that could serve as a means for economic advancement and a haven from racial oppression. Almost from the moment enslaved Africans were brought to the New World they sought to create communities of solidarity and refuge, from the Maroon settlements of North Carolina's Great Dismal Swamp, which sheltered thousands of people who had escaped slavery in the eighteenth and nineteenth centuries, to northern towns such as Brooklyn, Illinois, founded by free and fugitive Blacks in the 1820s. During the Civil War, the federal government aided these efforts, establishing freedmen's camps on plantations seized by Union troops. At Port Royal, South Carolina, more than ten thousand formerly enslaved people were provided land on which to harvest cotton, while at Davis Bend, Mississippi, the estate of Jefferson Davis's brother, Northern officers presided over a colony of freed Blacks that Ulysses S. Grant hoped would become "a Negro Paradise."

These camps were broken up after the war when Andrew Johnson granted amnesty to Confederate leaders and restored seized property to Southern landowners. And for the next decade, as Reconstruction temporarily brought the freedmen new rights and a prominent role in southern politics, the drive to establish separate Black communities stalled. But when Reconstruction ended in 1877 and a new era of racial terror dawned, Black people once again sought asylum from violence and economic subjugation. Between 1879 and 1881, more than twenty-five thousand Blacks fled to Kansas as part of the Great Exodus. Settling on barren plains, they attempted to scratch out a life for themselves in towns such as Nicodemus, an unforgiving scrap of land said to have been named after an African prince brought to America in chains before purchasing his freedom. Many settlers lived in earthen dugouts, with little food, little clothing, and little hope of supporting themselves. Gradually, as word spread that life there was grim and the future bleak, the stream of migrants to Nicodemus slowed. And when efforts to secure a railroad line failed, the flow reversed itself until hardly anyone remained in Nicodemus at all.

It wasn't long before another mass migration began, this time to the Oklahoma Territory. Spurred by the opening of land to settlers in 1889, Black promoters began planning new towns and selling lots to Black people across the South. The most famous of these promoters, Edward Preston McCabe, left Nicodemus to found the town of Langston. Situated on a hill forty miles northeast of Oklahoma City, Langston was one of the country's few successful Black settlements, reaching a population of two thousand in 1891. But McCabe had grander ambitions than simply building a Black town. A prominent

Republican and former Kansas state auditor, he wanted to transform Oklahoma into a Black state, with himself installed as governor. With that goal in mind, he traveled to Washington in 1890 and presented his plan to President Benjamin Harrison, who gave the idea serious consideration. But the numbers were not on McCabe's side. In spite of his promotional efforts, Black settlers never accounted for more than a tenth of the territory's population, and when statehood came in 1907 Oklahoma passed a series of discriminatory laws and voting tests that all but ensured the disenfranchisement of its Black residents and the slow demise of its thirty or so Black towns.

Soul City had much in common with both the utopian and Black-town traditions. Like its utopian precursors, it was born out of discontentment with the world as it existed and a desire to start over, on a completely blank slate. McKissick wanted to build a new kind of city, one with a stronger sense of community, a deeper regard for the well-being of others, and a more egalitarian distribution of wealth. He also hoped to incorporate the latest innovations in social policy and urban design, boasting that Soul City would be "a showpiece of democracy in a sea of hypocrisy."

But while many utopian communities had an abstract, theoretical feel to them, Soul City was a practical, hard-nosed endeavor. McKissick was not trying to achieve spiritual transcendence or the perfect relationship between man and nature. Unlike many utopian leaders of the nineteenth century, he did not aim to regulate every aspect of life in the community he was building. He did not want to eliminate sex or private property (as did the Shakers) or encourage open marriage (like the Owenites). He did not promise lemonade seas and the extinction of mosquitos (see the Fourierists). And he did not propose to build an elaborate, palatial structure like the "parallelogram" designed by the reformer Robert Owen or the "phalansteries" sketched by the French socialist Charles Fourier—self-contained cities in which groups of precisely 1,620 people would live and work in perfect harmony.

Nor was McKissick interested in providing a sanctuary for those who wanted to "turn on, tune in, and drop out," in the words of the psychedelic guru Timothy Leary. The people he recruited to build Soul City were not hippies or beatniks. They were, for the most part, professionals—architects, engineers, project managers, accountants, doctors, and nurses. And if they were not professionals, they had to have some skill, some concrete contribution they could offer the budding community. One young man, recently discharged from the air force, rode his motorcycle from Raleigh to Soul City in the spring of 1973 looking for a job, only to be told he needed a college degree. Returning a year later with degree in hand, he was once again rejected for lack of relevant experience. Not until his third attempt did someone take pity on him and find him a position in the office of the city planner.

In short, although McKissick wanted to build a new kind of community, he also wanted to provide something vastly more straightforward for the residents of Soul City—a chance at the American dream. There was a reason Black people were absent from the socialist utopias of the nineteenth century, and it wasn't just because they were being held in bondage. Even in the North, and even after the Civil War, most Blacks were indifferent to the message of the Shakers and Owenites for the simple reason that they couldn't take for granted the very things those movements sought to escape: materialism, ownership of private property, and middle-class respectability. The same was true a century later when white suburban dropouts flocked to communes in California and New England. McKissick mocked what he regarded as the frivolousness of white culture, telling the graduating class of a historically Black college in 1969, "I thank God that black kids today aren't swallowing goldfish or squeezing into phone booths or stealing panties and bras." Blacks had more pressing concerns, and so did McKissick. He wanted to take the American dream—the dream of opportunity, upward mobility, and self-determination—and make that dream available to a group of people to whom it had been denied. McKissick wasn't trying to create a place that didn't exist. The place he had in mind existed all around him. It just didn't exist for Black people.

In that sense, Soul City was closer in spirit to the tradition of

Black towns. When Edward McCabe founded Langston, he wasn't attempting to create a community for starry-eyed transcendentalists. Like McKissick, he hoped to build a town that would attract hardworking residents with traditional, even Victorian, values. Nor did Black-town developers shy away from the dictates of commerce, believing, again like McKissick, that manufacturing was the key to economic progress. The founders of Mound Bayou, a celebrated Black town in Louisiana, pinned their hopes for success on a cottonseed-oil mill, while officials in Boley, Oklahoma, invested in a brick factory and a carbonation works. In Langston, the L. L. C. Medicine and Toilet Factory manufactured blood remedies, cough balsam, and magic liniments and powders.

The Black towns and Soul City had something else in common. Both grew out of a larger vision of Black independence and Black Nationalism. This vision was as old as slavery itself. It inspired Paul Cuffee's attempt to colonize Sierra Leone in 1811, Marcus Garvey's "back to Africa" movement in the 1920s, and the so-called Republic of New Africa, a group of Black Power advocates in the late 1960s who demanded that the federal government hand over five southern states—Louisiana, Mississippi, Alabama, Georgia, and South Carolina—along with $400 billion in cash. Often, the vision was about separation, about withdrawal from white society and the creation of a distinctive and self-sustaining Black nation. That was the message of a song about Boley, which at one point had a population of seven thousand and was the largest Black town in America:

> Oh, tis a pretty country
> And the Negroes own it too
> With not a single white man here
> To tell us what to do.

Sometimes, though, the vision entailed a reversal of fortunes, where black was white and up was down, where those who had been high and mighty were brought down to size and those who had been oppressed were cast in the role of oppressor. This was the world described by Langston Hughes in his sardonic poem "Cultural Exchange":

Comes the COLORED HOUR:
Martin Luther King is Governor of Georgia,
Dr. Rufus Clement his Chief Adviser,
A. Philip Randolph the High Grand Worthy.
In white pillared mansions
Sitting on their wide verandas,
Wealthy Negroes have white servants,
White sharecroppers work the black plantations,
And colored children have white mammies:
    Mammy Faubus
    Mammy Eastland
    Mammy Wallace
Dear, dear darling old white mammies—
Sometimes even buried with our family.

There was certainly an element of this vision in McKissick's dream. By establishing his city on a former slave plantation, by taking ownership of the "big house," by naming the whole enterprise Soul City, he signaled the satisfaction he took in turning the tables, in flipping the script of American history. But he also made clear that he wanted Soul City to be more than an inversion of white supremacy. As his good friend the author John Oliver Killens wrote in *Black Man's Burden*, a collection of essays published in 1965, Black people were not simply "waiting for the day we can assume the role the white man played for centuries." Instead, McKissick hoped to set an example of how one race, finding itself in a position of power, could treat another race with respect and fairness. "We do not intend to adopt the white man's racism," he told the press in describing his venture. "Soul City will be an attempt to move into the future, a future where black people welcome white people as equals."

If Soul City was an heir to the tradition of Black towns, however, there were important differences. Most Black towns in the

nineteenth and early twentieth centuries were little more than agricultural service centers and trading posts, dusty little settlements that
grew up haphazardly, with little forethought or outside involvement.
Soul City was a meticulously planned, thoroughly vetted endeavor
that was supported by a number of prestigious universities, including
the University of North Carolina, Howard University, and the Massachusetts Institute of Technology. It also had something few other
Black towns could claim: the financial backing and organizational
assistance of the United States government. Aside from Port Royal
and a handful of other settlements established during the Civil War
(and, later, the Great Depression), the federal government had never
before supported the creation of a predominantly Black community.
It had certainly never backed a minority project on the scale of Soul
City. As McKissick liked to boast, at the time of its development Soul
City was the largest government-funded Black enterprise in American history.

SO WHAT HAPPENED? How did a project that once held such promise
and potential fall so depressingly short of its goals? Was Soul City an
impossible and misbegotten dream from the beginning, or was it a
brilliant idea that was thwarted by racism and ignorance? And how
might history have been different if Soul City had succeeded? Would
it have led us down the road of separatism and division, as its critics said they feared? Or would it have reinvigorated the civil rights
movement, as McKissick believed, giving Black people the economic
independence to match the political freedoms they had won in the
1960s?

These are among the questions I set out to answer when I traveled to Soul City that first time in 2014. It was a return home of
sorts: born in North Carolina the same year McKissick launched
his dream, I grew up just a few hours down the highway from Warren County and had often ridden past the exit that leads to Soul
City. But it was not until the spring of 1991, when I was a young
reporter at the *News & Observer* in Raleigh, that I first heard of the

town's existence. Working at my desk one day, I was approached by my editor, who relayed the news that Floyd McKissick had died. I knew the name but little else, so my editor filled me in, recapping McKissick's career as a lawyer and civil rights leader. At one point, he referred offhandedly to the "all-black city" McKissick had attempted to build in the 1970s. Back then, it wasn't possible to research a topic with a few clicks on a computer keyboard, so I filed the information in the back of my head and forgot about it. Not until many years later, when I was living far away and no longer working as a reporter, did I remember Soul City and begin to research its history. When I did, I learned that my editor's description had been inaccurate; Soul City was never meant to be all Black. I also learned that the *News & Observer* had played a significant role in fostering that misperception—and in bringing about Soul City's demise.

Since my first trip to Soul City, I have been back many times, to interview the residents who still live there, to picture the land as it was when McKissick arrived in 1969, and to imagine what it might look like today had things turned out differently. In the process, I have learned much not only about Soul City but about race, inequality, and the structural and political forces that tie the two together. I have also learned about the power of dreams, a power that can inspire people to greatness and result in crushing disappointment.

The disappointment of McKissick's dream resulted from many factors. Like all utopian projects, Soul City was in part a victim of its own ambition. Although McKissick's goal was modest—economic self-sufficiency for Black Americans—his method of achieving that goal was not. Attempting to build a city out of nothing but the red clay of the Carolina piedmont was a massive undertaking that would have daunted the most experienced and well-financed white developer. For a Black man without deep pockets or corporate backing, battling opposition from all sides, and facing one of the worst economic downturns of the century, it was a highly improbable venture.

But not impossible. Had it been that, the lesson of Soul City would be limited. It would tell us something about the longings and aspirations of Black people, but little about the forces standing in their way.

Soul City could have succeeded, though, as evidenced by the fact that other new cities of the period did survive—cities that faced many of the same challenges as Soul City, with one primary exception: they were built by white developers, financed by white corporations, and populated largely by white people. What doomed Soul City was not just the size of its ambition but, at least in part, the color. Like nearly every other effort to improve the lives of Black people, it was subjected to a level of scrutiny, second-guessing, and outright hostility that other ambitious ventures rarely encounter. Some of this scrutiny was motivated by blatant prejudice, but some of it is simply embedded in our social structures. If a project is designed primarily to help Blacks, it is automatically held to a higher standard of justification.

This is not to suggest that racism alone doomed Soul City. Again, that would be a simple story, and its lesson would be equally simple. Instead, the story of Soul City's demise is more complicated and more confounding. It is a story not just about white prejudice but about white power, about the control of white society over the lives of Black people. Many of the whites who opposed Soul City were not overtly racist; they were integrationists who simply thought Soul City was the wrong path to racial equality. But although not bigots, they failed to see that their opposition denied Blacks the one thing they desired most: self-determination. As one Black preacher presciently observed in 1973, "It's white folk, not black folk, who are going to decide whether Soul City will be a reality. It will come into being only if white folks want it to come into being."

The federal government deserves its share of the blame, too. After encouraging Soul City's development, it failed to offer needed resources and support. Moving at the pace of bureaucracy instead of business, it was responsible for costly delays and missed opportunities. Wary of public scrutiny and cowed by political opposition, it imposed conditions on Soul City that were not imposed on other new towns. And when the scrutiny and opposition intensified, the government lacked the conviction to stand by McKissick.

Nor can one overlook the self-defeating pride of McKissick himself. Determined that Soul City would be a monument to Black achievement, he sent contradictory messages about the racial makeup he desired. And although generally a pragmatist—as demonstrated by his alliance with Nixon—he was unwilling to compromise on the one aspect of the plan that may have doomed his dream: the town's name.

But my goal in telling the story of Soul City is not to assign blame. It is to understand the forces that led to its downfall and the lessons it offers for the pursuit of racial equality today. The need for these lessons is more urgent than ever. In the half century since McKissick launched Soul City, the financial gap between Black and white households has hardly budged. Blacks are still twice as likely as whites to be unemployed, while their median net worth is one-tenth that of whites. More importantly, they are still seeking the same self-determination McKissick hoped Soul City would provide in 1969. When protests erupted in Ferguson, Missouri, in 2014, Black residents were not just lamenting the death of Michael Brown, the young man shot by a police officer. Although that incident triggered the unrest, the frustration and bitterness had been building in Ferguson for decades, as the percentage of Black residents increased but whites retained control of all aspects of city government. By 2014, Ferguson's population was 67 percent Black and 30 percent white. Yet its government was staffed almost entirely by whites, from the mayor's office to the school board to the police department, which had only three Black officers out of a force of fifty-three. What Black residents in Ferguson, Baltimore, Charlotte, Minneapolis, and so many other cities are demanding today is the same thing McKissick was seeking five decades earlier: respect, dignity, and control over their own destiny.

SOUL CITY WAS one of the most ambitious and high-profile projects to emerge from the civil rights era. It was covered extensively by the local and national press, featured on NBC's *Today* show, studied at Harvard Business School, and watched closely by university planning departments around the country. Yet in the decades after its demise,

Soul City was almost completely forgotten. Every once in a while, a curious reporter or graduate student would sift through the archives and publish an article or thesis on Soul City. For the most part, however, it vanished from our collective memory. I have spoken to many historians and legal scholars who have studied the civil rights era and yet have never heard of Soul City. Its disappearance was so complete for so long that it seems almost intentional, as though the forces that conspired against Soul City were determined not merely to kill it but to erase it from history.

McKissick's effort deserves better. It deserves an honest reexamination and a prominent place in the history of the civil rights movement. In the popular imagination, that movement ended with Martin Luther King Jr.'s assassination in 1968. But once the protests and marches ended, there was still much work to be done. And Soul City was one man's attempt to carry the dream forward.

PART I

· 1 ·

"Black Boy in a White Land"

Where do we go from here?

That was the question on everyone's mind, and Floyd McKissick was certain he knew the answer.

It was May 1968, one month after the assassination of Martin Luther King Jr. For thirteen years, ever since the Montgomery bus boycott, King had been the moral conscience and public face of the civil rights movement. He had taken on Bull Connor and his dogs in the Birmingham campaign, inspired the nation with his soaring rhetoric in front of the Lincoln Memorial, and led the historic march for voting rights from Selma to Montgomery. His demand for freedom and integration had given the movement its sense of purpose, while his gospel of love and nonviolence had provided its strategic framework. The recipient of the 1964 Nobel Peace Prize, King had been the most influential Black man in America—perhaps the world. And although that influence had waned in recent years as a younger generation of activists embraced more militant and separatist agendas, King was still the closest thing to a unifying Black leader.

Now he was gone, gunned down on the balcony of a Memphis motel, and the civil rights movement confronted an existential question: What next? The immediate response to King's death had been grief and violence, with protests and riots breaking out in cities across the country. Already there had been nearly as many riots in 1968 as in any other year of the decade, itself the most tumultuous of the century. But the unrest was largely destructive, a way to release anger and frustration, not to chart a course forward. And as the fires burned out and the dust settled, the major civil rights organizations were debating which road to take and vying to show the way. Ralph Abernathy, who had assumed the reins of King's Southern Christian Leadership Conference, pledged to continue the Poor People's Campaign begun earlier that year. Leading a group of three thousand demonstrators, he set up a tent city on the National Mall and demanded $30 billion in poverty relief and an economic bill of rights that would give every American a guaranteed income. Whitney M. Young Jr., executive director of the National Urban League, called for a "White People's March" on the capital as a sign of interracial solidarity, while Roy Wilkins, head of the National Association for the Advancement of Colored People (NAACP), pushed for new jobs legislation and an "Adopt a Cop" program to improve relations between Black people and the police. The Student Nonviolent Coordinating Committee, more radical than its counterparts, deleted the word "nonviolent" from its name, urged Blacks to take up arms in self-defense, and contemplated a merger with the revolutionary Black Panthers.

The Congress of Racial Equality (CORE) rounded out the "Big Five" civil rights groups, and it, too, was trying to determine the next step in the struggle for Black freedom. For McKissick, who had been elected national director two years earlier, the answer was clear, and in the second week of May he called a meeting of CORE's National Action Council to share his vision.

They gathered in east Baltimore, which just weeks earlier had witnessed one of the worst riots in the country. For eight days, the city's Black neighborhoods had resembled a war zone, with residents smashing windows, looting stores, burning buildings, and throwing rocks and bottles at police and firemen. Cops in riot gear had marched through the streets, firing tear gas, exchanging shots with snipers, and rounding up lawbreakers and onlookers by the hundreds. When local officers proved unable to quell the violence, Governor Spiro Agnew declared a state of emergency and called up five thousand National Guardsmen, and when they, too, proved inadequate, President Lyndon Johnson dispatched five thousand soldiers to the area. It took more than a week and the arrest of six thousand people to restore order, and the final toll was devastating: six people dead, seven hundred wounded, and $12 million in property damage. Even now, as council members filed into the meeting, evidence of the riots was all around them: in boarded-up windows, burned-out storefronts, and the suspicious stares of newly armed shopkeepers.

Inside, McKissick quickly got down to business. He began with a report he had drafted with the help of his assistant director, Roy Innis. Titled "A Nation Within a Nation," the report argued that America was divided into two societies, one prosperous and white, the other impoverished and Black. A dam separated these two societies, and like all dams it held energy that could either create or destroy. The challenge was to channel that energy into a constructive program for the liberation of Black society. The prevailing approach had been to rely on government welfare, the report declared. But "handouts" were not the answer. Taxpayers disliked them because the recipients seemed ungrateful, while the recipients resented them because they offered no hope of permanent escape. Instead, the poor had to be given the same things everyone else wanted: jobs, opportunity, and control over their own destiny.

To achieve these goals, McKissick called for a sweeping program of economic development and urban reconstruction. At its heart would be a network of community corporations—nonprofit entities owned and managed by local residents. Funded by government-backed loans, these corporations would finance the creation of local businesses and provide job training for the unemployed. They would also use tax incentives to entice white companies to build plants in minority neighborhoods, train residents to operate the plants, and then sell them to the community after recovering their costs. The community corporations would use the revenue generated by the plants to invest in local businesses and pay for social services, thus creating a self-sustaining economic model. It was an ambitious and innovative plan that combined elements of free enterprise and social-ism. And with an estimated price tag of $1 billion, it was far more politically palatable than the $30 billion sought as part of the Poor People's Campaign.

But McKissick was not interested solely in urban reconstruction. In his view, the problems of the cities were inextricable from the problems of rural America. When the economies of rural areas col-lapsed, their residents poured into the cities in search of opportu-nity, which only exacerbated the overcrowding and destitution of the slums. Therefore, McKissick believed, it was vital to address rural poverty, too. And his proposal for doing so was even more ambitious than his program for urban renewal. Instead of simply providing subsidies to farmers or locating a few factories in the countryside, he wanted to build new cities across rural America. His proposal here was less detailed than his plan for community corporations. He didn't say exactly how the land for such an undertaking might be acquired, though he indicated it might come from the federal gov-ernment, which had plenty of surplus property. Nor did he explain how CORE might go about building new cities, though again he suggested that help might come from Washington, as well as from private foundations. If the details were lacking, however, McKissick's passion for the idea was not, and his plea to the council was personal and poignant. "This is me," he told the thirty or so members gathered that day. "This is what I believe in. This is what I'm willing to risk my life for, the same as I did when I led demonstrations."

The council's reaction was tepid. Some members were intrigued by McKissick's proposal, believing that new cities, built and run by Black people, could improve conditions in urban and rural areas. But they were skeptical of CORE's ability to acquire the land and assem-ble the staff necessary for such an ambitious venture. Others thought the whole plan too conservative, since it involved working within existing political and capital structures rather than overthrowing them. Still others were resistant to the entire economic thrust of McKissick's program, insisting that CORE should stick to its traditional methods of direct action and community organizing. The debate was long and tedious, reflecting a growing rift between the radical and traditional factions of CORE. And in the end, that rift doomed McKissick's plan. Although the council accepted his proposal for community corporations, it rejected what he viewed as the heart and soul of the program—the building of new cities.

Innis was furious. A month earlier, his thirteen-year-old son had been shot dead while playing on the streets of the Bronx, a tragic reminder of just how dangerous the cities had become. Venting his grief, he laid into the council members with a barrage of profanity. They were getting bogged down in details, he told them. They should put aside their differences and give McKissick the freedom to move forward in a bold new direction. McKissick was angry, too, but more than anything he was disappointed. The council had not just rejected a plan; it had rejected his dream. And if he couldn't pursue that dream at CORE, he knew he would have to leave. "I have never been one who wanted to be head of an organization that was not going in the direction I wanted to go," he explained later. He informed the council he would step down as national director as soon as it could find a replacement. The council, caught off guard by this news, did not respond at once. But three weeks later, at a meeting in Cleveland, it privately accepted his resignation. Then, as word of the shake-up began to leak, the council announced publicly that McKissick was stepping down and that Innis would take over temporarily, until a new leader could be found.

McKISSICK'S PRESENTATION TO the National Action Council was the first time he had formally pitched his idea of building new cities to promote economic equality. But the notion was far from new. In McKissick's telling, he had been thinking about it since 1945, when his army unit helped rebuild ravaged villages in northeastern France. If entire towns could be reconstructed in postwar Europe, he thought to himself, why couldn't Black people build new cities in the United States? Dreams are mysterious things, however, rarely emerging fully formed at a given moment in time. So although McKissick's dream may have taken shape at the end of World War II, its roots—the motivation and impulses behind it—can be traced to events further back in his life.

"Black, first. American, second." That is the opening line of the autobiography McKissick began at one point and never finished, and its meaning is clear. From his earliest days growing up in Asheville, North Carolina, he was aware that his skin color mattered more than his nationality.

Well, not exactly his earliest days. For a precious few years, McKissick had been oblivious to race, like the Zora Neale Hurston character who doesn't realize she's Black until the age of six, when she sees a picture of herself with a group of white children and wonders who that "dark chile" is where she's supposed to be. "Aw, aw! Ah'm colored!" she blurts out in astonishment. For McKissick, the realization came sooner, and in a more crushing way.

It happened in 1926, when he was four years old and riding the trolley with his aunt. He had never been on the trolley before, and as he climbed the steps he saw the conductor talking to two white boys, showing them how he operated the car. McKissick's aunt dropped her coin in the slot and walked to the rear, but he stayed up front, hoping to hear what the conductor said. When the man saw him standing there, he erupted in anger, ordering McKissick to get his "black ass" to the back of the car. McKissick, unaware that the conductor was talking to him, pointed to a handle and asked, "What's that?" to which the conductor replied by again ordering him to the back. Then, glaring down the aisle toward McKissick's aunt, he yelled, "Negress, you better come up here and get your black son of a bitch and take him back there with you." And as his aunt grabbed McKissick, half pulling, half guiding him to the rear of the trolley, the conductor added, "You'd better teach that boy some manners or he's going to get into a hell of a lot of trouble."

It was a small incident in some ways, the kind that was repeated every day in trolleys and buses across the Jim Crow South. But for McKissick, it was devastating. He saw the hatred on the conductor's red face, the white boys laughing at him, the tears running down his aunt's cheeks. "What did I do wrong?" he asked her in confusion. She just told him to hush, then reached into her purse for a handkerchief, kissed him softly on the head, and said, "One day, you'll understand."

Just as important as the incident on the trolley was what happened afterward, when he arrived home. His parents, aunt, and uncle gathered around him in the living room of their small house and told him over and over how much they loved him. "Just because you are black don't mean your people don't love you," they said. "They do love you and you ought to be able to do what anybody else can. You ought to be able to watch the trolley man work, but you will find that there are a whole lot of mean white people in this world." Later that afternoon, helping his father in the garden, he asked if all white people were mean. What about the man he had been named after, Floyd S. Bixler, a white merchant from Pennsylvania whom his father had met while working as a bellhop at the Battery Park Hotel and who had sent the family boxes of clothing, sheets, and towels every few months for a decade? Was he mean? No, his father replied. "He is an entirely different man, and as you grow older you will find out that there are two kinds of white people, good white people and bad white people. But there are a whole lot more bad white people than there are good."

McKissick never forgot that day. It was the day he first experienced the "double consciousness" W. E. B. Du Bois had described twenty-three years earlier, in *The Souls of Black Folk*. "It is a peculiar sensation, this double consciousness," Du Bois observed. "One ever feels his two-ness—an American, a Negro; two souls, two thoughts, two unreconciled strivings." Or, as McKissick put it in his autobiography, it was the day he learned he wasn't just a boy. He was a Black boy—"a black boy in a white land. And just by being alive, by getting born, I had inherited a world that hated me—a whole bunch of mean people I never saw, but who were waiting there to tell me, 'Get your black ass to the back.'"

Childhood was not all harsh lessons and bitter reality. As McKissick also wrote, "You can't be black full-time. Not as a child. The woods are green, even for Negroes." And for a Negro boy in the 1920s, Asheville was, all things considered, a surprisingly green wood. Nestled in the Blue Ridge Mountains, it was a small, close-knit community where everyone knew everyone; when Thomas Wolfe published his autobiographical novel *Look Homeward, Angel*, in 1929, even McKissick's parents recognized many of its characters. The second of four children and the only boy, McKissick was a rambunctious, sociable child who spent most days outside, roller skating down the city's treacherous hills, swimming in the creek that ran near his house, or fishing in the French Broad River. On weekends, he played baseball in Stumptown, a Black neighborhood where all the trees had been chopped down. And at night, he and his friends gathered in a grove across from his house and took part in that ancient boyhood ritual of insulting one another's mothers.

Within this world, McKissick was a leader, an instigator, and a prankster, the kind of boy who would run behind a peach truck, lower the tailgate, and catch the peaches as they rolled off. But mostly he was a hustler, in the best sense of the word. At various points growing up he worked as a busboy, a waiter, a bellhop, a window washer, and a field hand. He shined shoes and raked leaves, sold soft drinks and newspapers. In the fall, he would hike into the hills to pick apples and chestnuts, and on hot summer days he would buy a fifty-pound block of ice and pull it around the neighborhood in a wagon, selling it off chunk by chunk before it melted. His best customer was a bootlegger named Charlie Brown who lived next door. When a new batch of liquor arrived, Brown would tell McKissick to fetch some peaches to give it flavor. Then when the customers showed up, McKissick would bring ice for their drinks and fish to make sandwiches.

Racism wasn't as pronounced in Asheville as elsewhere in the South. White residents liked to boast that slavery had never existed in their town. That was a fiction: although the mountainous terrain made plantations impractical, most businessmen and professionals had kept at least one person in slavery, and by 1850 enslaved people made up 13 percent of the town's population. But unlike other areas of the South, Asheville's economy had not been built on slavery, so its support for secession had been lukewarm and its response to emancipation subdued. Asheville was also less physically segregated than many other southern communities. Instead of being confined to one or two neighborhoods, Black residents were scattered in pockets across town, the better to serve their white bosses. The McKissick home on Magnolia Street straddled one of these pockets, so that all their front-yard neighbors were Black and all their backyard neighbors were white.

Still, race was a defining fact of life in Asheville. And although McKissick had a happy childhood, he was continually reminded of the lesson he had learned on the trolley years before: he was a Black boy in a white land. It was a lesson he resented when he and his sisters visited their father at the hotel where he worked and were told to wait in a back room. A lesson he recoiled from when word spread that a white girl in the neighborhood had kissed him and her family was forced to move. And a lesson he rebelled against when he was turned away from the soapbox derby because of his skin color, only to sneak in anyway and finish in first place.

If these insults made clear to McKissick where he stood in American society, it was an incident several years later that persuaded him what to do about it. He was thirteen at the time, a member of a Black Boy Scout troop that was sponsoring a skating competition on French Broad Avenue, a gently sloping street near downtown. As one of the troop's best skaters, he was assigned to stand guard at the starting line and look after the younger kids. Wearing his uniform and a pair of metal skates strapped to his shoes, he was corralling the racers behind the line when one of them drifted into an adjoining street. McKissick darted out to catch the boy, and as he skated back to the starting line two policemen rode up on motorcycles and berated him. When he tried to explain what had happened, one of the officers became enraged. Removing a heavy glove and gripping it by the fingers, he slapped McKissick twice across the face, knocking him to the ground. "Don't talk back to me," he barked before ordering

McKissick to take off his skates. As McKissick pulled at the straps, he tried once more to explain and looked for an adult to confirm his story. The officer slapped him again and pulled out his nightstick. Before he could strike, McKissick removed his skate and swung it hard, knocking the baton out of the officer's hand. "You crazy black son of a bitch," the officer shouted. "Now I'll kill you." By this time, one of the scoutmasters saw what was happening and rushed over, pleading with the officer. "He's just a kid. He don't know no better." Soon other officers arrived to defuse the situation, and McKissick was handcuffed and taken to the police station.

He was met there by his father and a group of Black leaders who had heard about the incident and hurried to the station. The police threatened to throw McKissick in jail, but the leaders persuaded them to release the boy into his father's custody until trial. Two weeks later, McKissick appeared in court with his parents and the same group of Black men. One of them was a prominent minister who apologized on McKissick's behalf and begged the judge for mercy. McKissick's father also spoke, telling the judge (falsely) that he had already punished his son and would keep him out of trouble. The judge was swayed. Advising the elder McKissick to give his son a good thrashing, he dismissed the case and sent the boy home.

Prior to that moment, McKissick had planned to become a preacher, like his grandfathers on both sides; he had even promised his maternal grandfather he would follow in his footsteps. But the skating incident showed him the power of law and, more specifically, of lawyers. He saw that preachers had no authority; they could only beg and plead with white judges and prosecutors, who called them "boy" and made jokes at their expense. To be truly protected, one needed a lawyer. Lawyers were given respect and a voice within the system. But there were no Black lawyers in Asheville, and most white lawyers wouldn't represent Black clients. So McKissick decided he would become a lawyer and use the law to protect himself and the members of his race.

The skating incident also turned him into an activist. Although the judge warned him to watch his step, he could no longer ignore the injustices he saw. The day after his trial, a librarian at school handed him a copy of *The Crisis*, the magazine published by the NAACP. That same week he became a member of the organization. Soon, he was working with an NAACP investigator to document lynchings in the eastern part of the state. And several years later, when Asheville officials denied the actor and activist Paul Robeson a permit to speak at a public auditorium, McKissick joined a delegation to protest the decision before the city council. The protest failed, but McKissick emerged as the group's leader, proving that the trolley conductor had been right after all: he *was* going to get into a hell of a lot of trouble.

McKissick left Asheville in 1940 to attend Morehouse College in Atlanta. He was in his sophomore year when Japan bombed Pearl Harbor, and he enlisted in the army a month later. Despite a recruiter's promise that he could join the Army Air Forces, he was sent to the Field Artillery Replacement Training Center at Fort Bragg, where, because of his college background, he was assigned to teach math to white soldiers. From there, he was sent to the Thirteenth Engineer Special Brigade, which supported the tank divisions of the US Third Army, commanded by General George Patton. McKissick saw action in the battles of Metz and Rouen and was part of the Third Army's final push into Germany. During one engagement, he was hit in the head with shrapnel, for which he received a Purple Heart.

But the experience that affected him most came after the war, in French villages that had been destroyed by shells and aerial bombing. In the towns of Lille, Tourcoing, and Roubaix, along the Belgian border, McKissick and his unit helped clear rubble, pave streets, and repair town squares. And as he watched French engineers and planners slowly put their cities back together, he wondered why Black people couldn't do the same thing back home. "If we can spend all this time over in Europe building, we can sure go back down South and build," he told friends and relatives when he returned to the States in December 1946. But the reality of life at home made clear that his dream would have to wait. Although Blacks had played a critical role in the war, their status in America was unchanged. They

McKissick and his wife, Evelyn, shortly after
they were married in 1942.

were still discriminated against in jobs and public accommodations,
still sent to segregated schools, still turned away at the polls. The
likelihood that Congress would invest in new cities built by Blacks
was next to zero.

Besides, by that point McKissick was married, with two young
daughters to support. So he put aside his dream and returned to
Morehouse to complete his degree. Now even more committed to
racial justice, he joined the newly formed Progressive Party and campaigned for its candidate, Henry Wallace, in the 1948 presidential
election. He also got his first taste of nonviolent direct action, taking
part in the 1947 Journey of Reconciliation. Organized by a fledgling
civil rights group called the Congress of Racial Equality, the journey was designed to test a recent Supreme Court ruling that states
could not require segregated seating on interstate bus routes. For

two weeks, Black and white activists rode Greyhound and Trailways buses through Virginia, North Carolina, Tennessee, and Kentucky, defying demands that they separate. McKissick joined the group in Chapel Hill, then traveled to Asheville, Knoxville, and Washington, DC. The journey was dangerous and harrowing. In one town, a group of taxi drivers attacked the riders, then pursued them to the home of a local minister. At other stops, riders were taunted, harassed, and arrested. But the journey showed the power of nonviolent resistance and would serve as the model for a series of more famous bus rides fourteen years later.

After finishing at Morehouse in 1948 (the same year as King, who was seven years younger and thus avoided the war), McKissick enrolled at North Carolina College School of Law, an all-Black institution the state had opened to avoid integrating the University of North Carolina. There, he led protests demanding equal funding and the repeal of trespass statutes being used to thwart civil rights demonstrations. He also became the lead plaintiff in a lawsuit challenging segregation at UNC. Litigated by Thurgood Marshall, then head of the NAACP's Legal Defense Fund, the case ended up in the federal appeals court in Richmond, which ruled in the plaintiffs' favor. McKissick had already earned enough credits to graduate, but he enrolled in UNC summer classes anyway and left his family to live in a dorm on campus. His classmates were not kind. They hid snakes in his bed, poured water on his clothes, and knocked over his tray in the cafeteria. McKissick, as usual, fought back. After his tray was knocked over for the third time, he announced loudly that he wouldn't let it happen again (it didn't). And when he heard that the campus swimming pool was still segregated, he jumped in with his clothes on and declared, "It's integrated now."

With his law degree in hand, McKissick opened an office on Main Street in Durham. Like any young lawyer, he took whatever work came his way—property disputes, insurance claims, criminal defense. But his focus was civil rights law, and over the next decade he took on hundreds of cases challenging segregation and defending the right of peaceful protest. After the Supreme Court's 1954 decision in *Brown v. Board of Education*, he and his wife, Evelyn, filed suit to integrate the Durham public schools. The city prevailed on a technicality but, sensing the inevitable, it permitted a small number of Black students, including McKissick's two oldest children, to attend white schools in the fall of 1959. For the children, Joycelyn and Andree, it was a costly victory. Like their father, they faced the wrath of classmates, who cut patches out of their hair, spilled ink on their dresses, and doused their heads with cold water. But that was life as a McKissick, which blurred the line between family and the movement. Their modest frame house was not just a home; it was a staging ground for protests, a gathering spot for Black leaders, and a guesthouse for activists. At any moment, the children might be called upon to march, boycott, or go to jail (Joycelyn once spent a month behind bars rather than pay a fifty-dollar fine). They were also accustomed to the threats their father received by phone and mail. They would often come home from school to find a group of men on the porch, guarding the house with guns. And whenever they ate at a restaurant, they noticed that their father, like many Black leaders, never sat with his back to the door.

By the end of the 1950s, McKissick had become a controversial figure, hailed by some, despised by others. But his career in the spotlight was just beginning.

2

Scrambled Egg

The Montgomery bus boycott of 1955–56 is generally considered the start of the modern civil rights movement, and for good reason. It was the first time Black people successfully mobilized en masse to break the grip of Jim Crow. It was also the episode that thrust Martin Luther King Jr. onto the national stage, as he led the yearlong protest against segregation on the city's buses. But if one had to point to another moment that was equally important in launching the Black freedom struggle, it would be the Greensboro sit-in of 1960. Like the Montgomery boycott, the sit-in employed nonviolent direct action to protest segregation, this time at a Woolworth's lunch counter. But whereas the boycott was limited to Montgomery, the Greensboro sit-in spread quickly to other cities. Moreover, the sit-in was not the work of professional activists or community leaders. It was initiated by four unknown college students, thus foreshadowing the central role young people would play in guiding the movement over the next decade.

The Greensboro sit-in marked a turning point for McKissick, too. Prior to that moment, he had been mostly a statewide figure, serving as youth director for the North Carolina chapter of the NAACP.

But the sit-in introduced him to a broader, national audience. It also cemented his ties to the Congress of Racial Equality. Founded in Chicago in 1942, CORE was not the oldest of the major civil rights groups; both the NAACP (established in 1909) and the National Urban League (1910) were older. But those groups operated mainly through institutional mechanisms—the NAACP through lobbying and the courts, the Urban League through politics and corporate networking. CORE was the first civil rights group to rely primarily on direct action—the challenging of racial discrimination through protests, boycotts, marches, and other forms of nonviolent resistance. CORE's roots also set it apart. An offshoot of the Fellowship of Reconciliation, a Christian pacifist organization, it was for many years dominated by whites. Their goal was to abolish the color line, and early efforts were promising. In 1942, CORE integrated the Jack Spratt Coffee House in Chicago. Four years later, it ended the exclusion of Black skaters from the White City Roller Skating Rink.

After those initial victories, CORE floundered. Unlike the NAACP, which had a strong central office that organized national campaigns, CORE was a federation of autonomous chapters that shared a common philosophy but pursued their own projects. This limited the group's impact, since the chapters were only as effective as the people running them. CORE was also hindered by the red-baiting of the McCarthy era. Although it officially disavowed communism, several of its early leaders had links to communist groups, which scared away potential members. But as McCarthyism cooled down and the civil rights movement heated up in the wake of the Montgomery boycott, CORE regained its early momentum. It appointed an executive secretary to impose order on the organization, increased its fundraising, and expanded the number of chapters. It also hired a field secretary, a white activist named Gordon Carey who began looking for a way to boost CORE's national profile.

He found it the first week of February 1960. Three days after the start of the Greensboro sit-in, a local dentist mailed a postcard to the CORE office in New York seeking assistance on the students' behalf. Carey read the card and persuaded his superiors to send him to Greensboro. On the bus ride south, he learned that the demonstrations had moved to Durham and changed his destination. Arriving in the Bull City on February 7, he joined a sit-in the next day at a downtown lunch counter with a group of Black students. Police left the students alone but grabbed Carey by the collar and marched him down the street to jail. And the man who bailed him out a few hours later, waving a pocket copy of the Constitution, was Floyd McKissick.

Over the next few months, Carey and McKissick became close friends as they traveled the state together, training students in nonviolent protest, organizing sit-ins, and speaking at mass rallies alongside King. It was a heady time, especially for Carey, who was labeled an outside agitator and hounded by the media. As he put it in a letter to his bosses, "I can't move without the press covering my movement." But their courage and hard work paid off. The sit-ins spread rapidly, encompassing thirteen states and more than seventy thousand protesters. And though many groups played a part, CORE suddenly found itself at the center of the action.

The organization took off from there, appointing a Black activist named James Farmer as national director and finding new ways to dramatize the injustices of Jim Crow. It initiated boycotts against segregated stores and restaurants, fought discrimination in employment and housing, and pioneered the "jail-in," a strategy in which protesters stayed behind bars rather than post bail. But its most successful campaign came out of its past, and it was conceived, in part, by Carey. Traveling from South Carolina to New York in February 1961, he and another CORE staffer named Tom Gaither became stranded on the New Jersey Turnpike for twelve hours when their bus got caught in a snowstorm. Sitting on the bus with nothing to do, Carey pulled out a biography of Mahatma Gandhi and read about his famous march to the sea to protest the British salt monopoly. As Carey and Gaither discussed the march, they wondered whether a similar demonstration could be organized in the South. They knew about a recent Supreme Court decision barring segregation not only on interstate buses and trains but in stations and terminals as well. And they knew about CORE's 1947 Journey of Reconciliation, which

McKissick had participated in. So they decided to reenact the earlier journey with the goal of enforcing the Supreme Court's new ruling. And this time they came up with a catchier name: the Freedom Rides.

Launched that spring, the Freedom Rides propelled CORE to the forefront of the civil rights struggle. They also exposed a growing fissure within the movement. When the rides turned violent in Alabama, with white mobs firebombing one bus and brutally attacking riders on two others, moderates urged an end to the journey. At one point, King himself called for a halt, only to be overruled by more militant activists. Established groups also resented the attention CORE attracted with its confrontational tactics. While CORE got the credit and the glory, groups like the NAACP had to clean up afterward, raising money for bail and hiring lawyers to appear in court.

McKissick had long worked with both organizations. But as tensions between the two groups escalated, he was forced to choose sides, and, believing that desperate measures were called for, he chose CORE. The decision paid off when he was elected chairman of the group's National Action Council at the 1963 annual convention. The leading candidate had been Alan Gartner, a white activist who was head of the Boston chapter. But CORE's membership had become increasingly Black and demanded that its leadership reflect that. So during a tearful and emotional meeting, Farmer convinced Gartner to withdraw from the race. Then, at Carey's urging, he backed McKissick for the post.

THE NEXT FEW years marked the height of CORE's influence. With Farmer and McKissick leading the way, CORE established itself as the most visible and effective civil rights group in the country. Donations poured in, surging from $240,000 the year before Farmer took over to nearly $900,000 in 1964. The money enabled CORE to expand its staff (it had 137 paid employees at its peak) and finance a series of ambitious projects, including Freedom Highways, which targeted discrimination at hotels and restaurants along interstate roads, and Freedom Summer, a voter registration drive in Mississippi that attracted thousands of young out-of-state volunteers. Just one of several groups involved in Freedom Summer, CORE became the public face of the campaign when two of its members, along with a third volunteer, disappeared and were later found murdered, their bodies buried under an earthen dam.

Despite its growing influence, CORE was beset by strife. Although it was still the most interracial of the major civil rights groups, Black members were increasingly hostile to white involvement in the organization. Several white chapter heads and national staff (including Carey) were forced to resign, and in 1964, Blacks outnumbered whites in CORE for the first time. The group also began to rethink its commitment to nonviolence. When the Deacons for Defense and Justice formed in the summer of 1964 and announced their intention to defend Black neighborhoods with guns, CORE did not denounce the move. Instead it enlisted the Deacons to protect its field workers, in what Farmer described as "a partnership of brothers."

These conflicts took their toll on Farmer, and in the summer of 1965 he announced plans to resign. Once again, there was a fight over CORE's future, and once again McKissick prevailed. The moderate wing of the National Action Council favored George Wiley, a former chemistry professor at Syracuse University who had served as associate director under Farmer. The radical wing, seeking to strengthen CORE's relationship with poor Blacks, supported McKissick, in part because Wiley's wife was white. As one staff member explained, it was a choice between a "brilliant university professor married to a white woman and a down-home lawyer who sounded black." Farmer, himself married to a white woman, initially supported Wiley. But concluding that McKissick had the "empathy and ability to articulate the feelings of the ghetto," he changed his mind, and when the council cast its ballots in January 1966, McKissick won, twelve votes to eight.

When McKissick took over as national director, at the age of forty-three, CORE was still one of the nation's leading civil rights organizations, with an illustrious history, a membership of eighty thousand, and a flair for capturing headlines. But internally it was in shambles. Its expenses vastly exceeded its revenue, and as its agenda grew more militant McKissick struggled to raise money from white donors who had supported it in the past. In one month alone, donations plummeted from $44,500 to $19,900. There was also increasing friction between the national office, which wanted more control over CORE's direction, and the local chapters, which jealously guarded their autonomy.

McKissick spent the first several months of his tenure digging CORE out of its financial hole. He reduced the staff, cut back on travel, and offered creditors twenty-five cents on the dollar. He also moved the organization from its headquarters in the ornate Potter Building in downtown Manhattan to a third-floor walk-up in Harlem. In addition to saving a thousand dollars a month, the move signaled CORE's new focus on the problems of the ghetto. McKissick's roach-infested office was upstairs from Smalls Paradise, the legendary nightclub where Malcolm X once waited tables. From there, he launched a series of initiatives designed to help the urban poor, including an ambitious "target city" project, which sought to alleviate unemployment, hunger, and homelessness in the heavily Black cities of Baltimore and Cleveland.

McKissick also became increasingly outspoken, critical of the slow pace of change and skeptical of Lyndon Johnson's commitment to civil rights, which he thought was being overshadowed by the Vietnam War. In January 1966, he issued a statement condemning the war—more than a year before King announced his own opposition. Five months later, he stirred up trouble at the White House Conference on Civil Rights when he drafted a resolution demanding US withdrawal from Vietnam. That move threatened to derail the conference until Johnson made a surprise appearance to remind the 2,400 delegates that four centuries of injustice could not be undone in a single weekend. The White House also dispatched Arthur Goldberg, the US ambassador to the United Nations (and former Supreme Court justice), to argue against McKissick's resolution. And when McKissick formally introduced his motion, it was ruled out of order by James M. Nabrit Jr., the former president of Howard University and Goldberg's deputy, who declared, "I don't want to put that alba-tross around the civil rights movement."

It was a stinging defeat, but it showed that McKissick was a force to be reckoned with. And if his conduct at the conference alarmed moderates, it was nothing compared to what was to come. For in the months ahead, he would help pave the way for the next phase of the civil rights movement: the rise of Black Power.

BLACK POWER DID not emerge all at once, out of nowhere. It was an idea that had deep roots in African American thought and rhetoric. It was implicit in the writing of Paul Robeson and the speeches of Malcolm X, and it was explicit in the work of Richard Wright, who used the phrase as the title of a 1954 book about Africa's Gold Coast. But the event that marked the ascendance of Black Power as a ral-lying cry and a political force was the March Against Fear in June 1966. Launched by James Meredith, whose admission to the Univer-sity of Mississippi under armed guard four years earlier had gripped the nation, the march was intended as a departure from the typical civil rights demonstration. Instead of staging a massive rally led by the usual suspects, Meredith planned to walk the 220 miles from Memphis to Jackson, Mississippi, by himself. His goal was to show that Blacks would not be cowed by the threats and violence whites had unleashed in response to the Voting Rights Act of 1965. But the march showed just how pervasive that violence was. On the second day of his journey, Meredith was gunned down by a white man wielding a shotgun in a pickup truck. The gun was loaded with bird shot, so Meredith's injuries were not life-threatening. In some ways, though, the choice of ammuni-tion was particularly dehumanizing. As Meredith said afterward, "He shot me a like a goddamn rabbit."

McKissick knew Meredith well. They had met years earlier through the NAACP, and after McKissick moved his family to New York in early 1966, Meredith often visited their home in Harlem. So when McKissick heard about the shooting, he announced at once that CORE would continue the march on Meredith's behalf. The

Southern Christian Leadership Conference and the Student Nonviolent Coordinating Committee quickly agreed to join in, and by the next morning McKissick, King, and Stokely Carmichael (SNCC's newly elected chairman) were at Meredith's bedside in Memphis securing his blessing for their plan.

The three men resumed the march a few hours later, driving out to the spot where Meredith had been shot, linking arms, and taking off down the long, straight road. They didn't get far before they, too, were ambushed. About two hundred yards down the road, a group of highway patrolmen ordered them to the shoulder. When King attempted to explain what they were doing, one of the officers pushed him, and King toppled to the ground, nearly bringing the others down with him. Holding back their rage and doing their best to preserve their dignity, the three men reordered themselves in a single file and walked a few miles along the side of the road before driving back to the Lorraine Motel in Memphis to plot their strategy.

It was a daunting task, planning a journey over two hundred miles—four times the distance of the Selma-to-Montgomery march the year before. They had to decide where they would sleep each night, how they would transport food and other provisions, and how they would provide for the thousands of marchers they expected to pick up along the way. They also had to decide what they hoped to accomplish. The leaders of the NAACP and the Urban League soon joined the others in Memphis, and they argued that the march should be used to pressure Congress into passing the 1966 civil rights bill. Carmichael disagreed, believing the march should focus on voter registration. King sided with Carmichael, but the two men clashed on other issues, such as whether the march should be interracial and whether the Deacons for Defense and Justice should be allowed to participate. These struggles gave the march a chaotic and contentious atmosphere that led the *Washington Post* to refer to it as a "strange parade—half army of liberation and half civil rights carnival show."

For McKissick, the march was perhaps his finest moment. He

was funny and approachable, relating to the marchers on their own terms. When a pickup truck passed by with a group of teenagers riding in back, he called out playfully, "I got my mojo on ya, you gotta come!" (They did.) Another time, as the crowd set up camp for the night, he hopped onto an oil drum and explained that there was a men's tent and a women's tent—and severe penalties for fraternizing between the two. "Don't be surprised if your name is read into the Congressional Record for carrying on the process of integration," he jokingly warned. "You have a constitutional right to be human, but this is a movement of the *spirit*." And unlike King, whom young activists mockingly referred to as "de lawd" for his sometimes imperious bearing, or Ralph Abernathy, who would march just long enough to have his picture taken before getting back into an air-conditioned car, McKissick was willing to get his hands dirty. He walked nearly the entire distance from Memphis to Jackson, taking only a short break to fly back to New York for a fundraiser. Even physically, McKissick seemed more at home in rural Mississippi than either King or Carmichael. King was short and soft, with sensitive eyes and delicate hands. Carmichael was long and lanky, like a teenager who hadn't yet filled out. McKissick, standing six feet tall, had broad shoulders, a barrel chest, and a strong grip. He often served lunch to the marchers, then cleaned up afterward. He also got into long, philosophical discussions about the importance of nonviolence. As one historian wrote, "McKissick cast his arms wide, trying to pull everyone under the march's banner."

Yet even McKissick couldn't put a lid on the disagreements that were simmering beneath the surface. Ten days into the march, Carmichael was arrested for erecting a campsite on the grounds of a Black school. When he was released that night, he headed to a rally at a local park. Standing on the bed of a pickup truck, he railed against the forces of racism and inequality, urging the crowd to adopt a new slogan. "We been saying 'freedom' for six years and we ain't got nothing," he cried. "What we got to start saying now is 'Black Power!'" The crowd cheered wildly, repeating the phrase over and over, and soon there was a sharp divide among the marchers, with

McKissick (center) during the March Against Fear with Martin Luther King Jr. (left) and Stokely Carmichael (right).

King's followers chanting "Freedom now," and Carmichael's allies responding with "Black Power."

Events soon pushed McKissick into the latter camp. On the seventeenth day of the march, organizers requested permission to set up camp on the grounds of a Black elementary school in Canton, Mississippi. When white officials denied their request, the organizers went ahead anyway. But as the marchers erected their tents, a caravan of highway patrol cars pulled up, and seventy-five officers filed out. Wearing riot gear and armed with rifles and tear gas, they advanced to within ten yards of the crowd and donned gas masks. Some marchers fled, but around two thousand remained, and McKissick climbed on top of an eighteen-wheel truck to instruct the crowd in nonviolent resistance. Suddenly, the officers fired tear gas into the crowd, and an acrid smog descended on the field. As marchers ran to escape the smoke, officers struck them with rifle butts and kicked those who fell to the ground. One officer hit a priest, and when another marcher yelled, "He's a man of God," the officer responded, "I'll put him with his God," before striking the priest again.

During the attack, a gas canister hit McKissick in the knee, knocking him off the truck. When he landed, he heard a crack and felt a searing pain shoot up his back. Fighting back tears and nearly incoherent, McKissick let loose his anger. As one historian put it, "something shifted inside Floyd McKissick, both literally and figuratively." "I'm tired of having to *negotiate* for our constitutional *rights*," McKissick told a reporter for the *New Yorker*. "When the tear gas came, I fell off that truck like a scrambled egg. . . . They don't call it *white* power. They just call it *power*. I'm committed to nonviolence, but I say what we need is to get us some *black* power."

Because it took place at night and was hard to capture on film, the incident in Canton didn't receive the same coverage as the 1965 attack on the Edmund Pettus Bridge in Selma, in which civil rights marchers were mowed down by police armed with billy clubs and tear gas. But it was just as brutal and traumatic; those who were there referred to it as "the Night of the Valley of the Shadow of Death." As with the attack in Selma, though, it only reinforced the resolve of the marchers, who announced they would pitch their tents at the same school the next night. McKissick, meanwhile, lashed out at President Johnson for failing to protect the marchers. "We're sick and tired of begging," he said. "That man thinks you don't bleed, you don't cry, you don't suffer."

From that moment, McKissick became one of the most vocal advocates of Black Power—second in influence and visibility only to Stokely Carmichael. He declared the civil rights movement "dead," argued that nonviolence had "outlived its usefulness," and proclaimed that 1966 would be remembered as the year "when black men realized their full worth in society—their dignity and their beauty—and their power." So combative was his rhetoric that aides to King urged him not to attend CORE's annual convention in Baltimore that summer. As they explained, CORE was "yelling black power louder than SNCC." King's aides weren't the only ones who had noticed. The

FBI soon began surveilling McKissick, and many of the remaining white members of CORE resigned. One of them was Lillian Smith, a southern writer who had served on the National Action Council for two decades. Announcing her departure, she referred to the Black Power advocates within CORE as "the new Killers of the Dream."

3

"Look Out, Whitey!"

Critics often said it was unclear what "Black Power" meant, to which McKissick had a ready answer. Appearing on *Meet the Press* shortly after the March Against Fear, he pointed out that the phrase consisted of "two little bitty words in the English language." The first was "black," and "everybody who has gone through the sixth grade knows what 'black' means." The second was "power," and "everybody who has gone through the sixth grade knows what that means." Yet, McKissick went on, "I get a letter from a professor at Harvard saying, 'Explain black power.' That means putting power in black people's hands. We don't have any and we want some. That simply is what that means."

McKissick's protestations aside, there *was* confusion about the meaning of Black Power. Did it mean Black people were planning to rise up and launch a violent assault on white society? That was what many whites feared, and although few Blacks advocated violence, they were not above tweaking whites for their hysteria. (Thus the title of Julius Lester's 1968 book, *Look Out, Whitey! Black Power's Gon' Get Your Mama!*) Was Black Power about attaining political power through voter registration and redistricting? If so, that was less physically terrifying to whites, though still objectionable. Or was Black Power simply a slogan connoting racial pride—the wearing of African clothes and hairstyles, the elevation of Black culture?

According to a document issued by CORE, Black Power had six elements: economic self-sufficiency, political representation, an improved self-image, the development of Black leadership, the enforcement of federal laws, and the mobilization of Black consumers. McKissick embraced all six elements, but the one he emphasized most forcefully was economic autonomy. "Unless the Black Man attains economic independence, any 'political independence' will be an illusion," he wrote in his 1969 book *Three-Fifths of a Man*. Why? Because as long as Black people were economically dependent on whites, they would be too frightened to exercise their political rights. In northern cities and the rural South, "white storeowners withhold credit from Blacks who register to vote, creating a loss of tools and fertilizer, food and commodities," McKissick explained. "The alternative is obvious: don't register to vote and the lifeblood of credit becomes available; don't register to vote and the white racists can perpetuate themselves in power. The fear expressed by many poor Blacks at the thought of registering to vote is fully understandable—it is the fear of not having enough to eat."

McKissick was not the first Black leader to draw a link between economics and racial progress. Booker T. Washington had emphasized the importance of financial independence more than eighty years earlier, launching the National Negro Business League and urging Black workers to develop skills that would make them indispensable to white companies. "The opportunity to earn a dollar in a factory just now is worth infinitely more than the opportunity to spend a dollar in an opera house," he declared in his Atlanta Exposition address in 1895. W. E. B. Du Bois, who objected to Washington's narrow focus on industrial training, agreed with him about the value of economic self-sufficiency, arguing that Black consumers should shop exclusively at Black businesses. It was this spirit—along with discrimination by white proprietors—that led to the creation of Black Wall Street, a thriving commercial district in Tulsa, Oklahoma, that was a model of Black entrepreneurialism until white mobs destroyed it in a race massacre in 1921. The civil rights movement itself was born out of economic discontent. The first March on Washington Movement, in 1942, was triggered by the exclusion of Black workers from defense jobs and was called off only when President Roosevelt issued an order banning discrimination in all war contracts. And the 1963 March on Washington was a demonstration for "jobs and freedom," the former being thought indispensable to the latter. As a young John Lewis put it that day, "We march today for jobs and freedom, but we have nothing to be proud of, for hundreds and thousands of our brothers are not here. They have no money for their transportation, for they are receiving starvation wages or no wages at all."

Black leaders had also long recognized the leverage that economics gave them when demanding equal treatment. It was not the moral argument for integration that won the day after Rosa Parks was arrested for sitting in the front of a bus; it was the financial pain inflicted on Montgomery when Black residents boycotted the city's transit system. Likewise, private businesses such as Woolworth's and Howard Johnsons had reversed their policies primarily because of the economic pressure exerted by sit-ins, boycotts, and "buy black" campaigns.

Yet many of the most visible triumphs of the civil rights movement had not moved the needle on economic equality. As McKissick liked to say, what good was the right to sit at a lunch counter if you didn't have the bread to buy a burger? And Blacks still had far less bread than whites. In 1968, 29 percent of Black families fell below the poverty line, compared to 8 percent of white families. The median income of white families was $8,900, while for Black families it was $5,400. The unemployment rate of Blacks was double that of whites. The numbers went on and on, but as McKissick argued, "reciting the statistics of poverty is a sterile pursuit. Infant mortality, substandard housing, malnutrition—these are the polite terms of social scientists that blur the fact that babies are dying, families are crowded into rat-infested slums, and children are hungry." To make matters worse, school desegregation had largely stalled. In 1968, fourteen years after *Brown v. Board of Education*, 77 percent of Black students still attended segregated schools.

From the perspective of many Black leaders, then, the civil rights movement had been a double disappointment. Not only had it failed to achieve integration, it had done little to help Black people economically. By the mid-1960s, many Black leaders were responding to this reality. Even King, the civil rights leader most closely associated with integration, shifted his priorities, announcing the Poor People's Campaign in late 1967. And of course the reason King was in Memphis when he was shot at the Lorraine Motel was to support a strike by Black sanitation workers.

But no Black leader emphasized economic equality more than McKissick. The question was how to achieve it. McKissick knew that whites would never voluntarily give up their wealth and property. He also doubted that welfare could bring about systemic change (though he did support it as a means of temporary relief). If Black Americans were to achieve economic parity, McKissick believed, they would have to do so through the established mechanisms for accruing wealth. They would have to become entrepreneurs and businessmen, leveraging a system that had been used to exploit them into one that enriched them. In short, they would have to embrace capitalism, or, as it soon became known, "black capitalism."

McKISSICK DIDN'T LIKE the term "black capitalism." He preferred "black entrepreneurialism," or even "black socialism," believing those terms better captured the combination of wealth accumulation and redistribution he had in mind. But whatever the label, the drive to promote Black business emerged as a central front in the battle for racial equality. At the 1967 Black Power Conference in Newark, the organizers issued a statement demanding that Black citizens get a "fair share of American capitalism." The next year's conference, in Philadelphia, was sponsored by Clairol, whose president was a leading proponent of Black capitalism. Meanwhile, Black businesses sprang up across the country. In Miami, Muhammad Ali opened his

ChampBurger quick-service restaurant. In Los Angeles, two civil rights activists launched Shindana Toys, the first company to mass-produce Black dolls. And in North Philadelphia, the developer Leon Sullivan began construction on Progress Plaza, the first shopping mall in the country owned and operated by a Black man.

Black activists and businessmen weren't the only ones promoting Black capitalism. White philanthropists such as Henry Ford II and David Rockefeller endorsed the concept, believing it was key to solving the urban crisis. The conservative columnists Robert Novak and Rowland Evans were also sympathetic. Describing CORE's push for Black economic independence, they noted that it implied a degree of separatism "that makes white liberals still yearning for immediate racial integration heartsick." But, they added, "it strikes a responsive chord for Negro militants and has the indispensable virtue of attainability."

Perhaps the most surprising supporter of Black capitalism was Richard Nixon. In a campaign speech in April 1968, he argued that the rhetoric of Black capitalism had more in common with Republican values than Democratic ones. "Much of the black militant talk these days is actually in terms far closer to the doctrines of free enterprise than to those of the welfarist thirties," he declared in his "Bridges to Human Dignity" speech. "What most of the militants are asking is . . . to have a share of the wealth and a piece of the action. And this is precisely what the central target of the new approach ought to be. It ought to be oriented toward more black ownership, for from this can flow the rest—black pride, black jobs, black opportunity, and yes, black power, in the best, the constructive sense of that often misapplied term."

As many pundits observed, this sounded a lot like the rhetoric of McKissick and his assistant director, Roy Innis. Some commentators even accused Nixon of cribbing from CORE's press releases. Instead of being angered, however, McKissick and Innis were intrigued. So when a Nixon aide offered to set up a meeting with the candidate, they accepted. The meeting took place in early May, at Nixon's Fifth Avenue apartment in Manhattan. According to a letter written by one of his advisers, Nixon agreed to support CORE's effort to pass legislation giving Black residents control over their own communities. He instructed two aides to help Innis draft the bill, then directed his law firm to provide technical assistance. And when the measure, known as the Community Self-Determination Act, was introduced in Congress that summer, Nixon privately encouraged Republican legislators to vote for it. (The act was defeated by large margins in both houses.)

Despite the widespread support for Black capitalism, not all Black leaders were on board. Andrew Brimmer, the first Black member of the Federal Reserve Board, argued that the concept was "a cruel hoax" since the economy was moving away from small, locally owned businesses toward nationwide chains. Roy Wilkins, executive director of the NAACP, called Black capitalism "simple nonsense," claiming that for the foreseeable future "the bulk of all people who work will earn their living as workers—as employees, not as entrepreneurs." And Robert Allen, a California activist, maintained that Black capitalism would simply replace white exploiters with Black ones. "What CORE and the cultural nationalists seek is not an end to oppression," he wrote in *Black Awakening in Capitalist America*, "but the transfer of the oppressive apparatus into their own hands."

McKissick acknowledged the historical racism of capitalism. But he believed there was a difference between white capitalism, which was a "destructive, violent force," and Black capitalism, which was "designed to alleviate much of the poverty and powerlessness of the Black population of America." Yes, if Black businessmen conducted their affairs like most capitalists—engaging in cutthroat competition, refusing to pay fair wages, focusing only on the bottom line—they would be no better than their white counterparts. But as he explained in his weekly column for the *New York Amsterdam News*, the goal wasn't just to create a few Black millionaires. "It is rather a pragmatic response to the condition of the nation. It is a realistic means by which Black People can gain power."

· · ·

McKissick's early efforts to promote Black capitalism were modest. At the 1966 CORE convention, he announced the formation of the Harlem Commonwealth Council, which sought to acquire all commercial real estate on 125th Street in Harlem. The same year, he proposed a network of Black cooperatives across the South to protect civil rights activists from retaliation by white banks and businessmen. Over time, however, his ambitions grew, and he returned to his old dream of building new cities—cities where Black people would control the levers of power and capital. Twenty years earlier, on his return from the war, that dream had seemed premature. But now, with the limits of integration becoming clear and the Black community expressing a new sense of pride, the idea seemed ripe, and McKissick began to discuss it casually, as though trying it on for size. In December 1966, he testified before the Senate that one way of addressing the urban crisis was to build new cities that would relieve overcrowding, create jobs, and establish "a new environment fit for men, black and white, to live in." In July 1967, he issued the "Black Manifesto," a document that surveyed the demands of various Black groups, including those who desired separation, and argued that "with land the government now owns, or could acquire, new cities can, in fact, be built to be owned and controlled by Black People." Two months later, he told a reporter during an impromptu interview that CORE would soon announce plans "to develop a black community from the ground up."

With this last statement, McKissick was getting ahead of himself. It was true he had begun preliminary planning for a new city. He had recently received a grant from the Metropolitan Applied Research Center, a nonprofit founded by the psychologist Kenneth Clark, that would enable him to take a brief leave of absence to study the matter. But CORE was in no position to tackle such a project. Although McKissick had reduced the organization's debt and made it relevant again, there were still deep divisions within its ranks. Some members thought McKissick had gone too far in his embrace of Black Power, while others complained he hadn't gone far enough. The radical wing of CORE, seeking to end the group's reliance on white support, was angry that he had accepted a $175,000 grant from the Ford Foundation for a program in Cleveland focused on voter registration, job training, and leadership instruction. These tensions erupted at CORE's 1967 convention in Oakland, with the militant forces demanding a ban on donations from white organizations. McKissick pushed back, pointing out that CORE was still in the red and that foundation grants were essential to its survival. But in an effort to appease the insurgents, he agreed to eliminate the word "multiracial" from the section of CORE's constitution describing its membership. Defending the move to reporters, McKissick insisted it did not mean the exclusion of whites from the organization. Other members disagreed, declaring that the change had been made to "let the world know the direction that CORE is going."

Throughout the remainder of 1967 and early 1968, McKissick continued to emphasize economic equality and self-determination. In December, he joined King in support of boycotting the Olympics. In February, he argued that Black people must "have absolute power over the institutions in their own communities," while in March he called for the establishment of a separate school board in New York to address the needs of Black children. And on April 4, McKissick unveiled a plan in Cleveland to promote Black ownership of local factories. Designed by a San Francisco political economist named Louis Kelso, the plan was based on the idea that creating jobs for poor Blacks was not enough. In order to achieve true equality, Black Americans had to become owners, since most of the nation's wealth was a return on capital. "Our intention is not to establish a new welfare burden for present property owners and wage earners," McKissick declared. "Our intention is to establish a series of economic institutions whereby black residents of Cleveland can be owners of capital instruments rather than welfare recipients." The proposal was hailed by white executives, including Henry Ford II and William Schoen, a Detroit businessman who pledged $250,000 of 3M stock to CORE's Cleveland chapter.

But on the same day McKissick unveiled his proposal in Cleveland, King was shot dead in Memphis, and the civil rights movement was thrown into disarray. McKissick was nearly beside himself with rage. Speaking at a hastily arranged press conference in Cleveland, he declared King's death a "horror" that marked the end of nonviolence. "Black Americans will no longer tolerate this killing of their males," he told reporters, tears filling his eyes. Later that night, having flown to Washington, DC, he was even more emotional, telling a reporter, "The next Negro to advocate nonviolence should be torn to bits by black people." And the following morning, he caused a scene in a corridor of the White House when he angrily refused to attend a meeting of civil rights leaders with President Johnson because SNCC and other militant groups had been excluded.

The year before his death, King had published a book titled *Where Do We Go from Here: Chaos or Community?* It was his attempt to chart a path forward for the civil rights movement, to reconcile the demands of Black Power with the political realities of white America. Now, with King gone, that question was being asked again. But this time, it was accompanied by another question: Who

McKissick addressing a crowd of Garment District workers in New York City four days after King's assassination.

would take King's place at the head of the movement? In an article in the *New York Times*, the legendary civil rights reporter Claude Sitton recalled King's description of himself as a "drum major for justice" and asked, "Now that the drum major is gone, who will lead the crusade?" McKissick, he wrote, "speaks with a militancy and determination surpassed by few other nationally known Negroes." But CORE was a "ghost of its former self," with a shrinking membership, a dwindling financial base, and a national profile kept alive only by McKissick's frequent media appearances. Sitton was equally skeptical of the other candidates, describing Stokely Carmichael as the "high priest" of the "Black Power cult," dismissing Roy Wilkins and Whitney Young as "not equal to the challenge of today's problem," and asserting that Ralph Abernathy could not "hope realistically to provide the leadership on the national scene that the circumstances seem to demand." Ultimately, Sitton concluded, the problems of racial injustice and economic inequality could not be solved by any one organization or leader, but would require "massive" federal programs supported by "all Americans, black and white standing together."

It was a nice image, if not exactly realistic. By 1968, with spending on the Vietnam War at its height, the country's appetite for massive federal programs was waning. It took King's assassination and what remained of Johnson's political capital to pass the Fair Housing Act and the Housing and Urban Development Act of 1968, the last two pieces of Great Society legislation. Nor was the prospect of "all Americans, black and white standing together" very plausible. After the widespread riots that followed King's death, racial tensions were as bad as they had been since Reconstruction. Leading the country out of the morass would require visionary leadership and an organization with real credibility.

THIS IS WHY the stakes were so high when McKissick called a meeting of CORE's National Action Council in May, and why its rejection of his plan for building new cities was so disheartening. In the months after he announced his resignation and Innis took over the leadership role, CORE descended into turmoil. During the first week of July, it held its annual convention at the Sheraton Hotel in Columbus, Ohio. It was the twenty-fifth convention since the group's founding and, in many ways, its last. The gathering began smoothly enough, with rare appearances by Roy Wilkins and Whitney Young, both of whom pleaded for unity within the fractured civil rights community. Young even broke from his past rejection of Black Power, telling the delegates that America responded only to threats and pressure, not "to people who beg on moral grounds." There was also a dinner in McKissick's honor, attended by Muhammad Ali and James Baldwin. Speaking before a crowd of three hundred, McKissick grew nostalgic as he recalled his long association with CORE, from the Journey of Reconciliation in 1947 to the sit-ins of 1960 to the March Against Fear two years earlier. He also made clear just how difficult it was for him to resign, going so far as to suggest he might not be finished after all. "I might just step aside for a little while," he said, "but it would make too many white people happy if I leave."

From there, the convention went downhill fast. The same issues that had divided the delegates a year earlier—chapter autonomy, support from white foundations, the meaning of Black capitalism—surfaced again, this time in more intractable form. A group of delegates from Brooklyn and the Bronx, furious with Innis's imposition of a yearly assessment on all chapters, walked out on the last day and announced plans to form a splinter organization. Their departure prevented CORE from ratifying a new constitution and electing a national director. Two months later, the delegates reconvened in St. Louis to take care of unfinished business. After another walkout, this time by a Chicago group, the remaining chapters elected Innis as national director and approved a new constitution that excluded whites from active membership, thus completing CORE's transformation from a multiracial pacifist group to an all-Black association with separation as its goal. As Innis put it in his first press release after the convention, CORE had become "once and for all . . . a Black Nationalist Organization."

If McKissick had any doubts about his decision to resign, the events of that summer erased them. As he had predicted a year before, the era of the big civil rights groups was coming to an end. The movement might not be dead, but for McKissick—and the country—it was time to begin a new chapter.

· 4 ·

Dreams into Reality

When McKissick left CORE in the summer of 1968, he could have pursued any number of opportunities. With his national reputation and successful legal career, he could have joined a high-powered New York law firm, taken a job as a university professor, or run for a seat in Congress, as several friends had urged him to do earlier in the year. But McKissick was determined to prove the viability of Black capitalism, so he did what any good capitalist would do: he started his own business.

With a fifty-thousand-dollar loan from Chase Manhattan Bank, he founded McKissick Enterprises, a for-profit corporation designed to serve as a national clearinghouse for Black capitalism. Both a resource for other businesses and an investment vehicle itself, McKissick Enterprises had an ambitious goal: "to create and distribute profits to millions of Black Americans." To achieve this goal, the company would launch, and invest in, a variety of business ventures, from real estate to restaurants to retail. It would also assist other Black entrepreneurs, serving as a conduit to banks, providing technical advice, and leveraging McKissick's name on behalf of smaller firms. The corporation would be guided by a commitment to social justice but would need to generate profits to succeed. For that reason, McKissick made clear he would only invest in projects that promised a high rate of return. He also insisted the corporation would not become a tool of white oppression. As he explained in announcing his plan, "The Black Man and Woman will no longer be content to eat leftovers in the kitchen. We want to sit at our own table and carve the financial turkey with all its trimmings."

In spite of its grand ambitions, the headquarters of McKissick Enterprises was humble—a suite of rooms on the second floor of a two-story walk-up on 125th Street in Harlem, just down the street from the Apollo Theater. The offices were small, the furniture secondhand, and the bathrooms frequently out of service. But what it lacked in opulence, the office made up for with energy and a sense of purpose. It was led by Gordon Carey, the former CORE field secretary who had been ousted as part of the purge of white leadership. Occupying an office next to McKissick's, he served as an unofficial chief operating officer, managing day-to-day affairs and attempting to carry out McKissick's expansive vision. Working with him was a small staff of well-educated professionals, marketing and finance types who dressed in two-piece suits and took their jobs seriously. There was Froncell "Skip" Tolbert, a former marine and commercial lending officer who served as director of finance; Leslie Roberts, an alumnus of Harvard Business School who oversaw business development; and Lloyd Von Blaine, a public relations executive who owned a share of Frank's Restaurant, a Harlem institution where McKissick often held court in a corner booth. There were also three administrative assistants: Dorothy ("Dot") and Margaret Waller, unmarried sisters who had worked for McKissick in Durham, then followed him to New York when he took over CORE; and Jane Groom, a vivacious young mother of five from the projects north of the city. On a typical day, the office buzzed with activity—the sound of phones ringing, typewriters clicking, and staff dictating letters. The only thing that might break their concentration was a visit from some prominent civil rights figure—James Farmer, John Killens, or Stokely Carmichael, the last of whom would breeze into the office in a long, colorful dashiki and greet the secretaries in a loud, exuberant voice: "Hello, my beautiful African Queens. You are like flowers after a spring rain." The atmosphere was one of solidarity and optimism, an ethos best captured by a large poster that greeted visitors at the top of the steep stairs. Printed in black, red, and green, the colors of the Pan-African flag, it succinctly stated the mission of McKissick Enterprises: "Dreams into Reality."

During its first few months, the company launched a hodgepodge of business ventures: a publishing house called Thunder and Lightning, which purchased the rights to Robert F. Williams's Black Power manifesto *Negroes with Guns*; an import-export business, which sent Carey on a scouting trip to Mexico; a public relations firm targeted at Black companies; and a chain of restaurants and nightclubs featuring African-style food and entertainment. The firm also developed plans to build a shopping mall in Mount Vernon, New York, and McKissick joined Harlem Freedom Associates, a partnership of leading Harlemites (including Wilt Chamberlain and Bill Cosby) that purchased the Woolworth building on 125th Street, then leased it back to the store and used the profits to address community needs.

Based on his wide-ranging activities, one might have thought McKissick had set aside his dream of building a new city. After all, when he released a list of prospective projects shortly after filing for incorporation, the development of new towns appeared near the bottom, just above plans for Harlem Delight Coffee and a new line of hot sauce. But McKissick hadn't given up his dream. He was biding his time, waiting for the right moment to strike. And he soon received the encouragement he was looking for.

IT CAME FROM Washington. For many years, even before the riots of the 1960s, federal officials had been searching desperately for a way to improve living conditions in the cities. An influx of foreign immigrants and rural refugees since the turn of the century had placed heavy strains on the nation's urban centers. Public transportation was deficient, social services were stretched thin, and the housing stock was old, inadequate, and substandard. The postwar housing boom had only made matters worse. Instead of building new apartments in metropolitan areas, developers had erected sprawling housing tracts in the suburbs, luring the white middle class away from the cities. This didn't relieve the problem of urban overcrowding, however. As middle-class whites fled, poor Blacks from the South streamed in, and the resulting decline in tax revenue made it even harder for city officials to turn things around.

Congress had initially responded to this downward spiral with a program of urban renewal that provided money for local governments to demolish slums and build high-rise housing projects. In cities such as New York, Boston, and Chicago, entire neighborhoods were razed, and tens of thousands of poor, mostly Black residents were uprooted. Some were given apartments in the new projects, but many were displaced, with no choice but to move to other slums that had not yet been destroyed. As James Baldwin put it, "urban renewal" was really just "Negro removal." Not that those who remained behind were fortunate. Many of the new housing projects, such as the infamous Pruitt Igoe in St. Louis, quickly became slums themselves. Poorly designed, cheaply built, and badly maintained, they soon became overcrowded and run-down, infested with rats and roaches, breeding grounds for crime, illness, and delinquency.

It was these conditions, some social scientists argued, that had triggered the riots in the first place. People packed together like animals were bound to act like animals. One scientist even tested the theory, crowding rats into cages and documenting the pathology that ensued: a spike in aggression and mortality, a decline in fertility and social interaction. In a phrase that excited popular fears, he described rats living in such conditions as "going berserk." He also argued that overcrowding resulted in a "behavioral sink," a self-perpetuating descent into the abyss that inspired Tom Wolfe's 1968 ode to urban chaos "O Rotten Gotham—Sliding Down into the Behavioral Sink."

The worst was yet to come, sociologists warned. As more people moved to the cities in search of opportunity, unemployment and overcrowding would continue to rise, making life increasingly unbearable. According to the National Committee on Urban Growth Policy, the country would add a hundred million people by the start of the twenty-first century, and the vast majority would live in cities. Such forecasts sparked a revival of interest in the ideas of Thomas Malthus, the eighteenth-century British demographer who predicted that population growth would lead to famine and devastation. There was even a new Malthus, a Stanford University professor named Paul Ehrlich whose 1968 book *The Population Bomb* became a *New York Times* bestseller. Opening with the ominous declaration that "the battle to feed all humanity is over," the book described a dystopian future characterized by mass starvation and an alarming rise in the global death rate.

Since becoming president in 1963, Lyndon Johnson had taken a series of steps to address the mounting crisis. In 1964, he signed a bill creating the Department of Housing and Urban Development (HUD), the first cabinet-level agency focused on cities. A year later, he established the Task Force on Metropolitan and Urban Problems. Led by Robert Wood, a political scientist at MIT, the task force proposed a variety of initiatives for revitalizing the slums, including the popular Model Cities program, which provided infusions of cash to help communities combat the entire menu of urban ills—poverty, joblessness, crime, and shoddy housing. But revitalizing the slums was only part of the solution. Even if the cities became more livable, they were still incapable of absorbing the huge increase in population projected over the next half century. For that reason, Wood's task force concluded that the nation needed to do more than rehabilitate existing cities; it needed to build new ones as well. And because the task force believed private developers were unlikely to build those cities on their own, it recommended that the government oversee the effort itself.

As radical as this sounded, it was not without precedent. Seventy years earlier, at the close of the nineteenth century, a similar idea had taken hold in England. Known as the "garden city movement," it was the brainchild of Ebenezer Howard, a London court reporter who was appalled by the city's wretched living conditions and set out to find a solution. The problem, as Howard described it in his 1898 book *To-morrow: A Peaceful Path to Real Reform*, was that cities and rural areas offered mutually exclusive attractions. Cities had jobs, good wages, social interaction, and entertainment, but suffered from long commutes, overcrowding, inadequate housing, and a lack of nature. The country offered low rents, relaxation, proximity to nature, and fresh air, but lacked jobs, society, culture, and a communal spirit. These two environments were like magnets, pulling people in opposite directions. Instead of choosing between the two, Howard proposed merging them into a third setting—the "town-country magnet"—that combined the best of both worlds. To illustrate his theory, he sketched a diagram of three magnets arrayed around a group of people with the caption, "Where Will They Go?" To Howard, the answer was obvious. They would go where they could find high wages *and* low rent, natural beauty *and* human interaction, a field for enterprise *and* a flow of capital, freedom *and* cooperation. They would go to Garden City.

Howard's book had a utopian sensibility, but it was also quite specific. He had worked out all the details of what Garden City would look like. It would cover six thousand acres, would be "of circular form," and would have "six magnificent boulevards—each 120 feet wide," dividing it into six equal parts. At the center would be a garden surrounded by a series of grand public buildings, which would themselves be encircled by a 145-acre park. Next would come a glass shopping arcade called the "Crystal Palace," followed by concentric rings of houses, with an average lot size of 20 by 130 feet. The city would have a population of thirty thousand, while an additional two thousand people would live and work on an agricultural "green belt" surrounding it. Factories and workshops would separate the city from the green belt and would be linked by a circular railway, which would connect to a larger railway running to other garden cities. Howard had even devised a method of financing his cities, estimating that each resident would have to pay no more than two pounds a year to cover rent and maintenance.

Howard's proposal was hugely influential in England, leading to the creation of two Garden Cities—Letchworth, forty miles north of London, and Welwyn Garden City, halfway between the two. But his ideas were even more popular abroad, spawning replicas throughout Europe and inspiring the Swiss-French architect Le Corbusier, who attempted to translate the Garden City concept into a highrise modernist development called Radiant City. In the United States, Howard was embraced by a group of planners known as the Decentrists, who wanted to disperse the urban population to a series of small, self-contained communities linked by a network of highways. Although their plan never materialized, they did build two towns in the Garden City image—Sunnyside Gardens in Queens, New York, and Radburn, New Jersey, twenty miles west of Manhattan. Howard's ideas also shaped federal policy during the Great Depression. Faced with a sharp drop in agricultural prices and fearing that farmers would crowd into cities looking for work, President Franklin D. Roosevelt established the Resettlement Administration, an agency charged with building new communities. Under the guidance of Rexford Guy Tugwell, a Columbia University economist, the agency built three towns modeled on Howard's proposal: Greenbelt, Maryland; Greendale, Wisconsin; and Greenhills, Ohio. More than three thousand families moved into the towns, at a cost of $20 million. But the program came under attack for its hefty price tag and collectivist ethos (Tugwell, who had visited Russia in 1927, was nicknamed "Rex the Red"). And when a federal court ruled that it exceeded Congress's powers, the program was phased out, and the three towns were handed over to local homeowners' groups.

The drive to build new cities resumed in the wake of World War II as the return of soldiers and the baby boom created an urgent need for housing. This time, the private sector took the lead. In 1946, a group of developers in Illinois announced plans for Park Forest, a fully planned community thirty-five miles south of Chicago. Envisioned as a middle-class enclave primarily for veterans, Park Forest was one of the first successful new towns in the United States, reaching a population of thirty thousand by 1960. A few years later, Robert E. Simon, a wealthy real estate investor from New York, sold his interest in Carnegie Hall and bought nearly seven thousand acres of land in rural Virginia, eighteen miles west of Washington, DC. There, he broke ground on Reston (the name derived from his initials), a community designed as an alternative to the cookie-cutter houses and bland streets of most postwar suburbs. Built around a European-style village center, Reston relied on mixed zoning, high density, and open spaces to create an urban atmosphere in a pastoral setting. Meanwhile, thirty miles northeast of Washington, the shopping mall magnate James Rouse founded Columbia, Maryland. At fourteen thousand acres, Columbia was double the size of Reston and even more ambitious in concept. Instead of a bedroom community, Rouse set out to build a self-sufficient city of a hundred thousand people with its own economic base. He had already won approval from local officials and was about to begin construction on the first of Columbia's nine planned villages.

Despite the success of Park Forest, Reston, and Columbia, many private developers were reluctant to build new towns because of the high start-up costs and likelihood of failure. After purchasing a vast tract of land, a developer might spend several years and tens of millions of dollars clearing land, paving roads, and installing electricity, water, and sewer systems before generating any revenue. All the while, he had to pay off his debt, a burden that grew heavier as interest rates rose in the late 1960s. Both Reston and Columbia were backed by major corporations—the former by Gulf Oil, the latter by Connecticut General Life Insurance Company, Chase Manhattan, and the Teachers Insurance and Annuity Association. But even they faced financial difficulties. Reston nearly went bankrupt in its early years and was taken over by Gulf Oil in 1967, while James Rouse was forced to surrender half his interest in Columbia to Connecticut Life. Given the risk that a similar fate might befall them, most developers weren't willing to take the chance, choosing instead to build featureless suburban housing tracts such as Levittown, New York, and Daly City, California, the latter of which was caricatured in a famous folk song by Malvina Reynolds:

Little boxes on the hillside,
Little boxes all the same.
There's a green one and a pink one
And a blue one and a yellow one,
And they're all made out of ticky tacky,
And they all look just the same.

To remedy this problem, Wood's task force proposed federal support for new towns. Under its plan, the government would not give money directly to new-town developers but would use a system of mortgage insurance to guarantee loans made by banks and other investors. That guarantee, the task force believed, would attract investors not normally interested in new towns, since the risk of default would be borne entirely by the government.

Johnson included the group's proposal in his recommendation to Congress in January 1966, and a watered-down version made it into the Housing and Urban Development Act approved that year. But the provision for new towns was overshadowed by the Model Cities program, and over the next two years not a single developer applied for assistance under it. In the meantime, the administration continued to study the matter, consulting with universities, developers, lenders, and nonprofits such as the RAND Corporation. Then came the riots of 1967, and televised images of once-great cities such as Detroit and Newark being burned and looted created a new sense of urgency. One month after establishing the Kerner Commission to investigate the causes of urban unrest, Johnson created the Task Force on New Towns to revisit the work of Wood's group. Finishing its report in the fall of 1967, the task force expanded upon the ideas of the earlier group. Instead of merely providing mortgage insurance for developers, it proposed a more direct form of support: loans backed by government bonds. It also recommended a comprehensive system of federal assistance in which HUD would work directly with developers, and other agencies would supply grants to fund infrastructure projects such as water, sewerage, and electricity.

Johnson incorporated these proposals in the New Communities Act, which he submitted to Congress in February 1968. Part of a larger bill designed to add six million homes for low-income Americans over the next decade, the act called for the allocation of $500 million to build new towns across the country, with a cap of $50 million per town. Introducing the proposal from his ranch in Texas, Johnson described new towns as part of a two-pronged strategy to address the housing needs of the future. "Revitalizing our city cores and improving our expanding metropolitan areas will go far toward sheltering that new generation," he declared. "But there is another way as well, which we should encourage and support. It is the new community, freshly planned and built."

Congress was less certain. When the House voted on the bill, it omitted the provision for new communities. The Senate retained the provision, but not without a fight. During a contentious committee hearing, Senator John Tower of Texas complained that the program was too costly and speculative. Other senators wondered what the difference was between subdivisions, which were already supported by another program, and new communities. The bill's sponsor, Alabama Democrat John Sparkman, responded that a subdivision was simply a collection of homes, whereas a new town would have its own police station, schools, churches, and fire department—"everything necessary for the operation of a city." Sparkman also agreed to cut the price tag in half, to $250 million. That was enough to allay opposition, and Tower's motion to strike the provision was narrowly defeated. The House then agreed to reinstate the program, and on August 1, 1968, Johnson signed the New Communities Act into law.

MCKISSICK ENTERPRISES WAS incorporated that same month, but McKissick didn't initially grasp the implications of the new legislation. Not until Samuel C. Jackson, a longtime friend who had recently become assistant secretary at HUD, explained the details of the New Communities Act did McKissick fully realize what it meant. When he did, he quickly got to work. He assigned Gordon

Carey to draft a proposal for a new city while he headed south to look for land.

For Carey, who was thirty-six at the time, it was the perfect assignment. The son of an itinerant preacher who joined CORE in the early 1940s, Carey had spent his entire life immersed in the cause of social justice. As a boy, he met James Farmer at a Methodist camp his father ran in Michigan. In high school, he spent a summer working with the Quakers on the Cocopah Indian Reservation in Arizona. And at the age of eighteen, he volunteered on a cargo ship carrying livestock to war-torn Japan. Known as a "goat boat," the ship left San Francisco in January 1950 and arrived a month later in Okinawa. Once there, Carey and his crewmates spent a month as guests of the occupation government, frequenting the clubs established for American soldiers. Carey, who had led a sheltered life as a preacher's son, was disgusted by what he saw—gambling, drinking, prostitution—and began to question the integrity of the US government. He also began to flirt with anarchism, and when he registered for the draft, in 1950, he listed himself as a conscientious objector.

Carey was at a Quaker work camp in Mexico when the draft office notified him that he had been exempted from military service because of his religious beliefs. For most conscientious objectors, that would have been good news. But Carey was troubled. As he explained in a letter to the draft office, if he accepted the exemption he would be allowing someone else to be drafted in his place. That didn't seem right to Carey, who rejected the government's authority to force anyone to serve. The draft office, not surprisingly, disagreed. But it did make one concession: it sent Carey a new draft card. He was now listed as eligible for military service and ordered to report immediately for induction. When he failed to show up, a federal judge issued a warrant for his arrest.

What happened next was farcical. Carey was in Pasadena, California, by this time, living with his parents, and FBI agents staked out their house. The problem was the agents always arrived after Carey left in the morning and departed before he returned home. After a week, his mother became so annoyed she ratted out her son, telling the agents he was at his girlfriend's house across town. When they turned up there to arrest him, Carey refused to cooperate, letting his body go limp so that the agents had to transport him to jail in a wheelchair. The incident was so unusual in 1953 that the *Los Angeles Times* ran a front-page story about it the next day, complete with a photo of Carey sporting black-rimmed glasses, a pencil-thin mustache, and a high pompadour, with a loose strand of hair falling dramatically over his forehead.

Against the advice of the judge who heard his case, Carey represented himself, repeating the argument he had made in his letter: the government had no power to force men to serve against their will. The judge was no more sympathetic to this argument than the draft office. He sentenced Carey to three years in the Catalina Federal Honor Camp, a minimum-security prison in the mountains of Arizona. Established in 1933, Catalina housed low-level offenders who posed little threat of escape; instead of fences or barbed wire, a white line on the ground marked its boundaries. Carey worked in the infirmary, cleaning teeth, dispensing medication, and serving meals. But mostly he read. For a prison, Catalina was surprisingly well stocked with subversive literature. Carey plowed his way through works by Nehru and Trotsky, Emerson and Thoreau. The book that influenced him most was Tolstoy's *The Kingdom of God Is Within You*, a treatise on nonviolent resistance that had inspired Gandhi.

After a year in prison, Carey appeared before a parole board. Asked whether he had learned his lesson, he said he would do the same thing again. The board released him anyway, and Carey moved back to California, where he took classes at Pasadena City College. Already active in CORE, he was soon offered a job on the national staff in New York, working first as a field secretary, then as program director, and finally as assistant to the national director. During his six years there, he was instrumental in transforming CORE from a small, sleepy organization into one of the most visible and important players in the civil rights movement. In the end, though, the very changes Carey helped make possible within CORE led to his departure from it. As the organization moved away from its pacifist, interracial roots, his presence on the national staff angered some members, and he resigned in 1964. Carey wasn't happy about being forced out, but like many white activists he understood the desire of Black people to control their own struggle. "It was inevitable that the leadership had to move to a younger, Blacker group," he said later.

He felt the same way in August 1968 when McKissick asked him to draft a proposal for a new city, built by Blacks. As a civil rights activist, Carey believed wholeheartedly in integration. But he also believed that Black Americans had to "free themselves from the mental enslavement they were under." And he saw no contradiction between the two. Nor did he see any tension in his involvement with the project, since his job was to help McKissick achieve his dream, not to dictate its essence. "The only way Blacks can become independent is to become a nation, to overthrow the powers that be," Carey explained. "But that doesn't mean the races can't live together."

OVER THE NEXT couple months, Carey worked diligently on the proposal, reviewing the history of new towns, poring over government reports, and engaging in long talks with McKissick. The result, completed in October, served as the basis for all future proposals submitted to HUD. It began with the observation McKissick had been making for years: the crisis of the cities was linked to the crisis of the countryside. As opportunities dried up in small towns and rural areas, millions of poor people migrated to the cities in search of jobs. But the cities were unprepared to receive them. Built haphazardly, they had no plan for meeting the demands imposed by a flood of new residents. Thus, when the migrants arrived, often penniless

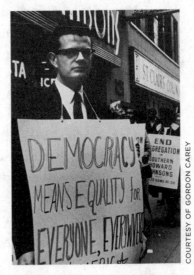

Gordon Carey at a CORE protest in the early 1960s.

and without skills or education, they found themselves in a situation nearly as bad as the one they had left. Instead of clean, modern housing, they were packed into dangerous, disease-ridden slums. Instead of community and connection, they found alienation and social anomie. Instead of rewarding, high-paying jobs, they found work that was menial and meaningless, if they were lucky enough to find work at all.

This situation affected all poor people, the proposal acknowledged, but it affected poor Blacks most of all. Because of housing and employment discrimination, Blacks were disproportionately relegated to the ghettos, where overcrowding, unsanitary conditions, and inadequate public services were most pronounced. That was one of the factors behind the spate of "urban rebellions" in recent years. With no way to make their voices heard, Black people had resorted to the only means available for drawing attention to their plight: violence and destruction. That violence had then triggered fresh confrontations with police, which only made the problem worse. "The end result," the proposal explained, "has been perpetuation of racial tensions and fears, themselves one of the root causes of urban blight."

What was the solution to this "self-perpetuating" problem? The Kerner Commission, established by Johnson to investigate the causes of urban unrest, had identified three possible responses: maintain the status quo; improve the "racial ghettos"; or relocate their residents to the suburbs. The commission ruled out the first option as a nonstarter, leaving improvements to the ghettos and relocation to the suburbs as the only possibilities. But in an article published in *Progressive Architecture* in August 1968, an architect named Ervin Galantay argued that this was a false choice. Titled "Black New Towns: The Fourth Alternative," the article noted that the commission had failed to consider another option: building new cities for Black Americans. To Galantay, this was the logical solution. The Model Cities program was destined to fail, he thought, because its resources were diluted across too many communities. But if the government put all its energy and money into one massive project—such as a new city—it might actually make a difference.

Carey had not read Galantay's article (and Galantay was apparently unaware of McKissick's plan), but their proposals were strikingly similar. Like Galantay, Carey first considered other answers to the urban crisis. Some Black leaders had suggested that all political and economic power in the ghettos be transferred to Black people, either individually or collectively. But this was only a partial solution, Carey explained, since the ghettos were in desperate straits. In any event, there was little chance white politicians and businessmen would agree to such a plan. A better answer was to start from scratch, to create new communities that would combine the best elements of urban and rural living. Countries such as England and Sweden had been experimenting with new cities for decades, the proposal pointed out. A handful of new towns had also been built in the United States. So far, however, Blacks had been largely excluded from these efforts. None of the new towns under construction were likely to achieve economic integration, much less racial balance. "The few blacks who may live in these communities," the proposal asserted, "will be lost in a sea of white suburbanites and will find themselves even further from the ability to determine their own affairs."

What America needed was cities built by and for Black people, cities that could provide "opportunity for Black youth," "new homes for Black families," "educational systems truly responsive to Black children," and "work for many Black unemployed and underemployed." Building "black-oriented cities," the proposal declared, would "provide an opportunity for the establishment of Black economic and political power without challenge to those already in control of existing cities." Moreover, these cities could serve as a testing ground for new ideas in urban planning. Unburdened by the mistakes of the past, planners could start fresh, rethinking the role of critical institutions, such as law enforcement, fire departments, and hospitals.

When it came to details, Carey's proposal was still thin. It suggested that the city would be developed in stages, eventually reaching a population of eighteen thousand, and that it would include everything found in a self-sustaining community: schools, churches, parks, recreation centers, industry, and job training. It also indicated that the city would be built in a rural area, far from an existing metropolis, since that would allow it to develop its own culture and identity. As for who would live there, the proposal maintained that the city would be open to people of all races. But it made clear that the majority of residents would be Black. "Persons of any color or persuasion will be welcomed as technicians for this city, and as residents," the proposal stated. "However, the town will be built with primary concern for the interest and welfare of Blacks and other disadvantaged minorities."

Anticipating the objections this might generate, Carey included a section titled "Black Orientation of the New Community." It was here that he attempted to justify the focus on Black needs and counter the claims of separatism. As a predominantly Black community, the proposal stated, "the new city will not further segregation, but rather provide a source of inspiration to Blacks throughout the country and a living proof to members of all other races that the Black man can hold his own in any modern economy, and can, in fact, exercise a role of leadership for the entire nation." If successful, the new city could be a model for other communities and an exporter of Black talent to the rest of the country. But its most important contribution would be psychological: "The tangible evidence of a new city, planned, built and operated primarily by Black people could bring hope to the most depressed areas of the nation."

The proposal ended with an action plan. It noted that McKissick had been in touch with James Rouse, the developer of Columbia, who had offered free training for McKissick's staff. McKissick had also been promised help by a number of other prominent institutions, including the business schools of Harvard and Columbia. Over the next few months, McKissick Enterprises would establish departments dealing with the full range of development activities: industrial and residential land sales, construction, educational systems, utilities, community services, finance, and marketing. The proposal also provided tentative cost estimates. The budget for the first six months would be a hundred thousand dollars. But that would cover only the most preliminary expenses. Ultimately, McKissick would need far greater sums to plan and develop his city.

At the moment, however, that city was just an abstraction, a vague dream without so much as a name. In order to make it a reality, McKissick would need land on which to build.

PART II

· · · · · · · · · · · · ·

5

Klan Country

In the fall of 1968, McKissick traveled to North Carolina to scout for property. For a developer hoping to build a new city, it was not an obvious place to look. California was a more logical choice, with an abundance of land, a growing economy, and several large projects already under way, including the planned community of Irvine in Orange County. New York State was also fertile ground for new cities, as was the area around Washington, DC, home to both Reston and Columbia. But McKissick was determined to build his new city in the South. Since most Black people in the North had migrated from below the Mason-Dixon Line, he reasoned, they were more likely to relocate there than anywhere else. And if he was going to build his new city in the South, he might as well return to the state where he'd been born and raised. Another Asheville native, Thomas Wolfe, wrote that "You can't go home again," but for McKissick home was the only place he wanted to be.

His reasons for choosing North Carolina were not just sentimental. McKissick believed the state's economic climate was conducive to his plans. With its first-rate universities, highly regarded banks, and pro-business culture, North Carolina was viewed as a model of the New South. Less dependent on slavery than the rest of the Confederacy, it had emerged from the nineteenth century with a more optimistic, ambitious attitude than its neighbors. Instead of clinging hopelessly to an antebellum plantation economy, it had invested heavily in industry, betting its future on textiles and furniture. The results were impressive. From 1900 to 1939, the value of its manufactured products increased more than that of any other southern state, and its total manufacturing value was second only to Texas, a state five times its size. In the words of the political scientist V. O. Key, North Carolina had demonstrated a "relentless forward determination."

From a political standpoint, the state was also attractive to McKissick. As Key observed in his 1949 book *Southern Politics in State and Nation*, North Carolina had been blessed with a record of stable and responsible leadership. "For a half century no scandals have marred the state administration. No band of highwaymen posing as public officials has raided the public treasury. No clowns have held public office—save the erratic and irrelevant Bob Reynolds—and there have been no violent outbursts by citizens repressed beyond endurance." Instead, the state had been guided by respectable, if stodgy, conservatives who were more interested in promoting business than fanning the flames of racism or pandering to populism. It had even produced a handful of leading liberals, including Frank Porter Graham, the US senator and past president of the University of North Carolina, and former governor Terry Sanford, who would soon become president of Duke University. For that reason, Key had labeled it a "progressive plutocracy," while a Black journalist who visited the state in 1947 wrote that it was "something of a living answer to the riddle of race."

Not that racism wasn't alive and well in the Old North State. It was still part of the South, with all the historical baggage that entailed. Although slavery had not dominated the state's economy, enslaved people still accounted for one-third of its population at the start of the Civil War. And although North Carolina had initially resisted calls for secession, it ultimately joined the Confederacy and then, after the defeat of Reconstruction, implemented a regime of white supremacy. When Black Republicans rebelled against that system, joining with populists to win control of the state government in 1894, white Democrats unleashed a campaign of violence that crushed the nascent fusion party. In Wilmington, an armed mob rampaged through the city, setting fire to the office of a Black newspaper, killing dozens of Black residents, and forcing the Republican mayor and city council out of office. It was the only successful coup d'état in American history, and Democrats moved quickly to ensure it would never be necessary again. Following the lead of other Southern states, they enacted a poll tax and literacy test designed to disenfranchise Black voters while grandfathering in poor, uneducated whites.

John Hope Franklin described the Wilmington insurrection as "the dying gasp of a reign of terror," and over the next half century the state avoided the worst excesses of Jim Crow as governors such as Charles Aycock promoted universal education for both Blacks and whites. Yet even as its policies became marginally more progressive, racism held a powerful grip on the state. Aycock was a white supremacist who thought Blacks were fit only for manual labor, and Sam Ervin, the state's longtime senator, was one of the signers of the 1956 Southern Manifesto, which condemned the Supreme Court's decision in *Brown v. Board of Education* and vowed to preserve segregation by all legal means. A graduate of Harvard Law School who nonetheless described himself as "a simple country lawyer," Ervin also led the Democratic Party's opposition to civil rights legislation during the 1960s. Maintaining that the federal government lacked the power to regulate racial discrimination, he famously argued that individuals were "entitled to their prejudices as well as their allergies."

So North Carolina was certainly "no picnic ground for its Negro citizens," as Key was quick to acknowledge. But with the possible exception of Virginia, it was more hospitable to Black people than any other southern state. And that "hospitality" had made possible something else that appealed to McKissick: a strong tradition of Black activism he could draw on for support. Not only had the sit-in movement been launched in Greensboro, the Student Nonviolent

Coordinating Committee had been formed at Shaw University in Raleigh. A number of influential activists had also emerged from North Carolina, including Ella Baker, the onetime aide to Martin Luther King Jr. who was known as the "Mother of the Civil Rights Movement"; Pauli Murray, the pioneering lawyer who coined the term "Jane Crow" to highlight the sexist dimensions of racial discrimination; and Jesse Jackson, a South Carolina native who made his name as student body president at North Carolina A&T, one of the state's many historically Black colleges. Perhaps most importantly for McKissick, the Black Power movement had strong roots in the state. One of the movement's earliest heroes was Robert F. Williams, a former marine who headed the NAACP chapter in the town of Monroe during the late 1950s and early 1960s. At a time when nonviolence was the rallying cry of most civil rights leaders, Williams sang a different tune. Fed up with the terrorist tactics of the Ku Klux Klan, he called for armed self-defense, forming a local chapter of the National Rifle Association and asserting that Blacks "must be willing to kill if necessary." Williams fled the country in 1961 after being brought up on trumped-up charges of kidnapping and was now living in China. But his legacy had inspired a new generation of activists, including the Pan-Africanist Howard Fuller, who would soon make news of his own with the opening of Malcolm X Liberation University in Durham.

For all these reasons, McKissick had settled on North Carolina as the home of his new city. But there was still the question of where within the state it would be located. The Blue Ridge Mountains, where he was born and raised, were too remote and inaccessible to attract the industry needed to create jobs. Besides, the Black population in the mountains had never been substantial; in 1968, fewer than 20 percent of Asheville's residents were nonwhite. The Coastal Plain, on the other hand, was heavily Black, especially in the northeast, where large plantations had been most prevalent and slavery most widespread. But this area, known as the North Carolina "Black Belt," was remote, in addition to having the most racist and conservative white population in the state. (It was a paradox of slavery that Black people were most oppressed in those areas where their numbers were largest, a consequence of white fears of insurrection.) That left the Piedmont, the vast middle region that separated the mountains from the lowlands. Encompassing the state's five largest cities—Charlotte, Raleigh, Greensboro, Winston-Salem, and Durham—and more than half its population, the Piedmont was the engine of economic growth in the state. It was home to the textile and furniture industries, the banking sector, and the burgeoning Research Triangle Park, which had recently landed its first major tenant in IBM. It was bisected by four major highways, boasted three commercial airports, and was the most politically moderate area of the state. If you were going to build a new city in North Carolina, especially if you were Black, the Piedmont was where you wanted to be.

McKissick knew the region well, having lived in Durham for two decades before moving to New York as head of CORE in 1966. He also knew from conversations with James Rouse that it was important not to reveal his intentions publicly before securing the land. Doing so could generate resistance to his plan and drive up prices as property owners sought to profit from his need for land. So instead of making the initial inquiries himself, he trusted the task to an old colleague, Theaoseus Theaboyd Clayton, known to friends as T.T. Eight years younger than McKissick, Clayton was a self-described "country boy" from Roxboro, a small town in the north-central part of the state. His family owned a large farm that grew tobacco, corn, and wheat, and Clayton spent much of his youth working the fields. But his father was determined to send all seven of his children to college, so Clayton left home at the age of eighteen and enrolled at Johnson C. Smith, an all-Black university in Charlotte. He did well enough there to gain admission to North Carolina College School of Law, the same school McKissick had attended before integrating the law school in Chapel Hill. Clayton worked briefly in McKissick's office after graduation, then entered into a partnership with a white lawyer in Warrenton, an hour northeast of Durham. An interracial law firm was practically unheard of in those days, but the white lawyer had represented suspected communists before Congress, so no whites would work with him. Clayton took on his own share of unpopular causes, representing Black parents who sued to inte-grate the Warren County schools and defending activists who were arrested for sitting in the white section of a movie theater. But he also got along well with local officials, developing a reputation as a smart, capable attorney. And he was married to an equally smart, capable woman, Eva M. Clayton, a fellow graduate of Johnson C. Smith who had made headlines earlier in the year when she ran for Congress. She lost to the incumbent, Lawrence H. ("L.H.") Fountain, who had held the seat for eighteen years. But her campaign boosted Black voter registration, and by winning nearly a third of the vote she established herself as an important new voice in North Carolina politics.

As an attorney who frequently handled land sales, Clayton was familiar with the region's real estate market, and he began making calls on McKissick's behalf. His first stop was a five-hundred-acre farm in Halifax County, on the eastern edge of the Piedmont. Owned by a prominent Black family that had made money in the funeral business, the farm was fertile and flat, with a large fish pond at its center. But when Clayton described the property to McKissick, the latter was unimpressed. "I don't know, T.T.," he said. "We need a *lot* of land." So Clayton contacted a state agricultural agent, who told him about a place called the Circle P Ranch, an 1,800-acre estate whose owner was eager to sell. Once a tobacco farm, the Circle P had in recent years been used for timber and cattle. It featured several creeks, a handful of barns and outbuildings, and an old white mansion on a hill. Best of all, it was located in Clayton's backyard—in Warren County, nine miles west of Warrenton.

Named after Joseph Warren, a Massachusetts doctor who died in the Battle of Bunker Hill, Warren County had at one point been the richest and most influential county in the state. Situated just west of the fall line that divides the Piedmont from the Coastal Plains, it had been home to the state's largest tobacco and cotton plantations during the eighteenth and nineteenth centuries. In its heyday, it had produced four governors, six state attorneys general, three state supreme court justices, five tobacco magnates, and the designer of the original Confederate flag. It was a destination, "the kind of place where Southern aristocrats came to relax," in the words of one journalist. "They bathed in the local hot springs and stayed at the Panacea Springs Resort and the Shocco Springs Hotel." Horace Greeley, the influential editor of the *New-York Tribune*, was married there, and Robert E. Lee's second daughter, Annie Carter Lee, was buried there.

By 1968, though, Warren County was a ghost of its former self. The tobacco and cotton farms had withered in the face of falling prices and foreign competition, while new technologies had eliminated many of the old field jobs. So, as was the case across the South, young Black men and women had headed north in ever larger numbers. They traveled by whatever means they could, the poorest by bus, the richest by car, and nearly everyone else by train. Most from Warren County took the latter, carrying a few belongings, a little money, and enough chicken to last the journey. It was this last detail that gave the train north its nickname: the Chickenbone Special. As one writer described its passengers, "Often they board with little more than the clothes on their backs, the paper bag of fried chicken, and an abiding faith that everything will be all right once they get North to where the jobs are. . . . Behind them is the near-certainty of nothing. Ahead, the nothing is at least still a gamble."

The Black exodus had a devastating impact on the South, draining it of the cheap labor it had come to depend on. In 1900, Black people made up a third of the region's population, and 90 percent of all Black Americans lived in the South. By 1970, only 19 percent of southerners were Black, and almost half of all Blacks lived outside the South. The pattern in Warren County was similar. From 1950 to 1970, one-third of the county's residents left, reducing the population from twenty-four thousand to just under sixteen thousand— the largest decline in the state. Most of the emigrants were Black, but many whites moved away, too. For those who remained, the situation was bleak. The median family income of five thousand dollars was about half the national figure, and one in three residents lived below the poverty level, making it the third poorest county in North Carolina and placing it in the bottom 10 percent of counties nationwide. The situation was even worse for Black residents, more than half of whom lived in poverty. If you visited the home of a Black family in Warren County in 1968, there was a 59 percent chance it lacked a proper kitchen, a 65 percent chance it lacked an indoor toilet, and a 68 percent chance it lacked connection to a public sewer or septic tank. As a reporter for the *Washington Post* noted upon touring the area a year later, "You have to study each shack to tell whether it is abandoned or not; until it falls down, an empty shack looks very little different from one that may house a large family."

The history of the Circle P Ranch mirrored that of the county at large. Originally named "Purchase Patent," it had once been a prosperous tobacco plantation owned by William Duke (progenitor of the famous Duke family) and worked by nearly a hundred enslaved people—fifty-three of them kept by William, forty-five by his son Green Duke. It was Green Duke who built the manor house in 1781, then passed it down to his son, Louis Duke, before the entire estate was sold to a planter named William Twitty in 1814. Renamed High Oaks, the plantation continued to profit from slavery until the Civil War, during which it served as a hospital for Confederate soldiers. In 1909, the Twitty family sold the estate to Samuel J. Satterwhite, a successful farmer who served briefly in the North Carolina legislature and fought bitterly against desegregation. He sold it to a lumber company in 1953, and seven years later it was acquired by Leon Perry, a businessman from the nearby town of Henderson, who changed the name to the Circle P Ranch (the P stood for Perry). By this time, the tobacco market was saturated, and the federal government was paying farmers not to plant the crop. So after stripping much of the land of timber, Perry used a quarter of the property to grow corn and the rest to graze cattle. For a while the estate was profitable again, and Perry had one of the largest beef operations in the state, with more than 2,500 head of cattle. But when the ranch started to lose money, Perry began looking for a buyer, which is how he and T. T. Clayton were introduced in the fall of 1968.

THE TWO MEN met at a small airfield near Henderson, where they climbed into a single-engine plane with Perry at the controls. The day was sunny and clear, and as they flew low over the sprawling ranch Clayton could see the white manor house surrounded by a cluster of barns and sheds, a network of red-clay roads, a few crooked creeks, and a dark herd of cows, like the shadow of a cloud, moving across the fields. Clayton was ecstatic, believing he had found exactly what McKissick was looking for. But Perry seemed puzzled. Although it wasn't unheard of for Black farmers to own large tracts of land in this part of the state, Clayton, well-educated and dressed in a business suit, clearly wasn't a farmer. Nor did he seem interested in lumber or cattle, the two other ways to profit from the land. At one point Perry's curiosity got the better of him, and he asked directly, "Hey, Clayton, who wants to buy this? What are you going to do with it?" Clayton simply gestured toward the rolling hills in the distance and offered a vague response. "That sure would make a beautiful golf course," he said.

After viewing the property, Clayton called McKissick and described what he had found. This time, McKissick was intrigued. In addition to Perry's 1,800 acres, there was an adjacent tract of 1,400 acres they could acquire, as well as several smaller lots. All told, Clayton estimated, there were more than 5,000 acres available—an area slightly smaller than Reston and about a third the size of Manhattan. That was more than enough land for a city, so McKissick flew down a few days later to inspect the property himself. Clayton picked him up at the Raleigh-Durham airport, and they drove north on US Route 1 in Clayton's long blue Oldsmobile. In those days, the suburbs north of Raleigh consisted mainly of farms and woodlands, and the monotony of the drive was broken only by the occasional crossroads community. Passing one of these junctions, they spotted a gorgeous spread of land sloping down toward the Tar River, a coffee-colored ditch that once ferried barges loaded with pine tar. "Is that it?" McKissick asked eagerly. "No, that's not it," Clayton replied. "But you'll like it."

And McKissick did. Using a survey Clayton had obtained from the register of deeds in Warrenton, the two men walked and drove the clay roads crisscrossing the property. It was just as Clayton had described: gentle hills, winding creeks, piney woods, and open pastures. There was a massive trench that held more than 1,700 tons of cow fodder, several large grain bins, and an assortment of farm machinery. At the center of the ranch, on the crest of a long incline, sat the old manor house. For several years, Perry's foreman, A. L. "Bud" Meek, had lived there with his son "Butch." They had since moved out, and the house was now in a state of disrepair, with broken windows, a sagging porch, and overgrown bushes blocking the entrance. Nearby stood a row of dilapidated outbuildings that looked as if they might once have stored food or supplies. But knowing the history of Warren County, McKissick and Clayton suspected they had also housed a different type of chattel. As Clayton put it, "It didn't take much imagination to know that a tract of land that large was owned by people who owned slaves."

In assessing the property, McKissick was aware of the challenges he would face building his city on the Circle P Ranch. For one thing, the land had none of the infrastructure needed to support a city. There was only one paved road in the area, and the clay roads were so dusty and rutted they were nearly impassable. The property had no water or sewer system, relying instead on wells and septic tanks, and there were only a few electrical wires running to the house and the main barn. As for Warren County, it didn't have much to offer, either. In addition to its poverty and shrinking tax base, the county's population was largely uneducated: 70 percent of adults hadn't graduated from high school, and only 178 residents in the entire county had a college degree. The school system was mediocre at best, and few residents had the skills needed by the industries McKissick hoped to attract. The county seat, Warrenton, had a population of less than two thousand. And although Blacks made up two-thirds of the county's population, whites controlled all the local institutions—the

county commission, the school board, and the local police department, which had only recently hired its first Black officer. There was
also a long tradition of white intimidation and violence, a legacy of
the slavery era, during which whites were significantly outnumbered
by Blacks. In 1802, fears of a Black uprising had swept the area, and
it was only eighty miles away, in Southampton County, Virginia, that
Nat Turner led his rebellion in 1831. In the twentieth century, whites
had held on to power through other means. As happened elsewhere
in the South, Black people in Warren County had been largely disen-
franchised through discriminatory application of voter literacy tests.
In 1939, only 110 Blacks were registered to vote, compared to 1,270
whites. And in the 1968 presidential campaign, the segregationist
George Wallace beat Democrat Hubert Humphrey in the county by
one vote, with Nixon receiving just one-eighth of the vote total.
Warren County was also the site of significant Klan activity, a fact
made glaringly clear by a sign on a nearby highway that read "You
Are in the Heart of Klan Country."

For all its drawbacks, McKissick saw several advantages to
Warren County. First, land was cheap, which was important if you

A sign greeting visitors to North Carolina in 1968.

needed a lot of it. Perry was asking only $215 per acre, and even if the price increased for subsequent tracts, it was unlikely to reach the $1,500 per acre paid by James Rouse in Columbia. Labor was also cheap; manufacturing wages in Warren County were below the state average, which was itself below the national average. And thanks to the state's aggressive right-to-work laws, union membership was the lowest in the nation, making the site attractive to industry.

Then there was its location. Although more than an hour away from the nearest city of any size (Raleigh, fifty-seven miles to the south, had 122,000 people, while Durham, fifty-four miles to the southwest, had 95,000), Warren County was situated in the desirable Piedmont industrial corridor. Within a five-hundred-mile radius, there were thirteen states, sixty-eight metropolitan areas, and a third of the nation's population. Access to transportation was also good. The Circle P Ranch was adjacent to Route 1, a rural highway once known as "America's Main Street" because it served as the primary corridor from Key West to the Canadian border. Route 1 had since been overshadowed by the massive Interstate 95, which lay thirty miles to the east, but hundreds of trucks still rumbled past the ranch every day. In addition, the new Interstate 85, which was slated to connect Montgomery, Alabama, with Petersburg, Virginia, was under construction less than a mile away. Perhaps most promising, the Seaboard Coast Line Railroad skirted the property's western boundary. Providing passenger and freight service from Florida to Washington, DC, the Seaboard Coast Line was the eighth largest railway in the nation, with more than nine thousand miles of track. If McKissick could persuade railroad management to build a siding at Soul City, he would have a direct shipping line to the entire Southeast.

The Circle P Ranch also had its share of natural resources. In addition to its three creeks—Rocky, Fishing, and Matthews—the property was just a few miles east of Kerr Lake, a fifty-thousand-acre reservoir created by a dam on the Roanoke River. One of the largest reservoirs in the Southeast—roughly the size of Cincinnati—Kerr Lake could supply water for both residents and industry, while also serving as a recreational site for boating, swimming, and fishing.

Finally, there was the history of the property. McKissick soon confirmed what he had suspected on his first visit: the ranch had once been a slave plantation, where Black men and women were passed down from white fathers to their sons. He also discovered that the estate had been owned at one point by Samuel Satterwhite, the segregationist legislator. For McKissick, there was a satisfying symbolism in building his city on such desecrated land. "I have wanted this land for a long time," he later told a reporter. "It belonged to the family of a state legislator who fought integration like a tiger."

Once McKissick settled on the Circle P Ranch, there was the question of how to go about purchasing it discreetly. In conversations with James Rouse, he learned how Rouse had acquired the property for Columbia through a series of shell companies with vague names such as "Alaska Iron Mines Company" and "Premble, Inc." McKissick now employed a similar strategy. First, Clayton negotiated a purchase price of $390,000 with Perry. Then, on December 19, Clayton signed an agreement with Perry, paying $4,000 for a sixty-day option to purchase the land. Finally, Clayton and McKissick entered into a contract whereby Clayton assigned his interest in the option to McKissick Enterprises. Both men being lawyers, they knew that for the assignment to be valid McKissick had to give Clayton something in return, even if it was only a nominal amount. They agreed on the sum of $10, McKissick wrote Clayton a check, and both men signed their names to the contract.

6

"Integration Blackwards"

McKissick's option to purchase the Circle P Ranch was good until February 19, 1969, and in a perfect world he would have completed the deal before going public with his plans. That's what James Rouse had done in 1963, unveiling his proposal for Columbia at a county board meeting after having secretly acquired title to over fourteen thousand acres. But circumstances forced McKissick to follow a bolder course. While scouting land in North Carolina, he had been in touch with Secretary of Agriculture Orville Freeman. In addition to regulating farm prices and food safety, the Agriculture Department was responsible for the economic health of rural America. And Freeman, the former governor of Minnesota, cared deeply about issues of poverty and social justice. During his tenure as secretary, he had helped establish the food stamp and school breakfast programs; had hired William Seabron, a former Urban League official, to eradicate racial discrimination within the department; and had even hosted a conference on the building of new towns across rural America. Thus, when Freeman read McKissick's proposal in late 1968, he offered to do whatever he could to help. The problem was, Freeman would soon be out of a job. On January 20, Richard Nixon would take the oath of office, and a new secretary would be appointed, one who might not be as sympathetic to McKissick's idea. So McKissick made a gutsy decision. In spite of the fact that he didn't yet have title to the land—and hadn't even secured a loan to pay for it—he called a press conference to announce his plans.

It took place on Monday, January 13, in Freeman's office in Washington, DC. McKissick, looking modish in a dark blazer over a white turtleneck sweater, sat behind a large desk arrayed with microphones. Freeman, in a conservative gray suit and black-rimmed glasses, sat next to him, while off to the side stood Seabron, Gordon Carey, T. T. Clayton, and several other McKissick aides. A small pack of television and newspaper reporters crowded into the room, waiting expectantly. Though no longer head of CORE, McKissick was still one of the most prominent—and quotable— Black leaders in the country, and journalists knew better than to miss one of his announcements.

They didn't have to wait long. After a brief word of thanks to Freeman and his department, McKissick dropped a bombshell: he

McKissick (center) with T. T. Clayton (left) and Orville Freeman (right) at the press conference announcing the launch of Soul City.

was planning a new city in rural North Carolina, a city "built and owned by black people." It would be named Soul City and would be located in Warren County, an hour north of Raleigh-Durham. McKissick Enterprises had already secured an option on 1,800 acres of land, in an area "blessed with beautiful scenery and numerous creeks and lakes." Soon, McKissick and his staff would begin planning and developing the city, which would have a population of eighteen thousand people within ten years.

In making his announcement, McKissick framed Soul City as a response, and a partial solution, to the urban crisis. That crisis had not begun in the cities, he argued. Instead, its roots lay in "the migratory pattern of people seeking to escape racism, oppression, and exploitation." Soul City would help arrest that pattern by creating new jobs and opportunities in one of the very regions Black people were fleeing. "We are doing more than building a town," he declared. "We will be helping to put new life into a depressed area where the median income is less than $2,000 per family—and we will be helping to stem the flood of migrants to the already over-crowded and decaying cities."

When it came to the racial makeup of the city, McKissick insisted it would "be open to residents of all colors, because we do not intend to adopt the white man's racism." He also made clear that he welcomed the participation of white America and anticipated support from the federal government, the state of North Carolina, and the nation's industrialists. But he left little doubt that the project was designed primarily to benefit Blacks, especially the poor and unemployed. He boasted that Soul City would create "new careers for black people," promote "the development of talent heretofore never employed or afforded opportunity," and enable Blacks to "determine their own futures." "White men have built other cities," he added. "Soul City will be an attempt to move into the future, a future where black people welcome white people as equals."

McKISSICK'S ANNOUNCEMENT MADE a splash. It was covered by all three television networks on the evening news, including *The*

Huntley-Brinkley Report, which dedicated a generous two and a half minutes to the story. The *Washington Post* published an article on its front page, while wire reports appeared in the *New York Times*, the *Philadelphia Inquirer*, and other major newspapers. For the most part, the coverage was positive. Press accounts emphasized the pledges of assistance McKissick had received from various entities, including Freeman's office, the Rouse Company, and the planning and architectural departments at the University of North Carolina, Columbia University, and MIT. They also repeated, without verification, McKissick's claim that the Nixon administration supported his plan and that four major industries had already expressed interest in building plants in Soul City.

In the days that followed, however, a tone of skepticism and hostility seeped into the coverage, particularly on the opinion pages. The editors of the *News & Observer* in Raleigh conceded that McKissick's idea was "fascinating" and would appeal to "people on all sides of the race issue who wish to see blacks running their own enterprises for their own benefit." But they found grounds for "some very justifiable pessimism." Not only would McKissick have to secure money to develop the land, he would have to recruit industry, train a largely unskilled workforce, and provide transportation, utilities, and a market for goods and services. "If Soul City's planners have looked reality straight in the eye," the editors cautioned, "they realize how difficult it is going to be to make this dream come true." The *Charlotte Observer* was equally dubious. Describing Warren County as "an economic desert island," it noted that the site McKissick had chosen was far from any "job-creating economic center." "Perhaps 'soul' can create a town where none exists and none seems likely to arise otherwise," the paper allowed. But absent "a massive, coordinated, government-backed" effort, Soul City was a gamble against the longest of odds.

The only thing the mainstream media seemed to fear more than the failure of Soul City was the possibility that it might succeed. Despite McKissick's claim that the town would be open to all races, many news outlets viewed the project as an experiment in separatism. The headline in the *Warren Record* blared, "All-Negro City Planned for Warren County Site," while ABC News described Soul City as an "all-black settlement." If such an experiment were to flourish, critics warned, it would have dire consequences for race relations in America. "A new bastion of racial segregation is the last thing this nation needs," argued the editors of the *Greensboro Daily News*. "It would encourage racial segregation just when most Americans have at last accepted that their greatest hopes lie in an integrated society."

Perhaps the most damning critique—and the one that would prove most consequential—came from Claude Sitton, recently appointed as editorial director of the *News & Observer* in Raleigh. A native of Georgia, Sitton had covered the civil rights movement for the *New York Times* from 1958 to 1964 before serving a four-year stint as the paper's national editor. Within the world of newspapers, Sitton was a legend, having taken over the "race beat" for the *Times* just as the movement was gathering momentum and having recognized, before many other journalists, the need for in-depth, continuous coverage of the subject. Driving and flying around the South from his home in Atlanta, he had reported on nearly all the major moments of the struggle—the sit-ins of 1960, the Freedom Rides of 1961, the Albany campaign, the Birmingham campaign, the showdown at Ole Miss, Freedom Summer. Indeed, if one wanted an eyewitness account of the movement's central years, one could simply read Sitton's articles from beginning to end.

Slight of build and prematurely bald, Sitton looked more like a bookkeeper than an intrepid correspondent. But beneath his unassuming appearance and low-key demeanor was a tough, dogged reporter who refused to parrot what white officials told him, instead venturing into Black communities to find the truth himself. A stickler for the facts who believed reporters should be objective, he didn't mistake that objectivity for blindness. He often portrayed civil rights protesters as well-dressed, polite, and respectable, while describing their tormentors as "teenage boys with duck-tail haircuts." In one of his most chilling reports, he recounted firsthand the efforts of police and angry whites to break up a voter registration meeting at a church in rural Georgia on a summer night in 1962. Sitting in the front row with two other reporters, Sitton recorded every detail of the intimidation campaign: how one policeman fingered his revolver while another slapped a heavy flashlight against his palm; how the officers took down the names of those in attendance and warned they wouldn't be able to protect them from the restless crowd outside; how the crowd shined lights in their faces as the attendees filed out into the darkness, then jeered when the reporters discovered that one of their tires was flat; how the reporters were followed for eighteen miles by a carload of whites before they stopped to write down the car's license plate number, only to discover the plate had been bent over to obscure it; and finally, how the reporters took their car to a mechanic the next day and learned that the gas tank had been filled with sand and the air valve on the flattened tire had been slashed with a knife.

Because of his sympathetic and thoughtful coverage of the movement, Sitton was widely admired by civil rights activists, many of whom carried his card as a talisman against violence and police abuse. He was equally respected by his peers in the press. In their book *The Race Beat*, journalists Gene Roberts and Hank Klibanoff described Sitton as the standard-bearer, "the best there was in covering, exposing, and interpreting the race story in the South." But as a Georgian, Sitton could also be defensive, pushing back against the assumption that all southerners were bigots. When James Baldwin criticized his review of a book about the civil rights struggle for suggesting that the author had overstated the extent of southern racism, Sitton responded forcefully, insisting that the White Citizens' Councils that had formed to oppose *Brown v. Board of Education* "do not reign supreme in all areas of the Deep South." He also argued that Baldwin's view of the South as a monolith was simplistic, asserting that the celebrated writer "would find more dissent on closer examination."

AP PHOTO/THE NEW YORK TIMES

Claude Sitton in 1965, one year after he gave up the "race beat" to become the *New York Times* national editor.

Burned out and tired of being away from his family, Sitton gave up the race beat in 1964 and moved to New York. As the *Times*'s national editor, he continued to oversee the paper's coverage of the civil rights movement and occasionally weighed in with his own analysis, as he had done in the wake of King's assassination. But Sitton disliked the internal politics at the *Times* and missed his native South. So when the *News & Observer* offered him the job of editorial director and vice president in the spring of 1968, he eagerly accepted. In his new job, he oversaw both the news and editorial sections of the *N&O*, as it was known, as well as the news department of its evening sister paper, the *Raleigh Times*. He brought to both papers the same insistence on accurate and thorough reporting, the same commitment to integrity, and the same determination to hold public officials accountable. But as head of the *N&O*'s editorial page, he had the power to shape opinion more directly. He also wrote a weekly column on local and national affairs, in which, on January 19, he shared his views on Soul City.

Titled "Soul City's Plan or Wilkins' Way?," Sitton's column juxtaposed McKissick's announcement with a statement issued the same week by Roy Wilkins, who had denounced a call by Black students for all-Black departments and dormitories on college campuses. Sitton acknowledged that, contrary to what the students proposed, Soul City would not be formally or legally segregated. But he suggested this was little more than a ruse to maintain eligibility for federal

funding. In spirit, he argued, Soul City was a descendant of other separatist ventures, from the Amish enclaves of Pennsylvania to Marcus Garvey's back-to-Africa campaign. "Such undertakings share an
unfortunate characteristic," Sitton charged. "They are 'sociological
sports.' They are spawned by an interruption of the normal processes
of human relationships, a sickness that infects both parent and offspring." Wilkins, by contrast, evinced a healthy and productive attitude toward race, Sitton argued. The longtime head of the NAACP
had not moderated his demands for freedom and equality. He was
still "an acid critic of American society," still insisted on the need for
change, for "a sharp alteration in methods" and an "acceleration"
of progress. But there was "none of the rejection, the defeatism and
withdrawal in the Wilkins initiative that one finds in that of McKissick," Sitton wrote. "Instead, it is characterized by faith in America
and in America's ability to change." This was important for whites
to recognize, for ultimately they would help determine the path that
Black people decided to take. And in Sitton's view, white society faced
a clear choice: "It can drift along in the indifference that has bred
Soul City and less benign social ills or it can show Negroes through
constructive action that Wilkins' faith in the system is justified."

Sitton's column—and the criticism it reflected—infuriated McKissick. When asked at his press conference whether his plan was part
of a trend toward separatism, he had responded coolly: "No, I think
it does the same thing as the Chinese have done in New York. They
built a Chinese area—Chinatown. It's a beautiful section of the town
that I admire." But as critics pressed the claim, he became increasingly agitated, convinced that the media were deliberately mischarac-
terizing his plan. Speaking to a group of students at North Carolina
College, in Durham, he blasted pundits' use of the word "separatist,"
calling it an example of "the semantics of racism—the language the
man uses to divide and conquer." He also pushed back against
the claim that Black people were the ones thwarting integration. "The
real separatists are those white people who years ago moved to the suburbs," he declared.

Still, he couldn't escape the perception that Soul City would be all-Black, if not in concept then at least in reality. Nor could he deny that he was partially to blame. Although he consistently maintained that Soul City would welcome whites, his rhetoric seemed designed to scare them away. At one press conference he declared, "Black people will own, control, and develop this city," while at another he announced, "We intend to be a majority, and we intend to control the new town." He also seemed uncertain about how to describe Soul City, using different language depending on his audience. Sometimes he called it "black-inspired," other times "black-built," and still others "black-oriented." Rarely did he call it "integrated." This was no accident. McKissick rejected the label "integrated" because it implied a preexisting policy of segregation. In his mind, there was no need to "integrate" Soul City, since it had never been segregated. "Liberals are all hung up on integration or segregation," he complained to the *Minneapolis Star*. "This is neither integration nor segregation, but letting black people do what they damn please, and go where they please."

He made a similar point in conversations with the Rouse Company. When a planner there questioned whether his approach was consistent with integration, McKissick responded sharply: "Everybody thinks of integration on white people's terms. Integration is fine when it's 80 percent white and 20 percent black. Nobody can conceive of integration where the blacks constitute 80 percent and the whites constitute 20 percent." In the end, McKissick conceded, white racism would probably make Soul City a predominantly Black town. But he didn't care if it was all Black or half Black or somewhere in between. What he cared about was giving Black people the same kind of opportunity and self-determination that white people took for granted. "The concept of Soul City is just as American as apple pie," he told the Rouse planner.

Some observers understood what McKissick meant. Shortly after his initial press conference, he received a letter from Henry H. Parker, a classics instructor at the University of Illinois who wanted to build a Black city in Iowa called King Town. In his letter, Parker referred to the work of Morris Milgram and Byron Johnson, two white developers who were trying to create an integrated community in Denver called Sunburst City. "These cats are groovy," Parker wrote, "but they're concerned with what I call 'Integration Whitewards.' I'm concerned, and it seems that you are too, with 'Integration Black-wards.' This means that we black folks make the plans, and call the shots."

McKissick concurred wholeheartedly. As he explained in his response to Parker, "We are convinced that if black people are to be liberated, they will have to liberate themselves. This is what we intend to do and we do not intend to fail."

IF THE MAINSTREAM press viewed McKissick's plan as too radical in its quest for Black control, some commentators thought it too conservative, relying, as it did, on the existing capitalist structure. Writing in the *North Carolina Anvil*, a progressive weekly in Durham, a journalist named Elizabeth Tornquist argued that Soul City, like any free-enterprise venture, would make its developers rich while leaving its workers poor. "Capitalism has always worked on the theory that the man who invests capital gets a larger return while the man who has only labor to invest gets a small return—enough, in the American system, to buy a house with a long-term mortgage, a car on the installment plan, furniture on credit, and plenty of hotdogs and cheap department store clothes for the children," Tornquist wrote. "But the system has rarely enabled men who invest their labor to purchase with it any sizeable stake in the company. It's difficult to see how the system, operating on the traditional principles, is going to achieve any different results in Soul City."

McKissick had an answer to this criticism, and on February 12— the 150th anniversary of Abraham Lincoln's birth—he unveiled it. Appearing at a press conference in Washington, DC, he explained more eloquently than ever before why it was essential for Black people to participate in the capitalist system. "People who teach economics are mostly white," he told the reporters gathered before him, "but the people who understand economics are mostly black. We know we're poor, and more important, we know why we're poor. We're poor because we don't own any of that thing—capital—that produces most of the wealth." Slavery had produced wealth, he noted, which was why Blacks had been enslaved in the first place. But like all laborers, they had been denied a share of that wealth. "Slavery taught us *who* had leisure, *who* had freedom, *who* had dignity. Not the slave, but the slave-owner. Not the sharecropper, but the landowner. Not the employee, but the capital owner."

That was why Soul City would be based on "slave ownership," McKissick announced, with Black people playing the role of masters. The difference was their "slaves" wouldn't be "weak and defenseless human beings." Their "slaves" would be "the non-human things that produce industrial wealth"—factories, stores, apartment buildings, hotels, warehouses, and machines. These "non-human things" would generate jobs, of course, many of which would be held by Black residents. But they would also create opportunities for Blacks to own capital and acquire meaningful wealth, the kind whites had long possessed. "It will take hard physical work to build a city where there is nothing now but woods and pastures," McKissick acknowledged. "We intend to work, and to work hard. But we do not intend *merely* to work. We intend to own."

Exactly how ordinary workers would acquire a share of capital in Soul City was a separate question. To answer it, McKissick introduced the political economist Louis Kelso, who had worked with CORE in drafting its proposal for community development corporations. Wearing a business suit and a polka-dot bow tie, Kelso didn't look like a radical. But he described his plan for Soul City as a form of "radical capitalism." Under the plan, a corporation that decided to build a factory in Soul City would establish an employee trust, which would borrow the money for construction and distribute the company's profits to employee shareholders. By using the trust form, Kelso maintained, the company could avoid corporate taxes, and employees would pay taxes only on the dividends they collected. The reporters were confused, wondering how Kelso's plan could be squared with corporate tax laws. They also questioned why a company would agree to turn over its profits to an employee trust. "I know it's hard to understand," responded Kelso, explaining that his plan would allow companies to build factories with pretax dollars. Even McKissick acknowledged the scheme was complex and idealistic. "Maybe you're right. Industry doesn't have a conscience," he told the press. "But we've had several companies show interest in this."

To his supporters, McKissick's reliance on Kelso's theories was evidence that Soul City would not be a typical capitalist venture. As David Godschalk, a planning professor at UNC, told a reporter, "It's halfway between almost socialism and the pure commercial concept of Reston and Columbia." Still, some critics weren't satisfied. Writing a few weeks later in *Hard Times*, another alternative newspaper, Tornquist argued that Kelso's concept of "radical capitalism" was an illusion that would soon be exposed by the harsh reality of the marketplace. "If McKissick doesn't make his profit soon, he runs a great risk of making nothing," she warned. And if that happened, the result would be disastrous. "Soul City will be the same patch of rolling countryside it always was, but instead of being called the Circle P Ranch, it may be known as McKissick's folly."

THE MOST POSITIVE reaction to McKissick's plan came from those he hoped to recruit to Soul City: Blacks themselves. In the days and weeks after his announcement, the Black press covered the story closely, with prominent articles appearing in the *New York Amsterdam News*, the *Chicago Daily Defender*, the *Baltimore Afro-American*, the *New Pittsburgh Courier*, and the *Los Angeles Sentinel*. Some Black papers responded directly to the doubts being expressed in the white press. The editors of the *Carolina Times*, in Durham, warned skeptics "to go slow before they conclude that the objective will never be reached." McKissick was not some "fool" with an "ill-conceived idea" but a "dynamic" and "intelligent" leader who knew how to get things done. As to the merits of his plan, the paper was also supportive. The plight of Blacks in Warren County was "pathetic," it asserted. No matter how hard they worked, they had never been given a say in their government. Soul City would change that, providing opportunity and autonomy for Black people throughout the region. "It is our hope therefore that every intelligent Negro citizen of the state, as well as others, will do everything possible to aid the Floyd B. McKissick Enterprise in the worthy goal it has set out to achieve."

For the most part, they did. A few days after McKissick's initial press conference, a group of Black schoolchildren on Manhattan's Lower East Side began a sidewalk collection to raise money for the new city. A few weeks later, both Howard University and North Carolina College offered their support for the project. And as news of McKissick's plan spread, it became clear that he was not the only southern transplant who longed to return home. In cities throughout the North, there were thousands—tens of thousands, maybe even hundreds of thousands—of Blacks who had not found what they were looking for. They had moved to Baltimore (or New York or Chicago or Detroit) because, as the saying went, it was better than hell. But as more and more Black southerners arrived in the North, conditions became increasingly desperate. Between 1940 and 1960, the Black population of New York City increased two and a half times, yet 85 percent of the newcomers were crowded into racial ghettos. The new migrants struggled to find work and housing, often paying a premium for the worst apartments. In the words of one journalist, "Gradually it became clear that Baltimore and Hell were often the same place." And so "the word began trickling back to the farms: stay where you are. The city is no place for people like us. The city is changing. You ain't gonna like it. Man, it ain't human up there."

It wasn't just that the North was inhospitable. Many Black transplants were homesick for the South. They missed the scent of honeysuckle in summer, the call of whippoorwills at night, the feel of cool earth in their hands. Most of all, they missed the sense of belonging, of community, of rootedness, which not even the suffering and persecution they had endured in the South could destroy. This helps explain why so much of the Black migration north during the twentieth century was not permanent. Instead it had a temporary, tentative quality to it, with many migrants returning home shortly after leaving and then repeating the experiment over and over until they either became accustomed to the North or resolved to stay in the South for good. This also helps explain why so many migrants sent their children home to live with grandparents, aunts, uncles, and cousins. As long as their offspring were being raised in the South, they could pretend their sojourn north was simply an extended leave that would one day allow them to return home.

McKissick's plan struck a chord with these transplants, disillusioned by the North and wistful for the South. Soon he was inundated with letters from Washington, DC, Pittsburgh, Philadelphia, Newark, Baltimore, Cleveland, Chicago, Detroit, and New York City. Some correspondents, such as F. N. Kurtz of Columbia, Missouri, wrote to offer encouragement. "Nothing is impossible after somebody does it," observed Kurtz, who hailed McKissick as "the Black Man's Moses." Others, like Robert E. Martin of Washington, DC, expressed an interest in being part of Soul City. Martin, an architect, and his wife, an unemployed manager, had read about the project and felt a "keen concern" for what McKissick was attempting. "In addition to living in Soul City, N.C., we would like to take part in the overall planning." John Council, of the Bronx, inquired about investing money in the project; Tody Foster, of Newark, sought work as an advertising writer; and Ronnie Collins, of Queens, sent the lyrics to a song he had written about Soul City:

> We are gone to live in peace and harmonie
> Cause I think that the way God mint for it to be

Not all the letters came from the North. Waved Ruffin, a school principal from Windsor, North Carolina, wrote to express interest in running a school in Soul City, while Isaac B. Markham, a contractor from Durham who described himself as a "brother of soul," asked whether he could bid on grading work for the project. Some of the letters were sent to McKissick Enterprises in New York. Other writers simply wrote "Floyd McKissick, Soul City, N.C." on the envelope, leaving it to the post office to figure out the rest. Those who were from Warren County relied on connections back home to put them in touch with McKissick. One man wrote to Ernest Turner, the owner of a gas station on the other side of the county. The man had left the area eight years earlier and was working as a supermarket manager in Washington. Now he wanted to return home and open a grocery store in Soul City. Could Turner help him out, he asked. Could Turner pull some strings?

McKissick was overwhelmed by the response. Speaking to reporters during his press conference with Kelso, he boasted about the volume of correspondence. He also reported that, in the weeks since his announcement, a stream of residents from nearby towns and counties had driven over to look at the property. "We could move in two thousand people right away on the basis of the letters we've received," he declared.

Not all Black leaders were sold on the plan. In early January, McKissick had sent a copy of his proposal to Whitney Young, executive director of the Urban League. McKissick and Young had often sparred over the direction of the civil rights movement, with Young urging a cautious, moderate approach and McKissick pushing a militant, confrontational agenda. Especially after the rise of Black Power, the two men had taken wildly divergent paths (though Young had moved closer to McKissick's position at the 1968 CORE convention). But McKissick did not hold grudges or let disagreements get in the way of personal relationships. Besides, he needed as many allies as possible to get Soul City off the ground. So his cover letter was all smiles, sending his best wishes to Young's "lovely wife" and suggesting that the Urban League could "play a major part" in the project.

Young was not swayed. Responding the same day as McKissick's announcement, he wrote that he had "serious questions" about the philosophy behind the proposal. Instead of building a new city, he wondered, why didn't McKissick focus his energies on one of the many Black communities already in existence, such as Harlem, East

Baltimore, or Watts? Doing so would eliminate the need to purchase land and attract residents, "since they are already there and anxiously waiting for you or someone to lead them to becoming the model prototype of how beautiful a black-run city can be." The Urban League had worked with a number of these communities, he added, and would gladly assist McKissick in revitalizing them. But "until we have made these cities succeed, I cannot get excited about starting another one."

Young's letter raised an obvious question. With so many Black communities struggling across the country, how could McKissick justify spending valuable resources building a new one? McKissick had an answer to this question, too. In his mind, there were psychological benefits to building something *new*, benefits that could spark the kind of creative, unconventional thinking that had inspired the civil rights movement itself. He agreed with Young that existing communities should not be forgotten and that Black leaders had a duty to address the problems of the urban poor. He had been as sensitive to those problems as anyone, launching renewal projects in Baltimore and Cleveland as head of CORE. But Young's insistence that all resources be pooled into one pot was "peculiar," he wrote, coming from someone who often "applauded diversity in methodology." In any case, McKissick argued, the land for Soul City was cheap, and it would ultimately cost less to build a new city than to resuscitate a dying one because he would not be burdened by the mistakes of the past.

While Young privately raised questions about Soul City, some Black leaders took their concerns public. Gordon B. Hancock, a sociology professor at Virginia Union University, offered a scathing assessment of Soul City. In a column for the *Norfolk Journal and Guide*, he accused McKissick of selling his race "down the stream to the segregationists for a mess of pottage—for a sop, if you please!" After fighting Jim Crow for a hundred years, Hancock argued, it would be suicide for Black people to embrace separatism now. "Let us hope that the Soul City project will die 'abornin,'" he wrote. "As soon as a Soul City is founded, if the hand-out is lucrative, there will be further Heart Cities, Head Cities, Hand Cities, Finger Cities, Big Toe Cities, Little Toe Cities, and so on!"

Stephen J. Wright, the gray-haired president of the United Negro College Fund, sounded a similar note. In a debate on the subject of all-Black dormitories and academic departments, Wright denounced separatism in all forms. Asked whether this included Soul City, he responded affirmatively: "That, too, is just another ruse to disappoint and delude the ignorant."

OF ALL THE reactions to McKissick's announcement, the one that mattered most was the reaction in Warren County. After all, that's where he planned to build his city. And although he didn't need permission to buy the land, he would need the approval of the Warren County Board of Commissioners to develop it. He would also need the support of local officials and businessmen to attract industry, improve the region's infrastructure, and ensure that Soul City was accepted by the larger community. So in the days and weeks after his announcement, McKissick and his staff watched anxiously as Warren County digested the news.

The initial reaction was mainly surprise. McKissick and Clayton had succeeded in keeping their intentions secret as they negotiated the option on the Circle P Ranch. As a result, residents of Warren County learned about Soul City at the same time as everyone else. Some heard about it on the radio while driving their cars. Some heard about it on the evening news. And some, including Amos Capps, chairman of the Warren County Board of Commissioners, heard about it by telephone. In Capps's case, the call came from the office of his congressman, L. H. Fountain, who wanted to know what all this talk was about a new city. Capps had no idea what Fountain was referring to, and his anger at being kept in the dark showed when he was interviewed later that day. "It did come as a shock to me to learn that a project of this magnitude was being planned without the knowledge of county officials," he told a reporter. Then, taking a shot at what he viewed as the separatist nature of the venture, he added, "They've been trying to get integration for 15 to 20 years and now it looks on the surface as if they are going to get segregation."

After the surprise wore off, officials and white residents cycled through a range of emotions not unlike the five stages of grief. Some were in denial, doubtful the project would ever come to fruition. Some were bargaining, wondering whether they could dissuade McKissick from following through on his plan. And some had reached the point of acceptance, arguing that if Soul City attracted jobs and industry it would be good for the area. Warrenton mayor W. A. Miles seemed to move through multiple stages in a single statement. "A $25 million project like this is too big in a poverty area like this," he told reporters. "If Soul City does materialize, though, then the county tax structure would get a real boost."

But the most prevalent emotions were anger and fear. The anger stemmed from the media's depiction of Warren County as a wretched and pitiable backwater. To many residents, especially those with deep roots in the county, this portrait was new and unfamiliar. To the Turners and Macons, the Braggs and Dukes— families that had been in the area since the eighteenth century— Warren County was the same charming, genteel place it had always been. Walking down Warrenton's historic main street, or driving past its stately mansions shaded by magnificent oak trees, they could convince themselves that nothing had changed, that their community was still as fashionable and smart as their parents and grandparents remembered it. So when reporters described what *they* saw while exploring its back roads or touring its crumbling estates, it came as a shock, like a former starlet seeing herself in the mirror for the first time in fifty years.

One of the most unflattering portraits appeared in the *Washington Post*. Titled "'Soul City' Stirs Its Future Neighbors," the article was written by a young reporter named Hank Burchard who visited the county in late January. Burchard recounted the same dreary facts that had appeared in other papers: the county's alarming poverty rate, its dismal median income, its rapidly shrinking population. But whereas most reporters had been content to leave it at that, Burchard went further, offering readers a sense of what those statistics meant in "human terms." The picture he painted was not pretty. The misery of Warren County, he wrote, "begins to come clear when one travels the dirt roads through the piney woods and sees shack after shack and the swollen-fleshed children with dull eyes that may light with fear of the unknown but seldom with curiosity. Neither brain nor body can grow properly on a diet of hog maws and overcooked greens."

The distress caused by Burchard's article was reflected in a response written by Bignall Speed Jones, the sixty-nine-year-old editor of the *Warren Record*. A descendent of William Duke, who had established the tobacco plantation on which Soul City was slated to be built, Jones was typical of the upper-class whites who had long ruled Warren County and the rest of the rural South. Viewing himself as more enlightened and progressive than the poor whites who worked the fields, he was nonetheless hesitant to disturb the status quo. When the Supreme Court handed down its decision in *Brown v. Board of Education*, Jones had encouraged Black residents not to push for integration because of the backlash it would generate. "The white people are determined that there shall be no mixed schools in this state," he wrote at the time. "Before they allow this to happen they will pull down the pillars of the temple." In recent years Jones had become more outspoken on the issue of equality, but he was not above displaying a casual racism. Asked by a wire reporter whether the *Warren Record* covered the local Black community, he answered proudly, "I carry all the nigger weddings. It's a fully integrated paper."

Like many residents, Jones was troubled by Burchard's depiction of Warren County. "Just as a mother feels her child is the finest child in the world and resents any suggestion that this is not the true state of affairs, many Warren County residents view their county," he wrote in his weekly column. But Jones had added cause to be upset, since he had spent half a day with the young reporter, answering questions, introducing him to locals, and showing him the county. In fact, Jones seemed to feel some responsibility for the impressions

Burchard had formed. He recounted how the two men had driven around together—"down the No-bottom Road, to Afton, by Jones Spring, Lickskillet, and back to Warrenton"—and informed his readers that Burchard had not taken notes, which may have accounted for his inaccuracies. "We saw many poor farms and some shacks that are a disgrace to the county," Jones acknowledged. "However, we did not see any persons in rags, or who appeared to be starving. I think it was here that Burchard used his imagination."

Mixed in with the anger felt by residents was a heavy dose of fear. For if local whites recoiled from the picture of Warren County that was being presented, they were even more frightened about what it might become. Although Black residents already made up two-thirds of the population, far more whites than Blacks were registered to vote, which meant whites dominated the polls and controlled the government. If Soul City succeeded, that electoral dominance would soon end. It was a simple matter of math: an influx of eighteen thousand people would more than double the current population. And if the bulk of those new residents were Black, the percentage of whites would plummet from 33 percent to 15 or 20 percent. No regime, no matter how entrenched or convinced of its own superiority, could permanently maintain power under such circumstances. "I can't say we don't deserve it," one official said when asked about the prospect of a Black takeover, "but I'd hate to see it happen."

It wasn't just the threat of becoming politically marginalized that scared white residents. It was the kind of people they feared Soul City would attract. When they heard McKissick describe Soul City as a sanctuary for poor Blacks fleeing the slums of the North, they imagined the worst. In their minds, Warren County would soon be invaded by a horde of violent "riff-raff" and "scum," bringing crime and disorder and a culture as strange as any foreign nation's. If that happened, they believed, all the "decent folks" would be forced to leave. McKissick and his staff attempted to assuage such concerns, making clear they were planning to recruit hardworking, law-abiding residents. At a meeting with the Warren County commissioners, Eva

Clayton described the project as an "opportunity city" that would attract intellectuals and ambitious young professionals. When asked by Capps, the board's chairman, whether it would draw hippies and hoodlums, she expressed puzzlement: "That's definitely not true." Still, some locals weren't persuaded. "We ain't got enough law and order to take care of our own," declared one resident. "When city rioters come, we'll have to move away."

As it turned out, the only person forced to leave was Leon Perry, the businessman who had sold Clayton an option on the land. After it became clear he was the seller, Perry received death threats from his neighbors in Warren County. Not wanting to risk a confrontation, he decided to lie low in Florida until tempers cooled down. Asked upon his return whether he would have agreed to the deal if he had known McKissick's true intentions, Perry was surprisingly defiant.

"Yes, I would," he said. "I'm glad someone's going to do something on it."

7

Green Power

In the weeks after his announcement, McKissick embarked on a hectic schedule, working feverishly to get Soul City off the ground. Five days after his press conference, he selected Ifill Johnson Hanchard, one of the country's leading Black architectural firms, to oversee the city's design. A few days later, he retained Hammer, Greene, Siler, a prominent consulting firm in Washington, DC, to prepare an economic analysis. He also announced a collaboration with the Department of City and Regional Planning at the University of North Carolina, which agreed to dedicate faculty time and resources to the project. And he traveled the country giving interviews and meeting with various groups and officials, including North Carolina governor Robert Scott and the National Association of Manufacturers, the country's largest industrial trade organization.

But the most critical task he faced that first month was finding money to buy the land. Throughout all the news conferences and interviews, no one had pressed him on how he intended to pay for the Circle P Ranch. That was a good thing, because McKissick wasn't sure himself. As of December 1968, McKissick Enterprises had a cash balance of less than three thousand dollars, which wasn't enough to renew the sixty-day option, let alone cover a down payment. McKissick's personal finances weren't much better. Although he had made a comfortable living as a lawyer and as national director of CORE, he and Evelyn had four children, two in college and two attending private schools in New York City. He also had mortgages on several rental properties in Durham and Asheville that could not be quickly or easily liquidated. All of this meant that if McKissick was going to exercise his option on the Circle P Ranch, he'd need outside financing, and he'd need it fast.

He had approached James Rouse in the fall, suggesting that the Rouse Company become involved as a partner or primary investor. But Rouse had his hands full with Columbia, which had broken ground two years earlier and was still in the midst of major construction. Although willing to provide training and advice, he could neither take on the project himself nor offer significant funding. McKissick had also contacted a number of banks, including First Pennsylvania and North Carolina National Bank, as well as Connecticut General Life, which had loaned Rouse more than $25 million to build Columbia. But while these sources didn't rule out the possibility of future support, none was willing to finance the initial purchase. That left Chase Manhattan as McKissick's best hope. Chase had already loaned him fifty thousand dollars to launch McKissick Enterprises, which meant it was familiar with his ideas about Black capitalism. It was also familiar with the new-town concept, having invested $10 million in Columbia a few years earlier. So on a winter day in early 1969, McKissick and Gordon Carey took a taxi from their walkup in Harlem to the sixty-story Chase tower in downtown Manhattan to make their pitch.

They met with a team of executives from the construction loan department and Chase's community development program. Operating informally at the time, the community development program would officially launch later that year with a mandate to aid Black businesses and disadvantaged communities. Though not a charity, the program was designed to provide loans to high-risk projects with social value, which should have made Soul City an ideal applicant. But when McKissick presented his proposal, laying out the long-term plan for Soul City and suggesting a thirty-year repayment schedule, the Chase team was skeptical. They couldn't loan him $390,000 to develop a city in a cow pasture, they responded. When McKissick reminded them they had invested $10 million in Columbia, the executives tried to explain the difference between the two projects. Columbia was a short drive from two large cities—Baltimore and Washington, DC—while Soul City was an hour from Raleigh-Durham, hardly a major metropolis. Howard County, where Columbia was located, was ripe for development, with several research facilities and federal agencies nearby, while Warren County was an economic wasteland that had been bleeding population for two decades. Finally, James Rouse was an experienced real estate developer who had proven himself on numerous earlier projects, whereas McKissick and his staff were novices, civil rights activists who had never built anything tangible in their lives. McKissick couldn't dispute the logic of these arguments, so he appealed to the executives personally, insisting that Soul City needed to be built and could be built. "Just work with me," he pleaded.

Coming from McKissick, it was an awkward plea. For years, he had savaged the banking industry for its racist past and exploitative practices. In a speech at the 1967 Black Power Conference, he had accused "a white, Anglo-Saxon Wall Street" of conspiring "to keep the black man in his place," while in his book *Three-Fifths of a Man* he harshly criticized Chase Manhattan for investing in South Africa and providing the economic base that made apartheid possible. He also attacked Chase's founder, John D. Rockefeller Jr., and the other "robber barons"—Andrew Carnegie, Jay Gould, J. Pierpont Morgan—for building their fortunes on the backs of the poor who "toiled in their mills and sweatshops." "By monopolizing the wealth and resources of the country, these families are probably the one group most responsible for the status quo," McKissick wrote. "They are the one group—these so-called philanthropists—most responsible for denying Black People the rights of self-determination, the acquisition of power and the control of their own communities. . . . They, more than anyone, are the enemy."

Yet now here he was, in the gleaming Chase tower, at the heart of Wall Street, pleading with the enemy for money. In truth, there was nothing unusual about this. Civil rights leaders had long depended for survival on the patronage of the very people whose business practices they blamed for the condition of Black America. McKissick himself had been in this position many times, and although he didn't enjoy it, he had always been self-consciously pragmatic in his approach. When more radical members of CORE objected to taking money from the Ford Foundation to fund the "Target City" project in Cleveland, McKissick had pointed out that the group had little choice: without the foundation's support, the Cleveland project would never get off the drawing board. He also recognized that banks and investors had tremendous authority in society and that policy makers often followed their lead. "They are the people with the influence to force other sectors of society to relinquish power," he explained.

Just because McKissick was willing to accept money from the rich, however, didn't mean he thought highly of their motives for supporting civil rights. "They do so to salve their guilt and sense of responsibility to the poor exploited by their corporations," he wrote. "They seem to feel that such philanthropy somehow absolves their sins and guarantees their moral right to their remaining millions." So when his personal plea to the Chase executives was met with silence, McKissick played on their sense of guilt, delivering a lecture on the plight of the Black poor and the obligation of white banks to help out. "You owe it," he told them bluntly.

The Chase team didn't reject McKissick's request on the spot, but he wasn't optimistic about his chances. Shortly after leaving the meeting, he called T. T. Clayton in North Carolina. "Those sons of bitches aren't going to lend me any money," he fumed. But McKissick had been more effective than he realized. Not long after that call, Clayton received another call, this one from an executive at Chase. "I know this is your friend, but he just made everybody mad," the executive said. "But in the end, we decided we're going to let him have it." He told Clayton that Chase had a relationship with a bank in Lumberton, North Carolina, 150 miles south of Warrenton. At ten o'clock the next morning, a bank officer would meet Clayton there with a certified check for two hundred thousand dollars—less than McKissick had requested, but still a good start. Stunned by the news, Clayton called McKissick's home in New York and reached his wife. "Evelyn, where's Floyd?" he said, to which she replied skeptically, "T.T., what do you want with him?" "I've got good news," he assured her, so she told him that McKissick had driven to the state university in Binghamton to teach a class on the Constitution. Reached in Binghamton later that day, McKissick was as shocked as Clayton. "I never thought we were going to get anything," he said. "I'm coming down tomorrow and we're going to look at the surrounding tracts of land and you'll do the title work."

The Chase loan covered only half the purchase price, so McKissick spent the next few days scrambling to raise additional money. Unable to secure another bank loan before the option expired, he proposed that Leon Perry finance the balance himself. Perry had previously turned down a higher offer from a group of dairy farmers because they wanted to pay him over twenty years and he needed cash immediately. But when McKissick promised he would retire the mortgage within a year, Perry agreed to the deal.

By the time those details were worked out, the February 19 deadline on the option was fast approaching. McKissick had scheduled a press conference in Warren County that afternoon to announce the filing of the deed, and he and Carey left on an Eastern Air Lines flight from New York that morning. On their approach to the Raleigh-Durham airport, however, there was a problem: the plane's landing gear malfunctioned. Although the control tower confirmed that the wheels were down, the light that was supposed to signal that they were locked in place was not on. As the plane circled the airfield, the copilot came into the cabin, got down on his knees, and pulled up a section of floorboard, as though looking for something. Eventually the plane turned west, and the pilot announced they were headed for

Charlotte, the nearest airport that could handle an emergency landing. As they descended, McKissick and Carey could see fire trucks and ambulances lined up on the tarmac and a layer of fire-suppression foam covering the runway. But when they touched down, the wheels held firm, and the plane coasted smoothly to a stop.

Once on the ground, the two men began looking for a way to Warren County. There were no flights scheduled from Charlotte to Raleigh-Durham that afternoon and no charter planes available. A stranger, overhearing their predicament, said he was flying east in his twin-engine plane and could drop them off at the airstrip in Henderson, fifteen miles south of Warrenton. They arrived late that night, and the next morning received word from Perry that the deal was still on in spite of the missed deadline. Even so, there was a tall stack of paperwork to complete, and by 5:00 p.m. they still hadn't finalized the transaction. The register of deeds in Warrenton kept his office open late, but at 5:25 Clayton phoned to say they would file the deed Friday instead. The deal was finally completed that night, and the next morning at ten o'clock McKissick walked into the county courthouse on Main Street and officially became the owner of the Circle P Ranch—the first Black man to hold title to the slave plantation William Duke had established almost two hundred years earlier.

Asked for comment by a group of reporters, McKissick's message was simple: "We're doing something good here for the whole country."

As IMPORTANT AS it was, the loan from Chase solved only a small part of McKissick's problem. Once he bought the property he still needed huge sums to prepare it for development—to turn pastures and woods into improved land, with water, sewer, electricity, and paved roads. Up-front costs in Columbia had run close to $50 million, while developers in Irvine, California, had spent several times that amount. Soul City might cost less, being located in an economically depressed region where land, labor, and materials were cheap. But even conservative estimates suggested McKissick would need at least $30 million. And in 1969, there weren't many places a Black man could get his hands on that kind of cash. As a headline in *Business Week* put it, "Soul City's Need Is Green Power."

The most obvious source of that power was the federal government. The New Communities Act not only provided loan guarantees of up to $50 million for new cities approved by HUD, it also offered planning grants to help developers put together all the documents—feasibility reports, environmental impact studies, population projections—required for HUD approval. Indeed, it was the New Communities Act that had encouraged McKissick to proceed with Soul City in the first place. But now that he had secured the land, McKissick was having reservations about relying on government loans. For one thing, he had been consulting regularly with James Rouse, who warned him about the pitfalls of doing business with the government—the bureaucracy, the scrutiny, the timidity. A 1969 case study of Soul City prepared by Harvard Business School also raised questions about the wisdom of participating in the HUD program. Noting that government assistance could often be "untimely and inflexible," the authors explained that most businesses prefer tax breaks and subsidies to active government involvement.

Aside from these practical concerns, there was a larger, more theoretical objection to government assistance. The whole purpose of Soul City was to promote Black self-determination, to give Black people control over their own destiny. Relying upon the government would necessarily undercut that goal. It would mean giving up a degree of autonomy and submitting to the supervision of white officials. This was another dilemma familiar to Black leaders, and one McKissick had often lamented. In an interview the previous year, he voiced frustration about constantly having to rely upon and report to whites. That was the reason he had started McKissick Enterprises: to end the cycle of financial dependence. "You've got to go to the man and beg him for every damn thing," he complained. "If you want money now there ain't no way for you to move for nothing without your going to the white folks for the money, including McKissick Enterprises. We ought to be able one day to get out of that bag."

There was also no guarantee the federal government would agree to fund Soul City. It was true that Orville Freeman had offered the Agriculture Department's full support when McKissick announced his plans in January. But Freeman had been replaced by Nixon appointee Clifford M. Hardin, the former chancellor of the University of Nebraska. And although Nixon had embraced Black capitalism during the presidential campaign—and had met privately with McKissick and Innis the previous spring—he wasn't sending positive signals now. Almost immediately upon taking office, he had gutted the Office of Economic Opportunity, the agency responsible for overseeing the War on Poverty, declaring that it was "time to quit pouring billions of dollars into programs that have failed." At the same time, he appointed as its director Donald Rumsfeld, a former congressman from Illinois who had opposed the creation of the office five years earlier. Then, in early March, Nixon issued an executive order establishing the Office of Minority Business Enterprise without consulting Black leaders beforehand and without yet allocating any funds for the new office.

Troubled by these actions, McKissick reached out to Bob Brown, an old friend who had recently become Nixon's top Black aide. Born in High Point, North Carolina, Brown had started his career as a police officer and federal treasury agent before opening his own public relations firm in 1960. Over the next decade, he built a lucrative business helping companies improve their relations with the Black community. He also formed close ties with many civil rights leaders, including McKissick and Martin Luther King Jr. When King was assassinated in 1968, Brown accompanied his wife, Coretta Scott King, to Memphis to retrieve his body, then joined the presidential campaign of Robert F. Kennedy. But after Kennedy was killed two months later, Brown was approached by a Black staffer on the Republican National Committee, who asked him to consult with the Nixon campaign. Although a Democrat, Brown had a favorable view of Nixon, recalling his 1957 trip to Ghana, the first time an American vice president had visited Africa. He accepted the offer and began doing advance work for the campaign. His most important assignment was in Rochester, New York, where Nixon was scheduled to give a speech in mid-October. A month earlier, the Democratic candidate, Hubert Humphrey, had been greeted in Rochester by hundreds of Black protesters lying in the streets. Hoping to prevent a similar spectacle from marring Nixon's trip, Brown spent several days negotiating with local activists, assuring them that if Nixon were elected he would make sure their concerns were heard. His efforts paid off: Nixon's speech to twelve thousand supporters at the Rochester Community War Memorial went off without a hitch. When Nixon learned who was responsible for averting a confrontation, he instructed a senior adviser to make sure Brown was with him for the remainder of the campaign. Relaying this news to Brown, the adviser told him, "You go on back home and get yourself together because you ain't going to be able to go home again."

After the election, Brown did go home, intending to resume his public relations business in High Point. He wasn't there long before he was called to the Pierre hotel in New York to meet with the president-elect. Upon his arrival, Nixon introduced him to the staff as his special assistant for urban affairs. Caught off guard by this announcement, Brown stayed silent. But after they talked for an hour about the needs of the Black community, and Nixon promised that Brown would answer directly to him, he accepted the job. He wasn't the only Black official in the Nixon administration. James Farmer, McKissick's predecessor at CORE, had been named assistant secretary at the Department of Health, Education, and Welfare, while Sam Jackson, a holdover from the Johnson administration, had stayed on as assistant secretary at HUD. There were other Black appointees scattered across various agencies—the labor department, the Equal Employment Opportunity Commission, the postmaster general's office. But Brown was the only Black official on the White House staff, which meant that when Black leaders had concerns about the administration they went straight to him.

McKissick lodged his first complaint with Brown in a letter on February 14. According to McKissick, the Office of Economic Opportunity had agreed several months earlier to transfer funds to

Bob Brown with Nixon.

the Small Business Administration to establish economic development centers in distressed urban areas; McKissick Enterprises had proposed such a center in Harlem. In spite of the agreement, OEO (now led by Rumsfeld) had not yet transferred the funds. "Can you determine for us the reason for the delay in the transmittal of these funds?" McKissick asked Brown. "Many organizations, like mine, are prevented from assisting the development of Black economic power, by the failure of immediate action on the part of certain agencies."

Six weeks later, McKissick followed up with a more pointed letter. "I have been disturbed by the course of events taken by the Nixon Administration the past few weeks," he began. "To my mind the Administration's actions have not reflected real concern for the concept of 'Black Economic Power.'" What precisely was McKissick disturbed about? First, in early March, Nixon had convened a meeting of Black leaders at the White House on the same day as a conference on Black economic development sponsored by the National Association of Manufacturers. When McKissick and other leaders pointed out the conflict, they were ignored, and when McKissick asked to send a member of his staff to the White House instead his request was denied. Nixon had also failed to consult Black leaders about who should lead the SBA and had reappointed the head of its New York office despite complaints from Black entrepreneurs that he was difficult to work with. "I am commencing to lose faith," McKissick confided in Brown. "Somehow the Administration does not seem to be getting the messages. The nation is still in the 'honeymoon' stage, but let us please get the channels of communication opened before the honeymoon ends."

Not content to criticize Nixon privately, McKissick took his concerns public. Shortly after Nixon's inauguration, he joined a group of prominent Blacks (including Jackie Robinson and the entertainer Dick Gregory) who gathered outside the White House to complain about the lack of access to the president. Two months later, he skewered the president during a visit to Minneapolis to promote *Three-Fifths of a Man*, telling a reporter that Nixon had "made an effort to hurt what is really black capitalism" by cutting back at the SBA. And in a radio interview with the journalist Victor Riesel, a noted labor advocate, he complained that the president had never defined his goals for Black capitalism. Attempting to remedy that oversight, McKissick explained that Black capitalism wasn't just about jobs. "It is about the right to have Black-run factories, Black-run plants, Black-run businesses and the right to be treated as equals in the commercial and political marketplace."

THUS, IN THE weeks and months after his Soul City announcement, McKissick had not only begun to sour on the idea of government assistance, he had harshly criticized the very administration whose assistance he would need. So he began to consider alternative sources of funding.

One possibility was to finance the project with investments from Blacks themselves. Although the overwhelming majority of Black people were poor, a handful of Black companies and entrepreneurs had prospered, especially in the insurance and hair products industries. McKissick had long advocated tapping into the wealth of this select group. As head of CORE, he had attempted to shift the organization's donor base from whites to Blacks, believing this would give him the freedom to chart his own course. As had happened then, however, his effort to raise money from Black investors fell short. Part of the problem was a lack of sufficient assets. Despite all the talk about Black capitalism, it was still mostly an aspiration. As McKissick liked to point out, if you combined all the Black businesses in the country, they wouldn't crack the *Fortune* 500. Nor were any Black-owned businesses listed on a major stock exchange. (Johnson Products became the first when it appeared on the American Stock Exchange in 1971.) Even Black corporations that did have significant resources—such as North Carolina Mutual, the nation's first billion-dollar Black insurance business—couldn't afford to take a risk on Soul City. As Mutual vice president J. J. Henderson explained in a letter denying McKissick's request for a $1 million loan, his company would consider providing assistance once Soul City had firm commitments from "national corporations, commercial, institutional, income producing properties and homes." Until then, Mutual didn't have the luxury of investing in such a speculative venture.

Another possibility was to rely on the same liberal donors and foundations that had helped finance the civil rights movement. McKissick had extensive contacts within this world, having spent much of his time at CORE sipping cocktails at the homes of wealthy patrons in Manhattan. But in raising money for Soul City, McKissick often found that liberals couldn't be counted on. Take Ted Kennedy: McKissick had been in touch with Kennedy about Soul City from the beginning, sending him proposals and reminiscing about his friendships with Kennedy's older brothers John and Robert. After Kennedy fled the scene of a fatal car accident on Chappaquiddick Island in the summer of 1969, McKissick wrote a column for the

New York Amsterdam News cautioning against a rush to judgment, then sent the young senator a note reminding him that leaders are forged in adversity. "No man is ever defeated until he admits that he is defeated," he wrote. Not long after that, McKissick and Carey visited Kennedy in his Washington office, laying out their plans and their need for a short-term loan of two hundred thousand dollars. At the time, Kennedy seemed supportive. He instructed the pair to call his cousin Robert Fitzgerald, a principal at Harbor National Bank of Boston, and promised to put in a good word. But when McKissick made the call, Fitzgerald said he had never heard from Kennedy and knew nothing about the project. The discussion ended shortly thereafter.

McKissick and Carey had a similar experience with Nelson Rockefeller, the liberal Republican who was then governor of New York. The two men met with Rockefeller in his Manhattan office, presenting their proposal and asking for financial help. Like Kennedy, Rockefeller responded positively and referred them to members of his staff. But as with Kennedy, those discussions went nowhere.

Sometimes McKissick and Carey encountered outright hostility. When they paid a visit to the Mary Reynolds Babcock Foundation, a North Carolina charity founded by an heir to the R. J. Reynolds Tobacco Company, the board responded that it couldn't support a segregated community. Dumbfounded, Carey looked around at the board's members, all of whom were white, then pointed out that he and McKissick were different races. No matter, they were told; the foundation didn't want to get involved. Neither did the Ford Foundation, which sent McKissick a letter expressing concern that Soul City would be virtually all Black and that McKissick's statements to the contrary were "pro forma disclaimers." When McKissick read those words, he erupted in anger. "To argue that you cannot support a new town which will provide education and training, good jobs, decent housing and an atmosphere of brotherhood and equality because you are afraid that Negroes may want to live there and might even constitute a majority would be absurd and comical except that it perfectly portrays the deep rooted latent racism of white America," he wrote back. "You can determine how you spend your money, but you cannot make us all one color and you cannot determine where all of us are to live."

The one exception to this pattern was Irving Fain, a Rhode Island businessman whose family had made a fortune in the textile and chemical industries. Fain was a longtime supporter of the civil rights movement, as generous with his time as his money. He had donated fifty thousand dollars to bail out demonstrators in Mississippi in 1965, had led the fight for fair housing legislation in Rhode Island, and had financed the construction of University Heights, a residential development in Providence that was racially and economically integrated. His support for civil rights stemmed from his Jewish faith, which he believed imposed a duty to do good, not just an injunction to avoid evil. In the words of the television journalist Fred Friendly, Fain "had soul long before it was fashionable." McKissick met Fain during his years at CORE, and the two men formed a close bond. Both were committed to relieving the misery of the urban poor, and both believed in the value of social experimentation. It was natural, then, that McKissick would turn to Fain for financial support, and it was characteristic of Fain that he would respond favorably. Writing McKissick a check for thirty-five thousand dollars in late January 1969, Fain agreed to loan him a total of two hundred thousand dollars in monthly installments over a period of six months. The loan was not intended to finance the purchase of the Circle P Ranch. Instead, it was "seed money" to pay for rent, salaries, taxes, and insurance. Fain offered liberal repayment terms to McKissick, explaining that he wanted the loan to be "as flexible as possible so that you will not be handicapped." He also offered a friendly warning, observing that McKissick's initial capitalization was "grossly inadequate," and that "the most common cause of difficulty in new business enterprises is lack of adequate capital. A word to the wise!"

Fain's loan was critical, helping keep Soul City afloat during the early touch-and-go days. But Fain made clear he was in no position to bankroll the entire project. In a series of meetings at McKissick Enterprises, he and other advisers insisted that McKissick had no choice but to seek a loan guarantee from HUD. The meetings were "real uptight," McKissick said later, and he was reluctant to accept the conclusion of his advisers. But in the end, he realized they were right. He was not James Rouse. No bank or insurance company was going to lend him $30 million. If he wanted to build Soul City, he would have to depend on the very thing he was trying to get away from: the beneficence of the federal government.

ONCE MCKISSICK MADE that decision, the next step was clear. Building on the proposal Carey had written the previous fall, he submitted an application for a $33 million loan guarantee to the New Communities Administration of HUD, which had been established to run the new-towns program. In most ways, the application mirrored Carey's draft. But there was an important difference. While the earlier version included a section titled "Black Orientation of the New Community," the new proposal deleted that section. It also pushed back against claims that Soul City would be segregated, insisting that the community would not be "a totally 'Black Town.'" It was true, the proposal acknowledged, that the developers were motivated by concern for the plight of racial minorities. But they recognized that "we live in a multi-racial and multi-ethnic society and that progress for any segment of the nation is dependent upon progress for all." They also understood that "a community does not exist in a vacuum, but exists as a part of a pattern of inter-dependencies with other communities." For that reason, the application stated, the developers would undertake an "extensive, honest, and in-depth effort" to recruit a diverse population, offering job training to poor whites, building economically integrated neighborhoods, and developing a range of social and cultural programs. "The number of white residents in Soul City will surprise the skeptics."

Soul City was not the first town that applied for funding under the New Communities Act. By the spring of 1969, HUD had received applications from more than a dozen developers and was on the verge of approving its first loan, a $21 million guarantee for the town of Jonathan, Minnesota. Proposed by a state senator and real estate mogul named Henry T. McKnight, Jonathan would be built on eight thousand acres of rolling fields and woodlands thirty minutes from downtown Minneapolis. If all went according to plan, it would have fifty thousand residents and fifteen thousand homes within twenty years.

But although not the first applicant, Soul City posed special challenges for HUD. For one thing, unlike most proposals, Soul City was designed to be a freestanding town, not a bedroom community. In that respect, it was more faithful to the intent of the law's sponsors, who wanted to encourage the building of completely new cities, not mere satellites. But Soul City's location in a rural area meant that McKissick would have to build the city's entire infrastructure from scratch. He would also have to create an economic base to provide jobs for the city's residents. Compounding these problems was the fact that McKissick, unlike many applicants, had no experience with large-scale real estate projects. Nor did he have access to the kind of money HUD ordinarily required developers to contribute as a condition of the loan guarantee. Thus, just like the bankers at Chase, officials in the New Communities Administration were initially skeptical of McKissick's proposal.

Then there was the issue of race. Soul City was the only new town proposed by a Black developer, and HUD staffers were acutely aware that the media had portrayed it as a separatist venture. They were also aware of the legal risks of supporting a racially identifiable city. Just four months before Congress passed the New Communities Act, it had approved the Fair Housing Act of 1968, which outlawed racial discrimination in housing. If HUD funded Soul City, and it became an exclusively, or even predominantly, Black community, the agency might violate the very law it was supposed to enforce. And if Soul City did not violate the Fair Housing Act, HUD might face pressure to fund exclusively or predominantly white developments. HUD had already received an application from a white developer near Memphis that raised precisely this concern. The agency therefore made clear it would only support Soul City if it were truly integrated. HUD was so concerned about the issue that it considered recruiting a white developer to join the project. In a memo never shared with McKissick, one HUD staffer argued that the addition of a white developer would give the city a more integrated, biracial feel.

HUD was also sensitive to the political implications of Soul City. Ordinarily, a member of Congress would jump at the chance to secure federal money for his state. But Soul City was no ordinary project, and instead of jumping on board, North Carolina's congressional delegation was running in the opposite direction. Representative L. H. Fountain, whose district included Warren County, wrote HUD secretary George Romney in June 1969 that he had received numerous letters opposing Soul City and had doubts about the project himself. Sam Ervin, the state's senior senator, was more blunt, urging Romney to reject McKissick's proposal because it was inappropriate to use taxpayer dollars to fund a private real estate development. "Manifestly, the taxpayers of the United States ought not to be called upon to finance directly or indirectly any such plans," Ervin wrote, ignoring the federal government's long history of supporting private real estate developments, many of them deliberately and exclusively white.

For all the opposition, however, McKissick had a powerful ally within HUD: his friend Sam Jackson, now the assistant secretary overseeing the New Communities Administration. Jackson and McKissick had known each other for years. Both were attorneys who had been active in the civil rights movement (Jackson's firm in Topeka, Kansas, had represented the plaintiffs in *Brown v. Board of Education*), and both were founding members of the National Conference of Black Lawyers. The two men were close enough that Jackson, concerned about perceptions of favoritism, assigned a young planner on his staff to communicate with the New Communities Administration about McKissick's application. Some HUD staffers also recognized the potential of Soul City. In an initial review of McKissick's application, one staff member argued that it presented a unique opportunity. "This project cannot be treated as an ordinary case," the staffer wrote. "It has implications of national and international importance.

We must use it creatively." Another HUD official acknowledged that the racial dimensions of the project cut both ways. "It's a problem," the official told a reporter for the Washington *Evening Star*. "On the one hand, we don't want to be in the position of encouraging a segregated community, and this will be, in effect, a de facto segregated town. On the other hand, here is a region in North Carolina that needs better housing, better community facilities, and this is something we should be encouraging."

The conflicting views within HUD—and the political pressure from outside—meant that Soul City's application was scrutinized more closely than others. After a preliminary review raised questions about McKissick's ability to attract industry, HUD sent the application back with a request for more information, including a cash flow analysis, an economic feasibility study, and demographic projections. It also suggested that McKissick apply for a planning grant under the New Communities Act to complete the studies and analyses HUD needed for a final decision.

Frustrated by this delay, McKissick launched the first of many lobbying campaigns, writing to Bob Brown at the White House and to Vice President Spiro Agnew, who had been a vocal proponent of new towns on the campaign trail. In late July, McKissick sent Agnew a copy of the Soul City application, along with a note emphasizing the project's unique nature. "This is not the traditional dormitory town which is dependent upon another city for its existence," he wrote. "It is designed to bring employment, housing, and new life to a rural, depressed area." Receiving only a polite response from one of Agnew's aides, McKissick wrote again a few weeks later, this time copying Daniel Patrick Moynihan, a White House adviser who had authored a notorious 1965 report placing the blame for Black poverty on the disintegration of "the Negro Family." Railing against bureaucratic procedure, McKissick complained about HUD's insistence that he obtain commitments from industry before receiving a loan guarantee. "Were we able to secure sufficient commitments from industry, in advance, it is questionable whether we would even require federal guarantee of the land development costs," he pointed out. What Soul City needed, McKissick continued, was a provisional commitment that would give industry the assurance it was looking for. "As it stands today, the potential sources of financing and the industrial sources of jobs all inquire as to whether the federal government will stand behind our program. Our answer now can only be, 'We don't know.'"

Having made the case in writing, McKissick and Carey traveled to Washington in September to meet with officials at HUD, OEO, the Commerce Department, and the Agriculture Department. A few weeks later, McKissick returned to the capital, this time with Jack Parker, the chair of City and Regional Planning at UNC. He also met with executives at Wachovia Bank, in Winston-Salem, who said they were willing to join a consortium of banks supporting Soul City. And he wrote again to Bob Brown, suggesting that the Nixon administration could repair its relationship with Black voters by giving the green light to Soul City.

The lobbying campaign appeared to work. Just as McKissick was beginning to lose hope, he received good news from Sam Jackson. Within a short period of time—perhaps by the beginning of the new year—HUD would approve the planning grant, and Soul City would be on its way. The change of attitude was striking enough that Carey remarked on it in a letter to a faculty member at UNC. "We had excellent meetings" in Washington, he wrote. "All of the governmental agencies suddenly seem to be warming up and ready to move ahead."

8

A Fresh Start

Most cities take shape gradually, organically. A trading post is established near a river or a crossroads, and if the location is propitious more traders arrive, turning the settlement into a town. Houses are built, roads are laid, a church is erected, a school opens, a government is formed. Seeking to attract more people, the government collects taxes to make improvements. It paves the roads, expands the school, builds a park, a library, a museum, and a hospital. It licenses utilities to provide water, sewerage, and electricity. It establishes a police department to keep the town safe, a sanitation department to keep it clean, and a fire department to keep it intact. As the town grows into a city, new amenities and services are added: theaters, restaurants, nightclubs, shopping centers, golf courses, swimming pools. And slowly, over the course of decades or even centuries, what began as a simple collection of pioneers and fortune seekers evolves into a complex and highly organized society.

In the case of Soul City, all this would have to happen at once, in a tightly compressed period of time. McKissick wouldn't have the luxury of building his city slowly and patiently, because the only way to finance such a project was to sell land, and the only way to sell land was to create a self-sufficient community that could attract residents and businesses. Nor could McKissick rely on a nearby city to provide services while he built his town. A development like Reston or Park Forest could postpone nonessential projects, such as museums, malls, theaters, and nightclubs, since residents could make the short drive to Washington, DC, or Chicago for those amenities. Soul City would have to provide everything residents wanted and needed by itself.

McKissick and his staff had always known, in a vague sort of way, how difficult this would be. But they had been so busy drafting the proposal, scouting for land, and negotiating the option that they hadn't fully considered the challenges that lay ahead when McKissick made his announcement in January 1969. The magnitude of the task didn't become clear until a week later, when they met with the faculty of the UNC Department of City and Regional Planning, a group of professionals who understood just how much effort and foresight was required to build a thriving community.

Even before announcing his plans, McKissick had reached out to Jack Parker, the department's longtime chair. Sixty years old, with a full head of wavy white hair, Parker was a distinguished figure in the academic planning world. A graduate of MIT, he had come to Chapel Hill in 1945 to establish the university's first planning department. Unlike most such departments, the program Parker created was grounded not in engineering and architecture but in the social sciences—in economics, law, public health, and environmental studies. Parker viewed planning as a humanistic endeavor, a means of creating sustainable, democratic communities that meet the economic and social needs of all people. Within his own realm, however, he was more of an autocrat than a democrat. Although he was warm and sociable, hosting lively parties at his home where he played piano and served bourbon "punch" (bourbon poured over ice in a crystal bowl), he ran the department like a fiefdom. When McKissick sent word through an intermediary that he was planning a new city and needed the department's help, Parker didn't waste time consulting his faculty. Instead, he dispatched a telegram to McKissick's office in New York declaring his interest in the project and requesting a meeting to learn more.

The meeting took place the Friday after McKissick's announcement, in the faculty lounge of Morehead Planetarium, an imposing redbrick building on the Chapel Hill campus. McKissick was accompanied by a handful of advisers—Carey, Clayton, two senior managers, and his newly hired architect, Conrad Johnson Jr.—while Parker brought along a dozen faculty members. Dressed in a three-piece suit, McKissick stood at the head of a long conference table strewn with ashtrays and spoke eloquently about the philosophy behind Soul City. But the planners wanted to talk details. They quizzed McKissick about land use, transportation, housing, utilities, recreation, and health care. And as they peppered him with one question after another, he and his staff began to realize what an enormous task they had undertaken. They also realized they could not accomplish that task while pursuing all the other ventures launched by McKissick Enterprises. So they put aside everything else—the publishing house, the public relations firm, the hot sauce line—and embarked on an intensive yearlong effort to plan Soul City.

They began with a series of conferences on various aspects of city planning. In February, they held a symposium at Howard University to discuss industrial recruitment. In March, they organized a summit in Warren County to explore educational policy. And in April, they cosponsored a seminar at Columbia Business School to strategize economic development. The schedule was hectic and demanding, and it began to wear on the faculty members, who were accustomed to a more academic pace. "There is yet another Soul City planning conference in the offing at the end of this week," a couple of professors grumbled to their colleagues that spring.

But McKissick was energized. At Howard, he spoke passionately about the potential of Soul City to provide a source of wealth for Black residents, while in Warren County he entertained the audience of a hundred academics, government officials, and activists with his unvarnished reflections on race and intelligence. Recounting the story of a Stanford professor who claimed that Blacks possessed just one type of intelligence and were therefore fit only for manual labor, McKissick cited his own experience as a rebuttal. "I've been to Harvard and Yale and even to Stanford and I know black folks and white folk, and I can tell you there are smart white folks and dumb white folk, and smart niggers and dumb niggers, and if the white folks didn't spend so much time trying to prove that niggers were dumb they'd realize that." Then, as his audience laughed, McKissick launched into a call and response with himself, as though he were in a church instead of a reception hall, addressing a congregation instead of a conference.

"Can Black folks do it?" he asked. "Yes!"

"Can niggers build a city? We can!"

"Will it be the best damn city in the country? It will!"

"And who's going to build it? Niggers!"

"With as much intelligence as whites? Yes!"

McKissick's conviction was infectious, leading others to believe in his dream as much as he did. "I never saw him hesitate," recalled David Godschalk, a UNC planning professor who worked extensively on Soul City. "He projected an air of total confidence that we're going to do this." That confidence was deliberate. McKissick believed that with enough determination, anything could be accomplished. "Belief in one's ability to do a thing is 'the' difference between success and failure," he had written in a law school essay titled "Will v. Reason." "For with the belief that a thing can be done, it will be done."

Yet even McKissick acknowledged the role of "reason" in confronting the obstacles in one's path. And in order to make his dream a reality, he had to reason through a series of difficult questions.

The first question was whether the Circle P Ranch could support a city. Was the soil stable and adequately drained, or would it shift under the weight of all that concrete, steel, and brick? Were there topographical features—rocky outcroppings, underground water sources, sensitive ecosystems—that would make development impracticable or unlawful? Would erosion or other environmental hazards threaten the long-term viability of the project? McKissick hadn't considered any of these questions before buying the land and didn't have the money to explore them now. So he turned to the Department of Agriculture for help. Although Orville Freeman had stepped down as secretary, his assistant William Seabron had stayed on, and he persuaded the Soil Conservation Service to provide McKissick with a soil survey, a contour map, a description of the watershed area, and aerial photographs. The work was time-consuming and tedious—a surveyor walked every square foot of the property, marking ponds, streams, hills, valleys, and dirt roads, while a scientist took test borings and analyzed the soil's mineral content—and would have cost two hundred thousand dollars on the open market. Fortunately for McKissick, the government did the job for free, and the results were favorable. The conservationists concluded that the land was stable and well drained, with a stream that ran year-round and no evidence of erosion or troublesome outcroppings. In short, they reported, "the property appears to present a minimum of development problems as a new town." A planner at UNC was even more encouraging. "The land is ideal for a city," he told the authors of the Harvard case study on Soul City. "There are just enough hills to make it attractive without making it difficult to build and live on."

McKissick also had to decide how big Soul City would be. He had initially projected a population of eighteen thousand within ten years, reasoning it would be unrealistic to aim larger. But it turned out that a bigger city would be easier to build. The larger the project, the more excitement it would generate, which would attract more interest from builders and industry. To aim big, in other words, was to project confidence, which was critical for a speculative development like this. So as planning moved forward, the population projections grew, first to forty-four thousand residents by 1990, then to fifty thousand people and twenty-four thousand jobs by the turn of the century. As Carey explained to reporters, "The very boldness of this project will generate far greater support from society than if it was less ambitious." Of course, there were risks to this approach.

The larger the ambition, the greater the expectations. And if those expectations weren't met—or weren't met quickly enough—the project would be labeled a failure, which would scare away the very investors and residents it needed to succeed.

The size of the project created other complications, too. If Soul City was going to support a population of fifty thousand, it would need a massive supply of water, both for drinking and for all the other routines of daily life: bathing, washing clothes and dishes, watering lawns and gardens. If each resident used eighty gallons a day (a conservative estimate), the city would need a supply of at least four million gallons daily. And that didn't even account for the water required by industry: a single factory might consume several hundred thousand gallons a day, and Soul City would need numerous factories to provide jobs for its residents. Then, of course, because what goes in must come out, the city would need an extensive sewer system to dispose of all that water, not to mention the solid waste generated by residents and the toxic waste generated by industry.

The Circle P Ranch had none of these things. The water for farming and ranching had come from a series of wells on the property, which provided only eighty-eight thousand gallons of water a day. The waste from livestock had been treated in septic tanks, which also had limited capacity. Warrenton, nine miles away, drew its water from Fishing Creek, a tributary of the Tar River that flowed just south of Soul City. But Fishing Creek wasn't big enough to provide water for both Warrenton and Soul City. As for sewer treatment, Warrenton relied on an ancient system that was already overburdened and in need of repairs; there was no way it could handle the additional waste from Soul City.

In addressing these challenges, McKissick and his staff had two choices. They could put together a patchwork of water sources—from Kerr Lake, the Roanoke River, and various ground impoundments—and discharge the city's waste into Fishing, Rocky, and Matthews Creeks. Or they could join with Warren County and its two neighbors—Vance and Granville counties—to build a regional water and waste-treatment system. The former approach was simpler since it wouldn't require the cooperation of local officials, many of whom had been lukewarm in their reaction to Soul City. But the latter approach would provide a more reliable, long-term solution. It might also make allies of the very officials who had been uneasy about McKissick's plans. Water and waste had been nagging problems for a number of nearby towns. Oxford, the county seat of Granville, had recently installed a temporary water line because of emergencies brought on by a dry summer, while Henderson, in Vance County, had been looking for an additional source of water to promote industrial growth. If Soul City could secure federal money to build a regional water and waste-treatment system, officials in those towns might view their prospective neighbor in a new light. "The mutual needs for water can be of inestimable value in fostering cooperation amongst the various municipal and county governments," the staff explained to HUD. McKissick therefore decided to pursue funding for a regional system, while making contingency plans in the event Soul City was forced to provide water and waste disposal on its own.

ONCE MCKISSICK DECIDED how big Soul City would be, there was the question of what it would look like. Would residential, commercial, and industrial uses be combined, as in large northeastern cities such as New York and Philadelphia? Or would they be strictly separated, as in many new suburban developments? How dense would the city be—low and sprawling, like Phoenix? Or vertical and compact, like San Francisco? Would residents rely on cars, or would they navigate the city by bus, bicycle, and foot? And what style of architecture and design would the city have? Traditional? Modern? Or something in between?

As with questions about soil, water, and sewerage, McKissick hadn't considered any of these details prior to announcing his plans. But he had decided one thing: he didn't want Soul City to be just another town, indistinguishable from the northern metropolises that were currently in turmoil. He was determined to build a new kind of city, one that would avoid the mistakes of the past and serve as a model for the future. As he put it in marketing materials, Soul City would offer residents—and the country—"a fresh start."

In pursuing this goal, McKissick was aided by a wealth of new thinking about urban design. The decades after World War II marked a coming-of-age for city planning in the United States. Spurred by the postwar demand for housing and emboldened by technological advances and a flood of federal money, planning had evolved from a quaint gentleman's pastime into a sophisticated profession. Dozens of new planning schools opened, student enrollment soared, and cities such as Philadelphia and Pittsburgh hired prominent architects to redesign their urban cores. Perhaps most emblematic of this evolution was the 1956 Urban Design Conference at Harvard, a historic gathering of two hundred city planners, architects, and critics who were determined to rethink how American cities were conceived and built.

One of the speakers at that conference was an obscure writer for *Architectural Forum* named Jane Jacobs. Filling in for the magazine's editor, Jacobs challenged the prevailing consensus that slum areas should be razed and replaced with massive blocks of high-rise apartments. To Jacobs, there was a "weird wisdom" in the chaos of urban neighborhoods, and she warned against attempts to impose an artificial order on them. "The city has its own peculiar virtues, and we will do it no service by trying to beat it into some inadequate imitation of the non-city," she argued. On the strength of that address and a subsequent article in *Fortune*, Jacobs received a grant from the Rockefeller Foundation to write a book on urban planning. The result, *The Death and Life of Great American Cities*, was published in 1961. In it, Jacobs attacked the entire premise of midcentury planning, which sought to create efficient, regimented communities where commercial and residential life were strictly divided. She argued that cities, as well as the districts and streets that comprise them, thrive on diversity—not racial diversity, although Jacobs certainly embraced ethnic pluralism, but diversity of uses. To generate and maintain this diversity, she believed, four principles had to be observed. City blocks should be short, to allow for frequent exploration of side streets; neighborhoods should serve multiple functions, to attract traffic throughout the day; buildings should vary in age and condition, to support a range of rents; and cities should be dense, to promote vitality. In making this last point, Jacobs distinguished between density and overcrowding, which most planners had conflated. Overcrowding exists when too many people live in a single residence, she explained, while density is a measure of how many people live on a given acre of land. Because building heights vary, low-density areas can be overcrowded, while high-density areas might have no overcrowding at all. The problems most planners were trying to solve—poor health, lack of sanitation, social disorder—resulted from overcrowding, not high density. Yet planners often treated the two as interchangeable.

Jacobs's book was groundbreaking, drawing lavish praise from reviewers. (William Whyte, author of the best-selling *The Organization Man*, called it "one of the most remarkable books ever written about the city.") And despite some resistance from the planning establishment, which dismissed its author as a "militant dame" with no formal training, it shook up the world of urban design, laying the foundation for what would eventually be called New Urbanism, a movement advocating mixed-use zoning, density, walkability, and environmental sustainability. But as Jacobs herself acknowledged, her ideas were relevant mainly to "great cities" such as New York and Chicago, not to suburbs, towns, and smaller cities, which posed their own challenges. There was also something slightly elitist and naive about her vision. She seemed not to fully account for how miserable life had been in the demolished slums. Yes, the massive blocks of high-rise housing projects were ugly and soulless. But they had indoor plumbing and proper ventilation, amenities their precursors lacked. Most importantly, Jacobs didn't explain how her vision of a diverse, dynamic city—reflected in her own Manhattan neighborhood of Greenwich Village—could be replicated on a scale large enough to absorb the projected surge in population over the next half century. Although she didn't explicitly reject the idea of new towns, her theory implied that it was folly. Because diversity required buildings of varying ages and conditions, a new town would struggle to achieve the mingling of uses she thought necessary for a thriving city.

McKissick and his staff were heavily influenced by Jacobs, especially her emphasis on walkability and vibrant street life. But they were even more influenced by James Rouse, who was in some ways the anti-Jacobs. Although Jacobs and Rouse were equally horrified by the high-rise housing projects and suburban sprawl that marked the postwar period, their solutions were wildly different. Whereas Jacobs favored large, dense cities like New York, Rouse thought many American cities had become too big, fostering a sense of "loneliness, irresponsibility, and superficial values." He preferred small, intimate towns where children walked to school and neighbors waved to each other from their front porches—towns like Easton, Maryland, where he had been born and raised. In addition, whereas Jacobs was suspicious of experts and planners, believing that "big plans can make big mistakes," Rouse thought the urban crisis could only be solved by a sociological approach. To Rouse, the problem wasn't too much planning but not enough. In a speech delivered in 1967, he assailed the haphazard development of the urban landscape. "Our cities grow by sheer chance—by accident, by whim of the private developer and public agencies," he complained. "Thousands of small separate decisions made with little or no relationship to one another, nor to their composite impact, produce a major decision about the future of our cities and our civilization—a decision we have come to label suburban sprawl. What nonsense this is! What reckless, irresponsible dissipation of nature's endowment and of man's hope for dignity, beauty, growth!"

To mitigate this problem in Columbia, Rouse convened an advisory group of fourteen experts from a variety of fields: education, psychology, sociology, public health, economics, and engineering. Meeting every other week for six months, the group issued recommendations on nearly every aspect of city life, from the optimal size of elementary schools to the best mix of commercial and civic institutions to the most effective way to provide health care. Rouse didn't accept all the group's recommendations, but its work informed his vision of Columbia as an environmentally friendly, racially integrated, and economically diverse community that would promote individual flourishing—or as he put it, "a garden for growing people."

Physically, Columbia aimed to combine the benefits of a larger city with the sense of community found in smaller towns. It consisted of nine villages arranged around a town center. Each village was divided into four or five neighborhoods, and each neighborhood consisted of a series of cul-de-sacs within walking distance of an elementary school. On paper, the villages resembled clovers, with the neighborhoods forming separate leaves. In the middle of each village (where the clover's leaves joined) was a small shopping center, a secondary school, a library, a medical center, banks, and restaurants. At the center of the entire city was a large shopping mall, a man-made lake, and a forty-acre park featuring an outdoor amphitheater. In an effort to preserve the beauty of the natural environment, power lines were buried underground, and large billboards were banned. But despite the involvement of some prominent architects (a young Frank Gehry designed the amphitheater), the physical environment was drab and uninspiring, consisting mostly of brown brick buildings and imitation Swiss chalets.

Rouse liked to refer to Columbia as "the next America," believing it would provide a blueprint for the cities of tomorrow. He was therefore generous with his time and resources, offering free advice to other developers and inviting them to Columbia to train with his staff. The arrangement was so popular it became known as Rouse University, and in the summer of 1969, McKissick and three members of his staff (Carey, Clayton, and finance director Skip Tolbert) enrolled. For two weeks they followed a regular course of study, meeting with the Rouse "faculty," touring the Columbia "campus," and tape recording every "class" as though preparing for a final exam. They learned the secret to creating a viable economic model ("The trick is to keep your major expenditures stretched out, so that your cash flow doesn't look so crumby"); the need to keep meticulous records ("because things you've never thought of are going to happen"); the value of a streamlined corporate structure ("Keep the organization simple, don't complicate it"); and the hazards of setting expectations too high ("The disenchantment can be appreciable").

They also learned the importance of creating a master plan before recruiting residents or industry. "You can't sell anything without a plan," they were advised. "Everybody in the world is skeptical. Projects like this go broke more than they succeed."

IN DRAFTING A plan for Soul City, McKissick had hoped to rely on Ifill Johnson Hanchard, the architectural firm he had retained shortly after his announcement. But it specialized in designing buildings, not cities, so McKissick began searching for a planner who could handle all aspects of the physical design, from housing to transportation to utilities. He found just the man at the MIT School of Architecture, which was advising Soul City on an informal basis. His name was Harvey Gantt, and he was exactly what McKissick was looking for. He was Black, so he furthered the goal of self-sufficiency. He was well-educated, so his intelligence could not be questioned. And he was a trailblazer, having made news as the first Black student to attend Clemson University (and on his way to much bigger things). Gantt's only weakness was a lack of experience. After graduating from Clemson with a degree in architecture, he had worked for a firm in Charlotte for just three years before enrolling in the master's program at MIT. But finding Black professionals with any real estate experience was a challenge. As McKissick told reporters, he had identified seventy-two job categories—from city attorney to sanitary engineer—in which Blacks were completely unrepresented. Besides, one of the goals of Soul City was to serve as a training ground for young Black professionals. So McKissick invited Gantt to Harlem for an interview and offered him the job. Gantt, who was being recruited by prestigious architectural firms in New York and Boston, was initially dubious. Looking around at McKissick's threadbare office, he wondered why a famous civil rights leader was building a new town.

But when McKissick explained the theory behind Soul City, Gantt was sold. Millions of poor Black southerners had moved north in search of a better life only to find disappointment, McKissick told him. Why not provide them with jobs and a decent place to live right where they were, in the South?

McKissick couldn't afford to offer Gantt a proper salary, so Jack Parker gave him a teaching position at UNC to supplement his income. Gantt's friends thought he was mad, passing up offers at established firms to join a fledgling company that couldn't even afford to pay him. They also worried McKissick was a modern-day Marcus Garvey, building an all-Black community that would undo the progress of the previous twenty years. Gantt insisted they were wrong. "Floyd's a civil rights leader," he told them. "He's not interested in separatism like Marcus Garvey. This is a different story."

Gantt was not in Columbia during the summer of 1969, but he made several trips there, and it strongly influenced his design. Like Columbia, Soul City would consist of a collection of villages arranged around a town center. Each village would have its own style and identity, but all would be racially and economically diverse, mixing single-family homes, town houses, garden apartments, and mid-rise residential buildings. At the heart of each village would be an "activity center," with a grocery store, a gas station, a library, a post office, a medical center, a barbershop, a beauty salon, restaurants, and banks. And at the heart of the entire city would be a town center providing citywide services, such as a central library, a museum, a hospital, a college, and a shopping mall. Just north of the town center, adjacent to the railroad tracks and I-85, would lie the industrial park. Consisting of eight hundred acres, it would be close to the villages, to shorten commute times (the goal was ten minutes), but separated from them by a man-made lake that would serve as both a buffer and a source of water for fire protection.

As for transportation, a major boulevard would bisect the city on a north-south axis, an inner loop road would link the villages, and a series of collector roads and local streets would wind through the residential neighborhoods. Speed limits would be low—thirty miles

SOUL CITY

SOUL CITY, NORTH CAROLINA

A tract plan of the first phase of Soul City shows Green Duke Village (bottom) and the industrial park, with a man-made lake separating them.

per hour on the boulevard, ten miles per hour on local streets—and sidewalks would be wide, to encourage pedestrian traffic. A network of bike paths would connect each village to the others. As the city grew, Gantt hoped most residents would forgo cars for walking and biking. He also envisioned an extensive public transit system, with regular bus service to the nearby towns of Henderson and Oxford and, eventually, light-rail service to Raleigh-Durham and Richmond.

Because Soul City was intended to provide urban amenities within a pastoral setting, it would feature a vast network of parks and open spaces. Gantt's design called for five community parks spread across the city, a large central park near the town center, and dozens of smaller playgrounds and picnic areas. In addition, one-third of the land would remain undeveloped, leaving wide swaths of woods, meadows, and wilderness available for recreation and animal habitats.

Gantt spent most of his time planning the city, not designing buildings, but early sketches suggest the prevailing aesthetic, which could best be described as 1970s contemporary. The buildings are low and modular, made of glass, brick, and precast concrete. There is little ornamentation—no columns, cornices, or arches—and the dominant colors are brown, tan, and orange, as in an episode of *The Brady Bunch*. But the renderings, with their clean lines and uncluttered facades, have a sleekness that contrasts with the squalor and disarray then prevalent in many big cities. Looking at Gantt's sketches next to archival photographs of East Baltimore or the South Bronx, it is easy to see how Soul City might have seemed like a welcome solution to the urban crisis.

IN ADDITION TO the physical landscape of Soul City, McKissick would also need to build a social and cultural landscape. Indeed, it was the creation of a thriving and egalitarian culture that he viewed as his most important challenge. "The greatest failures of America's cities have been in the field of human relations," he declared in his application to HUD. Therefore, the "primary innovative aspects of Soul City will be in the social arena." Existing cities were beset by crime, addiction, disease, poverty, pollution, and discrimination. The government had invested hundreds of millions of dollars to solve these problems, with minimal success. A new city, McKissick argued, could address such problems at the root, before they became unmanageable. He and his staff also believed this was one area where their experience as activists and organizers gave them an advantage. As they explained to officials at the Rouse Company, they might not know real estate or business, but they knew "how people live together in a community."

Imagine,
A city without prejudice.
A city without poverty.
A city without slums.
A city tailor-made for industry.
A city with a booming economy.
A brand new shining city.
With open spaces. Trees and grass. Rolling hills. Soft winds.
Fresh air. Clear skys. Where stars and moon are visible. Clean
water. Lakes. Creeks. Ponds. Springtime weather. Hardly any
snow. Yet distant mountains. Ample schools, hospitals, parking,
recreation. Well built, stylish housing. A master plan. But not
sterile and cold. For a city conceived with just an eye for bricks
and mortar is a city without a soul. Call the bold alternative
SOUL CITY.

An advertising flyer describes McKissick's vision
for Soul City.

To oversee this effort, McKissick established the Soul City Foundation, a nonprofit corporation funded by government grants and private
donations. Headed by Eva Clayton, the foundation was responsible for
planning all aspects of social life in the new community. But its most
pressing concerns were health care and education. Although Warren
County had several white doctors, the nearest Black physician was
one county away and in heavy demand, seeing as many as seventy-
five patients a day. Emergency care was also limited. Because of high
costs, the fire department had discontinued ambulance service in 1968.
County officials had scraped together enough money to buy a station
wagon that was operated by sheriff's deputies during the day and
volunteer firemen at night. But many of the drivers didn't have medical training, and if the vehicle was in use on one side of the county it
wasn't much help for an emergency on the other side.

As for education, the Warren County schools, like many rural systems, were underfunded and underperforming, with declining attendance rates and low test scores. They were also segregated. For a decade after *Brown v. Board of Education*, the school board had made no effort to integrate the schools. Black parents represented by T. T. Clayton eventually filed suit in 1963, and a federal judge ordered the county to submit a plan consistent with *Brown*. But after several years of stonewalling and halfhearted efforts on the part of school officials, only 2 percent of Black students were attending previously white schools, and no white students were attending Black schools. When the judge again ordered officials to adopt a new attendance plan, they persuaded the state legislature to create a separate school district for the town of Warrenton, where most students were white. The judge saw that move for what it was—a blatant attempt to evade *Brown* by splitting one multiracial district into two single-race districts—and declared it unconstitutional. But in 1969, school officials were still fighting integration, and it was unclear when, if ever, they would concede defeat.

McKissick knew that Soul City would need good schools to attract residents and industry. For that reason, he decided the city would eventually establish its own integrated school system, separate from Warren County's. But until there were enough students to support such a system, he would have to rely on the county schools. That created a dilemma. If Warren County was going to absorb the additional students Soul City attracted, it would need more classrooms. Yet it made little sense for the county to build new facilities if Soul City was one day going to construct its own. So the two sides reached an agreement: McKissick would help Warren County secure funding for a new school that would serve both populations until Soul City established its own system.

Finally, the city would need an organizational structure to govern itself. There were several options available, and the UNC Institute of Government drafted a two-hundred-page report analyzing each. The most obvious choice was to incorporate Soul City as a municipality, with the full range of powers that entailed—the power to tax, invoke eminent domain, share in federal and state revenues, and annex adjacent communities. But incorporating Soul City, especially at an early stage, would limit McKissick's flexibility, since it would put him under the control of whatever body was elected to govern the city. It was also unclear whether Soul City could qualify for incorporation: state law required a municipality to have at least five hundred residents, a benchmark Soul City wouldn't meet for several years. Alternatively, Soul City could be established as a privately owned town governed by a homeowners' association. This would give McKissick greater control, since as the association's creator he could appoint its board of directors. Both Columbia and Reston had adopted this approach, and there was a long history of privately owned towns in the United States. The problem was that private towns lacked many of the powers of incorporated cities. Although they could charge fees to pay for various services, they lacked the ability to share in various types of state revenue, such as sales and liquor taxes.

As a middle ground, the Institute of Government suggested a third possibility. Soul City could establish a special district—known as a sanitary district—that would oversee a range of services related to water and waste. Such a district offered many of the advantages of incorporation without sacrificing control. It could also be accomplished without meeting any population thresholds: McKissick would simply have to apply to the Warren County Board of Commissioners and the state board of health. So that's what McKissick did. He submitted a petition to create the Soul City Sanitary District, a taxpayer-funded agency that would provide water, sewerage, fire protection, and trash disposal for the town's residents. When the county and state approved that petition, the sanitary district would become the governing body of the new community.

DESIGNING SOUL CITY on paper was the easy part. The real challenge would be translating that design into reality, especially as costs increased and money became tight. Innovation is expensive, and the risk was that in an effort to build Soul City economically, many of its most creative elements would have to be sacrificed. Other developers warned McKissick about this. Writing to McKissick in the summer of 1969, Reston founder Robert Simon offered high praise for McKissick's proposal, which "greatly impressed" him. But he also offered a warning: "I have the impression that perhaps the compromises from the ideal that would be necessary to achieve economic viability have not been sufficiently taken into consideration."

Then, of course, once all the pieces were in place—or, more accurately, as they were being put into place—McKissick would have to attract residents to live in Soul City. And the key to attracting residents was to provide desirable, well-paying jobs, which meant he would also have to attract industry. As he put it in his application to HUD, "The entire project hinges on one single factor: the development of a job base of a sufficient size in Warren County to generate the demand for housing and services which will make the city possible." Columbia had struggled in its early years for lack of jobs. But then General Electric agreed to build a plant employing twelve thousand people, after James Rouse borrowed $19 million to supply it with the land. McKissick couldn't offer that kind of incentive, so the Department of Commerce identified a number of industries that might be interested in Soul City's cheap labor and proximity to Kerr Lake: textile companies, paper mills, printing plants, and beverage processors. McKissick had already talked with a handful of *Fortune* 500 companies, lunching with C. W. "Tex" Cook, the chairman of General Foods, and meeting with executives from General Motors. He had also made a pitch to Hanes, a clothing manufacturer owned by a Winston-Salem family with a progressive record on racial issues.

But just as residents would not move to Soul City unless there were jobs, companies would not locate in Soul City unless there were skilled workers to run their factories and safe, attractive neighborhoods for their managers to live in. As the Harvard case study noted, "In most situations, a business decides to locate in a particular area only after analyzing a series of existing economic and social conditions." In the case of Soul City, there was nothing to analyze except a plot of empty land, a stack of planning maps, and a proposal. This meant that any company investing in Soul City would need faith— faith in HUD, faith in Warren County, and, most importantly, faith in McKissick. "To locate in Soul City," the Harvard study concluded, business had "to be convinced that McKissick's dream for a new city would ultimately become an economic reality."

It was a classic chicken-and-egg problem, and it forced McKissick to pursue a strategy of concurrent development, building Soul City at the same time as he recruited residents and industry. "It's not a which comes first thing," McKissick explained to officials at the Rouse Company. "They both come first. They both come together, right now."

The stakes couldn't have been higher. If McKissick's gamble succeeded, it would pave the way for an entirely new type of development, making possible the creation of new cities across the country. If the gamble failed, McKissick's dream would die with it.

9

"The Salad Pickers"

During the first year of planning, Soul City remained uninhabited except for a few dozen cattle Leon Perry had left behind and a caretaker who had been hired to watch over the place. McKissick visited just twice: in March, to attend a planning conference, and again in September, when he and Carey spent a week on-site. It was not until this latter trip that he was able to fully explore the property he now owned. Walking the fields and red clay roads, he was struck again by the beauty of the land—its rolling hills, winding creeks, and verdant woods—and marveled at his good fortune. "It is land with a tremendous potential," he wrote to Perry upon returning to New York.

As 1969 came to a close, however, McKissick decided it was time to establish a physical presence at Soul City. He purchased five trailers from a dealer in Henderson—four for residential use, one for an office—and began moving members of his staff to the Circle P Ranch. The first to arrive was his former brother-in-law Duncan McNeill, who was divorced from McKissick's youngest sister, Jean. An electrical contractor by training, McNeill had given up his job in Durham to help McKissick build his city. Working with T. T. Clayton, he hauled the trailers to a site just a stone's throw from the old manor house and connected them to water and electricity. Then, in early January, he and his daughter Beverly, a student at Duke University, moved into one trailer, while Gordon Carey, his wife, Betye, and their four-year-old daughter, Kristina Lee, occupied another. Within a few weeks, they were joined by Jane Groom, the young secretary from McKissick Enterprises, who brought along her own large and boisterous family.

For Groom, the move to Soul City was a leap of faith and an act of desperation. Born and raised in Mount Vernon, a working-class suburb of New York City, she had been south just twice before, as a small child, to visit her grandparents. Like millions of other Black southerners, Groom's own parents had migrated north during the Great Depression in search of opportunity. They found it, or at least a glimmer of it, in Mount Vernon. Her mother worked as a maid for rich families in nearby Scarsdale, while her father taught himself radio repair. Between their two modest salaries they managed to get by for a while, renting a three-story house in the colored section of Mount Vernon and raising five children. Jane was the youngest, and the family home—with its large sun porch, French doors, and wrought-iron fence adorned with a B (for Ball, her maiden name)—made a powerful impression on her. She felt contented and safe there, with a backyard to play in, plenty of friends to play with, and the comforting smell of the ham hocks and navy beans her mother cooked mingling with the bleach she used to clean house. So when her family fell behind on rent and was forced to move into a dreary building nearby, she vowed she would never let the same thing happen to her.

But finding a decent home in Mount Vernon was not easy, and when Jane married her teenage sweetheart, Jimmy Groom, the couple rented a two-bedroom apartment in Levister Towers, one of the many high-rise projects built during the era of urban renewal. Relatively new and clean when the Grooms arrived, Levister Towers quickly deteriorated, graffiti spreading across its walls, roaches and rats infesting its apartments, and the stench of urine filling its hallways. Like her mother, Groom gave birth to five children, and she and

Jimmy struggled to make ends meet. He held a series of low-paying jobs (baker, school security guard), while she found temporary work as a secretary. It was a difficult life, and had they continued on the same path, they likely would have spent the rest of it in Levister Towers or some other vertical slum—pleading with management to make improvements, fearing for their children's safety, and wondering why they could never get ahead. But shortly after the birth of her youngest child, Groom glimpsed a way out. Reading the *Daily Argus*, Mount Vernon's morning newspaper, she came across an ad for a secretarial opening at McKissick Enterprises. A job in Harlem—working for a prominent civil rights figure—was just the kind of break she needed. Arranging child care with her mother, she applied for the job in the fall of 1968 and, after a typing test and an interview with McKissick himself, was offered the position.

Working for McKissick Enterprises was a revelation. Though long interested in the civil rights movement, Groom had been mainly a spectator, too busy raising children and helping support her family to take an active part. In her new job, she found herself at the center of the drama. She met famous leaders such as James Farmer and Stokely Carmichael. She typed up reports on the role of Black capitalism. And she learned about McKissick's plans for a new city in rural North Carolina. Like many people, Groom wasn't sure what to think of Soul City at first. The idea of a Black man building a new city on a former slave plantation seemed fanciful, like something out of science fiction. But as she became increasingly involved in the project, organizing conferences and working on grant proposals, she began to believe in its potential. So when McKissick asked for staff members willing to work on site, Groom eagerly volunteered. Her plan was to stay a few weeks, long enough to set up the office and train someone to run it. But in December 1969, shortly before she was scheduled to leave, her mother died suddenly. It was a shattering loss for Groom, who shared everything with her mother—her concern for her children, her hatred of Levister Towers, and her troubles with Jimmy, who seemed incapable of holding a job or remaining faithful. Desperate to escape her grief and looking for a way to salvage her marriage and her kids' future, she decided to take her family with her to Soul City, and to stay indefinitely.

They left on a blustery winter day in January 1970, seven of them and their belongings crammed into a Dodge Dart—the four oldest kids in the backseat, Jimmy behind the wheel, and Groom in the passenger seat with her two-year-old daughter, Amy, on her lap. The drive down was "a feat of sheer determination," Groom later recounted in her memoir, *The Salad Pickers*. Like the migrants who had traveled in the opposite direction for decades, Groom packed fried chicken for the ride, along with biscuits, sandwiches, and soda. For the first few hours she distracted the kids with books and games, and when they tired of those she told them to look for the Mason-Dixon Line (knowing full well there was nothing to see). By the time they arrived in Warren County, ten hours later, it was past midnight, and the children were asleep, heads resting on each other's shoulders. Jimmy pulled the car into the parking lot of a post office on Route 1, just across from the railroad tracks. He and Groom could see a dirt road disappearing into the woods and the outline of several small buildings nearby, but there were no people, no cars, and only a single streetlight standing guard. They waited in silence, listening and looking. When the clock turned two and there was still no sign of life, they decided to sleep in the car. Jimmy leaned back and dozed off at once, while Groom stared out the window, trying not to wake the child in her lap, until finally she fell asleep, too.

Almost as soon as she did, the sun nudged her awake, and what had been merely shapes and suggestions in the darkness came into focus. Next to the post office was an old brick service station. Across the street stood a red clapboard antiques store, and down the road lurked a small cinder-block building. Other than that, she could see only trees and fields, and as she looked around at so much nothing-ness she was gripped by panic. "Jimmy, take me home," she wanted to scream. But the children were beginning to stir, and as they, too, took in the desolate scene she decided to act. Spotting a truck coming toward them, she elbowed Jimmy, who flagged it down and told the driver they were looking for Soul City. "Well, let me see," the man replied in a deep drawl. "There are some development folks living on the old Satterwhite Plantation, but there sure ain't no city there yet." That was all Jimmy needed to hear. He asked for directions, and the driver motioned toward the railroad tracks, instructing him to follow the dirt road.

Jimmy did as the man said, steering the car across the tracks, then following the red-clay path as it twisted past pine groves and cornfields. And when, a mile down the road, they saw a "Welcome to Soul City" sign nailed to a tree at the edge of a pasture, Groom wondered again what she was doing here. But she kept her composure for the children's sake, and Jimmy pointed to a red barn. A few hundred feet past the barn, they came upon the old manor house, and behind the house, adjacent to a cornfield, they found the only evidence of a city under construction—the five single-wide trailers.

The first person to greet them was Gordon Carey. He came bounding out of his trailer with a big, welcoming smile. "Wow, Jane. This is your family," he said, as though in disbelief that she had really moved her husband and five kids to a farm in the middle of nowhere. But behind his astonishment, Groom sensed a newfound respect, and as she looked around again at the "endless green and brown fields," as she breathed in the "pure, sweet air" and listened to the "beautiful quiet," her initial despair turned to relief, then excitement. She thanked God for her family's safe arrival and decided she would stay and make a life in Soul City after all.

WHICH IS WHAT Groom and her family did. Moving into the smallest of the five trailers, they did their best to turn it into a home, furnishing it with a secondhand sofa from the Salvation Army and decorating it with books and pictures from Mount Vernon. The three older girls—Lianndra (age eleven), Sandra (nine), and Julia (seven)—shared a small room with bunk beds, while Jim-Jim, age four and the only boy, occupied another. Amy slept in a crib in the living area, with Groom and Jimmy in the room next door. The trailer was smaller than their apartment in Levister Towers, but it was new, there were

DOROTHY WEBB

The trailers where the Grooms and other early settlers lived.

no roaches, and it had an 1,800-acre backyard, which the children began to explore as soon as the car was unpacked.

But the three families—and others that soon joined them—had come to build a city, not just make a life. And over the next few months they began the most basic aspects of the job, cleaning out the red barn for use as an office and converting the old manor house into a preschool and community center. Both buildings were a wreck. In the barn, they found rusty pitchforks, feed buckets, broken pen gates, dried-up tobacco leaves, and a menagerie of insects, while the manor house had been taken over by roosting chickens. With a scarf tied around her head, Groom grabbed a mop and broom and began, in her words, "to sweep away the dust of past generations."

Life in Soul City was not glamorous. As Carey recalled, "The first year I was here we spent half of our time unfreezing pipes, pulling cars out of the mud, just getting the physical systems going." Like the Grooms, Carey and his wife had lived most of their adult lives in urban centers, first in Los Angeles, then in New York and Washington, DC. Now these city folks were thrust into rural North Carolina and, like the migrants traveling in the opposite direction, they had much to learn. A few weeks after arriving, the Grooms woke up one snowy morning to discover the taps were dry. Certain she had paid the water bill, Groom asked Jimmy to go outside and take a look. Crawling under the trailer, he discovered that the pipes had frozen. While he borrowed a blowtorch from the neighbors, Groom made a mental note to leave the faucets dripping on cold winter nights.

At times, the settlers' lack of experience was comical. When a herd of cattle broke through the fence and blocked the road, Carey and McKissick hopped into their cars and tried to round them up, like a pair of suburban cowboys. And when spring arrived and the settlers decided to plant a garden, they had to ask local farmers for help. Gathering on a warm Saturday morning with hoes, shovels, and rakes, they learned how to till the soil in straight rows, how much room to leave between crops, and how to bury the seeds gently under the earth so the rain wouldn't wash them away. It was all very serious until Groom, losing her balance with a hoe, fell backward onto the ground, spilling a handful of seeds and laughing uncontrollably. Still, they managed a successful harvest of cabbage, peas, collards, turnip greens, and tomatoes. The only crop that didn't survive were the potatoes. As Groom discovered later, she had planted the spuds upside down.

But their inexperience could also be dangerous. In late winter, not long after the first families arrived, Carey was burning trash in a field behind the manor house when the fire spread out of his control. As the wind blew the flames across the fields, he and Duncan McNeill tried frantically to contain them. But the two men were no match for the blaze, which jumped the property line in one direction and raced toward the trailers in the other. Fortunately, someone called for help, and both the volunteer fire department and the forestry service soon arrived. While the firemen doused the flames, the forest rangers felled a row of trees to create a firebreak. It was a terrifying incident, but it had one unexpected benefit: Carey and McNeill met dozens of their new neighbors.

Nature presented hazards of its own. Groom learned this one day when she was cooking in her kitchen with the door open and noticed something gray and bushy slip into the trailer. Rabbits and cats were abundant at the Circle P Ranch, but this animal was too large to be either. And its eyes, round and yellow, looked wild. Realizing she was face to face with a bobcat, Groom ran screaming out the door, an apron tied around her waist, a spoon still in her hand. She kept running until she reached the manor house. Only then did she turn around to watch as the bobcat fled across the fields.

It wasn't just the environment that was unfamiliar; it was the culture, too. In Mount Vernon, the Groom children had attended racially diverse schools where Blacks, whites, Hispanics, and Asians mixed easily. In Warren County, the school system was still reeling from a bitter fight over integration. Officials delayed the opening of the schools in the fall of 1970 and then, once classes began, canceled the free lunch program, which mainly served Black students. They also denied admission to Black children living outside the county, even though such children had been welcomed when the schools were segregated. And they rejected a series of demands by Black students—for Black history courses, Black administrators, and the right to organize a youth chapter of the NAACP. When Black students marched to the county school building to complain, the Board of Education responded by closing the schools for more than a week. Then, once classes resumed, Black students refused to return until their demands were met. They also organized a protest at John Graham High School, during which a curtain in the auditorium caught fire. No students were arrested at the scene, but that night police swore out fifty-eight warrants, which they served the next day. Ultimately, eighteen Black students were tried, convicted, and given suspended jail sentences. By the time they returned to school several weeks later, the entire community was on edge.

Things were even worse twenty miles down the road, in the small town of Oxford. In the spring of 1970, a white store owner and his two sons killed a Black man who allegedly made a flirtatious remark to the owner's daughter-in-law. The killing took place on a busy street, in the middle of a Black neighborhood, in front of several witnesses. And it was brutal. The white men chased their victim down the street, beat him viciously, and then, while he lay on the ground pleading for mercy, shot him in the head. When police failed to arrest the perpetrators for more than thirty-six hours, hundreds of Black residents protested in downtown Oxford, throwing bricks and bottles through storefront windows and setting several buildings on fire. Then, when the white men were acquitted because prosecutors couldn't prove who had pulled the trigger—though it was beyond dispute that one of them had—the Black community launched a crippling boycott of white businesses that turned Main Street into a ghost town.

No one in Soul City encountered any violence or overt harassment. As the staff noted in a memo to HUD, "There have been no hostile reactions, no vandalism, no crank calls, or letters." But there were small signs that not everyone welcomed them. On a trip to the grocery store in Norlina, a crossroads community a few miles away, Groom was so preoccupied with her children and shopping list that she left her wallet on the counter. Discovering her mistake as she drove home, she turned the car around and went back to the store. But when she asked the clerk whether he had seen the wallet, he shrugged and played dumb, as though he had no idea what she was talking about.

Evelyn McKissick had an equally infuriating experience at the Mammoth Mart in Henderson. Writing a check for $8.70, she was told by the clerk that the store didn't accept out-of-state checks. Evelyn pointed out that she had written checks at the store in the past and asked to see the manager, who repeated the clerk's message. But when Evelyn presented a check from Mechanics and Farmers Bank in Durham, the manager changed his story, saying that he would only accept checks from banks in Henderson. And when Evelyn asked him to call the Peoples Bank and Trust in Henderson, where she had just opened an account, he refused. Instead, growing angry and flustered, he told her he didn't want her business. What about the thousands of new residents who would soon be moving to Soul City, Evelyn asked. Didn't he want their business? No, the manager announced. He didn't care if anyone from Soul City ever shopped at his store.

Despite the difficulties, life in Soul City was filled with hope and joy. Neither the Groom children nor Kristina Carey had ever lived in the country before, and they were awestruck by the expanse of nature. They spent long days outside, playing hide-and-seek, making mud pies, climbing trees, chasing rabbits, and wading through creeks. On Easter, they hunted for eggs in the tall grass behind the trailers. And during the summer, they joined dozens of other kids from Warren County who packed into the manor house for a camp run by the Quakers.

The adults had joys of their own. On warm summer nights, they gathered on the concrete steps of their trailers to drink beer and tell stories. And on weekend afternoons, they took turns playing cowboy behind the manor house. In addition to the cattle, Leon Perry had left behind several horses and a tack room equipped with saddles, reins, and bridles. Gordon Carey was especially fond of riding. Prior to living in Soul City, he had been on a horse only once, years before, in Mexico. But there was a Black dentist in Warrenton who taught him everything he needed to know: how to fasten a saddle, how to hold the reins, how to feed and clean the animals. Carey was not a natural horseman. He could never get used to the horses' size, and he sometimes had difficulty controlling his mount. But he loved it nonetheless. He would often saddle up in the middle of the day to survey the land. Sitting high in the saddle and roaming the fields, he liked to pretend he was a rancher taking time each day to inspect the fences, look for strays, and explore pockets of the property too overgrown to reach by foot.

MCKISSICK DID NOT move to Soul City with the other members of his staff. He stayed in Harlem, managing McKissick Enterprises, negotiating with HUD, and trying to secure industrial commitments.

But he drove down every few weekends with Evelyn and one or more of their four children. Once there, he visibly relaxed, trading in his dress shoes for boots and donning a cowboy hat to protect himself from the sun. The change was evident even to strangers. "North Carolina seemed to bring out the best in McKissick," the author of the Harvard case study wrote. "Back home, freed from the stifling air of the urban north, he seemed to come to life. As he walked around the land that would be Soul City, he was simultaneously a highly competent businessman and a common man, talking to the case writer about equity financing and to the local farmer about hay and chickens."

Still, McKissick had much on his mind. In spite of Sam Jackson's optimism the previous fall, HUD hadn't yet approved his application for a planning grant, and McKissick wasn't sure what was taking so long.

One reason for the delay was that HUD had been inundated with applications. By the spring of 1970, nearly thirty developers had applied for funding under the New Communities Act. The proposals ran the gamut, from a retirement community nine miles west of Los Angeles called Beautiful City, to a lakefront development in

McKissick in front of the "big house" in the summer of 1970.

PETER W. SILVER

Utah named Stansbury Park, to an alcohol rehabilitation center for a Navajo tribe in New Mexico. HUD rejected the vast majority of proposals, usually because they weren't financially viable, but sometimes because of environmental concerns or lack of follow-through by the developers. It turned down Hamilton, a proposed town in California, because of its location along the San Andreas Fault, and Fountain Hills, a planned community near Phoenix, because the developer lacked a commitment to low-income housing. It rejected James Rouse and Robert Simon, both of whom applied for funding, on the grounds that the law was designed to support new communities, not existing ones.

When it came to Soul City, HUD continued to question the project's economic feasibility, fearful that McKissick would be unable to create the jobs needed to attract residents, sell land, and cover the costs of development. To address this concern, McKissick had hired Hammer, Greene, Siler, a Washington, DC, consulting firm, to prepare an economic analysis. It was a smart choice. In addition to being highly regarded in planning circles, Hammer, Greene, Siler was committed to social justice. The firm's founder, Philip G. Hammer, was an urban planner and civil rights activist who had worked for Robert M. La Follette, the progressive Wisconsin senator, before moving to Atlanta in 1946. There, he headed the Metropolitan Planning Commission, which oversaw the city's remarkable midcentury growth. Hammer later started his own firm, working with cities such as Norfolk, Charlotte, and St. Louis. He served as president of the American Society of Planning Officials in the 1960s and was appointed chairman of the National Capital Planning Commission by Lyndon Johnson.

Hammer's report on Soul City emphasized the state's industrial growth and vibrant labor market. Over the next two decades, it noted, North Carolina was expected to add 624,000 manufacturing jobs, most of them in the Piedmont, where Warren County was located. If Soul City captured even a sliver of that growth, it would easily meet its target of 9,000 manufacturing jobs, which would generate an equivalent number of service jobs. And that was without

taking into account the effect a newly built city might have on industrial recruiting. As for labor, the exodus of thousands of young people from Warren County over the past decade showed that the supply
of workers exceeded demand. Thus, if Soul City attracted industry,
it would have no problem finding workers, even without an influx of
new residents. None of this ensured that Soul City would succeed, the
report acknowledged. Many factors would play a role, including
the level of financing McKissick received and the effectiveness of his
team, which Hammer found "no reason to question." But the existence
of jobs and workers was an "absolutely essential pre-condition to
the undertaking, and the evidence would appear conclusive that this
pre-condition will be met."

McKissick submitted Hammer's report in January 1970, hopeful
it would allay doubts about the project's viability. But one month
later, HUD still hadn't approved the planning grant, and without
the grant—or some other source of funding—McKissick lacked the
resources to move forward. He had applied for another loan from
Chase, but executives there wanted assurance that HUD would ultimately approve the application. They traveled to Washington shortly
after the New Year to meet with Jackson. If he gave them that assurance, they explained, they were willing to loan McKissick $2.5 mil-
lion to stay afloat. Jackson was noncommittal, pointing out that
Soul City hadn't yet filed the application fee of $5,000. McKissick
promptly mailed in a check for that amount, assuming that would
resolve the issue. But HUD still refused to make any promises, and
the Chase executives began to suspect it wasn't serious about Soul
City. Meanwhile, McKissick's financial position was precarious. He
had been unable to pay anyone on his staff, including himself, for
more than a month. If he didn't get an infusion of cash soon, he
would be forced to shut the project down.

The situation called for another lobbying campaign, and McKissick
soon launched one. On February 6, he wrote to William Nicoson,
director of HUD's New Communities Administration, inquiring
about the cause of the delay. Ten days later, he wrote to Nixon,
explaining his predicament and asking for help. The next day, he

fired off a letter to George Romney, the HUD secretary, making a similar request. The day after that, he wrote Nicoson again, pressing for an answer to his earlier letter.

But he reserved his most urgent plea for Jackson. In a letter sent by registered mail, McKissick implored his old friend to tell Chase what it wanted to hear. "The critical period in our life is now," he wrote. "If the Government says we can get a guarantee, our problems are solved." Without a guarantee, Soul City would be dead in the water, unable to secure loans from banks, recruit industry, or attract investors. What was the point of the New Communities Act, McKissick asked, if HUD refused to make the very guarantees the law authorized? "No one is trying to get rich at the Government's expense," he assured Jackson. He and Chase were simply trying to fulfill Congress's goal of creating new, socially diverse towns. They had already invested more than half a million dollars as proof of their commitment. Now it was HUD's turn to reciprocate.

"Sam, you are a committed man; this I know," McKissick concluded. "These bankers who do not know want some evidence that you are going to move things—and move things right away."

WHILE MCKISSICK WAITED for an answer from Jackson, he reached out to state officials, hoping they might lobby HUD on his behalf. In March, he arranged a meeting with North Carolina governor Bob Scott. He had met with Scott the year before, shortly after announcing his plans for Soul City. But that had been an informational session, designed to answer any questions the governor might have. Now he was seeking Scott's support, and it was not an easy sell.

Elected in 1968, Scott was a descendant of the state's leading political family. His grandfather and uncle had both served in the North Carolina legislature, and his father, W. Kerr Scott, had been governor from 1954 to 1958. Longtime Democrats, the Scotts were no liberals. And their record on race was mixed. Kerr Scott had styled himself a moderate while governor, appointing the integrationist Frank Porter Graham to a vacant seat in the US Senate. But later, serving in the Senate himself, he had signed the Southern Manifesto opposing *Brown v. Board of Education*. His son, meanwhile, had distanced himself from the civil rights movement during his own campaign for governor. He had also angered Black residents with his response to student demonstrations at North Carolina A&T in the spring of 1969. After protesters exchanged gunfire with local police, Scott declared a state of emergency, imposed a curfew, and sent in five hundred National Guardsmen to sweep the campus for weapons—a move that resulted in the detention of more than two hundred students, the destruction of thousands of dollars' worth of personal property, and the discovery of only two functioning guns. Appraising the government's response, an advisory committee to the US Commission on Civil Rights declared the Guard's actions reckless and disproportionate to the danger posed.

Given this history, Scott was not an obvious ally for Soul City. And, as he candidly told McKissick during their meeting, he thought the project had little chance of success. But he was intrigued nonetheless. His administration had embraced regional planning as a way to improve the state's economic prospects. If Soul City could aid that effort, perhaps by helping secure federal dollars for the state, he was willing to back McKissick's venture—on two conditions. First, he wanted McKissick's application for a planning grant to be routed through the North Carolina Department of Administration. That way, state officials could monitor Soul City's actions. Second, in spite of that supervision, he wanted to keep the state's role in the project under wraps. He had already received numerous complaints from voters and local officials who opposed the building of a predominantly Black city. The last thing he needed was an announcement that the state was endorsing the project.

Scott's willingness to work with McKissick helped reassure HUD. Shortly after their meeting, Jackson and Nicoson paid a visit to Chase in New York. Although they didn't give the bank the promise it sought, they made clear that HUD was serious about Soul City and that if McKissick satisfied their requests the loan guarantee would ultimately come through. That was enough to loosen the purse strings. In April, Chase agreed to lend McKissick another $200,000. Not long after that, HUD approved a grant of $243,000 to the state of North Carolina. Of that amount, more than half was earmarked for the Warren Regional Planning Corporation, a nonprofit entity McKissick established to oversee the planning of Soul City.

And just like that, Soul City was back in business.

10

Naming Rights

With his immediate financial needs addressed, McKissick turned his attention to the most important factor in Soul City's prospects: recruiting industry. He and his staff had been in contact with various companies since his announcement more than a year earlier. But as planning progressed and HUD's support for the project grew, he redoubled his efforts, traveling the country to meet with corporate executives and search firms. Over the next year, he had discussions with more than twenty-five firms, including General Motors; General Foods; General Electric; Xerox; IBM; Sears, Roebuck; and Miller Brewing Company. In courting these companies, McKissick was often forced to compromise on his earlier ideals. Whereas he and the political economist Louis Kelso had once proclaimed that Soul City would be a model of "radical capitalism" in which employee-owned trusts would share in company profits, he now realized that such demands didn't play well with corporate America. You couldn't march into the headquarters of General Motors or Miller Brewing and tell company officials how to structure their finances, especially when you desperately needed their help. So, just as some of his liberal critics had predicted, McKissick gradually gave up on radical capitalism, making clear he would not insist on any particular form of ownership or profit sharing.

But there was one issue he was unwilling to compromise on: the town's name. In conversations with executives and recruiters, the name "Soul City" had emerged as a sticking point. The former head of American Electric Power Company told McKissick the name was "too poetic and fancy." An industrial recruiter in California said it was too Black. And officials at General Motors complained it was too unconventional.

This wasn't the first time concerns had been raised about the name. The authors of the Harvard case study argued that the name "denotes gimmicry and cultural segregation," while students in the UNC planning department thought it sounded "hard edged." HUD had also been dubious about the name. In their preliminary review of McKissick's application, staffers had recommended naming the city in honor of Martin Luther King Jr. or giving it "some other name that appealed to Black pride. This would establish Soul City not as a precedent for Black separatism, but as a preliminary experiment leading to a true multi-racial program of new community development." State planners in North Carolina were so uncomfortable with the name they referred to the project simply as "New City."

For all the controversy it generated, the name had not been well thought out. In fact, most people involved in the planning of Soul City don't remember exactly where it came from. According to one account, the name emerged from staff discussions about the kind of city they wanted to build. It should be attractive, they agreed, with stylish architecture, plenty of open space, and immaculate landscaping. But they also agreed that a great city was not simply a collection of beautiful buildings. It needed something more, some intangible essence that brought people together for a higher purpose. In a word, it needed "soul." And from that point on, staff members referred to the project as Soul City.

This account is certainly plausible. In his 1967 book *Cities of Destiny*, the historian Arnold Toynbee made a similar observation.

Explaining the difference between a real city and suburban sprawl, Toynbee argued that the key criterion was not size or population. "Los Angeles may swell physically to the size of a subcontinent, but the tropical luxuriance of its physical growth may never succeed in making a city of it," he wrote. "In order to become a city, it would have also to evolve at least the rudiments of a soul. This is the essence of cityhood."

Toynbee's book aside, there's little evidence to support this account of the name's origins. And some staff members dispute it. Carey believes McKissick chose the name himself, without any input. "I think it was a unilateral decision on the part of Floyd, and God only knows what went on in his head that led him to call it that." For his part, McKissick insisted that the name had religious connotations, not racial ones—a claim that many people, including Carey, dismissed. By 1969, they noted, the word "soul" and its various permutations— "soul music," "soul food," "soul brother"—had become inextricably linked to Black culture. For a time, some Black people even referred to Harlem as "Soul City."

Moreover, as late as December 1968, McKissick's staff was referring to the project as "Black City." In a memo written to McKissick on December 31, Harold Brown, senior vice president of McKissick Enterprises, recommended that the name "Black City" no longer be used and that the phrase "New City" be used instead. "I fear that the phrase 'Black City' may cause a reaction that will destroy or delay the project," he wrote. "Besides, there would be no federal assistance (and very little private assistance) to build a 'Black City.' I strongly recommend that we get the city built first before we attach the word 'Black' to it." McKissick appeared to accept this advice, for one week later, in a letter to the Rockefeller Foundation, he referred to the project as "New City." It wasn't until his press conference on January 13, 1969, that he began officially using the name Soul City.

Whatever the name's origins, and whatever people thought of it, McKissick had quickly become attached to it. In a fall 1969 interview in *CITY* magazine, he brushed off questions about the name, arguing that critics were trying to create controversy where none existed. Asked whether he would consider a different name, he became defiant. "All my life I've worked to keep my brothers from having to compromise what they believe to accommodate The Man," he said. "I believe in Soul City. If I change the name, I will have lived my life for nothing." McKissick also argued that there was hypocrisy behind the criticism. Lots of cities were named for white people or white culture, he pointed out. There was White City, Kansas; White Settlement, Texas; Whitesboro, Alabama. "God damn it's the White House and no one thinks of it as all white," he complained to Clayton.

The debate over the name was part of a deeper struggle over control and autonomy, over whose identity the city would reflect. McKissick was determined to make Soul City a monument to Black achievement. That would only happen, he believed, if the name reflected the role Black people played in building and sustaining it. There was also a long history of whites using names to control Blacks. For centuries, enslaved Africans had been stripped of their real names and given European names instead—names such as Thomas, Andrew, or Toby, the appellation bestowed on Alex Haley's African ancestor in *Roots*. Renaming the enslaved was a way of dominating them, denying them agency, and demonstrating that not even something as simple as a name would be theirs to choose. This domination continued after emancipation, as many Black people continued to bear the surnames of their former masters. McKissick was well aware of this history: his last name derived from a prominent family in South Carolina that had once enslaved his ancestors.

As with the charges of separatism, McKissick was exasperated by concerns about the city's name. But those concerns had been raised too frequently, by too many people, for him to ignore altogether. So in the spring of 1970, he wrote to his economic consultant Philip Hammer, asking whether he should change the town's name as a way to attract industry and lessen political resistance. If so, what should the new name be? Should he choose a generic American name like

"Cherry Hill," as the UNC students had suggested? Or should he name the city after a prominent Black leader, such as King, or perhaps even himself?

The answer came several weeks later, in a long, diplomatic letter. After debating the issue intensely, Hammer reported, his staff was split. On the one hand, most agreed the name had served a valuable function in quickly and clearly identifying the mission of Soul City. "In two words it has conveyed something of your basic purpose as a counterforce to migration to the urban ghettos." Moreover, that purpose was a worthy one that many businessmen and government officials applauded. It was true that some people objected to the idea of a new town, especially one focused on the needs of poor Blacks. But "there is no use trying to hide what Soul City is all about and the very use of the name 'Soul City' is a good way to lay it on the line."

The name served another function as well, Hammer noted. Although Soul City had to justify itself economically—which was what his firm had been hired to do—its basic appeal was "extra-economic." Corporations and banks were unlikely to invest in Soul City based on business considerations alone; the risk of failure was too high. If companies invested in Soul City, it would be because they believed in what McKissick was trying to accomplish. But if they took a chance on his dream, they would want some recognition in return. As Hammer bluntly put it, "There is no percentage in lending a helping hand if you do not get credit for it, and to a highly visible industrialist the identification with a town called 'Soul City' could spell instant credit."

Despite these benefits, Hammer explained, there were drawbacks to the name. For one thing, his staff had sensed some skittishness among the industrialists they had spoken with. Some were uneasy about being associated with a community that was perceived as separatist, while others thought the name had a flippant "less-than-solid" ring to it. "To many conservatives, the idea of a new town is radical enough without the social implications of a 'way-out' name." There was also a risk that the name would become a self-fulfilling prophecy—that by creating the perception of a separatist community, the name would impede efforts to attract white residents and businesses. "We know that the basic thrust of Soul City is 'majority black,' not all black," Hammer assured McKissick, "but the initial 'Soul City' momentum could push it in the latter direction."

For these reasons, Hammer wrote, the staff agreed that the name should ultimately be changed. The disagreement was over timing. Some thought it best to change the name now, while McKissick was trying to secure his first industrial commitment. Others worried that this would anger Black supporters—that abandoning the name so quickly in the face of white criticism would look like capitulation. Hammer thought McKissick would have a better sense than his staff of the potential fallout, but "at this particular time of tension and alienation, the step could have repercussions."

Hammer ended his letter with a "final hedge," a "personal post-script" that reflected his own instincts rather than the consensus of his staff. He advised McKissick to "travel along with 'Soul City' as far and as long" as possible, while remaining alert to the feedback he received from various quarters. "In short, if you really do run into persistent resistance in the business or banking community, and it looks serious, and it appears to jeopardize the success of your efforts, you ought to be ready and willing to change the name," Hammer wrote. "Up to that point (which you may of course not reach), I'd stick to 'Soul City' and play it for all it's worth."

That was all the encouragement McKissick needed. After receiving Hammer's letter, he informed his staff that, upon the advice of his economic consultant, he was sticking with the name Soul City. Carey was annoyed, believing that Hammer, like most consultants, had simply told his client what he wanted to hear. McKissick, on the other hand, was gratified, hopeful that Hammer's advice would finally put to rest questions about the wisdom of the city's name.

And for a while, at least, it did.

IN THE SUMMER of 1970, Soul City experienced its first tragedy. Odell Kearney, the handyman who had watched over the property before the first residents arrived and then helped them adjust to their new surroundings, died of a self-inflicted gunshot wound. It happened on a Tuesday morning in June, at his home in the small community of Ridgeway, just down the road from the Circle P Ranch. His wife was out shopping, and he was in the kitchen cleaning his gun when their children heard a shot. Rushing to the scene, they discovered their father on the floor, fatally wounded. Some speculated it was suicide, questioning how an experienced hunter like Kearney could shoot himself by accident. Others insisted Kearney would never have taken his own life, especially with children in the house.

Still grieving Kearney's death, McKissick soon received more bad news. In August, his friend and benefactor Irving Fain died of Hodgkin's disease, at the age of sixty-four. McKissick knew Fain was sick and had reached out to him several times in recent months to express his affection and gratitude. "My thoughts are with you constantly," he wrote in one letter. "Your support of my work here at McKissick Enterprises, and previously at CORE, has been of the utmost importance to me." Still, the news of Fain's death came as a blow. Not only had McKissick lost a close friend; he had lost an important adviser and patient creditor—a fact underscored six weeks later when Fain's estate sent McKissick a letter asking when he planned to repay the two hundred thousand dollars he had borrowed the year before.

McKissick was in no position to settle that debt, because he was still waiting on the loan guarantee from HUD. And on that front the news was mixed. Although his application hadn't been approved yet, the effort to build new towns was gaining steam. By late 1970, HUD had awarded guarantees to five projects. In addition to $21 million for Jonathan, Minnesota, it had authorized $30 million for Park Forest South, Illinois, an extension of the postwar community of Park Forest; $24 million for St. Charles, Maryland, a proposed town twenty-two miles southeast of Washington, DC; $18 million for Flower Mound, Texas, a suburb north of Dallas; and $7.5 million for Maumelle, Arkansas, a development just upriver from Little

Rock. HUD was also close to approving loan guarantees for several other developments, including Cedar-Riverside, a high-rise community near downtown Minneapolis that was inspired by Le Corbusier's Radiant City.

At the same time, there was a move to expand the program. Since passage of the New Communities Act in 1968, Washington's enthusiasm for new towns had only grown. In 1969, the National Committee on Urban Growth Policy issued a report titled "The New City." Denouncing the American metropolis as "monumentally ugly" and condemning suburban sprawl as "wasteful and destructive of the urban environment," the report called for a shift to comprehensively planned communities, pointing to Reston and Columbia as models. If the government built ten large cities (each with a population of one million) and one hundred smaller towns, the report asserted, it could absorb the population boom and remake the urban landscape. A year later, HUD issued a similar report, proposing the construction of ten new towns each year over the next decade.

Congress wasn't prepared to go that far, but it did double down on its support for new towns. In the summer of 1970, it passed the Urban Growth and New Community Development Act, which increased funding for new towns from $250 million to $500 million; established the New Community Development Corporation to oversee the program; and authorized a variety of grants for education, technical assistance, and social services. Nixon initially vetoed the bill because it was part of a larger package that exceeded his budget demands. But after extensive negotiations, Congress amended the bill, and Nixon signed it into law on December 31, 1970, just hours before the end of the legislative calendar.

With both HUD and Congress reaffirming their support for new towns, McKissick moved quickly to close the deal, scheduling a formal presentation before the New Community Development Corporation in February 1971. It was the most important moment yet in Soul City's short history, and he left nothing to chance. He brought along a team of a dozen planners, lawyers, accountants, and consultants, hoping to show strength in numbers. He also made sure the group was racially mixed (eight Black members, four white) to demonstrate the integrated nature of the project. They stayed at the Skyline Inn on I Street, a few blocks south of the Capitol and a short walk from the newly constructed HUD building, a curving concrete structure in the Brutalist style. To save money, the team slept two to a room, in single beds. For an extra twenty-five dollars, McKissick reserved a conference room, where he conducted a dry run the night before that lasted until two o'clock in the morning.

The preparation came in handy the next day, when the team appeared before a half dozen HUD staffers. McKissick spoke for roughly an hour, clicking through slides on an overhead projector and emphasizing Soul City's potential to spur economic development in a depressed region. He was followed by Harvey Gantt, who described the land-use plan, and Skip Tolbert, who detailed the financial projections. When it was time for questions, the HUD staffers had many. What kind of industrial commitments had McKissick secured? How would he cover the front-end costs of building a new town without taking on unmanageable debt? What kind of cooperation could he expect from local officials? McKissick parried the questions skillfully, his experience as a trial lawyer serving him well. Industry was enthusiastic, he explained, but was waiting for HUD to make a commitment. A loan guarantee of $33 million would ensure the project's economic feasibility even with no other funding. And local officials were coming around as they realized the benefits Soul City would provide for the entire area.

When the meeting ended, McKissick felt confident he had addressed HUD's concerns. But as weeks went by without an answer, he grew worried. In April, he wrote to William Nicoson to emphasize the need for a quick decision. "It should be clear that we are progressing on every front and that we have a high degree of cooperation from the State of North Carolina, regional government, local government, and from the various federal departments and agencies," he wrote. "What we need now to move ahead aggressively on industrial locations and additional federal support is announcement of the offer of commitment."

A few days later, he wrote to Nicoson's boss, Sam Jackson. He had talked with the Chase executives, who had recently been in touch with Jackson, and the message they relayed was not encouraging. The executives were under the impression that the project was no closer to approval than it was a year earlier, and McKissick blamed Jackson for giving them that impression. Now, Chase was insisting on a letter of intent from HUD before it would loan him more money. "Some persons cannot understand what they call the 'low priority' that this project has," McKissick wrote. "HUD's failure to give assurances that a guarantee would be forthcoming has most negatively affected our project."

Jackson responded informally in late April, then followed up with a formal letter on May 10, assuring McKissick that his presentation was "excellent" and had "favorably impressed" the staff. But there were still many questions to be addressed before HUD could approve his application. The economic analysis drafted by Hammer, Greene, Siler projected the number of jobs that would be created each year but provided no details about the types of jobs or how much they would pay. HUD also doubted the capability of McKissick's team, noting that it lacked "the extensive background in land development and sales normally assumed necessary for such an undertaking." For that reason, Jackson explained, McKissick should find a partner, preferably one with expertise in housing. In addition, the staff had numerous smaller questions, some of which were so nitpicky as to be almost comical. For instance, although Gantt's plan specified the number of parks in Soul City, HUD wanted to know the precise size of each one and where it would be located. HUD also wanted to know how much tickets would cost on the regional bus system, when the town would switch from bottled to natural gas, and how it would finance an ambulance service.

HUD's anxiety over Soul City stemmed mainly from its status as a freestanding town. Having never worked on a project so complex— and having received little guidance about how to proceed—the HUD staff was genuinely worried about making a mistake. To McKissick, however, the agency's demands seemed unfair, especially since other developers had not faced the same scrutiny. He also believed the new requests were counterproductive. As he explained to Jackson, he had recently been in negotiations with Certain-teed Products, a manufacturer of building supplies, about acquiring an equity stake in Soul City. But Certain-teed had somehow learned of HUD's insistence that he find a partner and had offered "quite unacceptable terms since they feel that we are over a barrel and must have them in order to proceed." Now, McKissick feared, it would be impossible to find a partner willing to put money into the project. "It is terribly embarrassing and expensive to us to work like hell and accomplish something only to find that we are no closer to the guarantee."

Despite his frustration, McKissick and his staff labored furiously over the next few weeks, researching industrial trends, meeting with HUD officials, and submitting follow-up reports. As part of a revised economic model, they slashed the amount of the requested loan guarantee from $33 million to $14 million. Chase, meanwhile, agreed to advance McKissick another $50,000 to tide him over until the application was approved. But as McKissick explained to Jackson, "It has already been spent to avert bankruptcy and we are broke again."

Finally, on June 9, the board of directors of the New Community Development Corporation gathered to discuss Soul City's application. The discussion was private, but the next day Jackson met with McKissick at John F. Kennedy Airport in New York to brief him on the outcome. On the whole, the news was positive. Jackson explained that most of the items raised in his letter were of a technical nature and that McKissick's staff had already addressed the bulk of them. As a result, the board had agreed to approve Soul City's application as soon as McKissick submitted an "acceptable equity position." But this condition was key. By "acceptable equity position," the board meant that McKissick had to put up sufficient cash, either his own or that of investors. Ordinarily, HUD required developers to put up 20 percent of the amount of the loan guarantee, a figure well within the reach of most large real estate firms. In the case of Soul City, an experimental town with a worthy purpose, the board would accept $1.5 million—or just over 10 percent. But even that was a stretch for McKissick Enterprises. Its main asset was the Circle P Ranch, which was heavily mortgaged. And, as McKissick had repeatedly told Jackson, most banks and insurance companies refused to make financial commitments until HUD approved the loan guarantee. Still, he was encouraged by the board's decision and left his meeting with Jackson determined to do whatever it took to meet this final condition.

WHILE McKISSICK AND his staff went back and forth with HUD, they reached out to a variety of other federal agencies. The New Community Development Act not only authorized HUD to provide loan guarantees for developers, it also established a network of grants to finance the planning and development process. McKissick took full advantage of this network, filing a steady stream of applications with an assortment of agencies. And in contrast to his frustrations with HUD, he had surprising success. The Department of Agriculture provided money to establish a summer feeding program for impoverished children in Warren County. The Office of Economic Opportunity contributed $98,000 for the planning of a comprehensive health program. The Department of Labor funded the hiring of twenty-seven college students as summer counselors. And the Office of Minority Business Enterprise awarded the Warren Regional Planning Corporation $190,000 for planning purposes.

These grants kept Soul City humming during the long wait for HUD's approval, providing jobs and resources for a community that had grown to more than twenty members. In addition to the Grooms, McNeills, and Careys (who had adopted a second child, an infant named Anthony), McKissick's longtime assistants Dot and Margaret Waller were now working on-site, as was Harvey Gantt. But the most prominent addition was McKissick himself. He and Evelyn moved down in the summer of 1971, exchanging the Harlem brownstone they had occupied since 1966 for a yellow trailer on the edge of a cornfield. Their only son, Floyd Jr., was away at college, but they brought along their youngest daughter, Charmaine, who was still in high school. It was a difficult move for a sixteen-year-old. In New York, Charmaine had attended the LaGuardia high school for performing arts (later made famous by the movie *Fame*) and spent most of her time singing, acting, and dancing. In Warren County, she attended John Graham High, which offered classes in bricklaying, welding, and vocational agriculture. Like her siblings, though, Charmaine took for granted that she would participate in whatever adventure her father embarked on. Besides, there was a consolation in moving to Warren County. On her visits to Soul City, Charmaine had begun dating Middock Kearney, the teenage son of the late caretaker. Handsome and full of life, Middock had eyes that seemed to change from gray to green depending on his clothes. He was just the kind of boy to make a girl forget what she had left behind in New York.

Also arriving that summer was McKissick's oldest daughter, Joycelyn, and her husband, Lew Myers. A native of Pennsylvania and a graduate of Franklin and Marshall College, Myers was working as director of Upward Bound at Harvard's Graduate School of Education when he met Joycelyn, who was studying for her master's degree in teaching. Two of the few Black students at Harvard, Myers and Joycelyn began dating in the fall of 1969 and married the next May. At McKissick's invitation, they spent their honeymoon in Soul City, making the twelve-hour drive from Cambridge in Myers's Volkswagen Beetle. The first thing Myers noticed when they arrived was the red clay, which, when not wet, coated everything in a coppery powder. "I didn't know whether to roll the windows up and suffocate from the heat or keep them down and suffocate from the dust," he recalled. But he was transfixed by the beauty of the land and by McKissick's vision of a city where Black people would control their economic destiny. So when his father-in-law offered him a job, Myers readily accepted. Like Gantt, he had to explain to friends why he was leaving Cambridge for a speculative venture in the middle of nowhere. "My friends said, 'Lew, you're crazy. You smoked too many joints. You're giving up Harvard to go to Warren County, North Cackalacky, to do what?'"

But Myers trusted his instincts, and he and Joycelyn moved into a trailer behind the old manor house. The couple cut a striking figure in Warren County. Myers was tall and lean, with a full beard and high afro, while Joycelyn wore bright dashikis and an African scarf wrapped around her head. To locals, they looked like H. Rap Brown and Angela Davis, Black militants on the FBI's "most wanted" list. Joycelyn was especially imposing. A writer and poet, she carried a black notebook everywhere, recording all that she saw and heard. But she was more than a silent observer. Like her father, she was outspoken and blunt, with a vocabulary so profane it had gotten her kicked out of Spelman College. As one staff member recalled, "She would come to a meeting and just cuss. And she wasn't even working on the project."

Myers was more affable, venturing out to talk with residents and picking up kids for the summer feeding camp in his Beetle. Yet even he baffled locals. One morning after a long run, he was stretching by the side of the road when a Black farmer in a pickup truck stopped and asked what he and the other folks at the Circle P Ranch were doing.

"We're building a new town," Myers answered.

"When are y'all gonna be done?" the man asked.

"Thirty years."

The man looked at Myers as if he was from Mars.

ALTHOUGH GRANTS KEPT Soul City alive, the HUD loan guarantee was the big prize, and McKissick kept his eyes fixed firmly on it. In August, he found a company willing to acquire an equity stake in the project. The National Corporation for Housing Partnerships, a for-profit company established by Congress to facilitate the building of low-income housing, agreed to become a general partner and invest five hundred thousand dollars in Soul City. The deal not only helped McKissick satisfy HUD's equity requirements; it also addressed concerns about his management capabilities. With more than five hundred field consultants, the NCHP had a wealth of expertise in housing and residential development.

No sooner had McKissick and his staff cleared one obstacle, however, than another appeared. HUD now had questions about the value of the Circle P Ranch, which McKissick had included in his equity statement. His accountants submitted an appraisal showing that the land had appreciated substantially since McKissick purchased it two and a half years earlier. But HUD questioned the accuracy of the appraisal. It also raised concerns about including the mortgaged land as part of McKissick's equity, even though Chase had agreed to subordinate its loan to any obligations Soul City accrued with the federal government.

Like most of McKissick's troubles, this difficulty was the result of an overly cautious bureaucracy. But at least one problem was self-inflicted. In August, a *Baltimore Sun* reporter named Walter R. Gordon traveled to Soul City. Whether he arrived with a jaundiced view of the project or formed one while there is unclear. But the article he published was highly skeptical, emphasizing the desperate poverty of the region ("In some ways, Warren County is worse off than any place in Mississippi"), the inexperience of McKissick's staff ("None of the people here has ever operated a large business enterprise, and it shows"), and the enormous challenges ahead ("The chasm dividing the present dream from the future reality could hardly be greater if Mr. McKissick intended to build this city on the moon instead of these gentle hills 10 miles from the Virginia border"). The article also suggested that Soul City would be segregated. "It is clear from conversations with Mr. McKissick and his aides," Gordon wrote, "that they visualize Soul City as a virtually all Black city, although there is no way they can legally exclude whites and they stop just short of saying they would like to do so." This statement might have been dismissed as Gordon's own interpretation, especially since, in response to a query about whether he wanted whites to live in Soul City, McKissick had responded, "That's a racist question." As an experienced trial lawyer, McKissick should have known to stop there, to leave well enough alone and not elaborate. But for some reason—perhaps out of exasperation, perhaps to be provocative, or perhaps because, after a lifetime of discrimination, he still felt like a "black boy in a white land"—he returned to the question later in the interview. "If you are asking me, do I want to live side by side with white people all my life, I don't," he said. "I want to live with my people."

That quote ended the article, and nearly ended McKissick's dream. HUD had made clear from the beginning that it would not—as a matter of law, could not—support a segregated community. Yet here was McKissick saying that's exactly what he wanted. When Sam Jackson read the article he was livid. He had been fighting on Soul City's behalf for two years, assuring everyone in Washington that McKissick was not a separatist. And now, in one sentence, McKissick had made him look like a liar. In an unusually stern letter, Jackson reminded McKissick that his application to HUD claimed Soul City would "seek to become America's first city where racism isn't tolerated." He then noted that McKissick's statement in the *Sun* conflicted with that claim. "Would you please verify the accuracy of the quotation," he wrote. "I am sure that you are aware of the fact that a project undertaken on the basis of the social policy reflected in the quotes would not qualify for Title VII assistance."

Responding to Jackson a few days later, McKissick did not address the accuracy of the quote. Instead, invoking his long history on the front lines of the movement, he argued that he shouldn't have to repeatedly defend his commitment to integration. "The record speaks for itself," he declared. He also argued that anyone who questioned Soul City's racial goals need only visit to see that whites were employed at every level and that his staff was working closely with state and local officials, who were mostly white. "This would not have been possible had our project been representative of the negativism and divisiveness indicated in the article by Mr. Gordon."

McKissick's response was enough to mollify Jackson, but other HUD officials were still uneasy. In mid-September, the board of the New Community Development Corporation met again to consider Soul City's application. Prior to the meeting, McKissick had submitted an updated equity statement that included his agreement with the National Corporation for Housing Partnerships, additional documentation on the value of the Circle P Ranch, and the promise of five hundred thousand dollars from a group of New York investors. With that issue addressed, he expected the board to finally approve an offer of commitment. He had even broadcast that expectation to his creditors, who were growing impatient. But when the board met, it deferred a vote on Soul City. Instead, as Jackson explained in a letter on September 28, it wanted a revised list of industrial prospects and more details about the interest they had shown in Soul City.

Now it was McKissick's turn to explode. On October 1, he dictated a long letter to Jackson, complaining bitterly about the imposition of yet another condition. "Each month a new hurdle is placed before us," he protested. "How can we possibly finish the race?" It wasn't just a question of finishing the race, however. It was a question of staying on his feet. The board's failure to approve the application had pushed McKissick to the edge of bankruptcy. In addition to owing back taxes in North Carolina and New York, he was heavily in debt. He had already been forced to close his office in Harlem and curtail operations at Soul City because HUD had not yet renewed the planning grant. In June, he had persuaded his creditors to hold off until September 1. On September 1, he had persuaded them to hold off until September 25. Now they were hounding him about what had happened at the board's meeting. Meanwhile, his staff was growing anxious. Harvey Gantt had recently departed to open his own architectural firm in Charlotte, and other employees were likely to follow. Perhaps most distressing, Carey's wife was scheduled to have a hysterectomy in the coming days, and the company's health insurance had lapsed. "Gordon is now forced to raise money to keep up the family," McKissick informed Jackson. As for himself, he didn't know how much longer he could last:

> Three years of my life have gone into this project. I'm now a very, very poor man having placed all of my property, as well as future

earnings, on the line for this project. Thus, I will be compelled to make some personal decisions within the next ten days regarding my future status. The embarrassment will be extremely difficult but at least sanity will prevail, good physical health and my family will then be stable. While I am not going to make a public announcement, I am sure my creditors within the next ten days will be on the attack unless McKissick Enterprises secures additional funds. They are ready, willing, and able to attack me, the republican party, and everyone else.

Then, in his own hand, he scrawled a personal postscript: "What really disturbs me is that people both black and white will long remember the failure of Soul City. Those who were on the verge of losing faith will [have] reason to lose faith."

Jackson must have sensed what was coming. For at 6:10 that night, before McKissick posted his letter, Jackson telephoned the office at Soul City. The board was meeting again in mid-October, he explained, and this time he hoped to have better news. A few weeks later, George Romney wrote McKissick himself, attempting to clarify the board's position and offer his own reassurance. "I would like to confirm to you that based on the information presently available to us, although incomplete as regards certain aspects of the project, the Board believes there is a good prospect that the project can be found deserving of Title VII guarantee assistance." As always with HUD, there were caveats. Romney noted that the environmental impact statement McKissick had submitted would need to be reviewed by a variety of government agencies, a process that could take three months. In addition, the board had sent McKissick's financial projections to an outside consultant for an independent analysis. Finally, any approval by the board would come with conditions that had to be satisfied before the money was actually released.

It was not a guarantee. But it was as close to one as McKissick had received. And it came not from his friend Sam Jackson but from the secretary of HUD, who had little reason to give him false hope. As if to confirm the positive implications of Romney's letter, McKissick soon received more good news: HUD had decided to renew Soul City's planning grant for another year. Having teetered on the brink of failure, he would soon have the money to keep his dream alive.

· 11 ·

"Theory of the Sugar Tit"

Not long after McKissick received Romney's letter, he sent his own letter to Bob Brown at the White House. McKissick had stayed in close contact with Brown since his announcement three years earlier, frequently asking him to intervene at HUD or put in a good word with other agencies. As with his letters to Jackson, his correspondence with Brown was often erratic, veering among indignation, flattery, and entreaty. Just a few weeks earlier, after the two friends had seen each other in Washington, McKissick had dropped Brown a note saying how nice it had been to talk with "an old home-state boy" before requesting that he make a "special thrust" to secure federal support for Soul City.

Now McKissick offered to do something for Brown. With the 1972 presidential election less than a year away, McKissick proposed that he, Brown, and Jackson launch an effort to mobilize Black support for Nixon's campaign. The Democratic Party was in disarray and had taken Black voters for granted, he explained. If Republicans emphasized the tangible benefits they had provided since assuming power, they could break the Democratic grip on the minority vote. Their effort should focus on the cities—on Cleveland, New Orleans,

New York, and San Francisco. They should assemble a staff, recruit other Black leaders, and spread their message through the media. Most importantly, they should make the administration's support for Soul City a centerpiece of their pitch.

McKissick's offer marked a fateful shift in both his politics and his struggle to build Soul City. A longtime Democrat, he had been critical of Nixon almost from the beginning of his presidency, denouncing his lack of follow-through on Black capitalism and his demagoguery on the issue of crime. In a column for the *New York Amsterdam News*, shortly after the 1968 election, he argued that Nixon had "no particular commitment to the black masses" and was indebted only to "large white corporations." In another column he condemned the administration's surveillance of radical groups, while in yet another he decried Nixon's approach to criminal justice, declaring him "one of the nation's leading proponents of law and order—racist style." But whatever his opinion of Nixon, McKissick needed help. In spite of Romney's letter, there was no guarantee HUD would ultimately approve his application. He had received numerous assurances in the past, only to find out later that a new request had been made or a new condition imposed. And even if HUD approved his application, he would need help dealing with the agency during the development phase. So he did what businessmen have been doing since the dawn of politics: he offered his support to those with the power to grant him what he wanted. As Eva Clayton explained later, "He was being expedient. He felt he had to do it."

McKissick's motive for supporting Nixon was irrelevant to Brown and Jackson, who readily accepted his offer. At a strategy session in January, the three men crafted a plan to reach Black voters, then spent the next few weeks working behind the scenes to implement it. McKissick threw himself into the effort, contacting potential supporters, pestering the campaign for resources, and drafting a confidential "Statement of Principles and Purpose." It was a starkly pragmatic document, arguing that the Democratic Party, "which admittedly speaks more directly to the problems of minorities," had a poor record of accomplishment; that minorities would be taken for granted if they failed to participate in the two-party system; and that the Republican Party, although more conservative in rhetoric, was "best suited to serve the needs of Black People" in the upcoming election. In fact, McKissick explained, it was the conservative nature of the GOP that made it an effective advocate for Black people. "Because the Republican Party seeks to maintain a public conservative posture, it has been able to throw many liberal rocks and hide its hands." To some, this might sound cynical, but to McKissick it simply reflected reality. "The game of politics is sophisticated," he wrote. It "cannot be dealt with in terms of rhetoric and non-accomplishments, but must be dealt with in terms of power, action and economics."

As if to demonstrate his own sophistication, McKissick's public pronouncements soon took on a different tone. Whereas before he had freely and vigorously criticized the president, he now held his tongue. When asked in March about Nixon's statement that Congress should pass a nationwide moratorium on school busing, McKissick initially dismissed the move as a political stunt. Then, apparently remembering his new loyalties, he demurred, telling the press he wouldn't say anything more about it.

McKISSICK'S DECISION TO support Nixon was only half the equation. There was also the question of whether Nixon would reciprocate, whether a president who had embraced the rhetoric of "law and order" and staked his political prospects on appealing to white southerners would welcome the endorsement of a Black militant. More to the point, would he be grateful enough to ensure the administration's support of Soul City? For most politicians, it would have been an impossibly fine line to walk. But Nixon had been walking that line his entire career.

As vice president, under Dwight Eisenhower, Nixon had been known as the GOP's "civil rights workhorse," in the words of *Jet* magazine. He had led the effort to eliminate discrimination in government contracts, praised *Brown v. Board of Education*, and condemned Southern Democrats bent on thwarting integration. "A political party at the national level cannot long endure or merit support when it's half for and half against equality of treatment," he declared in a 1956 speech in Harlem. When Ghana secured its independence from Britain that same year, Nixon traveled to Africa to mark the occasion. And when the Civil Rights Act of 1957 was in danger of failing in the Senate, he played a key role in pushing it past Southern opposition. Writing him afterward, Martin Luther King Jr. praised Nixon for his "assiduous and dauntless courage" and his "devotion to the highest mandates of moral law." The NAACP named him an honorary member.

Nixon continued to court Black voters during his 1960 campaign for president. In fact, for most of the campaign, he was viewed as more liberal on racial issues than John F. Kennedy. While Nixon promised to enforce *Brown*, eliminate literacy tests in voting, and end discrimination in housing, Kennedy assured southern officials he would not use federal troops to end segregation. It wasn't until the eve of the election, when King was jailed during a sit-in in Georgia, that the narrative flipped. Nixon resisted calls to intervene, fearing a backlash from southern whites. But Kennedy, at the urging of liberal aides, called Coretta Scott King to express his sympathies, while his brother Robert appealed personally to the judge in the case. When King was released shortly afterward and news of Kennedy's involvement spread, Black voters moved sharply in his direction. Even then, Nixon received 32 percent of the Black vote, a figure no Republican presidential candidate has come close to matching since.

During his years out of office, Nixon remained outwardly sympathetic to the cause of racial equality, urging Republicans in Congress to support the Civil Rights Act of 1964. But when he ran for president again, in 1968, he adopted a new strategy. Observing how Johnson's association with civil rights had alienated the Democratic Party's traditional base of white southerners, Nixon decided to woo those voters himself. Under the guidance of a young aide named Harry Dent, he pursued what came to be known as the "southern strategy"—an attempt to break the Democrats' century-old monopoly on the South with tacit appeals to white racism. Campaigning on a platform of "law and order," Nixon cast himself as the spokesman for the "silent center" (later rebranded the "silent majority") that was fed up with the protests of the civil rights and antiwar movements. His choice of Spiro Agnew as a running mate only amplified that message. As governor of Maryland, Agnew had publicly blamed Black leaders for the 1968 riots in Baltimore, calling them "caterwauling, riot-inciting, burn-America-down type of leaders."

Still, Nixon wasn't prepared to give up the Black vote entirely. In his "Bridges to Human Dignity" speech, in 1968, he had touted Black capitalism as an alternative to the liberal welfarism of the Great Society. He had also reached out privately to prominent Black leaders such as McKissick and Roy Innis and had hired Bob Brown to burnish his image in the Black community. His efforts didn't persuade everyone (Jackie Robinson warned that if Nixon were elected, "we as Negroes are in serious trouble"), but they were enough to make up some of the ground Republicans lost in 1964, when Barry Goldwater received only 4 percent of the Black vote.

Once in the White House, Nixon took several steps to appease Black voters. He created the Office of Minority Business Enterprise to promote Black entrepreneurialism and adopted the so-called Philadelphia Plan, which mandated affirmative action in government contracts. He also hired a handful of high-profile Blacks to serve in his administration, including James Farmer, who was appointed assistant secretary of the Department of Health, Education, and Welfare. And when Whitney Young, head of the Urban League, died of a heart attack in Nigeria, in March 1971, Nixon sent a plane to collect his body, then delivered a eulogy at his funeral.

To many Black critics, these were empty gestures. They noted that the Office of Minority Business Enterprise was severely underfunded and that Nixon had failed to appoint any Black officials to his cabinet. They also seized on a memo written by Daniel Patrick Moynihan, Nixon's domestic policy adviser, urging a policy of "benign neglect" on racial matters. At times, Nixon went beyond "benign neglect," as though determined to antagonize Blacks in his effort to pander to whites. When Supreme Court justice Abe Fortas was forced to resign in 1969 over conflict-of-interest charges, Nixon nominated the conservative southerner Clement Haynsworth to replace him. And when Haynsworth was rejected in a bipartisan vote, Nixon nominated G. Harrold Carswell, who had once run for the Georgia state legislature on a platform of segregation. (Carswell was also defeated, forcing Nixon to nominate the moderate Minnesotan Harry Blackmun.) Nixon also snubbed Black congressmen who sought meetings with him, attempted to dilute the Voting Rights Act of 1970, and called for a national moratorium on busing as a means of integration. James Farmer was so dismayed by the administration's record that he resigned less than two years into the job, while Bishop Stephen G. Spottswood, the chairman of the NAACP's national board, called the Nixon White House the first "anti-Negro" administration since Woodrow Wilson's.

And yet, such was Nixon's fear of losing that when he launched his reelection bid in 1972, he held out hope of attracting a subset of Black voters—what Moynihan termed "the silent black majority." Instead of appealing to these voters with coded rhetoric about "law and order," however, his campaign decided on a more direct enticement: money. Campaign aides had already outlined a plan to leverage the advantages of incumbency on the president's behalf. Known as the Responsiveness Program, the plan called for agency heads to channel grants and federal contracts to applicants who campaigned for Nixon. The program was designed to increase support among all racial groups, but special emphasis was placed on minority voters. In the words of one campaign document, "a selective funding approach will furnish encouragement incentives for Black individuals, firms and organizations whose support will have a multiplier effect on Black vote support for the President. This will call for working with OMBE, SBA, Department of Labor, OEO, HUD, HEW, and the Justice Department. What we do economically will be key politically."

Over the next few months, that's exactly what happened. The

Committee to Reelect the President (known officially as CRP, but mocked as "CREEP" by Nixon's detractors) established a Black voter division and hired Paul Jones as its executive director. A former Peace Corps administrator who once dated Angela Davis, Jones had campaigned for Hubert Humphrey in the 1968 presidential race. But like a number of Black Democrats, he accepted a job in the Nixon administration, believing he could do more for minorities within the system than outside it. Jones worked briefly at HUD and the Justice Department before moving to CRP in January 1972. There, he occupied an office next to G. Gordon Liddy, the former FBI agent who oversaw the break-in of the Democratic National Committee headquarters at the Watergate complex. Jones's duties were more mundane, if just as legally dubious. He spent much of his time working with Bob Brown to recruit Blacks who were already receiving federal grants and to funnel future grants to Blacks who agreed to come on board. Their efforts were described in a memo from White House aide Fred Malek to campaign chairman John Mitchell. "Bob Brown and his staff have identified all blacks who are receiving, or have received, money from this administration," Malek wrote. "These recipients will be utilized as a source of contributions and volunteers, and as a group of visible blacks to be used to reach the voters in their area of influence."

The Responsiveness Program was a success, both in terms of increasing support generally and in targeting minority voters specifically. One Black businessman who received a $2.1 million contract from the SBA sent letters to two thousand minority contractors, soliciting support for Nixon. Another made numerous donations during the course of the campaign after being informed that his ability to obtain future contracts was dependent on his support for the president.

But although the program had paid dividends, it had not yet attracted a major Black leader who was willing to speak on Nixon's behalf. James Farmer had received a $150,000 grant for a new think tank after assuring Jones and Brown he would support the president. But Farmer insisted on keeping a low profile, to protect his credibility, and never actually delivered on his promise. Thus, when McKissick expressed a willingness to support Nixon, the campaign welcomed him with open arms, appointing him to an ad hoc executive advisory committee and identifying him as the president's chief Black spokesman.

And once McKissick was in the fold, his application for Soul City moved quickly toward approval. In April, his staff met with HUD officials to go over the final details of its offer of commitment. In May, the Office of Minority Business Enterprise awarded Soul City a five-hundred-thousand-dollar grant to plan an industrial park named after the Black labor leader A. Philip Randolph. And in early June, the Office of Economic Opportunity approved a $1 million grant for the creation of HealthCo, a comprehensive health-care center for Warren and Vance counties.

Most significantly, McKissick heard from the man himself. According to T. T. Clayton, he and McKissick drove to Washington for an appointment with Nixon in the spring or early summer of 1972. They met alone with the president, Clayton recalled, and when McKissick expressed concern about the loan guarantee, Nixon assured him everything would be fine.

"Don't worry, Floyd," he said, "you're going to get your money."

Was there a quid pro quo between Nixon and McKissick? That would later become the narrative in the media, but the evidence is inconclusive. For one thing, there is no record of McKissick and Clayton meeting with Nixon in the Presidential Daily Diary, which recorded nearly all of Nixon's appointments and activities. And several people deeply involved in the project, including Gordon Carey and Lew Myers, say they never heard of such a meeting. Eva Clayton backs up her husband's account, describing T.T.'s visit to the White House as one of the highlights of his career. He told the same story for years, she says, often mimicking Nixon's throaty growl. McKissick's daughter Charmaine also recalls her father talking about the meeting with Nixon, though she is unsure whether it took place in 1972 or perhaps at a later point in McKissick's dealings with HUD.

Even if the meeting took place as described, Nixon's statement is ambiguous. Was he promising McKissick the loan guarantee in exchange for his support? Or was he informing McKissick that his application had been approved on the merits? The history of the Responsiveness Program would suggest the former, especially given Bob Brown's role and his close friendship with McKissick. But Brown steadfastly denied exercising improper influence on behalf of Soul City or any other project. "None of that was ever done, and there is nobody who can ever say that Bob Brown called him up and said we are going to give you a contract over here if you vote for the President," he testified before the Senate Watergate Committee. "There was no quid pro quo kind of deals made." And in the mountains of evidence the Senate later gathered about the Responsiveness Program, there is not a single reference to Soul City or McKissick's efforts to secure a loan guarantee from HUD.

On the other hand, there *is* evidence that HUD was on its way to approving the guarantee even before McKissick offered his support to Nixon. There are Sam Jackson's numerous assurances to McKissick over the course of two years. There is Romney's letter to McKissick the previous fall stating that "there is a good prospect that the project can be found deserving" of federal support. And, although it is unclear whether McKissick knew it, the board of the New Community Development Corporation had given his application tentative approval at its meeting in December 1971. The approval was conditioned on McKissick satisfying the terms laid out in Romney's letter, but in mid-May, Jackson informed the board that McKissick had done so and that he was preparing an offer of commitment. The board made no mention of McKissick switching parties. To the contrary, a HUD lawyer who attended the December meeting told colleagues that the board's decision was "based more on a desire to give a black developer a chance than anything else."

Instead of a quid pro quo, then, McKissick's endorsement of

Nixon might best be characterized as an insurance policy—a way to guard against the risk that HUD would back out of its commitment at the last minute. Doing so would be difficult if McKissick, rather than being a vocal critic of the president, was one of his staunchest allies.

Whatever the understanding between McKissick and Nixon, what happened next is clear. In late May, McKissick wrote a check to the Nixon campaign, buying five one-hundred-dollar tickets to a fundraising gala for Black Nixon supporters at the Washington Hilton. A few weeks later, he appeared at the gala to give the keynote address. It was a boisterous and star-studded affair. More than 2,500 guests packed into the hotel's grand ballroom, including Jim Brown, Jackie Robinson (who had overcome his earlier doubts about Nixon), and Betty Shabazz, the widow of Malcolm X. Music was provided by jazz legend Lionel Hampton, who introduced a dance number called "Do the Nixon," while his band played a new campaign song:

> We need Nixon
> Let's stay with Nixon
> He's the leader we can trust
> Our man is Nixon
> He's right on fixin'
> A better world for all of us.

The music was not the only entertainment. As the attendees tucked into their meals, they heard from an eclectic group of speakers. Jerome Green, a Vietnam veteran from Chicago, informed the crowd that there were seventeen thousand Black soldiers back home "ready to go all out for Mr. Nixon." Ethel Allen, a Philadelphia city council member, predicted that Black women would vote en masse for the president. And the Rev. William Holmes Borders, a prominent preacher from Atlanta, declared that Nixon "had done more for blacks than anyone since Jesus Christ," to which an audience member responded, "Now walk the water, Reverend!" The audience also heard from Nixon campaign manager (and former attorney general) John Mitchell, who was there with his famously outspoken wife, Martha. Touting the administration's record on minority issues, Mitchell urged the attendees to return to their communities and spread the word that a vote for Nixon would help the president realize his "goal of an America for all Americans."

McKissick spoke last. It was his coming-out party as a Republican, and he didn't disappoint. Wearing a white dinner jacket over a black dress shirt, he delivered a rousing speech written especially for the occasion. Titled "The Theory of the Sugar Tit," it explained why the former CORE leader had switched political parties, and why his audience should, too. According to McKissick, Black voters in 1972 faced many of the same problems as in 1932, when racism and economic deprivation threatened their very survival. In that earlier election, Blacks had abandoned their traditional allegiance to the Republican Party, throwing their support behind Franklin D. Roosevelt and the Democrats. Yet despite controlling Congress for forty years, despite controlling the White House for all but twelve of those years, and despite controlling the mayor's office in nearly every major city in the country, the Democratic Party had failed to cure the ills that afflicted the Black population—poverty, joblessness, crime, and lack of affordable housing. Instead, Democrats had attempted to pacify Black voters in the same way parents often tried to quiet their babies: with a sugar tit—a cube of sugar wrapped in cloth. "If you were a Southerner, and you knew what a sugar tit really is, it ain't milk," McKissick told the crowd. "It's a substitute for milk, and it's a pacifier, and it's something that makes you think you've got something when you ain't got it."

The sugar tit does not solve anything, McKissick explained. It makes matters worse, leading the parents to believe they are providing nourishment and making the baby forget what real milk tastes like. This is what had happened with Blacks and the Democratic Party. The party, believing it had met the needs of minorities with its empty rhetoric, had ceased trying to cure their ills. Black voters, meanwhile, had become so accustomed to a diet of sweet talk they had stopped pleading for real sustenance. The only way to break out of this dynamic, McKissick told the attendees, was to use their political leverage to demand results. And in 1972, he argued, the Republican Party was the only one with a record of accomplishment. It was the Nixon administration that had doubled funding for historically Black colleges. It was the Nixon administration that had created the Office of Minority Business Enterprise. And it was the Nixon administration that was trying to bring soldiers home from Vietnam.

"I guess some will still think we ought to hang on to the sugar tit," McKissick concluded. "That's ok. But me—I've tasted a little bit of cream and a little bit of milk and I know why I endured those fifty-two arrests and why my kids stood such abuse. There's food in the land—it's goodbye old sugar tit!"

McKissick's speech was a hit, drawing laughter and applause from the crowd. Even Mitchell, usually dour and grim-faced, couldn't repress a smile. "A lot of people are going to be surprised this year," Paul Jones told a reporter afterward. "The President only received 12 percent of the Black vote in 1968, but he's going to do much, much better this time because he's earned it."

As for McKissick, he had earned the gratitude of the Nixon campaign. Over the next few weeks, he received letters of appreciation from Jones, Bob Brown, and Maurice Stans, CRP's finance chair. But the most important letter came on July 28, from Sam Jackson. "Dear Gentlemen," it began, "You have applied under the Urban Growth and New Community Development Act of 1970 for a commitment to guarantee up to $14,000,000 principal amount of obligations . . ." The letter went on for several pages, dense and full of legalese. But buried in the second paragraph was the sentence McKissick had been waiting so long to read: "Based upon the information contained in your application and otherwise submitted by you to us, we have made the determinations required under the Act for purposes of the commitment hereby offered and are prepared, subject to the conditions specified below, to enter into an agreement providing for the guarantee under the Act of up to $14,000,000."

Setting aside the bureaucratic jargon and that worrisome reference to "conditions specified below," it was the sweetest letter McKissick had ever received. After three years of planning, negotiations, and an endless stream of excuses, HUD had finally approved his application to build Soul City. A dream that had once seemed fantastical to everyone but him was about to become reality.

Goodbye old sugar tit—hello milk!

PART III

12

Black Elephants

When McKissick offered to support Nixon's reelection, he had assured Bob Brown he would dedicate himself fully to the campaign. "As you well know, Bob, once I commit myself to a project, my commitment is total," he had written. "I am also one who believes in systematically executing that commitment."

Over the next several months, he made good on that promise. Three weeks after receiving Jackson's letter, he officially switched parties, changing his registration from Democrat to Republican. And three weeks after that, he attended his new party's national convention in Miami Beach. The Democrats had met in south Florida a week earlier, but whereas their convention was contentious and unruly, with bitter debates lasting through the night, the Republican gathering was placid and uneventful. There was no last-minute challenge to the front-runner, no drama over the selection of a running mate. Instead, the event was like a renewal of vows, with the delegates reaffirming their devotion to Nixon and the president promising four more blissful years. Even the protests outside the convention (staged by Students for a Democratic Society, the Yippies, and the

Southern Christian Leadership Conference) couldn't spoil the positive vibes inside.

The only surprising thing about the convention was its racial composition. One hundred and thirty-eight Black men and women took the floor as delegates, the most in party history. And although Black delegates still accounted for only 10 percent of the total, that was a dramatic increase from 1968, when just twenty-six Blacks had participated. Several Black celebrities were also on hand, including Sammy Davis Jr., who made headlines when he awkwardly hugged the president on stage during the nominating concert.

McKissick played a prominent role in the proceedings, working the halls of the convention center, attending a party for Black delegates at the Eden Roc Hotel, and testifying before the platform committee wearing a black elephant lapel pin engraved with the words "'72 Self-Determination." But his main reason for being in Miami was to promote Soul City, and he took full advantage of the opportunity, paying $250 to rent space in the grand lobby of the Fontainebleau Hotel, where many delegates were staying. There, under crystal chandeliers blazing in gilded mirrors, he set up a Soul City exhibit, complete with pamphlets, charts, maps, and a poster-size copy of a *New York Times* editorial praising the project. He and Carey took turns manning the exhibit, joined by Sam Tidmore, a former linebacker for the Cleveland Browns who had recently been added to the staff. It was an exhausting week—McKissick slept only a few hours each night—but highly productive. Hundreds of delegates passed by the booth each day, and by the end of the convention McKissick had scheduled meetings with eight firms interested in Soul City, including a box company, a hotel chain, a food-services supplier, an electronics firm, and a wigmaker.

A few weeks later, he was back in New York, where he launched the National Committee for a Two-Party System, a group designed ostensibly to encourage ticket-splitting among Black voters but in reality a vehicle to promote Nixon's reelection. To kick things off, the committee held a fundraiser at the Hilton Hotel in midtown Manhattan. It was another glamorous affair, featuring Nixon's younger brother Edward, boxing champ Archie Moore, and Juanita Poitier, the ex-wife of Sidney Poitier. And with five hundred guests paying twenty-five dollars a plate, it brought in a tidy sum for the committee's reelection efforts.

But if McKissick was enjoying the fruits of his relationship with Nixon, there was also a cost. Many Black luminaries who supported Nixon came under heavy criticism from the Black community. Sammy Davis Jr. was mocked by the Black press for embracing the president at the convention. James Brown performed to half-empty venues while protesters chanted "James Brown, Nixon's clown." And Charles Hurst, the president of Malcolm X College in Chicago, arrived at work one day to find his office riddled with bullets.

No one fired shots at McKissick, but he, too, was attacked. The leaders of the Congressional Black Caucus issued a statement condemning him and other prominent Black figures for supporting Nixon. "The President has bought them, and they have sold out," the caucus charged. Julian Bond, a Georgia state legislator and president of the Southern Poverty Law Center, was more blunt, describing McKissick and other Black Nixon supporters as "political prostitutes." A letter to the editor in the *New York Amsterdam News* went so far as to compare him to Judas Iscariot. "I can dig Brother McKissick's devotion to this project, but not at the cost of the nationwide Black Community," the writer stated. "At a time when blacks are trying to consolidate their political power to kick this turkey out of the White House, we are confronted by Negro leaders getting their pieces of silver."

McKissick was stung by the charges of selling out, but he didn't let on. Instead he embraced the criticism, referring to himself as a "happy hooker." He also fired back, arguing that it was George McGovern, not Nixon, who had betrayed the poor. During the Democratic primary, he pointed out, McGovern had embraced a guaranteed annual income with the slogan "$6,500 or Fight." But recently, after realizing he needed donations from Wall Street, the nominee had lowered his proposal to $2,500. Why were the members of the Black caucus so silent now, McKissick asked in a press release on September 1. "The answer is because *their* presidential candidate sold *them* down the river for a pat on the head from Big Business." And what about McGovern's running mate, Sargent Shriver, who had spent the past week in Louisiana boasting that his ancestors had fought with the Confederacy? If the members of the Black caucus "are a little sheepish today, well, that's understandable," McKissick stated. "They've got a plate of crow and humble pie to eat this morning."

Meanwhile, McKissick's alliance with the president went ahead full steam. That fall, the campaign published a full-page ad featuring a photograph of McKissick above the caption, "McKissick's Dream was Soul City. Democrats endorsed it. Republicans supported it. That's Action." The campaign also launched the "Black Blitz," a surrogate program in which Black leaders traveled the country giving speeches on Nixon's behalf. Armed with a fact sheet listing Nixon's accomplishments, the surrogates were advised to focus on Democrats and independents and to emphasize the theme of "Blacks as political hostage." McKissick was the chief surrogate, making trips to Louisiana, Illinois, Arkansas, Texas, and Georgia. Speaking at the historic Wheat Street Baptist Church in Atlanta, he told the congregation it was time to break the chains that tied them to a single party. "We must become able to change with the seasons," he declared. "So many of us are so rigid that we are unable to make a shift in strategy."

The message appeared to be getting through. In September, Nixon received an endorsement from Joseph H. Jackson, president of the National Baptist Convention, the largest Black organization in the country, with a membership of 6.3 million. A few days later, he picked up the backing of Jack E. Robinson, the president of the Boston branch of the NAACP. And a few days after that, Johnny Ford, the newly elected mayor of Tuskegee, Alabama, and a former campaign aide to Robert Kennedy, announced his support for the president. Endorsements also appeared in dozens of Black newspapers and magazines, including the *Cleveland Call and Post*, the *Atlanta Daily World*, the *Oakland Post*, and *Black Business Digest*.

It wasn't just the Black establishment that was coming on board. In

October, a group of young Black activists toured the country stumping for Nixon. Meeting with reporters in New York, the group's leader, Mary Parish, explained that she had worked for Shirley Chisholm in the Democratic primary but was fed up with the party's failure to deliver on its promises. "I have studied the record of black advancement since Nixon took office," Parish told the press, "and am thoroughly convinced that Mr. Nixon is 'The Man' for us in 1972."

Even some Black leaders who planned to vote for McGovern offered praise for the incumbent. Charles Evers, a civil rights activist in Mississippi whose brother Medgar had been killed outside his home in 1963, told reporters he understood why many Blacks were supporting the president. "Nixon has put more blacks in top positions of government than any other president," he said. "And you can't ignore the fact that blacks like Floyd McKissick and Sammy Davis Jr. have come out for the President." Jim Brown agreed. Referring to HUD's approval of the Soul City loan guarantee, Brown told reporters, "Ain't no Black cat ever got that much, and McKissick can create a lot of jobs for Black people."

The wave of endorsements buoyed the Nixon campaign, which was increasingly optimistic it would win a sizable share of the Black vote. To thank those who were responsible, the president invited his Executive Advisory Committee to the White House a few weeks before the election. In addition to McKissick, the group included Hurst, the president of Malcolm X College, and W. O. Walker, editor of the *Cleveland Call and Post*. As his visitors filed into the Cabinet Room, Nixon shook their hands and made small talk, noting that McKissick appeared to have lost weight. When McKissick responded that he was walking a mile every morning, the president quipped that he had given up exercise years ago. "I just got so tired after about a hundred yards," he said with a self-deprecating chuckle. Once they were seated, Nixon emphasized the progress his administration was making in the field of education and the opportunities he hoped to provide "without regard to skin color." McKissick, seated to Nixon's right, expressed his own hopes for the future. "We're changing the tide," he said, predicting that Black voters would move decisively in the president's direction.

When Election Day came, however, that prediction was not borne out. Although Nixon performed well in some cities (nearly one-third of Blacks in Louisville, Kentucky, voted for him), nationwide he received only 13 percent of the Black vote, barely higher than his 1968 total. By contrast, conservative whites in both parties flocked to the president. Democrats who had voted in the primaries for the segregationist George Wallace went for Nixon three to one in the South and six to five in the North. Nixon's dog whistle to whites, it turned out, was louder than his overture to Blacks.

Still, Nixon was grateful for McKissick's efforts. Shortly after the election, he offered him a job in the administration, suggesting the former soldier might like a position in the Department of Defense. McKissick declined, citing his commitment to build Soul City, but he was featured prominently at the inaugural festivities. He and Evelyn shared a box with Nixon and his wife, Pat, at a Kennedy Center concert the night before the inauguration, then watched the swearing-in the next day from the presidential viewing stand. They were also among a hundred guests invited to a state dinner at the White House in honor of the British prime minister.

McKissick moved quickly to capitalize on his newfound influence in the capital. Shortly after the inauguration, he and Bob Brown formed the National Council of Black Republicans, which secured three hundred thousand dollars in funding from the Republican National Committee. A few weeks later, McKissick met privately with the RNC's chair, a former congressman and United Nations ambassador named George H. W. Bush. Bush praised McKissick for his work on the campaign and pledged to build on his outreach to Black voters. "Things are in the process of change here at the National Committee," he assured McKissick. "I am determined that out of this will emerge a Republican Party with a sound record toward all Americans and with a much greater image of an open door."

· · ·

McKISSICK HAD WON the favor of party officials in Washington, but he still had work to do back home. That fall, voters in North Carolina had elected the state's first Republican senator since 1903: a television pundit and former political operative named Jesse Helms. And although he belonged to the same party as Nixon and Bush, Romney and Rockefeller, Helms represented an entirely new breed of Republican—one that had little enthusiasm for the kind of federal programs supporting Soul City, and even less enthusiasm for the project's goal of racial uplift.

By the end of his career, Helms would be one of the most powerful politicians in the country, "a maker of presidents and breaker of senators," in the words of one biographer. But his origins were humble. Born in 1921, a year before McKissick, he grew up in the small mill town of Monroe, just south of Charlotte. His father was a fireman and policeman with a reputation for roughing up suspects, especially if they were Black, and Helms was in awe of him. "My father was a six-foot, two-hundred-pound gorilla," he recalled as an adult. "When he said, 'Smile,' I smiled." Like McKissick, Helms worked hard as a boy, sweeping floors, jerking sodas, and covering high school sports for the local newspaper. He attended college briefly, first at a small Baptist school near Monroe, then at Wake Forest. But when he was offered a position on the sports desk of the *News & Observer* in Raleigh, he dropped out, believing he could learn more on the job than he could from any pointy-headed professor.

Due to a hearing problem, Helms was rejected for combat duty during World War II and served as a navy recruiter instead. It was the best thing that could have happened to him. Instead of storming the beaches at Normandy or patrolling the South Pacific, he honed his skills as a writer and public speaker, extolling the virtues of military service at high schools and civic clubs. He also received a crash course in radio broadcasting, traveling the state to interview sailors and their families. Helms was so enthralled with the new medium that when the war ended he left newspapers for good, taking a job as news director at WRAL, a Raleigh station owned by a conservative businessman named A. J. Fletcher. Fletcher treated Helms like a son, and his political beliefs—in free enterprise, small government, and an aggressive foreign policy—strongly influenced the young broadcaster. So when Fletcher backed a right-wing lawyer named Willis Smith in his bid to unseat Frank Porter Graham in the 1950 Senate race, Helms signed on, too, volunteering for the candidate in his spare time.

Smith's campaign against Graham was one of the nastiest in North Carolina history. Following the playbook of Senator Joseph McCarthy, who had recently launched his crusade of innuendo and insinuation, Smith's supporters implied that Graham, the former president of the University of North Carolina, was a communist sympathizer. They also suggested that a Graham victory would lead to racial intermixing. One of the campaign's most notorious ads featured a photograph of Graham's wife, smiling and dancing with a Black man. Another carried the warning "White People, Wake Up," followed by a series of rhetorical questions: "Do you want Negroes working beside you, your wife and daughters in your mills and factories? Negroes eating beside you in all public eating places? Negroes riding beside you, your wife and your daughters in buses, cabs, and trains? Negroes sleeping in the same hotels and rooming houses?" Graham favored all this and more, the ad asserted. "But if you don't, vote for and help elect Willis Smith for Senator. He will uphold the traditions of the South."

Helms later denied any involvement in the Smith campaign. But the evidence against him was compelling. The advertising manager of the N&O recalled Helms bringing him ad copy, including the picture of Graham's wife dancing. "I loaned him my scissors and he took and outlined around the figure of Mrs. Graham with a Negro," the manager said. Even close friends of Helms acknowledged his role in the campaign. One Smith aide who later served as a state judge reported that Helms was "up to his neck" in the campaign and that there was no "substantive publicity that he didn't see and advise on."

Whatever Helms's involvement, he was generously rewarded by Smith, who took him to Washington as his administrative assistant. Smith's office adjoined that of another freshman senator—Richard

Nixon—and Helms marveled at Nixon's unapologetic pursuit of suspected communists. He was equally enamored with Richard Russell, the longtime Georgia senator who used his mastery of parliamentary tactics to defend segregation; Helms even worked on Russell's ill-fated campaign for the Democratic presidential nomination in 1952. After Smith died suddenly in 1953, Helms returned to Raleigh, becoming executive director of the North Carolina Bankers Association. In addition to lobbying the legislature, Helms was responsible for publishing the association's monthly magazine, *Tarheel Banker*. Previously a dull little periodical consisting primarily of industry news and personnel ads, *Tarheel Banker* was transformed under Helms into a provocative platform for his conservative views. In editorials and personal columns, he attacked what he viewed as the creeping socialism of American politics and denounced the Supreme Court's decision in *Brown v. Board of Education*, declaring that the only reasonable response was to close the public schools. Helms also began a lifelong feud with his old employer the *News & Observer*, which he viewed as dangerously liberal. When "The Nuisance and Disturber," as he called it, criticized the state's banking industry, Helms responded in kind: "It is a shame that the Capital City of our State does not have a newspaper whose reliability and integrity are respected by our legislators."

Tarheel Banker established Helms's reputation in the business community, but it was not until he returned to WRAL as executive vice president, in 1960, that he became a statewide figure. By that time, the station had acquired a television license, and Helms delivered a nightly editorial on the events of the day. Wearing horn-rimmed glasses and speaking with a country twang that belied his political savvy, he pioneered the kind of paranoid, polarizing commentary that would later become standard cable-news fare. He attacked anything and anyone associated with the left—the United Nations, the War on Poverty, the civil rights movement—and saw communist plots everywhere. "The Congress of the United States yields to blackmail, and passes socialistic legislation," he warned. "The Supreme Court shackles the police, compounds confusion in the legislatures of the states, and turns loose murderers and rapists to repeat their evil deeds upon the innocent and law-abiding members of society. How much of this is the result of communist planning? Who can say? . . . The communists want law and order destroyed in America. They want riots in the streets and demonstrations on the campus. They want confusion in our courts, and frustration among our states. . . . The name of the game is now survival—and we will either win it or lose it."

Helms and his supporters denied that he was racist, but his editorials were filled with the kind of coded language easily decipherable by bigoted whites. In one diatribe on the civil rights protests he asked, "Is survival possible when civilization reverts to the law of the jungle?" In another he declared, "We must decide whether we will be ruled by sanity or ruined by savagery." Sometimes he spoke more bluntly, as when he referred to the "purely scientific statistical evidence of natural racial distinctions in group intellect" or when he described the Civil Rights Act of 1964 as "the single most dangerous piece of legislation ever introduced in the Congress." In case the message still wasn't clear, WRAL signed off each night by playing "Dixie."

Pundits at the *News & Observer* and elsewhere mocked Helms as a demagogic crank, but he found a constituency among the white farmers and factory workers who felt put upon by the bankers in Charlotte, the politicians in Raleigh, and the intellectuals at UNC (dubbed the "University of Negroes and Communists" by Helms supporters). To these "forgotten folks," Helms was a righteous warrior fighting to preserve old-fashioned Christian values. He might be harsh in his judgments, they acknowledged. But if he was mean, he was "mean for Jesus."

Like nearly all white southerners at the time, Helms was a lifelong Democrat. But when Kennedy and Johnson pivoted left on issues of race and economics, he abandoned party allegiance, proclaiming that the "fight is pitched not on party lines, but on sharply contrasting principles and ideals." He supported Goldwater in 1964 and Nixon in 1968. And when conservatives in North Carolina were looking for a Senate candidate in 1972, he agreed to run as a Republican.

His opponent was Nick Galifianakis, a congressman from Durham who styled himself as a new kind of Democrat who could appeal to independents, the young, and minorities. Helms presented himself as a traditionalist who would preserve the southern way of life. His campaign slogan—"Jesse: He's One of Us"—highlighted the contrast, asserting his own authenticity while slyly calling attention to his opponent's Greek heritage. The campaign was hard-fought and expensive, with Helms spending a record $654,000. Nixon's coattails were short that year, and Democrats scored impressive gains in the Senate. But Helms prevailed, defeating Galifianakis by a comfortable margin of eight points.

McKissick remained neutral during the race. When asked by reporters whether he supported Galifianakis or Helms, he was non-committal, though his silence was telling in light of his switch to the Republican Party. But when Helms won, McKissick was quick to

Jesse Helms at a victory celebration after winning his first Senate race.

offer an olive branch. On November 10, three days after the election, he sent the senator-elect a telegram congratulating him on his
"impressive victory" and requesting a meeting to brief him on Soul
City. "In spite of the fact no two men think alike," he wrote, "there
are many common things that we should work together on, and
many common things we should work together for."

It was a pragmatic gesture, emphasizing the interests the two men
had in common while downplaying their differences. And it showed
just how "sophisticated" McKissick had become. In *Three-Fifths of
a Man*, he had criticized the accommodationist philosophy of Booker
T. Washington, which was best represented by his famous speech at
the Atlanta Exposition in 1895: "In all things that are purely social
we can be as separate as the fingers, yet one as the hand in all things
essential to mutual progress." McKissick had argued that Washington was too willing to accept a secondary role for Blacks in exchange
for white cooperation. But his letter to Helms echoed Washington's
speech, stressing the mutual progress the two men could make despite
their fundamental differences.

In any event, Helms was not interested. He had long viewed
McKissick as a reckless agitator and CORE as a communist front.
And although Nixon had embraced both McKissick and Soul City,
Helms saw no reason to go along. "I'm not a Nixon Republican,"
he explained to reporters shortly after being elected. "I'm nobody's
Republican or anything else." So when he responded to McKissick's
telegram two weeks later, he left no doubt where he stood on Soul
City. "In fairness to you, I feel I should make clear that I do not
favor the expenditure of taxpayers' funds for the project known as
'Soul City,'" he wrote. "Moreover, at the appropriate time, I intend to
request a careful independent examination of expenditures to date,
in order that all citizens may have complete facts on which to base
their judgment of this type of federal spending of their tax money."

It was an ominous response, with its implication of financial misconduct and its threat of a federal investigation. But McKissick was
undeterred. Shortly after receiving Helms's letter, he followed up
with his own letter, in which he expressed his "mixed feelings" upon

reading the new senator's words. "I am delighted, of course, at any time to hear from a fellow republican whose opinion(s) on any issue may be in opposition to or in accordance with my own," he wrote. "But I am also keenly regretful that even without a visit to the Soul City Project and prior to the securing of facts and relevant data on the Project and before being sworn in as a senator for North Carolina, you have decided to launch an investigation of the Soul City Project." McKissick added that he had called Helms's office the day before to invite him to a briefing on Soul City and that he hoped the two men might meet soon to discuss the project. "In our telegram to you, we had requested a conference with you for this purpose," he concluded. "I again extend my request for a conference with you."

Over the next year, McKissick made numerous attempts to meet with Helms, sending him brochures and press releases, and phoning his office whenever he was in Washington. He never secured an appointment, but he did run into Helms once, in the rotunda of the Capitol. McKissick was there with T. T. Clayton, trying to drum up support in Congress while he negotiated the final terms of his deal with HUD. Walking through the cavernous hall, the two men spotted North Carolina senator Sam Ervin and approached him to make their pitch. Ervin had opposed Soul City from the beginning, urging George Romney to reject McKissick's application. But with no plans to run for reelection when his term ended in 1974, he seemed to have mellowed, and his response was encouraging. "Don't worry," he told McKissick, "I'm not going to hurt you."

McKissick and Clayton were feeling buoyed by that response when they saw Helms walking toward them. Before they could utter a word, the junior senator cut them off. "Floyd," he said in his tight-lipped drawl, "I want you to know I'm going to kill Soul City."

As Helms walked away, McKissick turned to Clayton and fumed, "Did you hear what that son of a bitch said?" To which Clayton could only respond, "I sure did."

13

Present at the Creation

In the fall of 1972, Bignall Jones was sitting in his dimly lit office at the *Warren Record* talking to a reporter for the *Charlotte Observer*. Squinting across the desk at his visitor, Jones reflected on the new city being built nine miles down the road on his family's old plantation. Once skeptical that Soul City would ever get off the drawing board, he was now bullish about its prospects, declaring confidently, "I think it's going to work." When asked what had changed his mind, his answer was simple: "About $14 million."

Jones's reaction was typical. In the months after HUD approved the loan guarantee, the public perception of Soul City shifted dramatically. Many who had once been opposed to the project were now grudgingly supportive, while those who had been skeptical were suddenly converts. Both the *New York Times* and the *Washington Post* published editorials praising McKissick's plan, while a headline in the *Greensboro Daily News* declared, "Soul City: No Scoffers Heard Now." Even some of McKissick's Black critics had come around. The NAACP's Roy Wilkins, who had once derided Black capitalism, lauded Soul City as Nixon's only true contribution to Black people. "I am constrained to believe that nobody in the administration intended it to be that way because I can't imagine this administration doing anything as positive as Soul City," he wrote to McKissick. "There must have been an injection of your own personality into the situation and Soul City comes out as a monument to your belief and perseverance."

Local officials also changed their tune. In October 1972, the Warren County Board of Commissioners met to consider a resolution endorsing the project. At first, those officials had been wary of McKissick's plan. Not sure what to make of Soul City—and doubtful it would ever get this far—they had listened to him and his staff without taking a firm position. But the loan guarantee cast Soul City in a new light. And when the board met that fall, it voted to approve Soul City and to offer McKissick whatever help he needed.

Around the same time, the towns of Henderson and Oxford agreed to cooperate with Soul City on construction of a regional water system. Funded by a mix of federal, state, and local grants, the system would provide ten million gallons of water a day, including at least two million gallons for Soul City. The project was so popular that even Representative L. H. Fountain, who had earlier written George Romney to express concerns about Soul City, agreed to throw his weight behind it. To McKissick, this was proof he could win support by showing how Soul City would benefit the surrounding area. "Sometimes in order to help yourself, you have got to help others," he explained.

But the strongest evidence of Soul City's changed image came from industry. In the months after the loan guarantee was approved, McKissick had promising conversations with a number of major corporations, including Borden Foods, Avon Products, and Burlington Industries. Whereas he once had to fight to get in the door of such companies, they were now coming to see him. And he soon landed his first catch. In November, a team from Morse Electro Products Corporation flew down to scout Soul City. Based in New York, Morse made sewing machines and stereo equipment and was planning a new factory on the East Coast. Executives spent several days touring the property, reviewing the development plan, and interviewing

McKissick and his staff. By the time they left, it was clear they were impressed. Still, even McKissick was surprised when, two days into the new year, he received a letter from company president Philip S. Morse, informing him that the board of directors was formally considering Soul City for its new plant. The facility would be large—about the size of six football fields—with a workforce of 350. And although many details remained to be worked out, such as training and housing for employees, Morse's letter indicated that the decision was all but made. He explained that the plant would open by the end of 1973 and that his public relations department would be in touch soon regarding an announcement. "We approach this move on the part of our Company with a great deal of enthusiasm and high expectation for the future," he wrote.

McKissick was elated. Although Morse was no General Motors, it was a well-regarded firm that was traded on the New York Stock Exchange and written about in the *Wall Street Journal*. A commitment from a company of its stature, so early in Soul City's development, would provide instant credibility, and McKissick did not attempt to hide his enthusiasm. "Your decision to choose Soul City as the site for corporate expansion will indeed be momentous," he responded to Morse. He invited the president to visit Soul City personally and emphasized that, as its first industrial tenant, Morse would have "the opportunity to work closely with us in the design of all aspects of this new town." He also explained that, as a result of recent developments, he had accelerated his construction timetable. "Within 60 to 90 days we will be in a position to begin installing the required roads and utilities and will simultaneously begin the construction of a number of community facilities," he assured Morse. "Well prior to the completion of your plant we can guarantee sufficient housing in a wide variety of types and price ranges."

As IT TURNED out, that estimate was wildly optimistic. Although HUD had approved the loan guarantee, there were still several conditions Soul City had to satisfy before the deal could be closed, including submission of an industrial marketing plan and the restructuring of its debt to ensure that all creditors were repaid. In addition, some officials in Washington continued to express doubts about the project's economic viability. One HUD administrator described it as a "poverty case" that was "marginal at best," an assessment seconded by the Office of Management and Budget. Edward Lamont, the newly appointed director of the New Communities Administration, disputed that characterization, arguing that Soul City was a worthwhile investment that would revive a struggling area. But even he was unwilling to waive the conditions that were holding Soul City up.

McKissick and his staff did their best to prod HUD along, pointing out that each month's delay was costing them twenty-five thousand dollars and increasing the government's financial risk. They also warned that failure to close the deal promptly could jeopardize the commitments they had already secured. "For three years, we have been told that jobs are the key to Soul City," Carey wrote to Lamont in mid-January. "We now have the promise of 350 jobs from Morse Electro Products and another 100 through our OEO-funded health program and clinic. Having achieved this we may now lose these commitments if we cannot assure Morse and OEO that this project is, in fact, going ahead now."

When their pleas to Lamont went unheeded, McKissick decided to go over his head. The problem was, many of his allies in the administration were now gone. Sam Jackson, who some thought might replace Romney as HUD secretary, had been passed over for the job. As a result, he had resigned and was now working at a New York law firm. Bob Brown had also departed, telling Nixon it was time he returned to High Point to resuscitate his public relations business. Brown had been replaced by Stanley Scott, a former journalist who was supportive of Soul City. But Scott lacked Brown's authority and knack for getting things done. So McKissick turned instead to Leonard Garment, a former law partner of Nixon who served as special assistant to the president. A Jewish New Yorker who had voted for Kennedy in 1960, Garment was an unlikely adviser to Nixon, whose anti-Semitism was already an open secret. But the two men had struck up a friendship at the firm where Nixon worked prior to the 1968 campaign, and Garment played a key role in his victory, helping to polish the candidate's rough edges and moderate his reactionary tendencies. Nixon rewarded him with a job in the White House overseeing civil rights and the arts. And though there were more influential advisers in the administration, Garment had carved out a niche as its "resident liberal conscience," which made him the logical person to petition on Soul City's behalf.

McKissick paid his first visit to Garment in early February, explaining his predicament. In addition to the costs of delay and the risk of losing industrial commitments, land prices in Warren County were on the rise. He had purchased several parcels adjacent to the Circle P Ranch, but still owned only 2,200 acres, far short of the 5,000 needed for Soul City. And now that HUD had approved the loan guarantee, property owners were taking advantage of the situation. Farmers who had once been willing to sell for three hundred dollars an acre were suddenly asking two to three times that amount. As one local businessman had explained, landowners intended to "make 'em pay through the nose."

Garment was sympathetic, and on February 5, he reached out to newly appointed HUD secretary James Lynn, requesting an update on Soul City. "I would appreciate it if you can confirm for me that the project is moving along," he wrote. "What are the next steps as you see them, and which are up to us and which to Mr. McKissick?" When Lynn failed to answer, Garment followed up with a more urgent note. "Reluctant as I am to bug my favorite Cabinet Member, I must ask you to get one of your staff to do something about my memorandum of last February 5 about Soul City," he wrote. "Floyd McKissick maintains he has done everything HUD has asked of him—and now his bankers are beginning to wonder if the government is ever going to deliver on a commitment made to him last June 29. He must be assured of FY 1973 money or a great deal goes down the tube."

Lynn finally responded on April 10, explaining that his staff was working with McKissick to satisfy the remaining conditions. But he noted that approval for certain matters had been held up by the

Office of Management and Budget, which was reviewing several HUD initiatives. So the next day Garment wrote to Paul O'Neill, associate director at OMB. "How soon will you be able to signal HUD that this project should move?" he asked. "My only interest is to give McKissick a definite answer. It looks up to now as though it has been 'yes' all along—but if FY 1973 funds run out because processing time is shrinking, then we have done him a real disservice."

In addition to pestering Lynn and O'Neill, Garment drafted a long memo to Melvin Laird, Nixon's chief domestic policy adviser. Garment conceded that Soul City posed greater risks than an ordinary satellite town that could rely on a nearby city for jobs. But unless the administration forged ahead with the project, how would it ever "find out whether a new town, beginning from scratch in an entirely rural area, can be made to succeed?" He also stressed the political implications of Soul City. McKissick was not only "one of the nation's best known black leaders" but "a political friend." "If we now say 'no' to McKissick we will stand accused not only of reneging on specific commitments to him, but of reneging on the President's commitment to the whole minority enterprise concept." Finally, Garment noted that McKissick had secured support from a wide range of public and private entities. "In my four years here, I have seen few projects in the minority development field which have put together as much as this one has. We should give Soul City the green light and inform the interested agencies that we have done so."

Garment's memo led the White House to reaffirm its commitment to Soul City. But HUD continued to drag its feet, and McKissick's fears were soon realized. He had stayed in close contact with officials at Morse, assuring them that everything was fine. At the suggestion of Chase Manhattan, he had even retained an outside public relations firm to promote the company's move. But as the months passed by without any action from HUD, Morse began to get cold feet. And when the company's board of directors met to formally consider the move, it decided to postpone the expansion until Soul City was closer to reality.

. . .

LOSING MORSE WAS a major blow, the kind of setback a fledgling community could ill afford. And McKissick was determined not to let it happen again. If HUD wouldn't close the deal voluntarily, he would force its hand. The Soul City Foundation had recently received a grant to help finance Soul Tech I, a manufacturing plant designed to attract small businesses willing to locate in Soul City but not in a position to build their own factories. There was no timetable for construction yet; the staff hadn't even chosen a site for the building. But McKissick needed a dramatic gesture to regain momentum. So he decided to use the grant as an excuse for a groundbreaking ceremony. Once shovels were in the earth, he reasoned, HUD would have no choice but to honor its commitment.

Over the next few months, the staff worked tirelessly on the groundbreaking, sending out invitations, booking music and entertainment, and lining up an impressive cast of speakers. For a while, McKissick held out hope that Nixon would attend. In July, he contacted Garment again, suggesting the president use the groundbreaking to tout his domestic policy achievements. Given Soul City's proximity to the Virginia border, he pointed out, Nixon could fly down by helicopter and return to Washington within two hours. Garment liked the idea and submitted a proposal to the president's travel office. "The Project has some risks but a decision has recently been made that the risks are worth taking," he wrote. "We are long overdue for projects with the President's participation; this is an excellent time and place and would be a dramatic change of pace."

The travel office felt otherwise, and its rationale was worrisome. "Although this project clearly has merit, it does contain considerable risk as referred to by Len [Garment] and there is a chance that because of budgetary problems, federal participation might have to be limited in the future," the office responded. "To commit the President at this time personally could lock us in on budgetary decisions which might have to be made in the future involving very substantial sums of money." In other words, although the White House had reaffirmed its support of Soul City, it was still hedging its bets. And if Nixon attended the groundbreaking, it would be that much harder to walk away later. So instead of a visit from the president, McKissick would have to settle for Stanley Scott.

As the groundbreaking neared, work crews prepared the site, mowing fields, erecting bleachers, and mounting signs on I-85 and Route 1 to mark the exit for Soul City. Jane Groom made her own preparations, pulling out her sewing machine and making herself a dress out of green polyester. Her children were getting too old for homemade clothes, so she took them to the mall in Raleigh and splurged on new outfits—pantsuits for the older girls, pinafore dresses for the younger ones, and a suit for Jim-Jim. Even her husband got in on the action, renting a pink tuxedo jacket and black pants. Then, the day before the groundbreaking, they gathered with the rest of the Soul City residents in an empty field. After a brief prayer, they each placed an object in a time capsule that was buried deep in the red soil. The children picked small toys and trinkets, but Groom chose something more meaningful: a copy of the "Dreams into Reality" poster from the offices of McKissick Enterprises in Harlem.

The groundbreaking took place on Friday, November 9. It began

A highway sign on Route 1 points the way to Soul City.

at nine thirty in the morning with a parade down Opportunity
Road, the only paved street on-site. A drill team from North Carolina A&T led the way, marching and twirling their weapons in a
blur of blue and gold. Following close behind was a long procession
of student bands—from Elizabeth City State University, John Graham High School, Norlina High, and the Central Orphanage in
Oxford. They marched to a dusty field, where an audience of nearly
a thousand stood before a large platform crowded with dignitar-
ies. There was Stanley Scott from the White House, Congressman
Parren Mitchell of Baltimore, the deputy regional administrator of
HUD, the general counsel of the Office of Economic Opportunity,
and the mayors of Warrenton, Oxford, and Henderson. Sam Jackson and Bob Brown were also there, as were McKissick's parents.
The speeches were triumphant and joyful. Lawrence Toal, a vice
president of Chase Manhattan, described the building of Soul City
as the work of "black, white, and green," while Tuskegee mayor
Johnny Ford teased McKissick for circumventing the traditional
path to municipal power. "If you can't be a mayor of your own
city," he told the crowd, "be like Floyd McKissick and build you
a city."

The high point of the celebration was the keynote address by the
state's new governor, James Holshouser. His predecessor, Bob Scott,
had always been ambivalent about Soul City, writing in his diary
that it had only a "50 percent chance" of success. Holshouser was
different. Just thirty-eight years old, with an earnest face and a boy-
ish haircut, he was the state's youngest governor since the Civil War.
He was also the first Republican elected to the office in the twentieth century. Both distinctions gave him an aura of destiny, and he
embraced Soul City with a fervor and idealism few other officials
displayed. Arriving at the Circle P Ranch by helicopter, he trekked
across the freshly mown fields with an entourage of aides and state
troopers, then took the stage to deliver a speech that sounded as
though it could have been written by John F. Kennedy.

"There are those who say there is nothing new under the sun, that
there are no new worlds left for man to conquer on this planet," he

began. "They should be here today." Soul City would be the first fully planned and freestanding new town in the United States, he noted. It would be a landmark in the history of urban planning, a milestone in the nation's quest for better communities. But Soul City was more than just a real estate development. It was "a tribute to man's ability to dream new dreams and to put those dreams to work." Like Columbus, like the Wright Brothers, like the astronauts who had recently landed on the moon, Floyd McKissick possessed a spirit that was rare and invaluable, Holshouser said. "It is a spirit of pioneerism, the same sort of spirit that has inspired man to open up frontiers, to go where man has never gone, to do what man has never done."

Of course, anyone could dream, Holshouser conceded. What set McKissick apart was the drive and determination with which he had pursued his dream. So deep was his passion, so complete his commitment, so contagious his enthusiasm that he had made converts of people who had once dismissed Soul City as a lark. Now, remarkably, McKissick had won the support of the federal government, the state of North Carolina, and all the local officials seated on the dais behind him. "Slowly but surely, those who doubted Soul City have become believers."

McKissick (right) and Governor Holshouser (center) on their way to the groundbreaking celebration.

As Holshouser spoke, his words were interrupted by the whistle of a train passing by on the edge of the property. Departing from his prepared remarks, he reflected on the role those trains had played in the demise of Warren County and the role they would soon play in its revival. "Those trains used to carry people from places like Warren County out to other cities where opportunity seemed greater," he reminded his audience. "Often they found disillusionment and unhappiness. I think Soul City will begin to reverse that trend and that soon trains will be carrying people back to North Carolina."

The governor ended with a flourish. "The eyes of this nation are on Soul City today because history is being made here," he declared. One day in the future, he would return to this site to observe the factories in operation, to see the thousands of people, Black and white, living and working together. In the meantime, "let Soul City serve as a lesson for all of us that man can go as far as his dreams take him, as long as he is willing to work to make those dreams come true."

When Holshouser sat down, the choir from Kittrell College stood up. There was only one song that could match the earnestness of the governor's speech: "The Impossible Dream" from the Broadway musical *Man of La Mancha*. The singers rendered it passionately, their voices building gradually from the first quiet notes to the stirring crescendo:

> *This is my quest, to follow that star*
> *No matter how hopeless, no matter how far . . .*

And the party was just beginning. That afternoon, Holshouser entertained three hundred guests at the governor's mansion in Raleigh, where he once again waxed eloquent on the day's events. "The groundbreaking for Soul City is probably a once in a lifetime thing for North Carolina," he told the Black syndicated columnist Billy Rowe. "It represents an idea and a dream that a lot of people have worked hard to make a reality, and it's obvious that it's becoming a reality." From there, the celebration moved to Durham, where three thousand supporters gathered at Cameron Indoor Stadium, home of the Duke basketball team, for the second annual Founders' Day Banquet. After more speeches, toasts, and salutes (Jack Parker, head of the UNC Department of Regional and City Planning, was awarded the Soul City Award "for service beyond the call of duty"), the crowd took to the dance floor as Jerry "Iceman" Butler and his Dynamic Show laid down one soulful hit after another. It wasn't until two o'clock in the morning that the last guests departed and made the long drive back to Soul City.

McKissick basked in it all. "On that day, I was happy because my mother and daddy were happy," he recalled later. "I had no doubt in my mind that what I was doing was correct. I was grateful to the president, I was grateful to the governor and I was grateful to all my friends and supporters who had come to see Soul City get started."

Jane Groom also reflected on the moment. As the shovels turned over the dirt, she thought of those in bondage who had once worked the same soil and wondered whether the "colored hour" had come at last. Then, being a realist, she began to think about what came next.

"There would be this weekend to celebrate, to laugh, to hold my shoulders a little bit higher," she wrote in her memoir. "But Monday was just a few days away. My children would return to school. Jimmy would go back to work; and we as a family would be strengthened to face our own personal challenges in the months and years to come."

14

Cream of the Crop

The groundbreaking was a public relations show, designed to pressure HUD into finalizing the deal. And it worked. Five weeks after the celebration, HUD notified McKissick that he had met all its conditions and could proceed to closing. Within a few months, he and his partners had formed the Soul City Company to oversee development of the project. And on March 6, 1974, the first $5 million in bonds were offered for sale on Wall Street. With repayment guaranteed by Uncle Sam, the bonds sold quickly, the bulk of them snapped up by Liberty National Life Insurance, a white-owned corporation based in Birmingham, Alabama. Speaking at a press conference in Washington, McKissick emphasized that the money from the bond sale was a loan, not a gift. "Nobody is giving Soul City any five million dollars," he told reporters. "All HUD is saying is that if we go broke, they'll guarantee our bond obligations to the investors, and I can guarantee to you that we're not going to go broke."

In addition to lighting a fire under HUD, the groundbreaking generated a fresh round of media coverage. In early January, the *New York Times* sent a reporter down to check on the progress of the new town. A few weeks later, a crew from NBC's *Today* show visited. Both reports were glowing, and McKissick was once again flooded with letters from Black transplants in the North. There was the middle-aged man from Pennsylvania who hoped to spend his golden years operating a ham radio station in Soul City, the young couple from Detroit who wanted to start a family in the new town, and the single mother from the Midwest who was planning to move south with her four-year-old son and two roommates. There was also a letter from Hattie Bell, a public school teacher in New York City whose twelve-year-old son, Laurence Fishburne, had recently made his television debut on the soap opera *One Life to Live*. Bell was intrigued by McKissick's vision for Soul City and requested information on schools, housing, jobs, and health care.

While some people wrote letters, many came to see Soul City for themselves. During one four-month period in 1974, Soul City welcomed nearly five hundred visitors, most from the South and Northeast, but some from as far away as Colorado and California. To handle the traffic, the staff converted an old shed into a welcome center stocked with brochures, maps, and souvenirs. When visitors arrived, they were greeted by a staff member, who showed them a clip from the *Today* story, then led them on a tour of local landmarks—the red barn, the manor house, Kerr Lake, Warrenton. Two years earlier, that would have been the extent of the tour. But the infusion of cash from the bond sale had given Soul City the bustling quality of a movie set. Work crews were busy clearing the land, grading roads, and installing underground electrical wires and streetlights. In August, HealthCo opened a temporary facility in a double-wide trailer. In September, construction began on the regional water system. And in October, ground was finally broken on Soul Tech I, the first of many planned buildings in the A. Philip Randolph Industrial Park.

But the clearest sign of progress was the influx of people. By the middle of 1974, more than seventy employees were on site, most living in a trailer park down the road from the manor house. Whereas McKissick had previously relied on a bare-bones staff of mostly inexperienced friends and family members, he now had a large team of

HAROLD VALENTINE/AP/SHUTTERSTOCK

McKissick with an architect's rendering of Soul Tech I.

highly qualified professionals. It was led by Charles Allen, who had been hired as general manager of the Soul City Company. A native of Virginia with a master's degree in urban planning from Columbia, Allen had moved to Soul City with his wife and three children after serving as director of development and planning in Gary, Indiana. He was joined by Donald Johnston, a former marketing executive at Montgomery Ward and General Electric, who was appointed director of industrial recruiting. With his silver hair, tailored suits, and contrasting collars, Johnston cut a distinguished figure amid the trailers and dusty roads of Soul City. The rest of the staff was equally impressive. George Williams, an air force veteran with a master's degree in planning from UNC, replaced Harvey Gantt as chief architect. Martin Doherty, a former Duke basketball player, served as head of finance. And Stan Roman, a graduate of Dartmouth College and Columbia Medical School, was hired as director of HealthCo. Like Johnston, Roman had an urbane manner that stood out in the rural atmosphere of Warren County. It didn't help that he drove a Mercedes convertible. But Roman was unapologetic about his lifestyle or his appreciation for fine things. "Many of the people here have reverted to the life style that is peculiar to this area," he told a reporter. "What is needed here is an infusion."

Although most of the staff was Black, about a quarter of the employees at Soul City were white, including Johnston, Doherty, and Dorothy Webb, who was hired as director of public affairs. A graduate of Vassar, Webb had received a master's degree from New York University, then served briefly as publisher of *CITY* magazine in Washington, DC. But what she really wanted was to join the civil rights movement, so when a friend got a job at Soul City she begged him to help her find work there. He obliged, recommending her to Carey, who offered her the public affairs job after a phone interview. Webb accepted without ever stepping foot in Warren County and moved down a few weeks later. Like many of the young people who left comfortable lives in the North to join McKissick's venture, she faced skepticism from relatives and friends back home. "My family thought I was crazy," she said. "But you have to remember any young woman who graduated from college at that time was considered crazy."

There were no trailers available when Webb arrived, so she spent the first three months at the Holiday Inn in Henderson. When a new shipment of mobile homes finally arrived, she moved into the trailer park with the rest of the staff. As a city dweller, Webb was often caught off guard by the hazards and peculiarities of country life. Once she was working in the red barn when a snake dropped from the ceiling and slithered down her blouse. Another time she was awakened in the morning by a violent rumbling that felt like an earthquake. When she ran outside, she realized it was just a herd of pigs rooting around under her trailer.

The staff could do nothing about pigs and snakes, but it did attempt to provide a sense of culture and community—transforming the second floor of the red barn into a library, establishing an Interfaith Committee to provide religious services, opening the manor house for dance classes taught by Charmaine McKissick, and publishing a monthly newspaper called the *Soul City Sounder*. Printed on a mimeograph machine, the paper carried updates on construction, profiles of staff and residents, personal interest stories, drawings, poetry, and humor.

The staff also put together a handbook to help newcomers adjust to life in the rural South. In addition to providing information about regional services, schools, and recreation, it translated local customs and idioms, explaining that "B-B-Q in North Carolina is chopped pork, not ribs," that "chili dogs are buns with chili," and that police cars used blue lights instead of red. And for those hailing from larger and less hospitable places, it noted that, in Warren County, "Everybody waves at everybody."

FOR THE MOST part, Black and white residents got along well. After all, everyone who lived in Soul City was committed to the goal of racial equality. But there were occasional tensions. Some Black staffers didn't like the fact that Carey's children called them by their first names, believing it showed a lack of respect. Others resented the father's influence with McKissick. Although Charles Allen had been hired as general manager, Carey was still McKissick's closest friend and most trusted adviser. The two men sometimes took off in the middle of the afternoon, grabbed a six-pack of beer, and drove over to Kerr Lake. There, sitting on a picnic table in what had once been the colored section of the beach, they hashed out whatever problems were bothering them that day. They also talked candidly about their families and their personal lives. "I probably knew Floyd better than I knew anyone else in the world," Carey recalled. When asked why they got along so well, he was uncertain at first. They believed in the same things, of course. And McKissick was outgoing and easy to talk to. But there was something more to it. "I think he trusted me," Carey finally offered. "He didn't have to keep any secrets. He didn't have to worry about anything. He could be himself."

It wasn't just the staff that resented Carey's relationship with the boss. McKissick's family was also troubled by his influence. Although they didn't doubt Carey's heart or his intentions, they worried that he lacked the pedigree and qualifications for the job. While the McKissicks were well educated, with multiple degrees from prestigious universities, Carey had never graduated from college. And in their book, that was a major liability. "My mother was not exactly a fan of Gordon Carey," Charmaine recalled. "She thought Floyd was just too nice to this white man that didn't have the same credentials as everyone else."

Not that Carey and McKissick got along perfectly. Like many Black leaders of the era, McKissick was sensitive about being controlled or upstaged by whites. Although he leaned heavily on Carey to run things at Soul City, he sometimes got angry when Carey departed from his instructions or contradicted him in front of others. He also bristled when white officials dealt with Carey instead of him. After all, he was the famous civil rights leader, not Carey. He was the one who had spoken at the March on Washington. He was the one who had appeared on *Meet the Press* and the cover of *Newsweek*. And he was the one who had secured the loan guarantee from HUD. So when members of the Warren County Commission or the Henderson city council addressed Carey as though he were in charge, it struck a nerve. A few times McKissick got so upset with Carey that he told him to pack his bags. But he always changed his mind the next morning, playing it off as though nothing had happened.

The two men were also different in important ways. Although McKissick could be warm and funny, telling tall tales and off-color jokes, his dominant trait was his intensity. He worked around the clock, had little patience for excuses and incompetence, and often lost his temper. Carey, though smart and committed, had a more whimsical approach to life. He referred to his list of things to do as his "FAT list," after the Frog and Toad children's story in which the hapless Toad makes a list of his planned activities only to promptly lose it. Jane Groom, who knew both men well, felt that their personalities complemented each other. "Gordon was the pillow," she reflected. "Floyd was the hammer." As for why Carey was more relaxed, Groom had an answer for that, too. "Floyd was the Black man," she explained. "When it comes down to it at the end of the day, he was the man who felt the color of his skin. Gordon didn't. That deep passion—the purple passion we felt within ourselves—Gordon's was bluish, and Floyd's was deep purple."

While the residents of Soul City got to know each other, they also made friends in the community. Some local Blacks still eyed them warily, turned off by their northern accents, modern hair styles, and foreign cars (in addition to Roman's Mercedes and Lew Myers's Volkswagen Beetle, Carey drove a VW Karmann Ghia). But others welcomed the newcomers, inviting them to dinner, dropping by with fresh-caught fish, and offering them rides into Warrenton. A few, such as Lucille Jordan, even joined the staff. Responding to an ad for a secretary, Jordan showed up at the Soul City office and handed her application to Jane Groom. When Groom asked how fast she could type, Jordan responded, "How fast do you want me to type?" Then, remembering her manners, she apologized and explained that she badly needed the job. Groom overlooked her cheekiness (and, as it turned out, her slow typing) and offered her the job anyway.

Local whites also grew accustomed to their new neighbors. A. D. Evans, who ran a service station on Route 1, initially feared Soul City would be "a cancerous sore" on Warren County. "But I don't feel like that now," he told a reporter. "They've got some of the cream of the crop in there." R. J. Collier, another store owner, took an equally sanguine view of the growing community. "The more people in the vicinity, the more business," he said.

Of course, this being Klan country, racial hostility was still prevalent. Driving down an unfamiliar road one day, Groom saw a sign propped against an old shed, with the words "Ku Klux Klan meeting here tonight" scrawled in red paint. She wasn't sure whether the sign was new or old, but she knew the Klan was active in the area. Not long before, she and a group of Soul City residents had attended a voter registration drive at the Snow Hill Baptist Church, just outside Warrenton. After a round of freedom songs and introductory remarks, they sat back to listen to the main speaker. Ten minutes into his address, he was handed a note by one of the organizers: threats had been made against the meeting. Groom felt someone grab her by the shoulder and say, "Jane, let's go." She didn't need to be told twice. She ran to the parking lot, got into her car, and followed the others in a caravan back to Soul City. As they sped down the long, dark road, she thought of the many civil rights activists who had risked their lives traveling on lonely southern highways like this one, "and for the first time I had the palpable feeling of what they must have felt during those years—fear."

And where there was fear, hatred was not far away. One day a reporter asked a white construction worker digging ditches at Soul City what he thought of the project. "Why I been for it all along," the man responded, with a knowing glance at his buddies. "I think all the niggers should move in there and we could put a fence around it and let 'em stay there."

As THE WIFE of the developer, Evelyn McKissick was the matriarch of Soul City. It was a role that suited her well. Like her husband, she had been born and raised in Asheville. But whereas his family clung tenuously to the middle class, her family sat comfortably atop it, having made a tidy sum on rental houses. The family's own house was perched on a hill above a tree-lined street. The McKissicks lived close by, but several rungs down the economic ladder. In fact, some members of Evelyn's family thought McKissick wasn't good enough for her. And although McKissick had plenty of drive himself, the status of his wife's family made him even more determined to succeed. Their marriage had thus been dominated by Floyd's career, with Evelyn playing the role of helpmate. When the family lived in Durham, she had provided beds for activists passing through town and bought extra gifts for visitors at Christmas. In Harlem, she had hosted parties for CORE staffers and employees of McKissick Enterprises. And in Soul City, she ran the preschool program in the manor house, entertained important visitors, and was elected head of the Sanitary District.

If Evelyn was the matriarch of Soul City, Jane Groom was everyone's little sister. Just twenty-eight when she moved to Soul City, Groom was energetic and cheerful, with bright eyes and a thousand-watt smile. She worked a full day, then came home to fix dinner and play with her children. She also enrolled in evening classes at North

FLOYD MCKISSICK PAPERS

Jane Groom (third from right) with other Soul City staffers.

Carolina State University in Raleigh, hoping to get the undergraduate degree she had always wanted.

But if life as a working woman and mother was fulfilling, Groom's marriage to Jimmy was not. The problems the young couple experienced in Mount Vernon continued in Soul City, due mainly to Jimmy's jealousy and violent outbursts. After one especially frightening incident, Groom's brother Buddy drove down from New York to check on her. Confirming that she was safe, he took her by the hand and led her on a long walk around the property. "Jane, I can walk with you and talk with you, but I can't solve your problems," he told her. "You and only you can change your life for the better."

Not long after that, Groom's older sister Jean moved to Soul City. Jean's marriage was also falling apart, so she packed up her three daughters and left Mount Vernon. An experienced bookkeeper, Jean got a job at the Soul City Company and moved into a trailer next to her sister. There, she fell in love with Augustine Howard, a graduate of North Carolina A&T who had come to Soul City to start a nonprofit. Named Andamule (after the promise of "forty acres and a mule"), the organization was designed to help Black people grow, harvest, and market sustainable crops. Howard was a master farmer and fisherman, but he also worked as a handyman and unofficial security guard, patrolling the grounds in his pickup truck to make sure everyone was safe.

As new residents arrived, some early settlers departed. McKissick's oldest daughter, Joycelyn, moved away in the fall of 1974. Her husband, Lew Myers, had entered the MBA program at UNC, so the couple rented an apartment in Durham. While Myers continued to work at Soul City, commuting two hours each day, Joycelyn gradually withdrew from her father's dream. In truth, she had never been all that happy at Soul City. With no job or purpose there, she felt superfluous and lost. Besides, she preferred poetry to planning, big cities to small. After a year in Durham she moved to Washington, DC, and she and Myers eventually divorced.

Gordon Carey's wife, Betye, also departed. Dissatisfied with the Warren County schools and tired of living in a trailer, she took their two young children and moved to Chapel Hill. Betye insisted she was leaving Soul City, not her husband, but the effect was the same, and they, too, soon divorced. For a while Carey lived in a trailer with Sam Tidmore, the retired football player, but it wasn't long before he met someone else, a young woman named Karen Wilken with two young children of her own. They were married in the summer of 1974 under a big cedar tree in front of the manor house. Karen carried a bouquet of wildflowers gathered from the fields, and Carey's father, who had flown in from California, performed the ceremony. It was the first wedding in Soul City, and it led to another first. The following January, the happy couple celebrated the arrival of their daughter Ramona—the first baby born in Soul City.

WHILE SOUL CITY made progress on the ground, it still faced headwinds from Washington. In finalizing its deal with McKissick, HUD had included a number of restrictions not imposed on other new towns. For starters, the $5 million from the initial bond sale could be spent only on infrastructure, such as clearing and grading the land, paving roads, and installing electricity. It could not be spent to build houses, stores, or factories—the very things that would be used to measure the city's progress. In addition, before McKissick could sell the remainder of the $14 million in bonds, he had to create at least three hundred manufacturing jobs. He also had to acquire additional land, complete the city's major roads, and raise sufficient funds for the construction of water, sewer, and storm drainage lines. These restrictions highlighted HUD's continuing anxiety about the prospects of a freestanding new town. Until McKissick showed an ability to attract industry, the agency was reluctant to allow him to begin building his city. But as McKissick continually pointed out, the lack of progress on the city was in turn frustrating his efforts to recruit industry.

Further complicating those efforts was the state of the economy. A year earlier, Arab oil producers had imposed an embargo on the United States in retaliation for its support of Israel during the Yom Kippur War. The embargo quadrupled the price of oil and, combined with a severe food shortage, plunged the economy into the worst downturn since the Great Depression. Unemployment soared, productivity stalled, and the stock market plummeted. And unlike most recessions, which feature low growth and low inflation, the slump of the early 1970s brought a rare mixture of low growth and *high* inflation—what economists called stagflation. It was the worst possible climate for a real estate development: rising prices increased the cost of borrowing while lack of growth made it nearly impossible to sell land.

The recession hit new towns hard. By late 1974, eight of the thirteen towns approved by HUD were in financial trouble, with several on the verge of bankruptcy. Park Forest South had already spent its $30 million loan guarantee and was seeking an additional $20 million. Gananda, a new town near Rochester, was also out of cash, having blown through $22 million in bonds. And Jonathan, Minnesota, was in such desperate shape that its founders were preparing to put it up for sale.

Soul City had only recently sold its first bonds, so it wasn't yet in financial distress. But the economic forecast portended rough seas ahead. McKissick's financial model assumed interest rates of 7.5 percent, yet inflation had already hit double digits. That not only increased his projected costs by millions but made it harder to attract industry, which would also have to borrow money at the higher rates. Add in the uncertainty over oil prices and the rising cost of construction materials, and most corporations simply weren't willing to invest in a speculative development like Soul City.

At the same time as the costs of new towns were rising, their benefits were being called into question. And, ironically, one of McKissick's key supporters was responsible. Two years earlier, the UNC Center for Urban and Regional Studies, an affiliate of Jack Parker's planning department, had received a federal grant to evaluate the status of new communities. Researchers at UNC collected data and interviewed thousands of residents from a cross section of new towns, some funded by federal loan guarantees, others financed by private investors. They then compared the results with data and interviews from conventional suburban developments, attempting to determine whether new towns performed better. The results were mixed. Although some cities, such as Columbia, Reston, and Irvine, showed higher levels of resident satisfaction than traditional suburbs, many new towns did not. Unfortunately, the media didn't grasp this subtlety. In a front-page article, the *Washington Post* simply reported the aggregate numbers, which showed little difference in resident satisfaction between new communities and ordinary suburbs. The newspaper also reported the study's recommendation that the federal government shift its focus from new towns to smaller developments in fast-growing urban areas. The problem was, this was a preliminary recommendation, which the *Post* had obtained from an anonymous HUD source. When the researchers issued their final report later in the year, they recommended that the federal government invest *more* money in new towns. But few people read the final report, and pressure began to build in Washington to end the new towns program.

Soul City wasn't mentioned in the *Post* story, but it had its own public relations problem. In late July, the *Wall Street Journal* ran an article with the headline "Search for 'Soul': Black Separatists

Get New Followers, Create New Towns." Printed on the front page, above the fold, the article was part of a series examining the status of Black people two decades after *Brown v. Board of Education*. The subject of the article was Black separatism, and it focused primarily on Oyo Tungi, an African-style village of fifty people in the South Carolina low country. Founded by a man named King Kabeyesi, Oyu Tungi was modeled after the Yoruba communities of Nigeria. Residents lived in plywood huts, raised goats and chickens, practiced voodoo and polygamy, and marked themselves and their children with three razor slices on each cheek. It couldn't have been further from the kind of modern industrial city McKissick was trying to build. Yet the article lumped Oyo Tungi and Soul City together, first in its subtitle ("Kabeyesi Rules Oyo Tungi, A Kingdom in Carolina; Big Plans for Soul City") and then in its body, casting them both as examples of Black separatism motivated by "dissatisfaction with white-dominated society." It even suggested a parallel between King Kabeyesi, a commercial artist from Detroit who had purchased Oyo Tungi for five hundred dollars, and McKissick, the former head of CORE who had received a $14 million loan guarantee from the federal government. And although the article acknowledged there was "a lot of difference" between Soul City and Oyo Tungi, the overall implication was that they were equally bizarre and pitiful attempts to achieve Black autonomy.

McKissick was furious. He had spent five years trying to build credibility among bankers and corporate executives who were already inclined to view his plans skeptically. And now, the paper of record for the business community was linking Soul City to a tribal community where women cooked food over open pits and the "king" had four wives. Shortly after the article appeared, he called Frederick Taylor, the *Journal's* managing editor, to demand a correction. When Taylor declined, McKissick followed up with a letter recounting the initial opposition he had faced from local residents and the many steps Soul City had taken—establishing a preschool program, running a summer feeding camp, spearheading the regional water system—to allay that opposition. "Our neighbors in Warren and Vance Counties are now realizing that Soul City is not a Black Power encampment, but a community of committed individuals who are here to upgrade conditions for the sake of everybody," he wrote. "What will happen to the carefully nurtured relationships we have built with area residents when they learn that the Wall Street Journal compares Soul City to a far-out tribal community where polygamy is practiced and the babies ritually mutilated?"

McKissick wasn't the only one who wrote to Taylor. Over the next several days, the editor received letters from Eva Clayton, Charles Allen, Gordon Carey, Philip Hammer, and S. J. Velaj, an executive at New York Life Insurance Company who served on the Soul City board of directors. All made the same point: Soul City was not the Black separatist venture described in the article. Meanwhile, Dorothy Webb, the director of public affairs, wrote directly to the author of the article, a young Black woman named Pamela Hollie. Hollie had stayed with Webb in her trailer for five days while working on the story. The two women had talked late into the night about life and love and had become close, Webb thought. So she didn't understand how Hollie could depict Soul City in such an unflattering light. In her letter, Webb noted that Soul City had for years been "the victim of the automatic and thoughtless assumption that a project sponsored by blacks is by definition a black separatist project." She was convinced that wasn't true before joining the staff, she told Hollie, and was even more convinced now. "Would I have uprooted myself from a rather comfortable urban situation to live in a dusty trailer in the middle of a field if I didn't feel that Soul City was a workable solution for white people as well as black?" she asked. "I cannot believe that you failed to notice that there are many whites, myself included, living and working in Soul City—you had ample time to observe us all and we certainly didn't attempt to direct your activities in any way. Therefore, I can't understand how you came to misinterpret so drastically what we're all about. What happened?"

When the *Journal* declined to publish a correction, McKissick threatened legal action. In a letter to Taylor, his attorney Steven Thal claimed that the article contained false and defamatory statements.

He demanded that the paper publish an article "focusing on the real purposes of this venture and presenting the true facts to the readers of your very influential newspaper." When Taylor rejected this demand, too, Thal wrote to Edward Cony, vice president of Dow Jones, the *Journal*'s parent company. His client's goal was to set the record straight, not collect damages, Thal explained. But McKissick had instructed him to file a lawsuit if the *Journal* did not meet his demands. He also suggested that officials at HUD were troubled by the article and were "asserting influence on various persons to do whatever is necessary to rectify this injury."

Despite the threats, the *Journal* did not give in to McKissick. Instead, it published two letters, one from McKissick and one from Eric Stevenson, a Yale-educated lawyer and banker who was deeply involved in issues of fair housing and urban development. Stevenson, who was white, described Soul City as "an important business and social venture" that should not have been equated with a "curiosity" like Oyo Tungi. McKissick was "not trying to show that blacks can and should 'go it alone,'" he explained, "but rather that they belong in the mainstream of large-scale real estate development, a field from which they have long been excluded because of prejudice."

Though unsatisfied with the *Journal*'s response, McKissick did not follow up on his threat to sue. As his lawyers explained, a lawsuit would be expensive and would only draw more attention to the original article. Besides, there was a good chance he would lose. So, reluctantly—and not for the last time—he swallowed his pride and dropped the idea of legal action.

McKissick was still dealing with the fallout from the *Journal* article when he received another blow. For two years, the Nixon administration had been under investigation for the burglary of the Democratic National Committee headquarters at the Watergate Complex. At first, it had seemed like a minor scandal, of interest only to a handful of reporters at the *Washington Post* and the *New York Times*. But as the investigation expanded, it ensnared numerous Nixon aides, including his campaign manager, John Mitchell, his former chief of staff, H. R. Haldeman, and the dirty trickster G. Gordon Liddy.

Throughout most of the investigation, McKissick had defended Nixon, confident the president would be proven innocent. Then, in July 1973, it was revealed that Nixon had taped his conversations in the Oval Office. When those tapes were released a year later, they showed what McKissick and many other Nixon supporters had been unwilling to accept: the president had ordered a cover-up of the burglary. Facing certain impeachment, Nixon resigned on August 8, 1974.

Nixon's departure was devastating for Soul City. Not only had McKissick grown fond of Nixon personally, but his influence in Washington depended heavily on the president's support. Now that support was gone, and McKissick's clout diminished accordingly. To make matters worse, the administration's chief proponent of new towns, Vice President Spiro Agnew, had stepped down amid his own scandal a year earlier. Thus, upon Nixon's resignation, the presidency passed to his new vice president, Gerald Ford, a man who had shown little interest in urban policy or new towns.

McKissick moved quickly to rectify that problem. Almost as soon as Ford was sworn in, McKissick sent him a long letter requesting a meeting to discuss the party's relationship with Black voters, which he believed had deteriorated since the 1972 election. Ford responded by convening a summit of Black leaders that fall and then inviting McKissick to attend his first budget message the following January. But the new president declined to throw his support behind the new towns program. And without that support, HUD caved to the political pressure that had been building over the past year and announced it would stop accepting applications for new towns. Officials attempted to give the decision a positive spin, insisting it would allow them to focus their time and resources on the projects already approved. To most observers, however, the decision was a clear sign that HUD was getting out of the new town business.

McKissick was deeply troubled by events in Washington. And just as he was discovering how much Nixon's resignation had hurt him, he found himself under attack from a completely different direction.

15

Blindsided

One day in the fall of 1974, a press release arrived in the third-floor newsroom of the *News & Observer* in Raleigh. Passing by the desk where such items were placed, an ambitious young reporter named Pat Stith picked up the release and read that the state department of transportation was preparing to build and pave several roads in Soul City, including a two-mile stretch known as Soul City Boulevard. The release was part of a marketing strategy to persuade skeptics that the new town was making progress. But for Stith, who was always on the lookout for stories of public corruption, the announcement raised a different question. Why, he wondered, was the state using taxpayer dollars to build roads for a private development? Determined to get to the bottom of the matter, he began calling government officials and pressing for an answer.

The result of his inquiries was a front-page article on November 3 under the headline "Private Roads Get Public Funds at Soul City." Its thrust was that McKissick had used his influence with the federal government to secure more than $500,000 for the construction of roads in Soul City. Most of the money had come from federal agencies such as HUD. But North Carolina had agreed to chip in

$166,000, even though doing so deviated from the state's transportation priorities. When Stith asked state officials why they had gone along with the plan, they said they felt pressured to do so. "It was the federal government people who came forth so eagerly to point out the HUD money and tell us . . . how to get it and everything else," one official told Stith. "We didn't dream that up."

The article made no claim of illegality. But it strongly suggested that improper influence had been brought to bear. Stith reminded readers that HUD had approved Soul City's loan guarantee only after McKissick announced his support for Nixon. He also pointed out that the new town had already failed to meet several benchmarks, implying that federal officials were propping up a failing venture. As of now, Stith reported, the only physical structures at Soul City were the old manor house, the red barn, and a smattering of trailers.

A few days later, the editorial page weighed in with a column titled "Soul City Gets Special Treatment." For the most part, the column repeated the claims in Stith's article: that the federal government had pressured the state to build the roads; that state officials had ignored their own priorities because of the lure of federal money; that McKissick had received the loan guarantee only after endorsing Nixon. But it also added a new claim, insinuating that the entire project was a scheme for McKissick to get rich. Citing McKissick's assertion that road construction would create jobs and expand the local tax base, the editors responded tartly, "What went unsaid is that the paving won't hurt Soul City's profit prospects in which he shares."

STITH'S ARTICLE WAS the second piece of negative publicity Soul City had received in the span of a few months, and McKissick was worried. One year after the groundbreaking, he was still struggling to recruit industry, complete the construction of Soul Tech I, and get HealthCo off the ground. The last thing he needed was a crusade against Soul City waged by the *News & Observer*.

Founded in 1880, the *N&O* was one of the oldest papers in the state and, at least politically, the most important. It grew out of the merger of two earlier papers—the *Raleigh News* and *Raleigh Observer*—and was purchased in 1895 by Josephus Daniels, an enterprising young publisher who had served in the administration of Grover Cleveland. Daniels was a progressive Democrat who supported trust busting, female suffrage, and labor rights. But like many progressives of the time, he was also a white supremacist who believed that the demand for racial equality was impeding progress in other areas. He endorsed the Democrats' campaign of violence and intimidation against Black Republicans in 1898 and was one of the leading advocates of a literacy requirement for voters. When some Democrats worried that the requirement would disenfranchise uneducated whites, Daniels assured skeptics that inclusion of a grandfather clause would protect whites while disenfranchising Blacks. He then published an editorial making clear that his goal was to keep Black people out of the voting booth. "Last November it was only by such a campaign as exhausted every resource of the white men in the state that White Supremacy was secured," the *N&O* wrote. "That victory was a signal one, but as long as there are one hundred thousand ignorant Negro voters entitled to kill the vote of an equal number of intelligent white men just so long are we in danger of being remanded to the terrible conditions from which we just escaped."

The literacy requirement passed, and Daniels emerged as a powerful figure in the Democratic Party, serving as secretary of the navy under Woodrow Wilson and ambassador to Mexico under Franklin Roosevelt. In later years, he expressed regret over the viciousness of his earlier racial attacks. But he continued to fight against civil rights legislation and warned against the social mixing of whites and Blacks.

As for the *News & Observer*, it was taken over by Daniels's oldest son, Jonathan, whose racial views gradually diverged from his father's. During World War II, Jonathan urged a patient approach to civil rights, arguing that "sometimes it is easier to ask people to give up their lives than to give up their prejudices." By the time the Supreme Court decided *Brown v. Board of Education* in 1954, however, he was convinced Jim Crow had to go. While other southern editors called for massive resistance to *Brown*, he condemned efforts to block integration. He was especially appalled by the closing of public schools as a way to avoid federal court orders. Those "who propose abandonment of the schools propose something beyond secession from the Union," he wrote. "They urge secession from civilization."

The news pages reflected Jonathan Daniels's evolving views. During the 1950s and '60s, the *N&O* covered the civil rights movement extensively, reporting on the sit-ins, profiling Black leaders, and documenting racial discrimination in the workplace. And when Jonathan Daniels stepped down as editor in 1968, he hired Claude Sitton, the legendary civil rights reporter for the *New York Times*, as the paper's vice president and editorial director. Sitton continued the paper's support for racial equality, embracing school integration and voting rights for Black people. But Sitton was no radical on the issue of race. He rejected the rhetoric of Black Power, which he once described as a "cult." And, of course, he expressed early opposition to Soul City, arguing that McKissick's proposal was characterized by "defeatism" and "withdrawal."

Because of that opposition, McKissick and Carey suspected Sitton was responsible for Stith's article and the paper's subsequent editorial. Carey reached out to Luther Hodges Jr., the son of a former governor and the chairman of North Carolina National Bank, which had loaned McKissick money in the early days of Soul City's development. What could they do to change Sitton's mind? Carey asked. "Nothing," Hodges replied. Sitton had taken a "negative position" on Soul City and "was so irascible and unreliable that there was no point in trying to talk with him."

Although Carey didn't dispute Hodges's characterization of Sitton, he had his own theory about the editor's motives. He had often crossed paths with Sitton while he was at CORE and Sitton was covering the race beat for the *Times*. For the most part, the two men had gotten along well. Sitton had written a glowing article about Carey's efforts to organize a training center for nonviolent resistance in Miami. And Carey, like most civil rights activists, revered Sitton for his sympathetic coverage of the movement. But there was one incident that lingered in Carey's memory. It occurred in the summer of 1961, after the first wave of Freedom Rides had been rocked by violence and some leaders, including King, were privately calling for a halt to the campaign. Sitton, relying on sources within King's circle, wrote a front-page article reporting that the rides would soon end. But King, despite his status, lacked the authority to make that decision. And the next day, the committee coordinating the rides met behind closed doors and voted to press on. Carey, who had conceived the campaign and was one of four permanent members on the committee, relayed the news to the media. As he stood before a crowd of reporters and announced that the Freedom Rides would continue, he looked defiantly at Sitton, as if to underscore the inaccuracy of his reporting. Sitton, who prided himself on getting the story right, was not amused. "You should have seen the look on his face," Carey recalled. The look was so angry that Carey suspected Sitton still held a grudge against him thirteen years later. And now, he believed, the editor was taking it out on Soul City.

Whether or not Sitton held a grudge against Carey, there was likely more to his opposition than personal rancor. Although Sitton had long been sympathetic to the struggle for racial equality, he had become disillusioned with the direction that struggle had taken. Like many white liberals, he was moved by King's gospel of love and non-violence, but turned off by the rhetoric of power and militancy that replaced it. He also never seemed to understand McKissick's vision for Soul City. Despite McKissick's insistence that the new town would be integrated—and despite the many whites involved in the project—Sitton clung to his initial belief that this was merely a ruse to secure federal funding. Decades later, when asked about Soul City for an oral history project, he referred to it as an "all-black city." Then, without prompting, he added, "I just didn't think that was right. I mean, I was an integrationist, and so we couldn't go along with that."

Nor was Sitton's opposition to Soul City softened by news of the loan guarantee. If anything, McKissick's alliance with Nixon only increased his hostility. A lifelong Democrat, Sitton had little regard for the Republican Party or its record on race. "Nixon was the guy who developed the Southern Strategy," he angrily reminded another interviewer. "For Floyd McKissick to get in bed with Richard Nixon—what has the Republican Party ever done for blacks, without going back to Abe Lincoln?" McKissick's view, of course, was that the Democratic Party had not done much for Blacks either and that it would continue to take them for granted unless they flexed their political muscle. But Sitton, for all his gifts, was not a subtle thinker, and McKissick's argument fell on deaf ears. As a profile in his own paper put it when he retired sixteen years later, "Claude Sitton often saw issues in absolute, black and white terms, recognizing few shades of gray. Even those with the utmost admiration for his integrity and iron determination recognized limits in his virtues."

Sitton was thus implacable in his opposition to Soul City. So when Stith proposed following up his article on road construction with a detailed investigation of Soul City's finances and progress, the editor readily agreed, giving his young reporter a long leash to dig up whatever dirt he could.

FOR STITH, WHO was thirty-two at the time, it was a golden opportunity. A dogged reporter with a nose for misconduct, he had begun his career at the *Charlotte News* covering local government before working his way up to investigative work. Stith scored several impressive scoops at the *News* and won a statewide press award for a series on pollution. But in the spring of 1971, he had a falling-out with the paper's editor. A local doctor had been mistakenly arrested for unpaid traffic tickets, and Stith wrote an article implying that the clerk of the court was to blame. Although his hunch turned out to be right, he had no evidence at the time, and the paper ran a retraction, stating that the story created "several false impressions." Stith was so incensed by the paper's disavowal of his work that he called the *News & Observer* the next day and applied for a job. Sitton, eager to poach a valued reporter from a rival paper, quickly snatched him up, and Stith moved his wife and three children to a suburb outside Raleigh.

Stith flourished at the *N&O*, developing a reputation as one of the best investigative reporters in the state. He outed the state highway commission for purchasing stone from a quarry owned by one of the commissioners. He forced the resignation of the chairman of the Alcoholic Control Board for making personal phone calls on the state's dime. And he exposed abuses in the judicial system that allowed state legislators to avoid punishment for traffic violations more frequently than members of the public. Stith was particularly drawn to stories of government waste. No instance of overspending or inefficiency was too small to escape his scrutiny. In one article headlined "Short Trees . . . Tall Price Tag," he questioned the state's decision to pay three hundred dollars apiece for thirteen Japanese maples planted in front of a government building. In another, he reported that the state's Department of Conservation and Development had paid five thousand dollars to cosponsor a professional golf tournament in Pinehurst, an expenditure he clearly thought unjustified.

Stith's fixation on waste and corruption stemmed, in part, from his childhood. The youngest of seven children, he grew up on a farm in Alabama, where he shared a double bed with two older brothers. When he was five, his mother died of colon cancer, and when he was nine, his father went broke and lost the farm. The family soon moved to Charlotte, where Stith's father launched a series of businesses—making hangers, demolishing houses, bottling syrup—that teetered on the edge of bankruptcy. Stith worked throughout high school and then enlisted in the navy, serving two years as a military journalist. With the help of a former employer, he got a scholarship to UNC and a job in the sports information office. But money was always tight. He married his high school sweetheart after his freshman year, and by the time he received his degree the couple had one child and twin boys on the way. Even after college, when he was working full-time at the *Charlotte News*, Stith moonlighted at his brother's box-making factory to help pay the bills.

It wasn't just Stith's upbringing that fed his obsession with

government malfeasance. It was
also the times. The late 1960s and
early '70s were a golden age for
investigative journalism. Reporters
such as Seymour Hersh and David
Halberstam had exposed the government's lies about Vietnam, while
Bob Woodward and Carl Bernstein
had helped bring down a president
with their reporting on Watergate.
Unlike many young reporters, however, Stith wasn't in awe of Woodward and Bernstein. He thought he
was just as good, if not better, than
they were. He also thought he was
destined to win a Pulitzer Prize. So

Pat Stith at the *News & Observer*
around 1974.

when he stumbled upon Soul City—a story that brought Nixon and
Watergate into his own backyard—he jumped at the chance to show
what he could do.

Over the next three months, Stith turned over every stone in his
investigation of Soul City, conducting more than a hundred interviews, filing multiple Freedom of Information Act requests, and
poring over thousands of pages of financial reports and government
documents. He made three trips to Soul City, walking the grounds in
his cowboy boots and peppering McKissick and his staff with questions. The staff answered his inquiries, confident they had nothing
to hide. A few were nervous, sensing Stith had already made up his
mind. "He wasn't listening," Eva Clayton said later. "He just wanted
to be able to say he had talked to me." But although Clayton feared
Stith's report would be damaging, neither she nor anyone else at Soul
City foresaw just how explosive it would be.

THE BOMB WENT off on March 2, 1975, with a front-page article
titled "Soul City: A Tangled Web." Accompanied by an editor's

note that this was the first in a series, the article read like a bill of indictment, laying out a long list of ostensibly damning allegations. It charged that Soul City was beset by conflicts of interest because McKissick controlled both the for-profit company that owned the land and the nonprofit corporations that had received federal grants to support the project. It alleged that nepotism and cronyism were rife at Soul City, pointing out that McKissick had hired friends and family members to work on his staff. And it asserted baldly that the loan guarantee was a reward for McKissick's endorsement of Nixon, quoting a Senate Watergate report that highlighted Bob Brown's role in the Responsiveness Program.

But the most pervasive and sweeping allegation was that, after six years and the injection of millions of dollars of federal money, Soul City had nothing to show for itself. Stith introduced this charge with a question about McKissick and his motives: "Has he been constructing a house of cards? Or has he been carefully preparing a solid foundation for a truly monumental venture in black capitalism?" It quickly became clear that the question was rhetorical. After claiming that McKissick had already spent more than $5 million in federal money, Stith described the current state of affairs at the Circle P Ranch: "There is no industry there, no shops, no houses—no Soul City."

It was a theme repeated throughout the series. Stith recounted over and over how much money the federal government had poured into Soul City: $5 million already spent, more than $19 million approved, and McKissick's staff "busily preparing applications for $5 million more." And yet, he reminded his readers, "there still are no homes, no shops, no industries in Soul City." A sidebar by another reporter was even more dismissive. The "main drag" of Soul City, the reporter noted, was "an undulating, rural unpaved road." Its only neighborhood was a collection of trailers "with scarcely any shrubbery about." And its skyline? "Only white mobile homes standing like sheep."

Taken out of context, there was some truth to this criticism. If one toured the grounds of Soul City, very little tangible progress was apparent. But considered in context, the criticism was patently unfair. For one thing, the time frame of six years, repeated again and again, was misleading. It was true that McKissick had announced his plans for Soul City in January 1969. But HUD did not approve his application until the summer of 1972, most of the grants were not awarded until 1973, and the first $5 million in bonds were not sold until March 1974, just one year before the N&O launched its series. Moreover, McKissick's contract with HUD barred him from using the proceeds of the bond sale to build residential, commercial, or industrial buildings—the very things the N&O faulted Soul City for lacking.

And yet even with those constraints, quite a lot *had* been accomplished. McKissick had purchased the land, assembled a staff, and completed the extensive planning necessary to build a city. He had participated in countless negotiations with local, state, and federal officials, met with dozens of executives, and established all the nonprofit organizations needed to support the project: the Soul City Foundation, the Warren Regional Planning Corporation, the Soul City Utilities Company, the sanitary district, HealthCo. And although he had not yet built any houses or stores, much of the infrastructure for the city was already in place. Construction crews had cleared the land, paved several roads, begun work on the regional water system, and nearly completed Soul Tech I. As a British planner consulted by HUD several months later observed, Soul City had accomplished as much in its short existence as any of the new towns built in England had in a comparable time frame. "I do not think there is a single British new town that has ever had much more than a sewage system, water supply, a few roads, one factory ready for occupation and a few other items of that sort after 2 years and that is exactly the progress so far made at Soul City," the planner wrote.

If Stith's claim about the lack of progress was unfair, many of his other claims evinced a lack of understanding of the New Communities Act. For instance, Stith implied that it was inappropriate for the Warren Regional Planning Corporation, a nonprofit entity, to receive a planning grant to help McKissick's for-profit company secure the loan guarantee. But Congress had envisioned just this type of arrangement, and HUD had specifically instructed McKissick to apply for the grant. Stith also noted that while the federal government was helping to fund the project, McKissick would be the one to reap the profits. Yet that, too, was part of the law's design. The task force that proposed the New Communities Act worried that private developers would not assume the financial risks of building new towns unless the government offered financial incentives. Yes, there was a chance McKissick would get rich off Soul City (although he had never suggested that was his goal). But that's what the government was banking on—that the prospect of making money would encourage developers to invest in new cities rather than the sprawling housing tracts that had done little to solve the urban crisis and much to exacerbate it.

Stith also suggested it was improper for McKissick to be involved in the various nonprofit organizations created to support Soul City. He noted that there was substantial overlap between the officers of these organizations and the officers of the for-profit firms that owned Soul City, using the term "interlocking directorates" so frequently it took on the quality of a smear. To illustrate this charge, the paper printed a diagram showing the connections between nine Soul City officials and the various organizations involved in the project. At first glance, the diagram resembled the "Tangled Web" of the main article's title, with a dark blur of lines crisscrossing the page. But a closer examination revealed that much of what the diagram showed was unremarkable. Three of the officials—Jane Groom, her husband, Jimmy, and Evelyn McKissick—were linked to just one organization each. Two others—Lew Myers and Charles Allen—were linked to just two organizations: Myers to the Soul City Foundation, where he worked, and the Soul City Sanitary District, to which he had been elected as a board member; Allen to the Soul City Company, where he was general manager, and the Warren Regional Planning Corporation, on whose board he sat. Why these connections were problematic the article did not say. It was true that McKissick was linked to nearly every organization participating in Soul City. But since he was the developer overseeing the entire project, it would have seemed strange had he not been.

There were other misleading claims, as well. Stith reported that McKissick paid $390,000 for the Circle P Ranch in 1969, then sold his interest to the Soul City Company in 1974 for $650,000, implying he had made a huge profit on the deal. In fact, McKissick sold the land for $600,000, and the transaction included an additional 250 acres he had paid $75,000 to acquire. Factoring in interest payments and taxes, McKissick's total cost was $598,000, making his profit just $2,000. And at the time of the sale, HUD had appraised the land at $727,300, which meant McKissick actually took a bath on the deal.

Stith also reported that the Warren Regional Planning Corporation had received a grant to plan an industrial park and persuade companies to move there, but had failed to recruit any industry. In fact, the grant said nothing about recruiting industry; it was geared strictly toward planning.

Finally, Stith reported that the Soul City Foundation had received a $90,000 grant to identify and apply for more grants, which it then used to secure an additional $723,000 in government funding. The implication was that the government had given money to the foundation for the sole purpose of obtaining more money—a sort of endless and self-perpetuating cash machine. In fact, the initial grant was designed to help the foundation plan for the needs of the town's low-income residents. And although one of the grant's objectives was to identify the financial resources available to execute this plan, there were three other objectives that Stith did not mention.

Some of Stith's criticisms were more on target. He reported that several of the agencies providing money to Soul City had not followed their own procedures and had failed to monitor how the money was spent. He revealed that the Warren Regional Planning Corporation had improperly provided life insurance and a loan to McKissick Enterprises. And he disclosed that HealthCo had opened eleven months behind schedule, had treated just 155 patients in its first month, and had been criticized by government auditors for purchasing supplies and services without competitive bids. These allegations were all correct. In fact, the problems at HealthCo were serious enough that a federal agency had labeled its performance poor. Yet even here, Stith omitted important details. One of the reasons HealthCo opened behind schedule was that government officials had refused to approve the purchase of a trailer until after the bond sale was complete, and due to delays at HUD that didn't happen until March 1974. In addition, although HealthCo treated only a small number of patients its first month, that number had doubled by the time Stith's articles came out (and would soon double again).

It went on like this, in article after article over the course of several weeks: allegations that were misleading, lacking context, or omitting important details. There were occasional quotes from McKissick or Carey contesting the charges. But to readers who knew little about Soul City or the New Communities Act or the urban crisis to which both were a response, the series left a clear and unmistakable impression: Soul City was a fraud and a failure, another example of the federal government flushing taxpayer money down the drain.

16

The Battle of Soul City

McKissick and his staff were devastated. They had no illusions that Stith was their friend or ally. Nor did they believe they were above criticism. They knew things had not gone smoothly, and they were as frustrated as anyone by their failure to attract industry and their inability to build houses, stores, parks, and all the other aspects of Soul City they had spent years planning. But they didn't understand how Stith could portray Soul City in such an unremittingly negative light. How was it possible, they wondered, to take all their hard work—their years of toil and sacrifice, of living in trailers, of battling opposition and misperceptions, of trying to bring prosperity to an impoverished area—and make it sound so self-serving, corrupt, and criminal? And so they reached what they thought was the only logical conclusion: the articles in the *News & Observer* were motivated by racism.

They weren't the only ones. The North Carolina Association of Black Lawyers accused the newspaper of "attempted character assassination" that was "racially inspired." "We believe this harassment of Soul City is part of a continuous effort to discredit and prevent black people from entering the economic mainstream of this state and the nation," the association declared. The *Carolinian*, a Black newspaper in Raleigh, argued that Stith and his editors had "ganged up to make McKissick look like a common criminal." "If those whites who have castigated him so hard and mercilessly would turn to being a black man (or woman) a while, they would realize that it takes a long, long time to get anything going in favor of Negro people, even with government financing." And a Black accountant from New York City wrote McKissick to say he was confident the allegations were motivated by fear and bigotry. "I am quite certain a black in control and command of such a large endeavor (millions of dollars) is too *much power*."

Sitton vigorously denied such claims, pointing out that the *N&O* had long ago embraced the cause of racial equality. His own record as a chronicler of the civil rights movement bolstered that defense. Stith's record was more complicated. In later years, he spoke candidly about having once held views he was now ashamed of. As a boy growing up in Alabama, he recalled, he had largely accepted Jim Crow, viewing segregation simply as "the way it was." And when he entered the navy at the age of eighteen, he told his superiors he didn't believe in "social mixing" of the races. Stith had also been turned off by the climate of protest and rebellion of the 1960s. While serving as managing editor of the student newspaper at UNC, he had fired left-wing reporters and imposed a ban on stories about "hippies." The one time he lifted the ban, running a picture of antiwar demonstrators on the front page, he wrote a caption that conveyed his true feelings: "Peaceniks gathered at the foot of the war memorial here yesterday to sing about freedom and how they didn't want to fight for it in Viet Nam."

When I interviewed Stith in 2019, he maintained that his views on race had evolved by the time he wrote about Soul City. He recounted a sociology class at UNC in which the students played a game of Telephone, relaying a story about a crime committed by a white man until, by the end of the exercise, the man's race had changed to Black. That class opened his eyes, Stith said, and he began to understand the evil of racism. As proof of his evolution, he pointed to an article he wrote for the *Charlotte News* in 1967 highlighting the lack of a modern sewer system in a largely Black community outside the city. The article put pressure on nearby white communities to come to the town's aid. Stith also told me that when he and his family moved to the suburbs of Raleigh in 1971, he was one of the few people in his neighborhood who voted in favor of a plan to integrate the local schools. Finally, he asked why, if he was motivated by racism, he so rarely turned his investigative eye on racial minorities. "I just didn't write about Black people because I wrote ugly stories about people in power, and they weren't in power," he told me. "Mostly what I wrote about were Democrats, white Democrats. Go back and look. Did I dislike Democrats? No, I'm a registered Democrat."

Stith did admit to one bias. "I've always favored the have-nots over the haves," he said. "If I'm guilty of something, that's where it is." So why wasn't he sympathetic to Soul City, which was designed to bring jobs and social services to one of the poorest regions of the state? "I thought it was impossible," he responded. And he was offended by the way McKissick had secured the loan guarantee from HUD. "Soul City was not funded on its merits," he said. "It was funded because we had a president who was willing to use the federal bureaucracy and to corrupt it for his own personal gain and we had a prominent Black leader who was willing to play that game to get what he wanted. I guess he figured the ends justified the means." When I suggested that the evidence did not establish conclusively that there had been a quid pro quo between McKissick and Nixon, Stith scoffed. "I believe right down to my toenails if he had not switched parties there wouldn't have been a Soul City."

Even if Sitton and Stith were not motivated by racism, the paper's attack on Soul City did play on racial stereotypes. A political cartoon on the editorial page depicted McKissick with exaggeratedly large lips. And the entire thrust of the series evoked classic tropes about Black people and money: that they can't be trusted, that they're incompetent, that they live beyond their means. Many of the *N&O*'s readers seemed to understand this. Stith received dozens of racist letters from readers who loved his stories about Soul City. The letters surprised him, because of both their ugliness and their volume, but they did not make him question the articles. "That did not please me," he said of his readers' reactions. "But I can't control them."

FOLLOWING THE ADVICE of HUD, McKissick said little in response to the *N&O* series. When Stith sought comment after the first wave of articles appeared, McKissick declined to offer any, referring all questions to his lawyer. But as the days went by and the paper continued to press its case against Soul City, he realized he had no choice but to publicly defend himself. On March 20, eighteen days after the series began, he called a press conference at the Howard Johnson Motor Lodge in Henderson. The staff prepared diligently for the event, putting together a thick press packet that rebutted many of the *N&O*'s claims and inviting a long list of local officials to attend. When McKissick took the microphone in front of a room packed with reporters, he was flanked by nearly a dozen allies, including the mayors of Oxford and Henderson, the executive director of the League of New Community Developers, and the director of the UNC Center for Urban and Regional Studies.

He began by going on the offensive. If anyone's integrity should be questioned, he said, it was that of Stith and his editors. He had spoken to several journalists, all of whom agreed the paper's series was unfair. One called it a "vendetta," another said it was "overkill." McKissick preferred the term "hatchet job." The *N&O*, he argued, had distorted the record, omitting certain facts and casting others in a misleading light. "We all know how deceptive a silhouette can be," he told the reporters. "You see something by its outline and you think you know what it is, but then when light is shed on the whole object, you may discover that it wasn't anything like what you thought of its silhouette." That's what the *N&O* had done. "It painted an outline but at the same time withheld the light which would have shown the whole situation in its true form and full face. All we intend to do at this press conference now is to shed that light which will reveal our whole condition."

To do that, McKissick recounted the obstacles he had faced in launching Soul City, the local, state, and national officials who had resisted his idea and had to be persuaded of its merits. That task was complicated by the fact that Soul City was the only new town in the HUD program located in a rural area, as well as by the fact that it was led by a Black man. Yet he had overcome that opposition by showing how Soul City could jump-start economic growth in the region. There was now overwhelming support for his project, as evidenced by the fact that officials in Vance and Granville counties had agreed to cooperate on a $12 million regional water system. The water system was a major accomplishment that alone justified the government's investment in Soul City, McKissick asserted. And it was only one part of the regional infrastructure Soul City would help create over the next thirty years.

McKissick acknowledged that the process of launching Soul City had taken longer than hoped. Five years had elapsed from the time he applied for HUD approval until the sale of the first bonds. But most new towns had taken at least three years, he pointed out. And in any event, what mattered was not the delay but the progress he had made in the past year, since the bonds were sold. With Soul Tech I nearing completion, construction of the water system underway, and key roads being paved, Soul City was as far along as anyone could reasonably expect.

As to the claim that Soul City had benefited from his switch to the Republican Party, McKissick did not expressly deny it. Perhaps his switch had hastened approval of the loan guarantee, he stated. But Soul City would not have been approved if it lacked merit. And if he had received favorable treatment, it wasn't reflected in the dollar amounts approved by HUD. To illustrate this point, he introduced the director of the League of New Community Developers, who displayed a chart comparing the grants and loans Soul City had received with those awarded to the twelve other new communities. Although Soul City had received more grants than some new towns, it had received less than others. And its loan guarantee of $14 million was near the bottom of the range, with all but three towns receiving more money, and one—The Woodlands, Texas—receiving $50 million, almost four times as much as Soul City's allocation.

McKissick also brushed aside the charges of nepotism. It was true that several family members were involved in the project. But there was nothing wrong with "competent nepotism," he argued, and everyone working at Soul City was competent. His son-in-law, Lew Myers, had an MBA from UNC and had previously worked at Harvard. His son, Floyd Jr., who worked part-time on the project, was studying for his master's degree in planning at UNC. And his wife, Evelyn, had run day care centers and preschools in Durham for years. Besides, Evelyn didn't receive a salary for her work as head of the sanitary district. McKissick also noted that there was nothing unusual about family members working together in a business. After all, the News & Observer had been a family business for eighty years.

McKissick ended by reminding his audience what Soul City was all about. "Years ago, I resolved to come back to my native state of North Carolina," he explained. "My roots are here and I wanted to do something which could stand as a symbol of black and other minority aspirations and bring new life to a region of this state which has been excluded from full participation in our wonderfully abundant society. Soul City is the symbol and reality of this desire. With the strong and uncompromising leadership of blacks and whites alike we are succeeding."

In addition to responding publicly to the N&O's attacks, McKissick and Carey appealed privately to Sitton. At a meeting in his office in downtown Raleigh, they complained that the paper had focused exclusively on the problems and delays at Soul City, ignoring the progress they had made and the resources they had brought to a desperately poor region of the state. Sitton listened to their appeal and seemed sympathetic. According to Carey, he promised that the paper would publish additional articles detailing the potential of Soul City. Those articles never appeared.

Instead, the paper published an editorial calling for a federal audit of Soul City. Reviewing Stith's allegations, the editorial said they raised serious doubts about the competence and integrity of McKissick and his staff. The only way to dispel those doubts was to subject Soul City to a thorough investigation. "An independent audit that can trace all the sources and expenditures of federally related funds in this project is essential before there can be any confidence in the development," it asserted. "Without this confidence, McKissick will never attract private industry to Soul City. And without job-creating industry, there will never be a community there."

THE NEWS & Observer could call for a federal audit, but only officials in Washington had the power to make it happen. Unfortunately for McKissick, there happened to be one person in Congress who had long wanted to launch just such an inquiry. Jesse Helms had been relatively quiet since threatening McKissick with a federal probe in the fall of 1972, perhaps because he wasn't yet ready to buck the Republican establishment that had endorsed Soul City. But with Nixon no longer in office and his old nemesis the N&O alleging corruption and mismanagement, Helms saw a chance to make good on his threat. Joined by Representative L. H. Fountain, the senator requested that the General Accounting Office, the investigative arm of Congress, conduct a full audit of Soul City. Not long after that, the North Carolina legislature commissioned its own audit, seeking to find out whether McKissick had mismanaged state funds.

In addition to investigations, the paper's series generated a wave of negative publicity, as the allegations were picked up by the national media, which repeated them without independent corroboration. Soon, Soul City was a laughingstock, fodder for political cartoons and sleazy tabloids. "A $19 million rip-off . . . and YOU pay," read the headline of an article in the National Enquirer. The series also stemmed the flow of money to Soul City. In early April, the Commerce Department announced that it would not provide additional funds to Soul City until the audit was complete. The North Carolina highway department also declined to endorse a mass transit study for Soul City, citing "questions being raised" about the project.

HUD stayed quiet in the immediate aftermath of the *N&O* series. But on May 6, it issued a vigorous response in the form of a letter to the editor. Written by Melvin Margolies, assistant administrator in the office of finance, the letter accused Stith of "preconceived bias" and claimed his articles were "often inaccurate, misleading or unsupported." From the moment Stith walked into HUD's offices, Margolies wrote, it was clear he had made up his mind about Soul City. His questions were abrasive, his conclusions erroneous, his implications unfair. And he showed little interest in the numerous ways Soul City had benefited the surrounding area. In addition to the regional water system, Margolies noted, Soul City had secured $2 million in education funding for Warren and Vance counties and $1.8 million for health care services. It was true the economic downturn had slowed Soul City's progress and that mistakes had been made. But it was inexplicable that the *N&O* would devote more than a dozen articles to the project "and not find a single positive point or offer a single rationale for its problems." "It would appear to me," he concluded, "that fairness would have required a more balanced attitude, investigation, and report."

The *N&O* published the full text of Margolies's letter, along with a rebuttal that was twice as long. If McKissick hoped that would mollify his critics, he was mistaken. Helms was incensed that HUD was continuing to support Soul City despite the GAO audit. On July 26, he introduced a bill barring HUD, or any other agency, from providing money to Soul City until the investigation was complete. HUD, seeking to forestall legislation that would formally tie its hands, assured Helms it would not approve additional funds for Soul City while the audit was pending. Satisfied with that response, Helms withdrew the bill. But he made clear his expectation that other agencies would follow suit. He also issued a blistering indictment of Soul City on the floor of the Senate, describing it as the offspring of "an intellectually and morally bankrupt doctrine, a doctrine that suggests that enough money thrown at any problem will make it go away, or thrown at any proposal will make it happen." "It just does not work that way," he declared. "There really is no such thing as a free lunch.

Somebody must pay the price. The taxpayers of my state are quite certain that they know who that 'somebody' is."

It was typical Helms, using the language of fiscal conservatism to justify his opposition to federal efforts to help minorities. But his argument did not go unchallenged. When Helms sat down, Senator Edward Brooke rose to speak. The only Black member of the Senate—and the first since Reconstruction—Brooke was part of the vanishing liberal wing of the Republican Party. He had coauthored the Fair Housing Act of 1968, opposed the nomination of Judges Haynsworth and Carswell to the Supreme Court, and been the first Republican to call for Nixon's resignation. Just three days earlier, he had taken on the Democratic Mississippi senator John Stennis, helping to defeat Stennis's attempt to weaken a key provision of the Voting Rights Act. Now, he faced off against another conservative southerner, albeit one from his own party. Responding to Helms's tirade, Brooke explained that he did not object to the GAO probe and would accept whatever conclusion the auditors reached. But until the investigation was complete, he argued, federal agencies should not withhold funding based on unsubstantiated articles in the press. "We do not hold up grants to any other agency, any other department of this government, any other town, or any other city merely on the basis of allegations made by a newspaper reporter," Brooke asserted. "When are we going to stop trying people and convicting them without evidence? This is a nation of laws, not of men. We have said it time and time again."

It was a valiant, if unsuccessful, defense, and when it was over Brooke wrote to share the exchange with McKissick. "As you know, Jesse Helms and I fought the Battle of Soul City on the Senate floor last Saturday," he wrote. "I thought you might be interested in reading the debate, so I'm enclosing a copy of the Congressional Record. You have my every confidence in your important work."

WHILE THE BATTLE of Soul City was being waged on the Senate floor, the GAO auditors diligently went about their work. State investigators had already completed their probe, finding nothing improper about Soul City's use of state funds. But the GAO's mandate was broader. Under a deal with Helms, it had agreed to evaluate the history and status of Soul City, as well as all federal, state, and local financing for the project. The investigation was costly and time-consuming; there were sometimes as many as twenty auditors at Soul City. They arrived promptly at nine each morning, pored over documents, interviewed staff members, and left precisely at five each afternoon. Everything about the operation was punctilious and precise. The auditors wouldn't so much as accept a cup of coffee for fear of being seen as friendly or compromised.

At first, the presence of so many strangers unnerved the staff. But they soon became accustomed to their guests and went about their work as usual. The problem was, there wasn't much work to do. As long as the audit was ongoing, there would be no more federal grants. And without the prospect of additional grants, it was impossible to recruit industry.

In fact, the investigation couldn't have come at a worse time. Soul Tech I was nearing completion, and McKissick was desperately looking for tenants. But with federal auditors on site, no company wanted to get near the project. In December, McKissick had met with Robert Thompson, a vice president of R. J. Reynolds Industries in Winston-Salem, about the possibility of building a food processing plant in Soul City. The meeting went well, and McKissick was optimistic about his chances of securing a commitment. But in April, Thompson wrote to say that Reynolds would not be expanding its operations in the near future. Thompson did not mention the *N&O* series, but McKissick, suspecting it was on his mind, sent him a copy of HUD's letter to the editor. "I hope the enclosed material will clear up some questions in your mind as it regards Soul City," he wrote.

An industrial recruiter McKissick had hired, Harry Payne, had a similar experience. Calling on contacts in Boston, Buffalo, and Chicago, he kept hearing the same thing: until the GAO audit was finished, no one wanted to touch Soul City. When he explained the situation to the governor's adviser for minority business, the latter was indignant. "I did not believe that a sincere prospect would be daunted by political allegations," the adviser wrote. Payne responded that he was surprised, too, but would follow up with his contacts at the end of summer. "During that time period, I would hope that our situation at Soul City would have been altered or cleared up to the point that I need not speak defensively."

As it turned out, the audit lasted much longer than that. The inspectors did not leave Soul City until September 1 and did not issue their report until the third week of December. For McKissick, it was almost worth the wait. After nine months and a cost of nearly five hundred thousand dollars, the GAO audit largely exonerated Soul City. Although the auditors confirmed the N&O's allegations of "interlocking directorships," they noted that there was nothing wrong or illegal about this arrangement and that HUD officials had been fully aware of it. The same was true of the paper's claims of nepotism. Some of the grants awarded to Soul City did bar the hiring of family members to work within the same department, the audit pointed out. But McKissick had not violated that rule. And the family members he did hire "had the education and experience to qualify them for their jobs."

As to the claim that McKissick had made insufficient progress in building his town, the GAO flatly rejected this charge, stating that "the physical development of Soul City was essentially on target." In reaching this conclusion, the report pointed out what the N&O should have made clear itself. "Although the idea for a new community was conceived in 1969 and the final application was made to HUD in 1971, it was not until early in 1974 that the loan guarantee was finally executed," the report stated. "Therefore the project, for all practical purposes, has been in existence for only about 18 months. Because the project was in its initial stages, most of the accomplishments were not visible in terms of shops and houses but were evidenced by more basic amenities, such as roads, utilities, and social services, required for the new community."

The audit did acknowledge that HealthCo had opened its doors eleven months behind schedule and had initially suffered from poor management and a lack of clear objectives. But over the past year, the report found, most of those problems had been resolved, and HealthCo was now treating an average of thirty patients a day at a cost of just forty-four dollars per patient.

The audit also faulted HUD and other agencies for deviating from established procedures in awarding several grants and contracts to Soul City. For instance, HUD had approved money for the regional water system in 1973, after Secretary Lynn announced the termination of the agency's public-facilities grants program. But as HUD officials explained, they felt a "moral obligation" to fund the water system in light of the offer of commitment made to Soul City a year earlier.

Finally, the audit raised "serious questions" about bookkeeping practices at Soul City. After sampling 349 expenditures, auditors found that about one-fourth—totaling $44,000—did not meet established procedures and were thus "unallowable." In the overwhelming majority of cases, the expenditures were "unallowable" because they lacked "adequate documentation," meaning travel vouchers or other forms hadn't been properly filled out. In some cases, however, money had been spent on items not covered by the applicable grant or contract. For instance, the Warren Regional Planning Corporation had paid $349 in penalties to the Internal Revenue Service and the state department of revenue even though its agreements with HUD barred it from using grant money to pay such costs. The auditors noted that a review of recent accounts at Soul City showed improvement, but "confirmed a need for a more businesslike approach to purchasing and recordkeeping." As a result, they recommended that agencies working with Soul City review all transactions made and recover any unallowable expenses. They also recommended that agencies put in place adequate safeguards "to prevent such unallowable expenditures in the future."

The audit did not minimize these concerns. Yet the overall impression it conveyed was strikingly different from that of the *News & Observer*. Where Stith and the editorial page saw corruption, fraud, and criminality, the GAO saw Soul City for what it was: an underfunded operation with an overstretched staff struggling to do its best and a federal bureaucracy still working out the kinks of the new towns program. There was no swindle or scam, the GAO made clear, just occasional shortcuts and sloppiness.

McKissick claimed victory. At a news conference on December 18, he noted that none of the principal charges leveled by the *News & Observer* had been substantiated by the audit. Asked about the finding of unallowable expenses, he blamed the problem on poor bookkeeping practices, which had since been addressed. "When Senator Helms and Representative Fountain first called for this audit by GAO, more than seven months ago, we publicly welcomed the audit and said then that we had nothing to hide and nothing to fear," he declared. "The GAO has validated that statement, and we find their report to be a very timely and welcome Christmas present."

If it was a victory, though, it was only a partial one. The finding of unallowable expenses gave critics something to seize upon. Indeed, the *N&O* portrayed the audit as a vindication of its reporting. In an article headlined "GAO Hits Handling of Soul City Funds," Stith led with the "serious questions" the audit raised about Soul City's expenditures. Not until the sixth paragraph did he acknowledge that the GAO had found no violations of federal law. And not until five paragraphs later did he concede that the GAO gave Soul City "what amounted to a clean bill of health." Other aspects of the report—such as the GAO's finding that Soul City was "essentially on target"— were buried deep in the article.

The editorial page was equally grudging. It emphasized the unallowable expenses without noting all the ways in which the audit had exonerated the project. It also blamed McKissick for damaging the reputation of the new towns program without acknowledging the role it had played in hyping the allegations and demanding an investigation. In fact, reading the editorial by itself, one might have thought its authors were as troubled by the attacks on Soul City as anyone. "Foes of federal efforts to assist minorities are always in the market for evidence of an effort gone astray," the editorial observed. "One such foe is Sen. Jesse Helms, who along with Rep. L. H. Fountain, D-N.C., requested the GAO audit following a series of Soul City articles in the *News & Observer*. If its fiscal record were perfect, Soul City wouldn't have an ally in Helms. Those who botched the effort have only helped to make their enemies more effective."

If the *N&O* would not acknowledge the truth of the GAO audit, the *Carolina Times*, in Durham, was happy to help. It ran an article across its front page with the banner headline, "GAO Audit Clears Soul City Project." On the editorial page, it asked a pointed question: "Is Helms Man Enough to Apologize?"

The answer, of course, was no. Although clearly disappointed with the audit, Helms maintained that its results were damning, going so far as to publicly ask the Department of Justice to review the case for possible criminal charges. "I am not an attorney, and I do not know what, if anything, that review will disclose," he declared the day after the report was released. "But whatever the result, an obvious fact will remain—Soul City is suspected by many citizens of my state to be the greatest single waste of public money that anyone in North Carolina can remember."

The Justice Department wasn't interested. After reviewing the GAO report, it concluded that the audit "had failed to reveal any violations of law" and that "the matter deserved no further prosecutive consideration."

PART IV

17

Good Place to Live

With the investigation behind them, McKissick and his staff attempted to regain the momentum they had lost over the past year. It was not easy. The *News & Observer*'s allegations had undermined morale and tarnished the project's reputation. Many companies were no longer willing to meet with McKissick, while others gave him a cool reception. In addition, two federal agencies decided to terminate funding for the project. First, the Community Services Administration, which provided grants to the Soul City Foundation, announced that it lacked the money to continue supporting the foundation. Then, the Department of Health, Education, and Welfare denied a request for seven hundred thousand dollars to fund HealthCo, citing the GAO's finding of "unallowable expenses," as well as the poor prospects for the town's future. "Evidence of growth of Soul City demonstrates no population potential in less than five to ten years that would justify a health facility," the agency stated.

But while CSA and HEW distanced themselves from Soul City, HUD reaffirmed its commitment. On the same day the GAO report was made public, the New Communities Administration announced a $445,000 grant to build sewer lines, storm drains, and roads. It was $3 million less than McKissick had asked for, but it showed that HUD had not given up on the project altogether. Governor Holshouser also reaffirmed his support. Dismayed by the suspension of funding to HealthCo, the governor appealed directly to HEW secretary David Mathews, arguing that medical care in Warren and Vance counties was "already at minimum levels" and that closing the clinic "would make it a critical situation." His plea was answered. On February 3, Mathews reversed his agency's decision, announcing that it would continue to fund HealthCo while evaluating the program's future.

McKissick also received good news from an old industrial prospect. In January, he met twice with executives from Morse Electro, who had gotten cold feet three years earlier because of delays in finalizing the loan guarantee. Morse was still interested in building a plant in Soul City, the executives said, and they tentatively committed to begin construction later in the year. In exchange, McKissick agreed to help the company secure government contracts and establish a minority division that would be eligible for a federal set-aside program. He also offered to display Morse products at the Soul City visitor center and to present Philip Morse with an award at the annual Founders' Day Banquet that summer.

And so gradually, step by small step, the development of Soul City began to move forward again. Soul Tech I had recently been completed, and McKissick finally landed his first tenants. The Warren Manufacturing Company, a newly created subsidiary of Hunter Outdoor Products, agreed to lease the bulk of the industrial space to make sleeping bags, field packs, tents, and other outdoor equipment, while American National Housing Company, a builder of low-cost modular homes, rented the remainder of the space. The Soul City Company also moved in to Soul Tech I, occupying ten thousand square feet of office space. It was the first real office the staff had occupied since arriving in Warren County, and the move from cramped trailers and dusty barns to a modern suite with glass walls and new furniture helped to reenergize a beleaguered workforce.

Elsewhere in Soul City, work crews were busy paving roads,

installing sewer lines, and digging storm drains. The regional water system was nearly complete, while construction was underway on the Magnolia Ernest Recreation Complex, the First Baptist Church of Soul City, a lake, a shopping center, and a permanent facility for HealthCo, which was operating at full capacity. At the entrance to the city, workers were erecting a steel and concrete monolith standing twenty feet high with the words "Soul City" engraved on both sides.

The most important development was housing. After the *N&O* series, HUD realized that its ban on the construction of housing had hurt McKissick's ability to demonstrate progress to industry and the public. So in 1976, HUD lifted the ban, and the staff began planning the city's first subdivision. They named it Green Duke Village, after the plantation owner who had built the manor house two hundred years earlier. But if the village's name served as a deliberate reminder of the legacy of white oppression, its street names were a tribute to the many Black figures who had fought for freedom. In addition to Turner Circle and Scott Circle, there was Walker Circle (named after David Walker, author of the famous antislavery tract "Walker's Appeal"); Allen Circle (for Bishop Richard Allen, founder of the African Methodist Episcopal Church); and White Circle (in honor of George White, North Carolina's first Black congressman). Other streets were named after sympathetic whites, including John Brown, Thomas Paine, and Oliver Otis Howard, a Union Army general and commissioner of the Freedmen's Bureau who helped establish Howard University.

With construction set to begin on Green Duke, McKissick suggested another groundbreaking celebration. But Floyd Jr., who was now working full-time in the planning office, talked him out of it. "It will be interpreted as more federal dollars being spent on new roads that will lead to nowhere," he wrote to his father. "Our current emphasis should be on building and creating a viable community here at Soul City. I say wait till we produce the jobs and the homes, then bring the press and they can report what actually exists here, not what's planned or under construction."

While the staff worked out the details of housing, McKissick began thinking about a home for his own family. Since 1971, when they left New York, he and Evelyn had lived in a trailer like everyone else at Soul City. It was not what Evelyn had envisioned. Although she had never questioned McKissick's decision to build Soul City, the move from a Harlem brownstone into a trailer in the middle of nowhere had not been easy for her. McKissick had promised to build a house within two years, a time frame that had been repeatedly pushed back, first because of delays with HUD and then because of the GAO audit. But now that the investigation was over and development was moving forward once more, McKissick was ready to deliver on his promise. He and Evelyn had already identified the site—a 3.7-acre tract across the road from Green Duke Village that he purchased from the Soul City Company for ten thousand dollars. In the future, the house would form part of a single-family neighborhood, just down the street from an elementary school. For now, it would stand alone at the end of a long driveway lined with dogwoods.

As for the design, McKissick left that to Evelyn. She had seen a house she liked in the newspaper, and the architects used that as the model. It was large, but not ostentatious. From the front, it looked like a California ranch, with double front doors, dark brown siding, and two stone chimneys. But it was built on a slope, so the rear of the house was two stories high. The decor was contemporary—parquet floors, shag carpeting, plaid upholstery—and there were several architectural touches, including a sunken living room and an interior courtyard surrounded by glass. In rural Warren County, where most homes were either shacks, trailers, or crumbling mansions, the McKissick home stood out. But in any middle-class suburb it would have seemed unremarkable.

McKissick wasn't the only one eager to build a house. Jane Groom had been waiting for this moment, too. The last few years not been easy for her. After struggling to make their marriage work, she and Jimmy finally separated. At one point, Groom and her children left Soul City, moving first to an apartment in Durham, then to Norlina. She continued to work in Soul City, however, and when construction

McKissick watches as a bulldozer clears land for a boulevard in Soul City.

began on Green Duke Village she was one of the first staff members to build a house. Unlike the McKissick home, hers was relatively small and modest, with three bedrooms, one and a half baths, and an eat-in kitchen. But it was the first house she had ever owned, and when she and her children finally moved in she felt as though a dream had been fulfilled.

As construction progressed, Soul City began to glow—literally. Work crews erected streetlights every twenty-five feet along Soul City Boulevard and Liberation Road. For those approaching the town at night, it was a surreal sight. Driving along US 1 in the dark, they would suddenly see a bright halo in the sky. Residents joked that it looked like a scene out of *Brigadoon*, the Gene Kelly movie in which two hunters lost in the Scottish mist come upon an enchanted village that appears once every hundred years. But there was an important difference between Brigadoon and Soul City. Brigadoon was untouched by the modern world, whereas Soul City was a beacon of modernity amid the decaying estates of Warren County.

The benefits of Soul City's development were felt beyond its limits. After sharp population declines in the 1950s and 1960s, Warren

County grew modestly during the 1970s, with the population increasing 3 percent. In addition, for the first time since Reconstruction, more Black people moved into the state than out. And some of them, such as David Carolina, came because of Soul City. "It's a pioneer city," said Carolina, who returned to the South from Newark and bought a house in Green Duke Village. "Just like the beginning of the whole doggone country."

For the hundred or so residents of Soul City life was good. On the Fourth of July, the town threw a massive Bicentennial celebration. That fall, it hosted the Miss Soul City pageant (won by Sandra Groom). And at Christmas, there was a holiday parade with more than fifty floats and automobiles. The mood was summed up by Carey's stepdaughter Kristina Renee Wilken, who published a poem in the *Soul City Sounder* titled "Good Place to Live":

> *I've lived in Soul City since I was seven;*
> *Floyd McKissick, I'm sure, will go to heaven.*
> *He founded Soul City and gave it a name*
> *The President could not have done the same.*
> *Soul City's for everyone, dark or light hue*
> *You've heard it, I know it, you'll have your chance too.*
> *The future Soul City is going to be bright*
> *For folks who have not yet seen the light.*

WHILE SOUL CITY forged ahead, the rest of the New Communities program was stuck in neutral. HUD's decision to stop accepting applications and focus on existing projects had not had the desired effect. The towns that had been struggling two years earlier were in no better shape, while most of the remaining towns were now in distress. In all, six of the thirteen projects were broke, obliging HUD to pay the interest on their bonds. Another five had money in the bank but didn't want to empty their reserves, so HUD paid their interest, too. The program's troubles were due largely to the recession of the early seventies, the effects of which continued to linger in the real estate industry. But mismanagement and local opposition had also played a role. Cedar-Riverside, a new community near downtown Minneapolis, had been stalled for three years because of a lawsuit over environmental concerns. Meanwhile, it was becoming clear that not all developers had the fortitude to stick with a project for the twenty or thirty years required for completion. Several were already in talks to sell their assets or transfer management to other firms.

The New Communities board had a decision to make. It could continue to support all thirteen towns and risk a catastrophic failure, or it could cut its losses. With political support for the program waning, the choice was easy. At a meeting in June 1976, the board instructed HUD staff to identify which projects were hopeless and which might still be salvaged. Although it stopped short of saying so, the implication was clear: projects in the former category would be abandoned, while those in the latter group would be given another chance.

Soul City was one of the few new towns not in immediate financial trouble, so McKissick wasn't worried about being shut down. But he had other grievances with HUD. The money raised from the sale of the first $5 million in bonds had been placed in an escrow account that could only be accessed with agency approval, and getting that approval was arduous. On one occasion, HUD demanded McKissick write a check for $1.10 before photocopying documents he needed. McKissick grew so frustrated with this nickel-and-diming that he threatened to sue the agency for violating the project agreement.

McKissick was also fighting with HUD to release an additional $5 million in bonds. Under the project agreement, release of the bonds was conditioned upon the creation of three hundred jobs, the development of key infrastructure, and the acquisition of additional land. With his recent industrial commitments, completion of the water system, and the purchase of a 1,400-acre tract adjacent to the Circle P Ranch, McKissick believed he had met those benchmarks. But at the very moment he submitted his request, Soul City became embroiled in an intraparty political dispute.

It began with Ronald Reagan's announcement that he would challenge Gerald Ford in the Republican presidential primary. That announcement threw the GOP into disarray, creating a rift between the traditional, moderate wing of the party and the insurgent conservative wing. In North Carolina, these two factions were represented by Governor Holshouser and Senator Helms, respectively. Holshouser, who was seen as a rising star by the moderates, came out strongly in favor of the incumbent. He believed the party had to broaden its appeal and unite behind a mainstream candidate. He also believed Reagan's challenge was hurting Ford's chances in the general election. His mistake was publicly saying so. Joining with nine other Republican governors, Holshouser issued a statement urging Reagan to quit the race for the good of the party. Instead of bringing the factions together, that move only deepened the rift, with Reagan making clear he had no intention of taking advice from Ford's supporters. And although Holshouser tried to delicately walk back the statement, he had made himself a target for Helms and the other insurgents.

The Republican primary in North Carolina thus became a referendum on Holshouser. Using money from the National Congressional Club, a powerful fundraising organization Helms had established three years earlier, the insurgents launched a vicious attack on the governor, disparaging his record and questioning his integrity. The main weapon in their arsenal was Holshouser's support of Soul City. The club mailed flyers to North Carolina Republicans reminding them of Holshouser's speech at the groundbreaking and suggesting that McKissick was pulling the governor's strings. It also produced radio ads alleging a backroom deal between the NAACP and Ford to make Edward Brooke his running mate. Brooke, of course, was Soul City's strongest supporter in the Senate. And there was in fact an effort to get him on the ticket; McKissick had even circulated a petition to that effect. But there was no backroom deal, and Ford ultimately chose Bob Dole instead.

Nonetheless, the campaign against Holshouser and Soul City was successful. After losing the four preceding state primaries, Reagan

A brochure depicting what life would be like in Soul City.

beat Ford handily in North Carolina. His victory didn't change the outcome of the primary—Ford ultimately prevailed in a contested convention—but it did resuscitate Reagan's image, helping propel him to the nomination four years later. It also established Helms as someone not to be crossed, a point driven home when he helped deny Holshouser a seat at the party's national convention that summer. Thus, when the New Communities board met in October, it deferred a vote on McKissick's request for additional bonds out of fear of drawing the senator's wrath. As explained in a memo written by James Dausch, the latest head of the New Communities Administration, the goal was to "put off the decision until after the November election, thereby avoiding perhaps (although I am not sure to what extent) the vigorous, adverse reaction from Senator Helms and the Raleigh *News & Observer*."

As it turned out, Ford lost the election to Jimmy Carter, meaning the board, made up of political appointees, would soon be replaced anyway. So with nothing to lose, board members voted on December 1 to release an additional $5 million in bonds to Soul City and to give the project preferential treatment in light of its experimental nature and social objectives. A few days later, the US Public Health Service announced that it would fund the increasingly busy HealthCo for another year.

As expected, those moves were blasted by Soul City's critics. In an editorial titled "Soul City Hits Taxpayers Again," the N&O argued that HUD's new "handouts" were further evidence that Soul City was "a wizard at shaking undeserved money out of the U.S. Government." McKissick, determined to let HUD know that Helms and the N&O didn't speak for everyone, organized a letter-writing campaign commending the board for its decision. Over the next few weeks, HUD received more than two dozen letters from a cross section of Soul City supporters, including the Southern Christian Leadership Conference, the chancellor of North Carolina Central University (formerly named North Carolina College), Holshouser's office, and local residents and officials. Linda Nesbitt, of New York, applauded HUD "for not succumbing to the pressures which a few narrow-minded racists have generated with their lies and innuendoes." Mary Richardson, of Warrenton, condemned the attacks on Soul City as "unwarranted." And Melvin Holmes, the city manager of Henderson, praised McKissick and his staff for their dedication to improving living conditions for the entire area. "I am sure you are receiving letters in opposition to the development of the project," he wrote to HUD secretary Carla Hills. "However, those of us who are interested in seeing our community made a better place to live, rejoice in your decision to continue supporting the development of Soul City."

18

Pride or Prejudice

The election of Jimmy Carter should have been good news for Soul City. In the two years since Nixon's resignation, the Ford administration had done little to aid the new communities program or address the larger urban crisis. And with the conservative wing of the Republican Party on the rise, it was unlikely a second Ford term would have been any different. Carter was no liberal on issues of race and economics; he had run as a centrist who disavowed the "tax and spend" policies of his Democratic predecessors. But he had also pledged to reduce poverty, improve health care, and increase jobs, a promise that won him the endorsement of many Black leaders, including Representative Andrew Young and Martin Luther King Sr. And once in office, he appointed more Black officials to high-level positions than any prior president. All of which made McKissick and his staff optimistic that Carter's presidency would benefit Soul City.

It didn't work out that way. For one thing, McKissick had supported Ford in the election, donating money to the campaign, attending a meeting of prominent Black Republicans, and papering the offices of the Soul City Company with Ford posters. And although he had not been as visible as he was during the 1972 election, when he traveled the country stumping for Nixon, he was still a registered Republican, which meant he didn't have much influence with a Democratic administration.

Then there were Carter's policies. When the new president took office, his primary concern was inflation. Prices had been on the rise throughout 1976, and with some economists predicting a double-dip recession, both candidates pledged to keep federal spending in check. Thus, a few months after taking office, Carter announced that he would initiate no new social welfare, health care, or educational programs. Instead, his national urban policy would promote economic development through existing loan programs and interest subsidies.

Soul City was also hampered by the turnover of staff and political appointees from one administration to the next. In the eight years since he had launched Soul City, McKissick had already seen three different HUD secretaries and four different directors of the New Communities Administration. Now, just as he was getting comfortable with Carla Hills and James Dausch, they were replaced by two new appointees. For secretary of HUD, Carter chose Patricia Harris, the first Black woman nominated to a cabinet position. A graduate of Howard University and George Washington Law School, Harris had a sterling résumé, having worked at the Justice Department, served as the US ambassador to Luxembourg, and been dean of Howard Law School. For the past seven years, she had been a member of Fried, Frank, Harris, Shriver, and Jacobson, one of the country's most prestigious law firms.

Still, some were skeptical of Harris's suitability for the post. When she appeared before the Senate banking committee for her confirmation hearing in January 1977, Wisconsin Democrat William Proxmire announced that he was troubled by her nomination. HUD was "in a shambles," he declared, its morale "low" and its accomplishments "pitifully inadequate." Ten years earlier, he reminded her, Congress had approved a plan to construct six million low-income homes over the next decade. But after a promising start, HUD had fallen far short of the goal. And to Proxmire, the reason was clear: instead of appointing administrators with experience in housing,

Nixon and Ford had appointed "scholarly lawyers" such as Harris to lead the agency. Proxmire did not doubt Harris's intelligence or character, and he acknowledged she was likely to be confirmed easily. But he questioned her priorities and her knowledge of the country's housing crisis. Just a few months earlier, he noted, she had called for an abandonment of public housing projects, arguing that they should be replaced with government housing vouchers to individuals. That was not the attitude HUD needed in a secretary, Proxmire declared. It needed "someone sympathetic to the problems of the poor."

Harris defended herself, pointing out that she was the daughter of a dining-car worker and just eight years earlier would have been unable to buy a house in the nicer parts of Washington, DC. "I started, Senator, not as a lawyer in a prestigious law firm, but as a woman who needed a scholarship to go to college," she told Proxmire. "If you think that I have forgotten that, you're wrong."

While Proxmire questioned Harris's experience and empathy, Jesse Helms tried to poison the well for Soul City. After asking the nominee whether she was familiar with its history, he asserted that "citizens and leaders of all political parties and philosophies have strongly criticized this project." He also cited the GAO audit, claiming it had found "numerous irregularities, including nepotism, interlocking directorships, many HUD deviations from its own rules and regulations, improper loans, improper expenses, and an average of approximately 25 percent of transactions not meeting the test for allowability." In light of these findings, he asked if Harris would agree to conduct a personal reevaluation of Soul City "for the purpose of objectively determining whether the project should be abandoned, or made subject to radical revision, or at a very minimum curtailing the abuses noted in the GAO report."

Harris responded coolly that she had no "preconceived notions" about Soul City or any other new town, but would certainly fulfill her duty to monitor the program. Edward Brooke was less restrained. Speaking out of turn, he quickly corrected Helms's characterization of the GAO audit. "The Senator and I debated this on the floor," he reminded Helms. "We spent several hours on it at least but I understand that the GAO has made a report which exonerated them of all charges. Now there may have been some criticisms. I trust in your review that we're talking about the same report when you're asking the Secretary to review it. I think there's only one GAO report."

Helms: "Well, I have seen only one, and it certainly was anything but an 'exoneration.' I have already stated the findings of the GAO audit, and I stated them accurately."

Brooke: "Well, I say to the able Senator from North Carolina, if we read the same report we read it differently, but anyway we'll be very glad to have your review of it."

Helms: "In any case, Mrs. Harris, will you keep both Senator Brooke and me advised?"

Harris: "Yes."

From there, the senators moved on to other topics, with a young Joe Biden asking Harris about the role of the housing industry in the economic recovery. But the colloquy between Helms and Brooke lingered over the hearing, making clear to the incoming secretary just how politically contentious Soul City had become.

PROXMIRE WAS RIGHT: Harris was confirmed quickly and easily in late January. But the rest of the HUD bureaucracy turned over more slowly. It wasn't until April that William J. White, a Boston real estate executive, was confirmed as director of the New Communities Administration. And it wasn't until October that the new board of directors met for the first time. In the meantime, McKissick was left in limbo, unable to obtain approval for key decisions.

Then, once the board did meet, its main focus was deciding which of the new towns to shut down. White had prepared a report recommending the closure of seven of the thirteen towns. Soul City was not on the list, but some board members suggested it should be. Victor Palmieri, a California lawyer who had made his fortune overseeing corporate restructurings, argued that McKissick's application had been approved not because it made sense economically, but because of reasons having to do with "equal opportunity." Now, he believed, the agency was "nursing it along," knowing full well it had little chance of success. White pushed back, pointing out that Soul City had provided many benefits to the surrounding area, including the regional water system and HealthCo. But he agreed that the board needed to decide whether it would continue to treat Soul City as a "special experiment" or insist that it "fly on its own." Harris, who was under continuing pressure from Helms to provide an update on Soul City, attempted to mediate. She asked White and his staff to study the project further and report back to the board in January.

When McKissick got wind of the board's discussion, he instructed his own staff to prepare a memo for White, hoping to influence his report. Because White was new to HUD, the memo began by educating him about Soul City's distinctive nature. Besides being the only new town built by a Black developer, Soul City was the only project true to the original intent of the New Communities Act, which sought to encourage freestanding towns, not mere bedroom communities. This distinctiveness had created difficulties not faced by other new towns—difficulties that HUD had exacerbated with foot-dragging and red tape. The eighteen-month delay between the offer of commitment and the sale of the first bonds had cost Soul City a commitment of 350 jobs from Morse Electric. (Morse's latest commitment had also fallen through, this time because of financial problems at the company.) And the ban on housing had hurt Soul City's ability to attract residents and demonstrate progress to the media and industry. Yet in spite of such obstacles—not to mention the recession, the attacks by the N&O and Jesse Helms, and the GAO audit—Soul City was better positioned than almost any other new town, with much of its critical infrastructure in place, $2.8 million in the bank, and another $4 million still available from the loan guarantee. The only thing needed now was industry, and the key to attracting industry was HUD support. As a consultant from Arthur D. Little had recently explained, "the single greatest barrier to industrial jobs was the lack of clear, long-term commitments from HUD." Soul City's fate was thus in HUD's hands, the memo asserted. By signaling its support in clear, unequivocal terms, HUD could give industry the assurance it needed to build in Soul City. And once industry came, the rest of the pieces would fall naturally into place.

The memo worked. When White submitted his report to the board in January 1978, he recommended it support Soul City "to the fullest." He acknowledged that the project was ambitious and that Soul City had struggled to create jobs. But he praised McKissick for bringing needed infrastructure and services to an impoverished region. He also pointed out that Soul City was consistent with "the President's determined effort to advance the cause of minority groups." The question was how HUD could maximize the project's chances of success. According to an analysis by his staff, Soul City's long-term prospects depended not just on attracting industry but on securing grants from federal agencies. Over the next twenty-five years, McKissick would need anywhere from $29 million to $46 million in grants to remain solvent. HUD could provide some of that money, but much of it would have to come from other agencies. And like industry, those agencies would support Soul City only if they believed HUD was fully behind the project. Thus, White concluded, the board should reaffirm its commitment to Soul City and communicate that message clearly to the rest of the federal bureaucracy.

The board remained skeptical. At its January meeting, some members pointed out that Soul City had been approved by the Nixon administration, so Republicans would take the blame if it failed. Others argued that the amount of money needed to sustain Soul City was "unbelievable." Palmieri, who confessed to not reading the report, described the project as a "disaster." "This is Viet Nam. It really is," he told his colleagues. "It's harder each day to get out."

Much of the debate focused on solutions. Neva Kaiser, the daughter of Chase Manhattan chairman David Rockefeller, wondered whether HUD might persuade NASA or another agency to build a research facility in Soul City. Palmieri dismissed that idea, arguing that the government couldn't locate a federal facility "out in nowheresville in a rural black community." Instead, he suggested using federal money to lure a European firm to Soul City. Perhaps

Harris could talk to one of the big German chemical companies that was struggling to meet environmental standards back home. Now it was Kaiser's turn to object. "Is this going to look like a Tongsun Park activity if we pay them $20 million to locate there?" she asked, referring to a South Korean lobbyist who had recently been charged with bribing members of Congress to keep troops in his country. "I wish you hadn't put it exactly in those terms," Palmieri responded. "I'm not even going to answer it."

The most logical solution, board members agreed, was to recruit an American company. White reported that General Motors was seriously considering Soul City for a manufacturing plant that would provide five hundred jobs. A site evaluation team was scheduled to visit soon, and White had recently spoken with Thomas Murphy, the company's CEO. The problem was, Murphy wanted a letter from HUD stating that it was committed to Soul City for the long haul, a promise White was not in a position to make.

Neither, it turned out, was the board. Although Palmieri agreed it would be unfair to pull the plug prematurely, he refused to support an indefinite commitment to Soul City. Instead he asked the staff to make contingency plans in the event that HUD and McKissick could not turn things around. "You take definitive action to produce the strenuous economic event that has to happen," he said. "You also take definitive action to gear up for the cutoff."

In the end, the board voted to foreclose on seven of the thirteen new towns, including Jonathan, Minnesota, the first development HUD had approved, and Park Forest South, one of the most expensive. But it would continue to support the remaining six towns: St. Charles, Maryland; Maumelle, Arkansas; The Woodlands, Texas; Harbison, South Carolina; Shenandoah, Georgia . . . and Soul City.

In announcing the decision, Harris blamed her predecessors for the program's problems. "There was a total lack of support from the Nixon administration," she told reporters. "There was mismanagement and there were bad decisions. Not surprisingly, there were financial failures." But not all the new towns were lost causes, she added, and HUD would "not close out those existing communities that are viable and are meeting national and local goals. We not only intend to support them, but to make them stronger."

When asked why Soul City was among the projects to be salvaged, Harris emphasized the social mission of the project. "It is an area where clearly there is a need for low and moderate-income housing," she responded. "We are not prepared at this time to say that we should cease our efforts to make Soul City viable."

It was not a ringing endorsement. But it was enough to give McKissick hope, and to give his critics cause to snipe. In an editorial that read as though it could have been written by Jesse Helms, the N&O sneered that Soul City "seems to have more lives than a cat. Its longevity as a 'new community' can only be attributed to steady injections of political plasma in the form of U.S. dollars during the Nixon-Ford administrations. Now, the Carter administration appears ready to take over the doctoring with taxpayers' dollars." None of this was justified, the editorial argued, for Soul City had been a "spectacular failure." Instead of the forty-four thousand people promised (nine hundred of whom were already supposed to be living there), "Soul City boasts a current population of 94, a job count of 129, and 14 single-family houses, with 11 occupied." And while "all the interlocking companies and organizations involved at Soul City" had created jobs for McKissick and his family, they had done "precious little for others."

The paper consoled itself with the fact that HUD had not pledged to throw any more money into the sinkhole that was Soul City. "But rest assured McKissick and his consultants will keep the lines hot to Washington," it warned. "About all the taxpayers can do is salute in the direction of their investment as they zip by on I-85."

GRANTED A TEMPORARY reprieve by HUD, McKissick renewed his efforts to recruit industry to Soul City, writing to every *Fortune* 500 company in the country and hiring an industrial marketing consultant named Walter Sorg. At fifty-one, Sorg had a long and impressive résumé in both the public and private sectors. From 1969 to 1976, he had been assistant director of the Office of Minority Business Enterprise, where he was responsible for helping minority firms raise capital. As part of that effort, he had created the National Minority Purchasing Council, an organization designed to connect minority businesses with large corporations that would buy their goods and services. In its short existence, the council had funneled more than $3 billion in sales to minority firms. Sorg left OMBE after Carter's election and started his own consulting firm. When McKissick asked him to work for Soul City, he agreed without hesitation. Although white and conservative, he believed deeply in Soul City's goal of Black economic empowerment. He also thought highly of McKissick and his staff, telling an executive at Honeywell that Soul City "has been exceptionally well-managed" and "has consistently met all its financial obligations."

Without the money for an extensive advertising campaign, Sorg spent the next year reaching out to personal contacts at dozens of companies, including General Motors, Standard Oil, Sears, Levi Strauss, Quaker Oats, Borden, Philip Morris, J. C. Penney, and Ford. Sorg was most optimistic about GM, which was considering Soul City for one of twelve expansion possibilities. "I think we'll get one of them," Sorg predicted. But he also had high hopes for several other companies. Standard Oil had expressed interest in purchasing limited partnership shares in the Soul City Company. And Sears had promised to "push" one of its affiliates to locate in the new town, perceiving "benefits in a 'Soul City Connection' which go somewhat beyond the economics involved." "It just takes that first commitment—and everything else falls into place," Sorg explained to the director of equal opportunity at Sears. "But oh, the agony of getting that first commitment."

In Soul City's case, the agony was exacerbated by several factors, the most prominent of which was the lack of a sewage treatment plant. By 1978, the regional water system was fully operational, providing ten million gallons of water a day, including at least two million gallons for Soul City. But although workers had installed a network of sewer lines, there was still no system for treating the waste. Instead, Soul City was pumping its sewage through an eight-mile force main to Warrenton. That was only a temporary solution, however, since Warrenton's plant could handle no more than 250,000 gallons a day from Soul City—about one-eighth of its water supply.

For industry, this was a major problem. If a factory used 100,000 gallons of water a day, it had to dispose of almost an equal amount. Yet with a capacity of only 250,000 gallons, Soul City could barely handle one plant. Already, the lack of sewerage had hurt industrial recruiting. Miller Brewing Co. had been scouting sites for a plant that would consume five million gallons of water a day. Although Soul City's engineers thought they could find enough water to handle the input, the lack of a treatment system meant there was no way to process the output. So Miller went elsewhere.

The staff pressed Warrenton to improve its sewerage. Carey even walked the sewer lines with local utility workers, discussing the problem and looking for a solution. But Warrenton's system was overburdened, with untreated waste spilling into nearby creeks. And when Soul City suggested expanding Warrenton's system by installing a new treatment plant upstream, local officials objected. As Lew Myers put it, "Warrenton didn't want drinking water we were pissing and shitting in."

The obvious solution was to build a new sewage plant in Soul City. To pay for one, McKissick applied for a grant from the Environmental Protection Agency, which provided funding for local sewerage projects. But EPA's formula for approving such grants was based on the number of residents who lived in a given area, and, at the moment, Soul City's population was only around a hundred. McKissick explained that the sewage plant was needed for *future* residents, but the EPA had no formula for taking such a factor into account. Thus, as had happened at other stages in its development, Soul City confronted a catch-22. It needed a treatment plant to attract industry, which was needed to attract residents. But without residents, it couldn't obtain funding for the plant. And without industry or residents, McKissick couldn't sell land to pay off the loans that had been guaranteed by the same government that was declining to fund the sewer system.

The lack of sewerage wasn't the only problem. Soul City lacked its own schools, shopping centers, cultural institutions, and all the other amenities that make a community attractive to industry. Globe Union, a maker of automotive batteries, had cited "livability" as the main factor in its recent decision to build a plant in Winston-Salem rather than Soul City. To make matters worse, the economy had plunged back into a recession, with inflation once again hitting double digits. But the inability to provide sewerage was critical. "Without sewerage, you're nothing," Carey said in analyzing Soul City's downfall years later. Myers put it more concretely: "If we had sewerage and were able to get Miller Brewing to put a plant in there, we might not be having this conversation."

IF MCKISSICK HAD little control over the lack of sewerage, there was one problem he could address: the city's name. Although he hoped questions about the name had been put to rest years earlier, they surfaced again as the staff made a renewed push to attract industry. In January 1978, an executive at Honeywell told Sorg there was a "disconnect" between the city's name and its location, adding that his company didn't want to get caught up in a "potentially volatile situation." Around the same time, officials at General Motors informed McKissick that the name was a potential problem and that he should consider a change. It was the third time GM had flagged the issue, and senior staff decided it was time to act. They had already persuaded McKissick to change the name of the A. Philip Randolph Industrial Park to the Warren Industrial Park as a way of erasing any racial connotations. Now, in a series of memos, they proposed renaming the city itself.

The first memo was written by marketing director John P. Stewart, who had joined the staff two years earlier and was a frequent target of McKissick's temper. On January 23, he wrote to McKissick identifying four "changes that should be made immediately." At the top of the list: renaming the town. "The times have changed," Stewart wrote, "and I personally feel the name is currently becoming more of a disadvantage in attracting industry, as it was an advantage in the late '60's and early '70's."

A day later, McKissick received a similar memo from Billy Carmichael, an outside marketing consultant. The son of a prominent UNC official, Carmichael was well connected in the state's political and business circles. And he left no doubt that the town's name had become a liability. "In concept Soul City is an integrated community," he wrote. "In the public's mind, Soul City is a black city." A new name would change that perception, giving McKissick a chance to "dramatize to the public the true concept and mission of the project."

Three weeks later, Carey added his voice to the chorus. In a memo to McKissick on February 14, he argued that it was time to make some "hard decisions." The name Soul City had been "an important symbol during the years when we were dealing primarily with symbols," he wrote. "The nature of our work, however, has changed from creating dreams to executing them." And in the execution stage, it was important to listen to what others were telling them. In addition to Honeywell and GM, HUD had long advocated a name change. "Frankly, I think that part of the problem with HUD today is that they feel they are being asked to take extraordinary steps to support us, but that we are not willing to do those things necessary to insure our own success." Carey insisted that changing the name would not mean surrender. To the contrary, failure to change the name might very well doom McKissick's dream. "We talk of Soul City being an interracial project, but we sometimes appear to do those things which will preclude white participation," he concluded. "Of the few dozen lots purchased in the subdivision, not one has been bought by a white homeowner except purchases by staff of our own Company."

Carey did not coordinate his effort with Stewart and Carmichael. But that is surely how it must have looked to McKissick. Moreover, he could not have failed to notice that the three men pushing him to change the name were white, once again raising questions about control and identity. So it was hardly surprising that he resented the effort. "Those who have problems with the name, I submit, also have problems with Black folks," he responded in a memo of his own. "While I agree that it might be easier to sell land by changing the name, it would probably be easier to achieve our personal goals if we were white. Just as we cannot change from Black to white, I do not think we should change the name." Then, in a personal jab at the three men, he added: "I think that the name change is a good excuse for people's inability to accomplish specific objectives and job assignments."

Undeterred by McKissick's response, Stewart asked Carmichael to prepare a report with suggestions for choosing a new name. Sent to McKissick in late February, Carmichael's report rejected the idea of a contest to rename the city, which some staffers had suggested. A contest would take control away from McKissick and leave the name in limbo for a period of time. Instead, he urged McKissick to announce a preselected name with a major publicity campaign, possibly tied to some milestone in the city's development. As for the name itself, Carmichael argued that it should have no racial or ethnic connotations, should be capable of standing the test of time, and should invoke the idea of the New South. "South City" and "Genesis" were both possibilities, but Carmichael preferred "Sunrise." With its image of a new day dawning, "Sunrise" would give McKissick's dream a truly fresh start.

As McKissick stewed over the issue, he received input from friends and business colleagues. Julian Madison, a Black Cleveland architect who had invested in Soul City along with his brother Robert, argued in favor of a new name. "After four years of discussion, debates, opinions, positions, and lectures on the subject of the name, I have come to the conclusion that it should be changed," he wrote. "I take this firm position mainly because I want to give those who have used the name as an excuse for non-production of industry an opportunity to 'produce or shut up.'" As an alternative to "Soul City," Madison proposed "Kerr Lake," which he thought might attract residents to the recreational and leisure features of the area.

But Harvey Gantt, who now had his own architecture firm in Charlotte, took McKissick's side, arguing that "it would be a big mistake to change the name of the project at this stage." Soul City had been closely followed by Black people around the country who were concerned about problems of equality and opportunity. Renaming the city now would disappoint all those people who had cheered McKissick on. Besides, Gantt was not convinced a name change would have much effect on industry. "Anyone who is using the name 'Soul City' as a reason for not locating is merely reflecting traditional racism," he wrote. "I hope you will not be seduced by the siren call to switch horses in midstream."

Irving L. McCaine, a longtime friend of McKissick and chairman of the board of McKissick Enterprises, offered a similar assessment. He had surveyed numerous people about the name and heard a variety of opinions. Some disliked it, saying they wouldn't want "Soul City" on their business letterhead or their child's birth certificate. Others felt differently, arguing that the name was an "ear catcher" that would attract residents. McCaine wasn't sure who was right on the merits. But he was sure about one thing. "In my opinion, a name change would indicate to America that the proponents of Soul City have no backbone and succumbed to the power of racism in order to make a buck," he wrote. "An obligation rests with Soul City people and it must not falter from its original goal, including its name."

On every other issue concerning Soul City, McKissick had been a pragmatist, doing whatever it took to realize his dream. He had switched political parties. He had endorsed Richard Nixon. He had given up on his plans for "radical capitalism." Yet on this one issue he refused to budge.

Carey believes it was stubbornness. "Once he got it out there and the newspapers talked about Soul City, there was no turning back," he said later. And McKissick *was* stubborn. But that obstinacy had not prevented him from making a thousand other compromises. In the end, his refusal to change the name wasn't just about stubbornness. It was about pride. McKissick wanted Soul City to be regarded as a "black accomplishment." He wanted to prove that Black Americans could achieve something monumental. To remove the word "Soul" from the project, he believed, would undermine that message. It would suggest that Black people could only be accepted if they erased their Blackness, if they denied the part of their identity that had been used to enslave and dehumanize them. And if there was any way McKissick could avoid that, he was determined to do so. Thus, whether out of pride, principle, or a belief that nothing would help at this point, McKissick rejected his consultants' advice and resolved to keep the name.

As if to vindicate that decision, McKissick soon received positive news. In April, a textile manufacturer named Wilmetco announced that it would begin operations in Soul City that summer. Based in Long Island, the company agreed to lease manufacturing space in Soul Tech I, where it would make backpacks for the consumer market and duffel bags for the military. Eventually, Wilmetco projected, it would have three hundred employees in Soul City and an annual payroll of more than $2 million, a huge infusion of cash for an impoverished area.

A few months later, Standard Oil invited McKissick to speak at a management retreat in the Northwoods of Wisconsin, paying him a $1,500 honorarium and flying him up the night before in a company jet. Appearing before a group of seventy senior managers at the exclusive Red Crown Lodge, McKissick praised the company for its social conscience and touted free enterprise as the best hope for solving the problems that afflicted racial minorities. Black people were not looking to destroy the system, he assured his audience; they wanted "to become part of it, and once we become part of it, to fight to make the system include all people." The managers received him warmly, and afterward the chairman of the board sent McKissick a note expressing his desire to personally visit Soul City.

Not long after that, Sorg received a letter from Phil Drotning, Standard's director of corporate social policy, who reported that Amoco Chemical, one of the company's divisions, was interested in locating a minority-owned plastics operation in Soul City. Relaying the news to McKissick, Sorg suggested this might be the break they had been waiting for. "Although Phil couldn't give me a timetable," he wrote, "my guess is that things will be popping in the next couple of months."

19

Maseratis and Microwaves

As Soul City entered its sixth year of physical development, it was finally starting to feel like a real city, or at least a city in progress, with 124 full-time residents, 135 jobs, and work crews everywhere. Green Duke Village had sprung to life, with thirty-four houses either built or nearing completion and another forty-three lots ready for construction. As a Christmas gift, the Soul City Company had planted two saplings in every yard, letting residents choose among dogwood, red maple, oak, sweet gum, and cedar. Across Liberation Road, workers were paving roads and laying underground electrical lines in Pleasant Hills Village, which would have ninety-one lots. And soon bulldozers would begin clearing land for the third village, Haliwa Hills, named after a Native American tribe that had been in Warren County since the early eighteenth century. At the Warren Industrial Park, new roads were being paved and water and sewer lines installed, while down the road a construction crew was laying the foundation for a six-thousand-square-foot fire station, which would house the city's signature light blue fire trucks. The new HealthCo ambulatory care clinic was also up and running. With two doctors, two dentists, and a handful of nurses and technicians, the clinic was handling more than ten thousand patients annually across Warren and Vance counties. Behind HealthCo stood a small shopping center, with a drugstore, gift shop, and pharmacy. There was even progress on a new sewage treatment plant. After protracted negotiations, McKissick had secured $4.2 million in funding from a consortium of federal and state agencies. Construction would begin soon, with an expected completion date in the spring of 1981.

It was all very different from how it had looked a short time ago. "The change which has occurred in a brief few months is just staggering," Sorg wrote to McKissick in late 1978. Sorg had traveled down from Washington a few days earlier to inspect the site and was struck by the transformation of Soul City "from a state of repose to one of vitality." The years of hard work had paid off, he assured McKissick. Even the staff seemed to have recovered its old vigor. It was like the old days when they had worked out of trailers and the red barn, overworked and understaffed but energized by a sense of mission and urgency.

"I have been optimistic about Soul City since the day you outlined your dream in my office in 1969," Sorg added. "For most of those intervening years, my optimism was based on a lot of faith and trust in the ability of you and Gordon to convert dreams (nightmares at times?) into hard-nosed reality. But the tangibility of my optimism only became evident last Thursday. We've spanked a bottom. A baby has been born. It's alive and kicking and beautiful."

Not everyone was enamored with the infant. Around the same time as Sorg's letter, McKissick received word that General Motors had ruled out Soul City as a possible location for a new plant. It was a devastating blow. After courting the company for eight years, he had come up empty-handed. Even more crushing was the explanation he received from a source within GM: the city's name. Frustrated and angry, McKissick asked Sorg if there was anything they could do to reverse the decision. Sorg suggested they write to CEO Thomas Murphy. He even drafted a letter from McKissick to Murphy asking directly whether the name had factored into the company's decision. If so, the letter charged, "it casts a cloud over an otherwise

McKissick (front center) poses in front of the monolith with some of Soul City's 124 full-time residents.

unblemished record of G.M. support for minority enterprise." But there would be no reconsideration of the decision. GM was not coming to Soul City.

Perhaps for that reason, HUD's view of the project quickly soured. In December, it rejected Soul City's budget for 1979, demanding that McKissick submit a revised budget in January. At the same time, it declined McKissick's request to release the final $4 million in bonds. In a letter explaining these decisions, William White, the director of the New Communities Administration, informed McKissick that Soul City was no longer a financially acceptable risk. But White had not discussed the letter with Secretary Harris. And when she confronted him about the matter, he quickly backtracked. He did not mean to imply that the project was not economically feasible, he assured her. He had simply concluded that the agency could not justify releasing the final $4 million in bonds. Of course, failure to release the bonds might itself render the project unfeasible. Therefore, Harris announced the appointment of a task force to evaluate the project's future. On the surface, her announcement was encouraging. The task force would "seek to develop possible ways to encourage investment in Soul City," she stated. But beneath the surface were troubling signs. Harris charged the task force with reviewing "current and future conditions which impact on the viability and success of Soul City." She also requested that it estimate "the number of jobs, land sales, and housing starts needed on an annual basis to make Soul City a success."

It didn't take a genius to realize that the task force would decide whether the infant city lived or died.

WHILE THE TASK force began its work, McKissick flew to Washington, DC, to indulge in a rare bit of nostalgia. On Saturday, March 3, he emceed a testimonial dinner for James Farmer at the Sheraton Park Hotel. Speaking to a crowd of four hundred, McKissick praised Farmer for his leadership and bravery during the civil rights battles of the 1960s. Farmer brushed off the praise, denying he possessed any special courage. But with a patch over his right eye (he had recently undergone surgery for glaucoma), he looked every bit the old soldier. And when he told the audience it was time to form a new civil rights organization because "the war is just starting," it was possible, if just for a moment, to envision him and McKissick leading their troops into combat once more.

After spending two days back in Soul City, McKissick was scheduled to return to Washington on Tuesday, March 6. He had a meeting at HUD on Wednesday and, as he often did, had made reservations to fly up the night before. It was dusk when he got behind the wheel of his Pontiac sedan for the sixty-mile drive to the Raleigh-Durham airport. He had driven this route hundreds of times over the past decade and, on most nights, probably could have made it blindfolded. But on this night, approaching the town of Butner, just north of Durham, he swerved to avoid a deer and drove off an embankment. The car rolled over and landed on its roof, trapping McKissick inside. When the paramedics arrived, they worked frantically, prying open the car door with a hydraulic spreader, cutting McKissick out of his Yves Saint Laurent suit, and rushing him to the Durham County General Hospital.

It was too late, a local radio station reported. McKissick was dead. Another great civil rights leader had perished, this one in a tragic accident three days shy of his fifty-seventh birthday.

Not until several hours later did listeners learn the truth: McKissick was alive, albeit in critical condition. His youngest daughter, Charmaine, was the first to see him. Living in Durham at the time, she received a call from her mother, then rushed to the hospital and found McKissick on his way into surgery. He looked as if he had been in an explosion, his head covered in bloody bandages, shards of glass embedded in his face, his collarbone, shoulder, and arm all fractured. But as soon as he opened his mouth, she knew he was going to be fine. "Doodlebug, they fucked up my suit," he joked, using his pet name for her. He told her to drive to the impound lot and retrieve his briefcase. Then, drawing her close, he instructed her to find his cowboy hat and run her fingers along the inside band. There, she would find ten one-hundred-dollar bills he always carried in case of emergency.

McKissick stayed in the hospital for several weeks, undergoing tests, working with a physical therapist, and gradually recovering his strength. After the first week, he was well enough to read some reports and take a few calls (including one from Ronald Reagan, who phoned to check on his condition). But he wasn't able to keep tabs on everything that was happening at Soul City. And the timing was terrible. The task force was busy gathering information from the staff at Soul City, and its early assessment of the situation was not encouraging. In April, Floyd Jr. attended an event with Secretary Harris at Harvard's Kennedy School of Government, where he was pursuing a master's degree in public administration. During the event, he sat next to Bill Wise, HUD's assistant secretary for public affairs, who ticked off a handful of reasons HUD was likely to shut the project down. For Floyd, it was an alarming conversation. He tried desperately to rebut what Wise said, then called his father to warn him. As he recalled later, "I remember leaving there and calling my dad up and telling him what I had heard and we needed to get this guy some good data, get him some good information because he obviously was headed in the wrong direction."

OVER THE FOLLOWING months, Soul City faced a barrage of new attacks from old enemies. It began in March, shortly after McKissick's accident, when the *Wall Street Journal* published an article under the headline "Mixed Fortunes: Black Leaders of the 1960s Have Come Out Better Than Segregationists." Its premise, as the headline implied, was that opponents of integration had fallen on hard times while the civil rights leaders they once tormented were prospering. As an example of the former, it cited former Arkansas governor Orval Faubus, who had once blocked Black students from entering Little Rock's Central High School but was now being treated for a heart condition in Houston. The article painted equally sad portraits of George Wallace (once a presidential candidate, now confined to a wheelchair after an assassination attempt); Lester Maddox (the former Georgia governor who had branded a pistol to keep Black people from eating at his fried chicken restaurant, now "subdued by a heart attack and seriously in debt"); and James Clark (the Alabama sheriff who led the attack at Selma, now facing a two-year prison sentence for smuggling a planeload of marijuana into the state).

If the article's depiction of the segregationists was oddly sympathetic, its portrait of former civil rights leaders was even stranger. Coretta Scott King, widowed at the age of forty, was portrayed as a wheeler-dealer who had raised $15 million for the Martin Luther King Jr. Center for Social Change in Atlanta. Andrew Young, a former King aide who was now ambassador to the United Nations, was said to be earning nearly fifty thousand dollars a year and living "in a lavishly decorated, four-bedroom apartment at the Waldorf Towers with a chauffeur at his beck and call." And Vernon Jordan, once a lowly law clerk making thirty-five dollars a week, was now head of the Urban League, reportedly earning a hundred thousand dollars in annual salary and corporate directorships.

As for McKissick, he was "another obviously affluent black" who had made money off his career as a civil rights leader. The article highlighted the millions of dollars Soul City had received in federal money and its failure "to lure sufficient blacks or industry" to rural North Carolina. "The founder, however, obviously is doing well, though he won't discuss his income," the article reported. "Mr. McKissick's wife and son also hold jobs at the project. All drive expensive automobiles. And they occupy a rambling house that a builder says couldn't be duplicated for $300,000."

It was the old narrative about uppity Blacks living above their station, and it apparently caught the attention of another reporter at the *Journal*, a staff writer named Susan Harrigan. Not long afterward, she traveled to Soul City to report on the town's progress. Harrigan spent five days on-site, touring the property, interviewing staff and residents, and reviewing numerous documents. In spite of their previous experiences with the *Journal*, the McKissicks welcomed her warmly—inviting her into their home, feeding her dinner, driving her to the airport—and after she left they felt certain that Harrigan, unlike the reporters before her, would give them a fair shake.

They were disappointed. Her article appeared on the front page under the headline "An Old 'New Town' Hangs On, Sustained by Federal Money." The title was unobjectionable, and much of the article was a straightforward account of the difficulties Soul City had encountered. It quoted McKissick on the red tape of the federal bureaucracy; Bignall Jones, the editor of the *Warren Record*, on the importance of Soul City to the local economy; and a businessman from nearby Henderson who wanted the Ku Klux Klan to burn Soul City down. And although Harrigan seemed determined to play up the town's lack of progress with cheeky comments about the cement foundation of the "unbuilt fire station" and the Pleasant Hills subdivision consisting only of "pleasant, empty hills," she did quote local resident Johnnie Johnson, who said, "Soul City is like a dream to me," and Henry Chew, who compared living in Soul City to being a "Forty-Niner" on the frontier.

But there was a subtext to the story, one alluded to in its subheading—"Floyd McKissick's Soul City Is Lacking People, Jobs; The Leader Lives in Style"—and developed more fully in the article itself. It was the same subtext that had run through the *News & Observer* series four years earlier: the entire enterprise of Soul City was a clever exercise in nepotism, conflicts of interest, and personal enrichment. Harrigan pointed out that McKissick controlled the company that owned the land in Soul City; that he drew a salary from that company but wouldn't say how much it was; that his wife ran the town's sanitary district and was part owner of Soul City's only store; that his son was planning director; and that the lake was named after his mother-in-law. Harrigan also implied that while the rest of Soul City was struggling, McKissick and his family were getting rich. "His wife drives the family Maserati," she wrote, "while he has a Pontiac Bonneville and his son operates a Mercedes-Benz." Her description of the McKissick home was equally insinuating. "There is a large cabinet containing silver and china in the living room. There is a big microwave oven in the kitchen and a tall stone fireplace in the sunken living room."

The facts were mostly correct. Evelyn did drive a Citroën SM (a Citroën body with a Maserati engine). And the family did have a microwave oven (as did about ten million other American households). But the implications were misleading at best and malicious at worst. Every private developer under the New Communities Act owned the land on which the towns were being built; the whole point of the law was to encourage private developers to build new cities with public support. Evelyn did run the sanitary district, and Floyd Jr. had taken over as planning director. But as had been pointed out repeatedly, Evelyn received no pay, and Floyd Jr. was amply qualified for his position. More to the point, it was unlikely his father could have found anyone else for the same salary. Finally, McKissick had secured millions of dollars of federal money, but much of that money benefited the surrounding area, not just Soul City. And it wasn't just the government that had invested in Soul City; McKissick had invested nearly all his own assets in the project, too.

McKissick was incensed by the article. In a long letter to the paper's editor, he argued that his lifestyle was irrelevant to the progress of Soul City. What difference did it make what kind of car his wife drove or what their house looked like, especially since they had lived in a mobile home for their first five years in Soul City? He also disputed the article's suggestion that Soul City was receiving special treatment from the federal government. "Almost every American city, hospital, large farm, railroad, and housing development is in one way or another sustained by federal money, as are many of our large and small businesses and corporations," McKissick wrote. Besides, Soul City was sustained by more than federal money. It was sustained by private capital, including $1.5 million invested by the partners of the Soul City Company. "It is sustained also by a belief that even poor Americans and black Americans are part of the system and should be afforded the opportunity to build and to live in nice houses and decent communities, and to make a profit."

Not satisfied with a letter, McKissick threatened a lawsuit. But as had happened five years earlier, when the *Journal* compared Soul City to the tribal village of Oyo Tungi, his lawyers talked him out of it, noting that a lawsuit would only "keep the thought of the original article alive in the minds of readers." So McKissick tried his best to put a positive spin on the article. In a letter to William White, he argued that the *Journal*'s attack was a form of flattery. "We must be doing something right or we would not merit the attention of the press," he wrote. He also attempted to use the article as leverage, urging White to approve construction of another industrial building. "The only real way to answer this kind of attack is to show concrete evidence of progress."

A few weeks later, the *News & Observer* piled on with a new series by Pat Stith, who had continued to file a steady stream of Freedom of

Information Act requests with HUD. The lead article reported that Soul City had met only 10 percent of its population, housing, and job goals and would need massive infusions of cash to survive. A second article declared that "Uncle Sam has treated Soul City like a favorite nephew, forgiving its shortcomings and sending more money." And a third article charged that McKissick and his wife had "found the good life at Soul City." Picking up where the *Journal* left off, it reported that McKissick's salary had increased from fifty thousand dollars to seventy thousand dollars over the past four years, that Floyd Jr. was earning twenty thousand dollars as planning director, and that Lew Myers was being paid twenty-one thousand dollars as director of corporate and institutional development.

Stith's articles prompted another blistering editorial in the paper, which argued that the "sad story of Soul City threatens to discredit all manner of social programs" and that "HUD has no sustained obligation to fulfill every wish of the hustling Floyd McKissick." Instead, the editors insisted, HUD had a duty to "take an open-eyed look at Soul City's dubious and pessimistic prospects and to turn off McKissick's money spigot." In case that image wasn't vivid enough, the paper ran a cartoon showing one HUD official pouring a sack of money out an open window while another official speaks into a phone: "Another couple-a-million? Sure, Mr. McKissick . . . It's on its way."

McKissick did not respond directly to the *N&O*, but he did hold a press conference at a hotel in nearby Rocky Mount to address the recent spate of news coverage. Wearing a white beret to cover the bald spot where he had recently received eighty stitches, he argued that Soul City had made substantial progress compared to the other towns supported by the New Communities Act. And it would have made even more progress if not for repeated attacks by the *N&O* and the state's congressional delegation. "I wonder, really, what we could have accomplished for the state of North Carolina . . . if I had had (their) ongoing assistance."

While McKissick battled the press, prominent supporters came to his defense. Daniel Pollitt, a distinguished law professor at UNC, wrote a letter to President Carter praising Soul City's efforts, while the editors of the *Carolina Times* encouraged Black people "to rally around the project." Both Pollitt and the *Carolina Times* had been allies of Soul City from the beginning, so their support was not surprising. More intriguing was an editorial by Bignall Jones in the *Warren Record*. In the ten years since McKissick announced his plans, Jones had come a long way, from skeptic to optimist to evangelist. He had glimpsed how Soul City could improve the fortunes of Warren County. He had also gotten to know the people building it. Just a few months earlier, he had attended his first cocktail party at Soul City and discovered it wasn't much different from any other party. "It looks to me like they hold a cocktail glass the same" as anybody else, he told a reporter. Now, Jones pushed back against the *N&O*'s attacks. In a column headlined "Without Soul City's Help," he recounted all the good things Soul City had brought to Warren County: the health care clinic, the regional water system, the funding for a new sewage treatment plant. He lavished particular praise on HealthCo, which not only provided affordable medical services to local residents but also helped secure government funding for the Warren County Health Department. And although HealthCo was financed by federal grants, "no one can believe that without Soul City's connections there would ever have been a HealthCo in Warren County and without it Warren County would be poorer." It was true that Soul City had "not met the dreams of its founders yet," Jones acknowledged. "But Soul City has meant a great deal to Warren County and we feel will mean more in the years to come."

Lew Myers sent a copy of Jones's column to Claude Sitton, requesting that he reprint it in the *N&O*. Sitton declined, explaining that the paper had already covered McKissick's press conference in Rocky Mount and that Jones's piece would not "add significantly to our readers' understanding of the Soul City situation."

The media wasn't McKissick's only problem. Seizing on the various news reports, Jesse Helms took to the floor of the Senate to once again condemn Soul City as a boondoggle that was contributing to the massive federal deficit. "Mr. President, how can such use of the taxpayers' money be justified?" Helms asked, returning to his familiar pretext of frugality. "It cannot." A few days later, in an interview with Stith, he declared his intention to cut off all federal funding for Soul City through an amendment to an appropriations bill for HUD. "I think it can be done," he said. "I think there will be some problems from a parliamentary standpoint, but I think I have found a way around it."

As the attacks on Soul City intensified, the staff attempted to hold things together. On May 4, Dot Waller wrote a memo urging McKissick to ignore the media and Helms, both of whom were clearly enemies. Instead, she urged him to attend to business at home. The Soul City office was a mess, she pointed out, and visitors weren't being welcomed properly. A week later, Carey fired off a series of memos complaining that the bike paths were not being maintained, that the pool was not ready for summer, and that at 8:35 a.m. on a recent morning only a few people were in the office.

McKissick continued to search for solutions. In March, he reached out to Coors Brewery, which was scouting for a new plant on the East Coast. In May, he suggested to HUD that Soul City be marketed as a retirement community until it could attract industry. And in mid-June, he and Myers traveled to New York to drum up interest in home sales. For two days, they camped out at the St. Regis Hotel in midtown Manhattan, meeting with hundreds of Black residents eager to move to the South. They spoke with Elaine Alexander, a retired factory worker from Georgia who was "tired of the noise, the crowds, and the fear of walking the streets or into your hallway." "I want to dig in the dirt again and go fishing when I feel like it," she said. They met with Irene Gregory, a medical technician who lived "in one of the best parts of Brooklyn" but was still "scared much of the time." And they talked to Ron Cornwall, a thirty-one-year-old lawyer who summed of his view of Soul City in four words: "The future is there."

Despite the enthusiasm, few people were willing to invest their savings in a development that was under review by HUD. And as the situation grew increasingly dire, McKissick began to run out of options. He reached out to Nigerian and Liberian officials about the possibility of establishing an African-American cultural and trade center in Soul City. He canceled disability insurance for himself and Carey, saving nearly three thousand dollars in annual premiums. Finally, he considered doing the one thing he had long refused to do. Talking with Carey in private one day, he raised the issue of the city's name. Maybe they should change the name after all, he said. Perhaps that would buy them time and goodwill with HUD. It was a sign of just how desperate he was. Never before had he been willing to compromise on this aspect of his dream. But now, like a man bargaining for his life, he offered the only thing he had left: his soul. Carey just shook his head. "It's too late," he responded. "It won't help."

Still, McKissick kept fighting. On June 5, he wrote to Senator Birch Bayh of Indiana. "We are involved in a difficult and massive economic development program in conjunction with a variety of governmental and private entities within our region," he wrote. "All we ask is a fair hearing and that we not be tried and convicted in the press." A few days later, he wrote to North Carolina's newest senator, Robert Morgan, and Representative L. H. Fountain with a similar request. And when the *Warren Record* published another editorial on June 7, praising Soul City as "a good neighbor," McKissick sent a copy to Helms and pleaded with him one last time to visit Soul City.

Dear Senator Helms:

I cordially invite you to visit Soul City in order that you might see what we have accomplished thus far and our objectives in the immediate future. I am sure you will agree that first-hand information is better than reliance upon press reports. I have also extended an invitation to Senator Morgan and Representative Fountain to visit us at the time of your visit.

  Much of the information you have about Soul City we believe to be distorted and I would welcome the opportunity to present additional facts for your information—facts which do not and cannot fit into a letter or form.

Enclosed for your information are two recent editorials from THE WARREN RECORD, along with news stories about a resolution by the Warren County Chamber of Commerce and Democratic Party supporting it.

Thanking you in advance for your cooperation.

Very Truly Yours,
F. B. McKissick Sr.

Helms did not respond to McKissick's letter. Nor did he ever visit Soul City. Soon there wouldn't be much left to see.

WHILE MCKISSICK WORKED frantically to rally support, the HUD task force went about its work, reviewing McKissick's five-year development plan and hiring Avco Community Developers, a California consultant with experience in new towns, to evaluate the project. At first, it looked as though Soul City might get another reprieve. In early April, McKissick met with the task force and laid out a four-step plan that included approval of the remaining $4 million in bonds, additional infrastructure grants, funding for two more industrial buildings, and a campaign to improve the town's public image. The task force was impressed; in late April it approved Soul City's 1979 budget and tentatively decided against foreclosure.

Then, on June 21, Avco submitted its report. Although Soul City was not yet broke—it still had $1 million in the bank, plus $4 million available in unissued bonds—the report concluded that it was no longer financially viable under any conceivable restructuring program. The authors pointed to a number of problems that had hindered the project's success: the economy, the location, the lack of amenities. But one problem stood out: the city's name. "The average prospective white buyer sees Soul City as having a negative connotation," the report stated. "He conceives of it as a community built by Blacks for

Blacks and is concerned that he would be living in an alien atmo-sphere."

The next day, the task force met again and reversed its earlier decision. Soul City was no longer a financially acceptable risk, it con-cluded, and thus not eligible for further assistance from HUD. Har-ris accepted the group's conclusion and directed White to develop a plan for acquiring Soul City, either by deed or through foreclosure proceedings.

Although McKissick had no warning of the decision, he had grown nervous when officials at HUD did not return his calls the previous week. "When you call the federal government, and you can't reach nobody, you know something's up," he said. Still, he was caught off guard when three members of the HUD task force walked into his office at 12:30 p.m. on June 28—seven years to the day since the loan guarantee had been announced. "We hate to tell you this, but we're here to tell you that we're withdrawing," one of the mem-bers said. With his quick temper and sharp tongue, one might have expected McKissick to erupt in anger and profanity. But he kept his cool, listening to the officials and then ushering them out the door. When they were gone, he called his staff together and broke the news. The mood was grim, recalled Dot Waller. "It was like someone had passed away, like the entire staff had died." For Floyd Jr., it was also awkward. A producer from *60 Minutes* was on-site working on a story about Soul City, and he spent the entire day showing her around without mentioning what had happened. It was a pointless deception; the producer would hear the news as soon as she turned on the television or read the paper the next day. Floyd wasn't even sure why he did it. Maybe it was because the news didn't seem real, and by not sharing it he could pretend for a few hours more that it wasn't.

Jane Groom was out of the office when the announcement was made, having driven to Henderson to run some errands and pick up lunch. As she drove back to Soul Tech I, she noticed how beautiful the day was, with white puffs of clouds in the sky and wild roses growing along the side of Soul City Boulevard. She parked her car in the lot and headed for the employee entrance. A familiar voice called out behind her. "Hey, Jane, wait up." It was Lew Myers, walking quickly, briefcase in hand, a grave expression on his face. "It's over," he told her. HUD was closing down the project. Construction would cease immediately, and they would all soon be out of work. Groom was speechless. "I just couldn't believe it," she recalled. "I was like, 'But why? We're just beginning.'"

The official announcement came later that day, at a press conference in Washington. Speaking to a room full of reporters, assistant secretary Bill Wise explained that HUD would pay off the $10 million in debt, then seek to negotiate a takeover of the land owned by the Soul City Company. Asked why the project had struggled, Wise did not blame McKissick. "The lesson is it is very tough to develop a new community from scratch and particularly in a rural, isolated area." William White, who joined Wise at the podium, agreed with that assessment. "This has been very difficult," White said. "The man put his life into it. But an analysis of our options showed clearly there was no way for the project to succeed." When reporters pressed him to say whether the project had been mismanaged, White demurred. "It's not a question of mismanagement. The area itself just didn't work out. There was not enough of a market to draw from."

As for what would happen next, White wasn't sure. "We're hoping to work out with McKissick a friendly foreclosure," he told reporters. "I don't know how he will react."

He soon found out. McKissick's initial response was muted. In a statement issued the day of HUD's announcement, he said only that he was surprised by the decision, given that Soul City was not in default. The next day, his tone changed. Interviewed for a front-page story in the Washington Post, McKissick blamed Soul City's lack of progress on HUD. "The way this was done, it's like cutting off a man's hand and then condemning him because he can't pick up anything." Asked whether he was going to accept HUD's decision, he was defiant. "No, I'm not going to give up on Soul City," he said. "I'm a fighter. I've just got to fight this."

McKissick's defiance inspired the rest of the staff. Initially resigned to Soul City's closure, they decided to fight, too. "It was really bad there for a while, and then we decided we wouldn't let it die," said Dot Waller. "We would just continue until we couldn't continue anymore."

20

"Sorrow's Kitchen"

And so began the last chapter in Soul City's history—an uphill battle to reverse HUD's decision and keep McKissick's dream alive. Known as the Save Soul City Campaign, it was coordinated by the North Carolina Black Leadership Caucus and supported by the Southern Christian Leadership Conference. Over the next few months, the campaign generated a flurry of activity, issuing reports and press releases, circulating a petition addressed to President Carter, and hosting a picnic at Soul City to raise money for the effort. The response was encouraging. More than fifteen hundred people from thirty states signed the petition, while a crowd of a hundred and fifty Black leaders trekked to Soul City for a day of swimming, tennis, and fishing.

Those who could not attend in person wrote to offer their support. In the months after HUD's decision, McKissick received hundreds of letters from ministers, journalists, educators, and activists. Rabbi William Feyer of Woodbridge, Virginia, noted that he was a CORE veteran who had attended the 1963 March on Washington and served as a poll watcher in Mississippi. "I now read that Soul City is being threatened with a cut-off of federal support," he wrote. "What can I do to help?" Malvin Russell Goode, a television reporter with the National Black Network in New York, explained that he had written to his local congressman and was ready to do whatever he could to "stem this tide." Some writers encouraged McKissick to keep the faith, while others offered ideas for the property. "Hang onto all the land: start an organic vegetable farm," advised Katherine Heaton Daye of Lexington, Kentucky. "There is going to be a greater market for food locally produced."

Numerous supporters also wrote to HUD and other federal officials on Soul City's behalf. One of them was Walter Sorg, who appealed directly to Helms. Sorg made clear that he had not initially been a fan of the new communities program, which he thought an unwise interference with market forces. But once the government invested millions of dollars in the program, he believed, it should support those towns that had a chance to succeed, including Soul City. "I personally have *no* doubts concerning the future value of the property known as Soul City," he told Helms. "Its strategic location in a state which is exploding industrially ordains that it will ultimately be a winner."

Sorg also expressed his views about why Soul City had struggled: "Industry was afraid to come in." And why was industry afraid? First: "Skepticism that the feds would not back their bet and thus leave them high and dry if they (the feds) pulled the plug." And second: "Uncertainty concerning John Q. Public's reaction to a company which so closely identified itself with a 'black operation.'" Industry's skepticism about the government's commitment had been proven right, Sorg argued. As for concerns about the public's reaction, he wasn't so sure. "It is my belief that a company with enough guts to take the plunge would have derived a substantial plus for itself, as well as making a statement on behalf of the corporate community."

"I am the last to find fault with your senatorial record," Sorg concluded. "You have been a consistent, articulate spokesman for a return to a set of principles which could result in getting Big Brother off our backs. For this you have my thanks and appreciation. But on the issue of Floyd McKissick and Soul City, I just can't support your logic."

Many people did, though. In a letter to the *N&O*, Eric Chandler of Raleigh argued that Soul City was doomed from the start because it perverted the normal process of urban development. Instead of building a town where people had already struck gold, he asserted, McKissick had built his town first in the hope that gold might one day be discovered there. And the "liberal social experimenters" in Washington had funded the whole thing. "The arrogance with which they spend the money forcibly taken from us is equalled only by their profound, almost unfathomable ignorance and by the insincerity of the mea culpas which follow the collapse of each and every one of their untenable schemes," Chandler wrote.

Two days later, Helms echoed that argument on the floor of the Senate. Troubled by news that McKissick was mounting a campaign to reverse HUD's decision, Helms introduced a provision forbidding the agency from providing additional money to Soul City. Noting that this was the eighth government-sponsored new town to go under, Helms argued that the entire program was a silly and wasteful enterprise. "Soul City and the other failures are dismissed by some observers as worthwhile dreams that simply never materialized," he declared. "It is high time, however, that the Congress of the United States realize that the hard-pressed American taxpayers are sick and tired of paying for foolish dreams." The last time Helms had introduced legislation targeting Soul City, Edward Brooke rose to its defense. But Brooke was no longer in the Senate. During his 1978 reelection campaign, it came out that he had lied about his finances during a bitter divorce from his wife of thirty-one years. That revelation led to a criminal investigation overseen by a young Massachusetts prosecutor named John Kerry. Although no charges were filed, Brooke's reputation was badly damaged, and he lost to Democrat Paul Tsongas. Thus, Helms's attack on Soul City went unchallenged, and the Senate approved his proposal by a voice vote.

Helms was not finished. In an interview with the *News & Observer* the same day, he returned to his earlier claims that Soul City was a fraud designed to line its developer's pockets. Asked whether he would support a settlement between HUD and McKissick, he responded skeptically. "If it's going to further enrich anybody down there, we'll have to see about that," he said. "I think McKissick and his family have profited enough from this venture."

Carey was livid. In a memo to McKissick, he declared that Helms's statements were "so racist, vindictive, irresponsible and untrue as to be beyond belief or comprehension." Given the personal nature of the attacks, he argued, McKissick should respond forcefully and should seek support from his allies in Congress. McKissick did just that. In a telegram to members of the Congressional Black Caucus, he described Helms's provision as "yet another unwarranted vindictive and personal attack upon me and the partners of the Soul City Company." Pointing out that Soul City was not currently in default, he urged the caucus to reject the provision when it came before the House. "The Senator is using his high office to deny me and other Black Americans due process, equal protection of laws and the right to be a successful entrepreneur in the free enterprise system."

AT THE SAME time McKissick was fending off Helms's attacks in Congress, he was attempting to negotiate with HUD. In July, he flew to Washington for discussions with the staff of the New Communities Administration. When he left, he was optimistic the two sides could reach a deal to keep Soul City alive. But the next day, HUD announced it was terminating several regional projects in Warren County, canceling all construction contracts for Soul City, and withdrawing nearly $1 million it had pledged for the new sewage treatment plant.

Believing he had been betrayed, McKissick turned to the only recourse left. On August 17, he filed a lawsuit in federal court in Washington, DC, alleging that HUD had breached its contract with Soul City by failing to provide adequate support, thwarting his efforts to build needed infrastructure, and refusing to release the final $4 million in bonds. The allegations were plausible enough that the court issued a temporary restraining order in McKissick's favor. The order blocked HUD from foreclosing on the property, terminating existing grants, or taking any steps that would deny essential services to the residents of Soul City or push the project into default.

Over the next few months, McKissick battled on, lobbying his supporters in Washington and preparing for his trial against HUD. But privately he wondered whether it was all futile—the lawsuit, Soul City, the civil rights movement itself. Responding to a letter from an old friend named David Stith (no relation to Pat Stith), he sounded weary. "Tell me, David. Do you think we have made very much progress? Do you think times have changed any? Sometimes I think it is only the personalities that change and nothing else."

While McKissick sought comfort from one old friend, he cut ties with another. Relations between him and Carey had been tense since the car accident in March. Some family members thought Carey, who had been in charge while McKissick was in the hospital, had not done enough to make a favorable impression on the task force, and they blamed him for the shutdown. McKissick had not shared that view with Carey, but he now made his displeasure known. On July 12, he sent Carey a notice of termination, effective in two weeks. Typed on company stationery and signed by McKissick, the letter was cold and impersonal. It conveyed regret at having to let Carey go, but noted that "the financial situation is out of our hands." It also thanked Carey for "a very good performance during your time here," and expressed confidence that he would find work elsewhere. "The Company approves your taking all the time off required during this interim to look for another job," the letter concluded. "If we can be of any assistance, please feel free to call."

Carey was not surprised by the decision. He knew McKissick could no longer afford to pay him, could no longer justify his presence on staff. Still, he was hurt that McKissick didn't break the news in person. They had been friends for nearly twenty years, ever since McKissick had bailed him out of jail during the sit-ins of 1960. They had fought one battle after another together, facing angry crowds and skeptical allies. And now their relationship was ending with a form letter. "I knew that Floyd could no longer have me on staff. He couldn't pay me. I knew that," Carey said later. "But it would have been nice if he'd walked in and been cordial."

As it turned out, that letter was not the worst part of the experience. Sometime later, McKissick sent Carey another letter, this one far more personal and hurtful. Carey did not save the second letter, and apart from calling it "nasty" and a "tirade" he is reluctant to describe it in detail. "My feelings were so mixed at that time (as were Floyd's) that I think it would be unreasonable to try to recreate much about the missing letter," he told me in an email. "Clearly he was angry, but it was then (and now) difficult to take his charges seriously. As I said earlier, his world and dreams were falling apart and he was having difficulty thinking analytically. In my response, as I recall, I did not answer him point by point but did say that I disagreed with the thrust of his letter."

In any event, Carey had little time to dwell on the pain. With five kids to support and his wife in her second year at Duke's law school, he had a more pressing problem: putting food on the table. He and Karen had built a house in Soul City, but there were no jobs for someone with his qualifications in Warren County. So he decided to start his own consulting company, advising on real estate developments. Carey spent the next year working on a project in Trinidad and Tobago while Karen finished law school. When she graduated, in 1981, she took a job at a law firm in Raleigh, and the couple sold their house to Charles Worth, a former Soul City staffer who had become the Warren County manager.

Carey had little contact with McKissick during his last two years in Soul City. Looking back later, he said he wasn't angry at his old friend. He simply felt that chapter of his life was over.

"I wasn't exactly happy, but I'm not one to get bitter," he said. "I saw it for what it was. I think we all just realized that that dream had ended and that we had to go on with our lives somehow."

THE LAST MONTHS of Soul City were not pretty. Despite his initial victory in court, McKissick held a losing hand. With his access to funds cut off, he lacked the resources for a protracted legal battle. HUD's lawyers knew as much and signaled their intention to litigate until McKissick ran out of money. Seeing the writing on the wall, he indicated a willingness to talk, and the two sides sat down to negotiate a settlement.

Yet even as he negotiated with HUD, McKissick continued his efforts to attract industry. And in January 1980, he finally caught a break. Perdue Foods agreed to buy five hundred acres in the Warren Industrial Park for a chicken hatchery and processing plant that would employ 1,200 people. Touting the deal as the spark that would finally lift Soul City off the ground, McKissick pleaded with HUD to reconsider its decision. But HUD had no interest in continuing to support Soul City, or any other new town. It was trying desperately to get out of the new-town business.

On May 16, the parties agreed to terms. McKissick would drop his lawsuit so that HUD could foreclose on the property. In exchange, the government would let McKissick and his partners keep eighty-eight acres of land, including the mobile home park and Soul Tech I, both of which were heavily mortgaged. HUD also agreed to pay the Soul City Company $167,000 to help satisfy outstanding debts. As for current residents, they would be permitted to stay in their homes, with management of the community reverting to a private home-owners' association.

The settlement left McKissick with little to show for eleven years of hard work and a personal investment of more than a half million dollars. "I was way out there on a limb," he told an interviewer later. "Everything that I owned was in hock one way or the other." Roy Gast, HUD's project manager for Soul City, backed up that assertion. "He was certainly taking it on the chin," Gast said. "A lot of developers in the same situation didn't put up the kind of money he put up, nor expose themselves to the risks he exposed himself to on behalf of the project. It was a percentage of what his worth was, and it was 100 percent. You can't ask for more than that."

Yet the *N&O* viewed the settlement as one more example of McKissick's ability to fleece the government for personal gain. In an editorial titled "No Taps for McKissick," it maintained that he had once again displayed "an uncanny knack for gaining advantage from the federal government." After all the money the government had lost on Soul City, the paper stated, the settlement was "not a bad ending for McKissick, whose project never came close to the goals he himself set and that formed the basis for federal sponsorship." The paper applauded HUD for finally ending its involvement with Soul City. But it showed little sympathy for McKissick, arguing that the project benefited him far more than the general public. "The government's settlement with McKissick seems so handsome," it concluded, "that there need be no taps or tears for the impresario of Soul City."

With the settlement finalized, McKissick began the painful process of closing up shop. There was no one left on staff, so he did most of the work himself, answering mail, taking out the garbage, cleaning up the office. Recalling this period later, he said he had never worked harder in his life. "I was the janitor, the bell-hop man, the trash-can man." And yet, unlike every other job he had held, there was no satisfaction in the work because it was designed to destroy, not create. "Taking something down is more difficult than beginning something," he observed. "Here you know that you aren't going to get paid anymore. You've got all your obligations and you lost twelve years of your life. And now it all goes down the drain."

Jane Groom felt the same. She spent long hours walking around the property "disgusted, sad, and angry." She tried to stay positive. When she recalled a line from Zora Neale Hurston—"I have been in Sorrow's kitchen and licked out all the pots"—she resisted the urge to give in to self-pity. But she couldn't escape the feeling that a verdict had been rendered and that the foreclosure of Soul City was like a death sentence. "In my head," she wrote, "it seemed the gavel had been slammed down, vibrating onto a cold, steel table."

ON JANUARY 29, 1981, Roy Gast climbed the steps of the Warren County Courthouse. It had been almost twelve years since McKissick mounted the same steps to take title to the Circle P Ranch. Now the ranch and other property he had acquired was on the auction block as part of a foreclosure sale, and Gast had come to bid on the government's behalf. He had been authorized to make an initial offer of $1.5 million and to increase it "in his sound discretion" up to $11.5 million. But there was no need to go beyond his opening bid. Aside from a small group of reporters, the courthouse steps were empty. And when the trustee opened the auction, Gast was the only bidder. His offer of $1.5 million was quickly accepted, and the federal government officially became the owner of Soul City.

Except Soul City no longer existed. Not long after the foreclosure sale, the Warren County Board of Commissioners requested that the state department of transportation remove the signs on I-85 and Route 1 that marked the exits for Soul City. The commissioners had once embraced Soul City, believing that McKissick's dream would revive the county's fortunes and help it reclaim some measure of its past glory. Now they were taking the first step in a process that would eventually wipe Soul City off the face of the map. As board chairman Walter J. Harris explained after some residents objected, "We felt there was no such place. It was just a name put on a tract of land."

Mixed Blessings

In January 1983, the latest director of the New Communities Administration, Warren T. Lindquist, made an announcement. After fifteen years and the expenditure of $570 million, HUD was terminating the program. It had not been a successful experiment. Of the thirteen new towns approved for loan guarantees, the government had foreclosed on nine and left three more on the verge of bankruptcy. The details of each failure varied, but the broad outlines were the same: inadequate funds, halfhearted support from HUD, overly optimistic projections, and an economic climate that made large-scale real estate development a losing proposition. The lone survivor was The Woodlands, an exurb of Houston that had been launched by the oil magnate George P. Mitchell and received a $50 million loan guarantee from the federal government, the most of any new town and four times more than Soul City. Today, The Woodlands is a thriving municipality of 120,000 people, 88 percent of them white. No one thinks of it as separatist.

Outside the HUD program, the new-towns movement fared better. In California, Irvine became the catalyst for staggering growth in Orange County, while on the East Coast, both Reston and Columbia realized their founders' visions. In some ways, Columbia has become a version of what McKissick hoped Soul City would be: a thriving, racially diverse city with well-planned neighborhoods, good jobs, and a strong sense of community. But although diverse, Columbia is not a predominantly Black city. It has also struggled to achieve economic integration, with many of its poorer residents relegated to villages near the city center. And, of course, Columbia differs from McKissick's dream in this crucial respect: it was the accomplishment not of Black men and women but of white.

ALTHOUGH THE FEDERAL government gave up on the new-towns concept, McKissick never did. After reaching his settlement with HUD, he continued to look for ways to salvage his dream. When Ronald Reagan was elected president in November 1980, McKissick briefly held out hope the new administration might revive the project. But McKissick no longer had the same connections in Washington he'd once had. His alliance with the Republican Party had frayed. And the party had changed. Once capacious enough to embrace liberals such as Nelson Rockefeller and Edward Brooke—politicians who believed in the power of government to improve people's lives—it had been taken over by Jesse Helms and other conservatives whose primary goal was to cut taxes, shrink government, and end welfare, and who made no real attempt to attract minority voters. Some civil rights icons, such as Ralph Abernathy, did support Reagan, but Abernathy was labeled a "modern Judas" and a "senile turncoat" by Black critics. McKissick, who had once felt such wrath himself, wasn't afraid of being called names. But he couldn't bring himself to support the Republican Party anymore, especially since it wasn't willing to support Soul City. So in the early 1980s, he switched his political affiliation again and rejoined the Democratic Party.

When McKissick's efforts to salvage Soul City faltered, he returned to his roots: practicing law. He rented a storefront office on Oxford's Main Street, across from a Hardee's fast-food restaurant. There, he took on the kind of unglamorous cases he had handled as a young lawyer: criminal defense, personal injury, and the occasional civil rights case. It was a steep fall for a man who had once marched arm in arm with Martin Luther King Jr., socialized with James Baldwin and Muhammad Ali, and shared a box at the Kennedy Center with Richard Nixon. But McKissick needed money, and, like many other civil rights figures, he discovered that there was no longer much demand for leading marches and planning protests.

McKissick also fulfilled a childhood vow: he became a preacher. It was the vocation he had planned to pursue before the back of a policeman's glove pushed him into law. But he had never entirely abandoned the calling. In some ways, his career as a civil rights leader had been a type of ministry. Instead of giving sermons and presiding at Sunday services, he had delivered speeches and organized demonstrations. Soul City itself had been something of a spiritual quest. Whether or not one believed McKissick had chosen the name for religious reasons, the project had an undeniably devotional feel to it.

What finally brought McKissick to the pulpit was his car accident in the spring of 1979. While waiting for the paramedics to pull him from the wreckage, he thought back over his life and recalled the promise he had made as a child. He also reflected on "the overwhelming power of God," in whose hands his life rested. The paramedics worked on his body, but McKissick's mind was elsewhere. "I was talking with God," he said. "I was conscious and I was aware that they were working to get me out of there. But I was talking with God. God told me to preach for him."

It didn't take long for McKissick to answer that call. In August 1979, while fighting with HUD over the future of Soul City, he delivered a trial sermon at Union Baptist Church in Durham. Titled "Should We Pay Taxes to Caesar, or Who Is Caesar Today?," the sermon built on an argument McKissick had been making for years: in order to change the system, one must work within it. His audience, which included Durham's Black elite, answered enthusiastically with shouts of "Amen," "All right," "Go ahead and preach," and "Tell it like it is." Encouraged by their response, McKissick enrolled in divinity school at Shaw University in Raleigh, and when he completed his studies he began preaching at the First Baptist Church of Soul City.

Those who saw McKissick during the 1980s describe him as weary and diminished. He was too proud to complain about his situation, too dignified to ask for help. But his confidence was shaken. "He was never quite the same after that," recalled Bob Brown. "He lost a lot of his fire."

Not all of it, though. In 1982, McKissick roused himself to lead one more protest against the forces of discrimination and oppression. The state of North Carolina had announced plans to dump soil contaminated with cancer-causing PCBs in Shocco, an African American township in Warren County. Officials made the decision without consulting the community, and local residents believed they were being discriminated against because of their race. So they fought back, with McKissick leading the way. As trucks loaded with toxic waste rumbled down the road, protesters lay on the pavement, blocking their path. More than thirty demonstrators were arrested, including the sixty-year-old McKissick. Dressed in a suit and employing the tactics of nonviolent resistance he had helped pioneer, he let his body go limp as highway patrolmen carried him to a waiting bus and charged him with impeding traffic. It was the last of many times in his life he went to jail for the sake of the cause.

Five years later, in an oral history interview, McKissick again showed flashes of his old passion and commitment. Asked whether he was ready to give up on Soul City and move elsewhere, he responded defiantly. "I will never leave, period, because I believe in the concept. I see it taking root, and the new-town concept is a valid concept notwithstanding what anyone says."

Two years after that, he gave his last speech, a graduation address at his alma mater, North Carolina Central's law school. Like most of his speeches, a copy of this one was stored in a cardboard box in his garage in Soul City. More than twenty years later, his daughter Charmaine began the process of organizing the papers. As she went through the box, she noticed a curious thing. McKissick's final speech bore the same title as the first one he had given, almost four decades earlier: "Am I My Brother's Keeper?" Many years had passed, and much had changed, both in the country and in McKissick's life. Yet he was still asking the same question he had asked as a young man and still arriving at the same answer. "Yes," he concluded. "I am my brother's keeper."

But McKissick's time was running short. His lifelong cigarette habit had taken its toll. For several years, his throat had been raw, his voice rough. He ignored it for as long as he could, sucking on lemons to soothe the pain. Eventually he could ignore it no longer. In 1989, he went to a doctor and received the diagnosis he knew was coming: lung cancer.

A few months later, McKissick was appointed to the North Carolina District Court by the state's newest Republican governor, James G. Martin. He was the first Black judge to serve in the Ninth Judicial District, a four-county area encompassing Warren County. The appointment was a kind of redemption for McKissick, who had faded from the public eye, and it energized him. He had once believed that the most effective route to social justice ran through the law, and as a young civil rights leader he had placed much of his hope for change in the power of the Supreme Court. But he believed even more in the power of trial courts. These were the courts poor people were most likely to find themselves in, since they rarely had the money to appeal to a higher tribunal. "If America is to save itself, it must do so through a legal system that is designed to aid Black Men and poor men and represent their interests," he had written in Three-Fifths of a Man. "Unbiased legalism is the way to mediate between men. We need dedicated social engineers to point the way."

McKissick was not able to fulfill that role himself. By the time of his appointment, his health was failing, and when he took his seat on the bench for the first time, he did so with the aid of an oxygen tank. His tenure on the court was short-lived. He heard his last case in early 1991, and on April 28, only ten months after taking his seat, he died at his Soul City home. His final days were difficult. He struggled to breathe and came to loathe the taste of Ensure, the only nourishment he could consume. But there was a certain peace to his death. It came one evening after dinner. He sat in his favorite chair in front of a large picture window. Outside, he could see the rolling hills, the fields and forests he had fallen in love with more than two decades earlier. They were still there, waiting to be developed, waiting for his dream to become reality. Charmaine watched from across the room. "He took a deep breath, and that was it."

McKissick's death was widely reported. The *New York Times* described him as a "civil rights maverick," while the *Washington Post* quoted Jesse Jackson's assessment that McKissick was "one of the giants of the civil rights struggle." He was buried in Soul City, near the entrance to his home. The funeral, which was held at Union Baptist Church in Durham, was presided over by Benjamin Chavis, now the most prominent civil rights leader in the state. There were tributes from James Farmer, Jesse Jackson, and Bob Brown. Shirley Caesar sang. Selections were read from the Book of Isaiah and 2 Timothy. Printed inside the program was the poem "Invictus" by the nineteenth-century British writer William Ernest Henley. A tribute to stoicism in the face of suffering, the poem is best known for the line "My head is bloody, but unbowed." But for those mourning McKissick, the last stanza was most poignant:

> It matters not how strait the gate
> How charged with punishments the scroll
> I am the Master of My Fate
> I am the Captain of My Soul.

AMONG THE MOURNERS at McKissick's funeral was Gordon Carey. After leaving Soul City, Carey had gradually put his life back together, working first as a consultant, then starting his own software development company. In the 1980s, he and Karen had moved from Raleigh to Winston-Salem, where she became a partner at a prominent law firm. Carey was happy and content, raising five children from two marriages. But he missed his old friend. When I asked him, years later, whether he had seen McKissick in the years before his death, he looked away and grew distant, as though he were lost. "No, I didn't," he finally said. "I didn't really." During my many interviews with Carey, he was forthcoming about nearly every aspect of his life. He relished talking about Soul City and was proud of his involvement with it. He had always wanted to live an interesting life, he told me, and felt he had done so. But whenever I asked about his falling-out with McKissick, he became evasive, as though it was one of the most painful memories of his life—too painful to regard with his usual detachment. I noticed something else during the course of our many interactions. When I first communicated with Carey by email, in 2014, the quote beneath his signature line read, "Enjoy life—it is too short to be taken seriously!" It was typical of Carey, who is quick to find humor in even the most difficult circumstances. But at some point during our conversations, he replaced that quote with a more somber one. His emails now ended with William Faulkner's famous line about the timeless nature of history: "The past is never dead. It's not even past."

Carey wasn't the only one deeply affected by his time at Soul City. Although the town never became the engine for economic growth McKissick envisioned, it did provide training for Black professionals, many of whom went on to distinguished careers. One of the most prominent was Eva Clayton, who in 1992 was elected to the US House of Representatives, becoming the first African American to represent North Carolina since Reconstruction. Clayton served five terms in the House, providing crucial leadership on the problems facing rural America. After declining to run for reelection in 2002, she was appointed assistant director-general of the Food and Agriculture Organization, a division of the United Nations dedicated to ending hunger around the world.

Floyd Jr. also entered politics, serving in the North Carolina Senate for thirteen years. As chairman of the legislative Black caucus, he was a strong voice for voting rights, health care, and criminal justice reform. He moved away from Soul City decades ago but remains proud of the work he did there and shares his father's sense of hope and idealism. On the wall of his Durham office hangs a quote that would have fit in perfectly at McKissick Enterprises: "Never laugh at anyone's dream. People who don't dream don't have much."

Probably the most famous alumnus of Soul City is Harvey Gantt, the young architect who created the master plan for the town. In 1983, he became the first Black mayor of Charlotte, serving consecutive two-year terms. Smart and charismatic, Gantt was considered a rising star in the Democratic Party, someone who might one day run for national office. So in 1990, the party nominated him for a seat in the United States Senate. His opponent in the general election: Jesse Helms.

Since the fall of Soul City, Helms's profile had only increased. He was a key player in Ronald Reagan's 1980 presidential victory and had established himself as a leader of the modern Republican Party. In fact, it is fair to say that Helms, with his focus on deregulation and his cultural conservatism, paved the way for Reaganism, which in turn gave rise to the Tea Party and the Freedom Caucus. Throughout the 1980s, Helms had also burnished his foreign policy credentials, taking hard-line positions on communism and nuclear deterrence. And he had reaffirmed his hostility to minority interests, leading a sixteen-day filibuster in opposition to the creation of Martin Luther King Day. His rise had not gone unchallenged. In the 1984 campaign, he battled Democrat James Hunt, a popular former governor, a race Helms won by a slim four-point margin. Now he faced another tough test against Gantt, a dynamic African American who had run the state's largest city.

Having been on opposite sides of the Soul City battle, the two men found themselves locked in a vicious contest. It was one of the most expensive campaigns in Senate history and was watched closely for its national implications. Many observers thought a Gantt victory might signal a weakening of the Republican stranglehold on the South, and for a while it looked as though he might win, with polls showing a race too tight to call. But in the last weeks of the campaign, Helms returned to the kind of race-baiting he had employed on behalf of Willis Smith in 1950. In one ad, he suggested that Gantt had gotten rich at taxpayer expense while working as a planner at Soul City. Another ad showed the hands of a white man crumpling a rejection letter while a narrator explained that the job he applied for had been given to a less qualified minority. "Is that really fair?" the narrator asked. "Harvey Gantt says it is." The ads were blatant appeals to racial resentment. And they worked. When the results came in, Helms won, 53 percent to 47 percent. Six years later, the two men squared off once more, and again Helms prevailed, 54 percent to 46 percent.

After that campaign, Gantt retired from politics and returned to his architectural practice in Charlotte. But he continued to think about what makes a city vibrant and successful. And every so often, while driving his car or working at his desk, he would think back to his days in Soul City and marvel at the boldness of McKissick's vision. "How audacious was that?" Gantt reflected when I interviewed him in his downtown office. "To think that we could build a city in rural America, in the heart of one of the poorest sections of North Carolina, that we could attract people who were previously farmers and domestic workers and bring in factories and the kinds of jobs that would pay decent wages and see a lifting of their quality of life and economic circumstances . . . There are a lot of days I've sat and wondered, 'Why did I think that was going to succeed?'"

But Gantt believes Soul City could have succeeded, if not for the timidity of industry, the foot-dragging of HUD, the opposition of Helms and the *News & Observer*, and the economic downturn of the 1970s. "There was an opportunity there. There really was an opportunity. He just needed some more help, and not just federal government help. He needed some more risk-taking developers." And if Soul City had succeeded, what would it have meant? Gantt paused to consider. It might have changed the history of race relations over the past half century, he said, expanding the country's focus beyond civil rights to the even more challenging issue of economic equality. "Had it been successful and we'd seen Black capitalism really at work in a thriving, growing entity, not just somebody who's a great

entertainer, a great athlete, but a group of people who were instrumental in developing a really viable city that attracted both Blacks
and whites, I think it would have done wonders for the psyche of
Black Americans and Americans in general, and that model would
have been replicated in other counties across the country."

While Gantt retired from politics, Helms served another term in
the Senate, continuing to push far-right policies. He helped to tighten
trade sanctions against Cuba, railed against federal funding for controversial art, and opposed government spending on AIDS research
(a position he later reversed). He also added to his reputation for cru-
elty and bigotry. Finding himself in an elevator one day with Carol
Moseley Braun, the first African American woman elected to the Senate, Helms told his white colleague Orrin Hatch, "Watch me make
her cry" before whistling "Dixie." He held up the confirmation of a
HUD official because, as he put it, "she's a damn lesbian." And when
Bill Clinton advocated that gays be allowed to serve openly in the
military, Helms warned that if the president visited North Carolina
he "better have a bodyguard."

For all that—and for everything he did to destroy Soul City—it's
easy to view Helms as a villain who deserves only contempt. But
McKissick had a different view. Asked about Helms after the federal
government pulled the plug on Soul City, McKissick was philosophical. "No one can afford the luxury of hating any man," he responded.
"I never did hate Senator Helms, who was made in the image of God.
He makes me look around and think: study the devious devices of
people. So thank God for Senator Helms."

AT THE *NEWS & Observer*, Claude Sitton and Pat Stith continued
their efforts to uncover government waste and misconduct. And
their work finally received the recognition some thought they
deserved. In 1983, Sitton won the Pulitzer Prize for Commentary
for his weekly column. Among the articles included in his submission was one blasting the "Dixie demagoguery" of Jesse Helms.
Thirteen years later, after Sitton had retired, Stith was part of a

team that won the Pulitzer Prize for Public Service for a series on the environmental damage caused by North Carolina's massive hog industry. I was a staff writer at the *N&O* at the time and knew Stith, although not well. To a young reporter still learning the ropes of daily journalism, he was a gruff and distant figure. But he was deeply respected in the newsroom, and the Pulitzer was seen as a long-overdue reward for a lifetime of hard work. By the time he retired, in 2008, he had become a legend among investigative reporters. According to the 2016 book *Democracy's Detectives*, Stith's reporting was responsible for the resignation of eighteen public officials, the firing or demotion of another nineteen, and the indictment of six. His work also led to the passage of thirty-one laws in North Carolina, the hiring of forty-six officials, and the transfer of millions of dollars. One story alone led to the recovery of $2.4 million when twelve thousand state workers were forced to repay the state because of an accounting error.

When I interviewed Stith for this book, he defended his work on Soul City. Although he acknowledged that his stories weren't as clear as they could have been, he said he had done the best he could in light of the constraints he was operating under. "I did an honest job," he said. "Could it have been better? Well, yeah, you give me another shot at any story I ever did, I'll do better if I get a second shot at it. Can't you do better on a second shot? That's a given. But did I write a basically error-free story? Basically. And I say basically because I'm allowing for some errors somewhere, I just don't know what they are. Yes, I did. Did somebody lay it all out for me? I guarantee you they did not. It was hunt and peck and find this and that and the other little scrap of a lead and go over and find that contract and whatever."

When I suggested that there are errors of commission and errors of omission, Stith agreed. "I really think it's possible to write a story . . . that contains no error but the story itself is untrue," he said. But he dismissed the idea that his stories fit that description. He also said he was not bothered by the attacks on him for his stories about Soul City. "People could say anything to me, I didn't care. They could say,

'You work for a rag' or 'Your work's no good.' It's like pouring water on a duck's back. I didn't care."

AND THEN THERE is Soul City.

In the mid-1980s, a sportswear manufacturer moved a cut-and-sew operation into Soul Tech I, and the community's population increased to around three hundred. But if McKissick feared that another developer would swoop in and capitalize on the groundwork he had laid for Soul City, he needn't have worried. Many of the same obstacles he confronted in the 1970s—a lack of jobs and skilled workers, a mediocre school system, rural isolation—also thwarted later developers. In 1989, a group of investors bought a hundred acres of former Soul City land with the intention of building an industrial park that would provide 1,300 jobs and 85 single-family homes. But like McKissick, they were unable to attract industry, and the project never got off the ground.

Thus, for many years nothing much happened in Soul City. And then, something did. In 1994, the state of North Carolina announced plans to build a medium-security prison in Warren County, on land that had once belonged to Soul City. The prison would be located just off Soul City Boulevard and would house up to six hundred inmates. It wasn't exactly what Soul City residents had hoped for, and many protested. Others were resigned. After all, a prison would provide jobs, which were still sorely needed in Warren County. So after overcoming limited resistance, the state moved forward with its plan, and in 1997, the Warren Correctional Institution opened for business.

The real blow came several years later. By this point, the sportswear company had closed its operation, and Soul Tech I sat vacant. This gave prison officials an idea. The building, which was just down the road from the prison, was ideal for a small manufacturing plant. And the state had been expanding its prison factories in an effort to raise revenue and provide work for inmates. So officials purchased Soul Tech I and converted it into a factory making janitorial supplies.

Now in operation for well over a decade, the Correction Enterprises Janitorial Products Plant has been a resounding success. I toured the plant in October 2015 with Karen Brown, the director of Correction Enterprises, and Forest Fesperman, the plant manager. They greeted me in a small cinder-block building just outside a barbed-wire fence, then led me through an interior courtyard shaded by trees. On the other side of the yard, we entered a reception area furnished with round Formica tables, black office chairs, and a wooden bookshelf displaying the products made inside—disinfectant, laundry detergent, tile and grout cleaner, and bars of soap imprinted with the Correction Enterprises logo: the figure of a person holding a star over the words "Not Just Making It Right. Making It Better."

Inside the plant, Fesperman showed me the equipment and explained how it worked. The inmates worked steadily, if not briskly, bottling detergent, cutting bars of soap, bagging powder. The majority were Black, but about a quarter were white—roughly the same racial makeup as the Soul City staff. They watched us indifferently, though one older prisoner did approach and tell me his story: how he had

Inmates working at the prison factory that used to be Soul Tech I.

been framed for murder and spent six years on death row before having his sentence reduced to life in prison. Fesperman listened quietly, with the expression of a man who has heard it all before. A textile chemist by training, he worked as a salesman for several years before helping to open the plant. He's proud of the operation, and for good reason. It's well run and gives inmates a sense of purpose. It also generates about $6.5 million in yearly revenue for the state. Of all the things that have come out of Soul City, Correction Enterprises may be the most successful.

But for those who remember what Soul Tech I once was and what it represented, the plant is like a wound. Even today, McKissick's daughter Charmaine can't bring herself to drive by it. In 2007, three years after her mother died, she moved into her parents' house with her husband, Tyrone Melton. Both work in Durham (she as a professor of communications at North Carolina Central University, he as a director for the North Carolina Association of Educators) and make the hour-long drive several times a week. But Charmaine never enters Soul City through the main entrance, which would take her past the plant. Instead, she takes a longer route that winds past fields planted with soybeans. And when she gives directions to visitors, she sends them along the back route, too.

Not that the rest of Soul City is much to look at. The maintenance of Green Duke Village is managed by the Soul City Parks and Recreation Association, which is funded by homeowners' dues. As more and more residents moved away during the 1980s and '90s, there was less money to maintain the streets, the bike paths, the manor house, and the pool. The situation eventually became so dire that Warren County agreed to assume control of the Magnolia Ernest Recreation Complex. Local officials paid for needed repairs and opened it up to the entire county. The complex is now in good shape. On summer days, the water in the pool is blue and the nets on the tennis court are intact. But the rest of Soul City is slowly crumbling. The streets have not been repaved in decades, the manor house is in desperate need of repair, and only a handful of streetlights work. What once looked like a scene out of the movie Brigadoon now resembles a ghost town. The Soul City monolith has been repeatedly defaced with spray paint, and a vandal once fired two bullets into the middle of the "o." In the mid-2000s, a woman bought the property on which the monolith stood and announced her intention to destroy it. Sickened at the thought, Jane Groom and other residents pleaded with county officials to do something. Their pleas were heard: Warren County paid to move the monolith to the entrance of Green Duke, where it still stands.

One of the most demoralizing developments was the closure of HealthCo. Even after the federal government foreclosed on Soul City, HealthCo continued to operate for three decades, serving Warren, Vance, and surrounding counties. For many poor residents, it was the only viable form of health care, since transportation was free and costs were subsidized by the government. At one point, it had seven full-time doctors and two dentists, as well as a large staff of nurses and technicians. But in 2009, it was shut down amid an inquiry into mismanagement of funds. Once HealthCo closed, it seemed as if the last remaining part of Soul City had died.

ABOUT TWO HUNDRED people live in Soul City today. Many arrived after the federal government foreclosed in 1980 and know little about the community's history, but there are still a handful of early residents. On a summer afternoon I meet with two of them—Jane Ball-Groom (as she is known now) and her cousin Voyette Perkins-Brown—along with a newer resident, Ihsan Abdin, in the multipurpose room of the Scott Mitchell Apartments. An affordable housing complex built in the late 1980s, Scott Mitchell consists of six one-story buildings huddled near the entrance to Green Duke Village. Most of the residents are elderly or disabled, and the multipurpose room resembles a nursing-home lounge, with linoleum floor, folding tables covered with plastic tablecloths, and a large television set.

We are joined by Ihsan's four-year-old grandson, who sits quietly as we talk. At one point, Voyette reaches into her purse, and I hear a rattling sound that I assume to be a bottle of pills. Instead, she pulls out a Tic Tac container and offers it to the child. He takes a few and sucks on them for a while, then lays his head on the table, puts his fingers in his mouth, and sleeps soundly while we talk for an hour and a half.

Voyette tells me about moving to Soul City in 1974, after she and her husband divorced. She had been living in Yuma, Arizona, and when the movers arrived with her furniture, they looked around at the trailer park, then looked at her. "The truck driver said to me, 'Ma'am, I have been in the moving business for twenty years and I have never interfered in a decision, but I have a question. You left Yuma and moved yourself and your son here. May I ask why?'" Voyette recalls. "And I asked myself that for the next ten years."

But she grew to love Soul City. A medical technologist by training, she got a job counseling migrant workers in Henderson. And with the help of a Federal Housing Administration loan, she purchased a home in Green Duke Village, where she still lives. "For me, the dream has been fulfilled. I came here and I raised my son. I have a home— peace, contentment—that's what everyone's looking for."

Ihsan came to Soul City in 1989, long after the government fore- closed. She knows some of its history, but not all, and she asks Jane to describe what Soul City was supposed to be like. Jane describes the villages, each with its own activity center and schools, the parks, the theaters, the stores. "It was going to be a beautiful place to live."

After our conversation, I drive around Green Duke Village again. I have been here several times since my first trip and know it well, but I still make new discoveries on each visit. Today, I notice how the loop road rises and falls as it curves around the subdivision, like a slow-speed roller coaster. I also notice a cluster of red, yellow, and pink flowers growing beneath the Green Duke Village sign.

When I drive past the recreation complex, I see that it is open, so I park the car on the street and walk past the basketball courts, where a group of five children, all Black, are playing a game of pickup. At the pool, a middle-aged white man sits in the lifeguard chair under a royal-blue umbrella. Seated near him on the edge of the pool is a white teenager in a hot-pink bikini. They are listening to a portable

ANDREW MOORE

Ihsan Abdin tends the grass at the base of the Soul City monolith.

radio, which is playing "Small Town," John Mellencamp's valentine to rural America. Nodding to the lifeguard, I continue down the sloping field toward the lake. As on my first trip, it is still overgrown and littered with trash, but it is easy to imagine how beautiful it must have looked when completed in 1977. There is a rumble overhead. I look up and see the white traces of an airplane streaking across the clear blue sky. Had history turned out differently, I think, that plane might have landed here, in Soul City, bringing executives, bankers, tourists, and prospective residents. Instead of a ghost town, Soul City might now be the booming city Bob Brown, James Holshouser, and many others once predicted it would become. And instead of writing about a lost dream, I might be documenting another great American success story, this one conceived and built by Floyd Bixler McKissick, no longer a Black boy in a white land but just a man, at home in his own country.

Because at bottom, I believe, that's what McKissick wanted. Soul City, the March Against Fear, the sit-ins, the Journey of Reconciliation—each battle he fought was a response to a particular injustice and followed a particular logic. But all sprang from the same motivation and the same desire: to reverse the hierarchy of identity he had become aware of on the trolley all those years ago. Not Black first and American second, but *American* first, so that to live in a town named Soul City, to drive down a street named Liberation Road, to work in an industrial park named after A. Philip Randolph would be viewed not as separatist or defeatist or some "sociological sport," but would be, in McKissick's words, "just as American as apple pie."

I return to the car and drive around a while longer. On my first trip to Soul City, I felt a pit in my stomach brought on by a mixture of sadness and pity. Now, as I leave Green Duke Village, passing the manor house and the monolith, I feel something different. The sadness is still there, but the pity has been replaced by admiration for McKissick and all who followed him to Soul City. I want better for them, but I don't feel sorry for them. I feel sorry for those who lack the vision and courage they displayed in taking a chance, in pursuing their dream and refusing to accept falling short as a sign of failure.

I remember something Jane Ball-Groom said to me on that earlier trip. She had invited me into her home and offered me a bologna-and-cheese sandwich. Sitting in her colorful living room, painted mauve and decorated with books and paintings, I listened to her reminisce about all that had happened since that winter day in 1970 when she and her husband piled their five children into a compact car and drove ten hours to arrive in the middle of the night. She spoke with affection and pride about her role in building Soul City. "It's not a mansion on the hill by a river," she said. "But it's a far cry from the projects. To me, it was a blessing."

NOTES

PROLOGUE: "COMES THE COLORED HOUR"

1   **"I can just see 'ole massa' now":** James T. Wooten, "Integrated City Rising on an Old Plantation," *New York Times*, July 25, 1972, 21.

2   **lacked indoor toilets:** US Bureau of the Census, 1970 Census of Housing, Housing Characteristics for States, Cities, and Counties, vol. 1, North Carolina, part 35, "Structural, Plumbing, Equipment, and Financial Characteristics for Counties: 1970," Table 60, issued August 1972, http://www2.census.gov/prod2/decennial/documents/38148036v1p35.zip.

2   **lacked a high school diploma:** US Bureau of the Census, 1970 Census of the Population, vol. 1, Characteristics of the Population, North Carolina, part 35, "Educational and Family Characteristics for Counties: 1970," Table 120, issued March 1973, http://www2.census.gov/prod2/decennial/documents/1970a_nc.zip; Hank Burchard, "'Soul City' Stirs Its Future Neighbors," *Washington Post*, January 26, 1969, 35.

3   **"a Camelot built on racism":** "McKissick's Camelot," *Roxboro Courier-Times* (Roxboro, NC), reprinted in *Warren Record* (Warrenton, NC), February 6, 1969, 2.

3   **"liberation through violent revolution":** Floyd B. McKissick, *Three-Fifths of a Man* (New York: Macmillan, 1969), 47.

3   **"go get some bread":** McKissick Enterprises, "Floyd B. McKissick Announces a New Program for Economic Development," press release, October 3, 1968, McKissick Papers, folder 5135; Floyd B.

McKissick interview with Robert Wright, October 16, 1968, 22, Bunche Collection.

4   **under surveillance by the FBI:** Jack Anderson, "Black Activists Are FBI Targets," *Washington Post*, May 16, 1972, B15.

5   **stop "sucking the sugar tit":** Floyd B. McKissick, "The Theory of the Sugar Tit," speech delivered June 10, 1972, personal papers of Charmaine McKissick-Melton, copy on file with author.

5   **double his share from 1968:** Ronald Taylor, "2,500 Blacks Meet to Plan Ways to Re-elect President," *Washington Post*, June 11, 1972, A2.

5   **"cancer of hectic urbanization":** "'Soul City': A Vital Experiment," editorial, *Washington Post*, July 6, 1972, A16.

5   **"practical as well as imaginative concept":** "A Not Impossible Dream," editorial, *New York Times*, July 8, 1972, 24.

5   **"best thing that has happened to Warren County":** Caption on the back of a photograph of Henderson city manager Melvin Holmes, McKissick Papers, folder P-4930/9.

6   **"into a booming American city":** "Soul City Praised on Anniversary," *News & Observer* (Raleigh, NC), July 22, 1972.

6   **"what 'ole massa' would have to say now":** Wooten, "Integrated City," 21.

10   **about fifteen cents an hour:** Karen Brown, director of Corrections Enterprises, interview with the author, October 15, 2015.

10   **Soul City was not ... "a City upon a Hill":** Chris Jennings, *Paradise Now: The Story of American Utopianism* (New York: Random House, 2016), 6, 138.

10   **Nor was Soul City ... become "a Negro Paradise":** Janet Sharp Hermann, *The Pursuit of a Dream* (New York: Oxford University Press, 1981), 46; Norman L. Crockett, *The Black Towns* (Lawrence: Regents Press of Kansas, 1979); Katherine Franke, *Repair: Redeeming the Promise of Abolition* (Chicago: Haymarket Books, 2019); Sundiata Keita Cha-Jua, *America's First Black Town: Brooklyn, Illinois, 1830–1915* (Chicago: University of Illinois Press, 2002); Carter G. Woodson, *A Century of Negro Migration* (Washington, DC: Association for the Study of Negro Life and History, 1918).

11   **These camps were broken up ... remained in Nicodemus at all:** Crockett, *Black Towns*; Kenneth Marvin Hamilton, *Black Towns and Profit: Promotion and Development in the Trans-Appalachian West, 1877–1915* (Urbana: University of Illinois Press, 1991); Hannibal Johnson, *Acres of Aspiration: The All-Black Towns in Oklahoma* (Austin, TX: Eakin Press, 2007); Nell Irvin Painter, *Exodusters: Black Migration to Kansas after Reconstruction* (New York: W.W. Norton, 1986); Morris Turner, *America's Black Towns and Settlements: A Historical Reference Guide* (Rohnert Park, CA: Missing Pages Production, 1998); Woodson, *Century of Negro Migration*.

11   It wasn't long . . . thirty or so Black towns: Crockett, *Black Towns*; Hamilton, *Black Towns and Profit*; Johnson, *Acres of Aspiration*; Woodson, *Century of Negro Migration*.

12   a tenth of the territory's population: Crockett, *Black Towns*, 98.

12   "a showpiece of democracy in a sea of hypocrisy": "Architectural Firm Chosen for 'Soul City' in Carolina," *New York Times*, January 19, 1969, 76.

12   But while many utopian . . . work in perfect harmony: Jennings, *Paradise Now*, 7–8.

12   "turn on, tune in, and drop out": Robert Greenfield, *Timothy Leary: A Biography* (Orlando, FL: Harcourt, 2006), 281.

13   One young man . . . office of the city planner: Glenn Powell, Soul City resident, interview with the author, March 6, 2015.

13   "stealing panties and bras": "McKissick Backs Separatist Movement," *Durham Morning Herald*, March 9, 1969.

14   The founders of Mound Bayou . . . liniments and powders: Crockett, *Black Towns*, 131, 144.

14   It inspired Paul Cuffee's attempt . . . $400 billion in cash: John Hope Franklin and Alfred A. Moss Jr., *From Slavery to Freedom: A History of African Americans*, 8th ed. (Boston: McGraw Hill, 2000), 111, 188, 395–96; Peniel E. Joseph, *Waiting 'Til the Midnight Hour: A Narrative History of Black Power in America* (New York: Henry Holt, 2006), 54–55, 219, 278; ". . . We Also Want Four Hundred Billion Dollars Back Pay," *Esquire*, January 1, 1969, 72.

14   "Oh, tis a pretty country": Johnson, *Acres of Aspiration*, 80.

15   sardonic poem "Cultural Exchange": Langston Hughes, *The Panther & the Lash* (New York: Alfred A. Knopf, 1967), 82–83.

15   "the role the white man played for centuries": John Oliver Killens, *Black Man's Burden* (New York: Trident, 1965), 116.

15   "welcome white people as equals": Paul Jablow, "Soul City Has to Start with the Spirit Itself," *Charlotte Observer*, March 30, 1969.

18   "only if white folks want it to come into being": "Students March Down Franklin in 3rd Annual Cates Memorial," *Chapel Hill Newspaper*, November 20, 1973, 1.

19   In the half century since McKissick . . . one-tenth that of whites: Valerie Wilson, "Black Unemployment Is at Least Twice as High as White Unemployment at the National Level and in 14 States and the District of Columbia," Economic Policy Institute, April 4, 2019, https://www.epi.org/publication/valerie-figures-state-unemployment-by-race/; Kriston McIntosh, Emily Moss, Ryan Nunn, and Jay Shambaugh, "Examining the Black-White Wealth Gap," Brookings Institution, February 27, 2020, https://www.brookings.edu/blog/up-front/2020/02/27/examining-the-black-white-wealth-gap/; Ta-Nehisi Coates, "The Case for Reparations," *Atlantic*, June 2014.

19   **By 2014, Ferguson's population . . . a force of fifty-three:** Matt Pearce,
          Maya Srikrishnan, and David Zucchino, "Protesters and Police Face
          Off in St. Louis Suburb Over Shooting," *Los Angeles Times*, August
          11, 2014, https://www.latimes.com/nation/nationnow/la-na-missouri
          -st-louis-police-shooting-teen-20140811-story.html.

20   **an article or thesis on Soul City:** The most extensive accounts of Soul
          City can be found in Herman Mixon Jr., *Soul City: The Initial Stages,
          the Genesis and First Two Years of the Soul City Project, with Ques-
          tions for the Future* (Chapel Hill: Center for Urban and Regional
          Studies, University of North Carolina, 1971); Foon Rhee, "Visions,
          Illusions, and Perceptions: The Story of Soul City" (thesis in fulfill-
          ment of Honors in History, Duke University, 1984); Emily Webster
          Madison, "Objections Sustained: The Conception and Demise of Soul
          City, North Carolina" (essay submitted for Honors in History, Uni-
          versity of North Carolina at Chapel Hill, April 1995); Biles, "The Rise
          and Fall of Soul City: Planning, Politics, and Race in Recent America,"
          Journal of Planning History 4, no. 1 (February 2005): 52–72; Timo-
          thy J. Minchin, "'A Brand New Shining City': Floyd B. McKissick Sr.
          and the Struggle to Build Soul City, North Carolina," *North Caro-
          lina Historical Review* 82, no. 2 (April 2005): 125–55; Christopher
          Strain, "Soul City, North Carolina: Black Power, Utopia, and the Afri-
          can American Dream," *Journal of African American History* 89, no.
          1 (Winter 2004): 57–74; Devin Fergus, *Liberalism, Black Power, and
          the Making of American Politics, 1965–1980* (Athens: University of
          Georgia Press, 2009); and Zachary Gillan, "Black Is Beautiful But So
          Is Green: Capitalism, Black Power, and Politics in Floyd McKissick's
          Soul City," in *The New Black History: Revisiting the Second Recon-
          struction*, edited by Manning Marable and Elizabeth Kai Hinton
          (New York: Palgrave Macmillan, 2011), 267–86. Soul City has also
          been chronicled in one self-published memoir: Jane Ball-Groom, *The
          Salad Pickers: Journey South* (Morrisville, NC: Lulu, 2012). And it
          was the subject of a short 2016 documentary, *Soul City*, directed by
          Monica Berra, SheRea DelSoul, and Gini Richards. Shorter accounts
          of Soul City include Amanda Shapiro, "Welcome to Soul City: Explor-
          ing the Remains of a Black Power Utopia," *Oxford American* 80
          (Spring 2013); and Roman Mars, "Soul City," April 5, 2016, an epi-
          sode of the podcast *99% Invisible*, produced by Katie Mingle, https://
          99percentinvisible.org/episode/soul-city/.

1: "BLACK BOY IN A WHITE LAND"

24   **the most tumultuous of the century:** Peter B. Levy, *The Great Upris-
          ing: Race Riots in Urban America during the 1960s* (Cambridge, UK:
          Cambridge University Press, 2018), 9.

24   **every American a guaranteed income:** Ben A. Franklin, "'City' of the Poor Begun in Capital," *New York Times*, May 14, 1968, 1; Sylvie Laurent, *King and the Other America: The Poor People's Campaign and the Quest for Racial Equality* (Oakland: University of California Press, 2018).

24   **improve relations between Black people and the police:** Peter Kihss, "A March on Capital by Whites Proposed by Whitney Young," *New York Times*, April 24, 1968, 1; Paul Hofmann, "NAACP Drives Against Violence," *New York Times*, April 9, 1968, 37.

24   **a merger with the revolutionary Black Panthers:** Claybourne Carson, *In Struggle: SNCC and the Black Awakening of the 1960s* (Cambridge: Harvard University Press, 1995), 279–90.

24   **For eight days, the city's Black neighborhoods . . . $12 million in property damage:** Peter B. Levy, "The Dream Deferred: The Assassination of Martin Luther King Jr., and the Holy Week Uprisings of 1968," in *Baltimore '68: Riots and Rebirth in an American City*, ed. Jessica Elfenbein, Elizabeth Nix, and Thomas Hollowak (Philadelphia: Temple University Press, 2011), 3–25.

25   **Titled "A Nation Within a Nation" . . . the Poor People's Campaign:** "A Nation Within a Nation: CORE's Proposal for Economic Development and Control of Black Areas," McKissick Papers, folder 6970.

26   **"what I'm willing to risk my life for":** Rhee, "Visions, Illusions, and Perceptions," 22.

26   **The council's reaction was tepid . . . building of new cities:** Rhee, "Visions, Illusions, and Perceptions," 22–24.

27   **his thirteen-year-old son had been shot dead:** "Mayor Attends Funeral for Son of Roy Innis," *New York Times*, April 19, 1968, 42.

27   **he knew he would have to leave:** Rhee, "Visions, Illusions, and Perceptions," 24.

27   **until a new leader could be found:** Rudy Johnson, "McKissick Resigns as Head of CORE," *New York Times*, June 26, 1968, 33.

28   **why couldn't Black people build new cities:** McKissick interview with Jack Bass, December 6, 1973, Southern Oral History Program Collection, University of North Carolina at Chapel Hill, 9–10; Harold Woodard, "Floyd McKissick: Portrait of a Leader" (master's thesis, University of North Carolina at Chapel Hill, 1981), 22; Mixon, *Soul City*, 13; Rhee, "Visions, Illusions, and Perceptions," 5.

28   **"Black, first. American, second":** McKissick, unfinished autobiography, personal papers of Charmaine McKissick-Melton, copy on file with author.

28   **"Aw, aw! Ah'm colored!":** Zora Neale Hurston, *Their Eyes Were Watching God* (New York: Harper Perennial Modern Classics, 2013), 9.

28   **It happened in 1926 . . . "more bad white people than there are good":** Woodard, "Floyd McKissick," 12–13; McKissick, unfinished autobiography; Ernest and Magnolia McKissick interview with Louis

Silveri, August 2, 1977, Southern Highlands Research Center Oral History Collection, University of North Carolina at Asheville, 20–22.

29   **"two unreconciled strivings":** W. E. B. Du Bois, *The Souls of Black Folk* (Chicago: A.C. McClurg & Co., 1907), 9.

30   **Childhood was not all harsh lessons . . . insulting one another's mothers:** Woodard, "Floyd McKissick," 2–3, 7-12; McKissick, unfinished autobiography; McKissick, autobiography transcripts, January 13, 1986, personal papers of Charmaine McKissick-Melton, copy on file with author; Ernest and Magnolia McKissick interview with Louis Silveri, 19–20.

30   **Within this world . . . fish to make sandwiches:** Woodard, "Floyd McKissick," 3–5; McKissick, autobiography transcripts, 13; "Assignment in Asheville," Memorandum from Jane Groom to FM, August 23, 1973.

30   **although the mountainous terrain . . . response to emancipation subdued:** John C. Inscoe, *Mountain Masters: Slavery and the Sectional Crisis in Western North Carolina* (Knoxville: University of Tennessee Press: 1996), 59–86, 211–58.

31   **backyard neighbors were white:** McKissick transcripts, 12; Ernest and Magnolia McKissick interview with Louis Silveri, 23–24.

31   **Still, race was a defining fact . . . finish in first place:** Woodard, "Floyd McKissick," 13–14; McKissick, outline for autobiography, personal papers of Charmaine McKissick-Melton, copy on file with author.

31   **If these insults made clear . . . protest the decision before the city council:** Woodard, "Floyd McKissick," 14–17; McKissick, unfinished autobiography; McKissick interview with Robert Wright, 1–2.

33   **McKissick left Asheville . . . received a Purple Heart:** Woodard, "Floyd McKissick," 18–23.

34   **But the experience that affected . . . built by Blacks was next to zero:** McKissick interview with Jack Bass; Woodard, "Floyd McKissick," 22; Mixon, *Soul City*, 13; Rhee, "Visions, Illusions, and Perceptions," 5.

34   **by that point McKissick was married . . . the 1948 presidential election:** Woodard, "Floyd McKissick," 21–25; McKissick interview with Robert Wright, 9.

34   **He also got his first taste . . . more famous bus rides fourteen years later:** August Meier and Elliot Rudwick, *CORE: A Study in the Civil Rights Movement, 1942–1968* (Urbana: University of Illinois Press, 1975), 33–39; McKissick interview with Robert Wright, 8.

35   **After finishing at Morehouse . . . ruled in the plaintiffs' favor:** Woodard, "Floyd McKissick," 26–29; McKissick interview with Bruce Kalk, May 31, 1989, Documenting the American South, University of North Carolina at Chapel Hill, 3–4; Biographical sketch, Floyd McKissick, April 1967, Papers of the Congress of Racial Equality, Reel 5.

35   **"It's integrated now"**: McKissick interview with Bruce Kalk, 5–7; McKissick interview with Robert Wright, 6–7.

36   **For the children ... with his back to the door**: Rhee, "Visions, Illusions, and Perceptions," 4; Charmaine McKissick-Melton, interview with the author, July 18, 2016; Floyd McKissick Jr., interview with the author, October 12, 2015; "McKissick Led Way in Civil Rights," *Herald-Sun* (Durham, NC), undated clipping from Daniel H. Pollitt Papers, folder 131.

2: SCRAMBLED EGG

37   **The Montgomery bus boycott ... over the next decade**: Taylor Branch, *Parting the Waters: America in the King Years, 1954–1963* (New York: Simon & Schuster, 1988), 143–205, 271–75; William H. Chafe, *Civilities and Civil Rights: Greensboro, North Carolina, and the Black Struggle for Freedom* (New York: Oxford University Press, 1981); Tomiko Brown-Nagin, *Courage to Dissent: Atlanta and the Long History of the Civil Rights Movement* (New York: Oxford University Press, 2011), 133–41; Aldon D. Morris, *The Origins of the Civil Rights Movement: Black Communities Organizing for Change* (New York: The Free Press, 1986), 40–76.

37   **youth director for the North Carolina chapter of the NAACP**: Woodard, "Floyd McKissick," 30; Chris D. Howard, "Keep Your Eyes on the Prize: The Black Struggle for Civic Equality in Durham, North Carolina, 1954–63" (undergraduate honors thesis, Duke University, 1983), 47–53.

38   **Founded in Chicago in 1942 ... boost CORE's national profile**: Meier and Rudwick, *CORE*, 1–98; Nishani Frazier, *Harambee City: The Congress of Racial Equality in Cleveland and the Rise of Black Power Populism* (Fayetteville: University of Arkansas Press, 2017), 3–25, 53–58; Brian Purnell, *Fighting Jim Crow in the County of Kings: The Congress of Racial Equality in Brooklyn* (Lexington: University Press of Kentucky, 2013), 31–36.

38   **He found it the first week ... at the center of the action**: Meier and Rudwick, *CORE*, 101–12; Morris, *Origins*, 198–200; Purnell, *Fighting Jim Crow*, 36–40; Gordon Carey, interview with the author, August 21, 2015.

39   **The organization took off ... catchier name: the Freedom Rides**: Meier and Rudwick, *CORE*, 113–36; Carey interview, *Eyes on the Prize I* interviews, Washington University Digital Gateway, November 6, 1985.

40   **Launched that spring ... to appear in court**: Meier and Rudwick, *CORE*, 137–58; Branch, *Parting the Waters*, 452, 557–58.

40   **McKissick had long worked ... backed McKissick for the post:** Meier
      and Rudwick, *CORE*, 282–94; transcript of McKissick interview
      with Eugene E. Pfaff, Greensboro Voices/Greensboro Public Library
      Oral History Project, August 9, 1982, 1–6, http://libcdm1.uncg.edu
      /cdm/ref/collection/CivilRights/id/863; Howard, "Keep Your Eyes,"
      62–65.

40   **The next few years ... under an earthen dam:** Meier and Rudwick,
      CORE, 145–149, 170–71, 213–328; William L. Van Deburg, *New
      Day in Babylon: The Black Power Movement and American Culture,
      1965–1975* (Chicago: University of Chicago Press, 1993), 133; Tay-
      lor Branch, *Pillar of Fire: America in the King Years, 1963–65* (New
      York: Simon & Schuster, 1998), 440–41.

41   **Despite its growing influence ... commitment to nonviolence:** Manning
      Marable, *Race, Reform, and Rebellion: The Second Reconstruction
      in Black America, 1945–2006,* 3rd ed. (Jackson: University Press of
      Mississippi, 2007), 84; Meier and Rudwick, *CORE*, 294–373.

41   **"partnership of brothers":** Roy Reed, "The Deacons, Too, Ride By
      Night," *New York Times*, August 15, 1965, SM10; Lance Hill, *The
      Deacons for Defense: Armed Resistance and the Civil Rights Move-
      ment* (Chapel Hill: University of North Carolina Press, 2004), 133–49.

41   **These conflicts took their toll ... twelve votes to eight:** Meier and
      Rudwick, *CORE*, 374–408.

41   **When McKissick took over ... of Baltimore and Cleveland:** Meier
      and Rudwick, *CORE*, 409–13; Van Deburg, *New Day in Babylon*,
      132–33.

42   **McKissick also became increasingly outspoken ... "the civil rights
      movement":** Aram Goudsouzian, *Down to the Crossroads: Civil
      Rights, Black Power, and the Meredith March Against Fear* (New
      York: Farrar, Straus and Giroux, 2014), 3–5; David J. Garrow, *Bear-
      ing the Cross: Martin Luther King, Jr. and the Southern Christian
      Leadership Conference* (London: Jonathan Cape, 1988), 473; McKis-
      sick interview with Robert Wright, 34–35.

43   **Black Power ... Africa's Gold Coast:** Goudsouzian, *Down to the
      Crossroads*, 142; Joseph, *Waiting 'Til the Midnight Hour*, 1–131;
      McKissick interview with Robert Wright, 24–28.

43   **"like a goddamn rabbit":** Goudsouzian, *Down to the Crossroads*, 47.

43   **McKissick knew Meredith well ... blessing for their plan:** Goudsouz-
      ian, *Down to the Crossroads*, 27–30; McKissick interview with Rob-
      ert Wright, 31–34.

44   **The three men resumed ... allowed to participate:** Goudsouzian,
      Down to the Crossroads, 31–102; Garrow, *Bearing the Cross*, 473–
      79; Joseph, *Waiting 'Til the Midnight Hour*, 133–40; Taylor Branch,
      At Canaan's Edge: America in the King Years, 1963–68 (New York:

Simon & Schuster, 2006), 476–77; Hill, *Deacons for Defense*, 245–50; McKissick interview with James A. DeVinney, *Eyes on the Prize II* interviews, Washington University Digital Gateway, October 21, 1988, 2–3.

44   "civil rights carnival show": Nicholas von Hoffman, "Mississippi Marchers to Cut West into Delta," *Washington Post*, June 13, 1966, A1.

45   "you gotta come!": Goudsouzian, *Down to the Crossroads*, 66.

45   "movement of the *spirit*": Goudsouzian, *Down to the Crossroads*, 104.

45   referred to as "de lawd": Marable, *Race, Reform, and Rebellion*, 68.

45   willing to get his hands dirty: Goudsouzian, *Down to the Crossroads*, 102.

45   He walked nearly . . . "everyone under the march's banner": Goudsouzian, *Down to the Crossroads*, 102, 103; Renata Adler, *After the Tall Timber* (New York: New York Review Books, 2015), 88–89.

46   allies responding with "Black Power": Goudsouzian, *Down to the Crossroads*, 143; Garrow, *Bearing the Cross*, 482–84.

46   Events soon pushed . . . "something shifted inside Floyd McKissick": Goudsouzian, *Down to the Crossroads*, 198–202; Garrow, *Bearing the Cross*, 485–87.

47   "get us some *black* power": Adler, *After the Tall Timber*, 88–89.

47   "That man thinks you don't bleed": Goudsouzian, *Down to the Crossroads*, 203–6.

47   most vocal advocates: Tom Adam Davies, *Mainstreaming Black Power* (Oakland: University of California Press, 2017), 137.

47   declared the civil rights movement "dead": United Press International, "Kennedy Clashes with CORE Chief," *New York Times*, December 9, 1966, 1; "The Civil Rights Movement Is Dead," undated manuscript, Papers of the Congress of Racial Equality, Reel 5.

47   nonviolence had "outlived its usefulness": Meier and Rudwick, *CORE*, 414; Branch, *At Canaan's Edge*, 519; Thomas J. Sugrue, *Sweet Land of Liberty: The Forgotten Struggle for Civil Rights in the North* (New York: Random House, 2009), 340.

47   "when black men realized their full worth": Marable, *Race, Reform, and Rebellion*, 94–95.

47   "louder than SNCC": Joseph, *Waiting 'Til the Midnight Hour*, 145.

48   "new Killers of the Dream": Meier and Rudwick, *CORE*, 417.

3: "LOOK OUT, WHITEY!"

49   "two little bitty words": Floyd McKissick, interview by Edwin Newman, *Meet the Press*, August 21, 1966, transcript available in NBC online archives, https://archives.nbclearn.com/portal/site/k-12/flatview?cuecard=48789.

50   the mobilization of Black consumers: "McKissick Asserts 'Shock' Is Necessary to Gain Negro Goal," *New York Times*, October 2, 1966, 69; Woodard, "Floyd McKissick," 32–33; Mixon, *Soul City*, 7.

50   "the fear of not having enough to eat": McKissick, *Three-Fifths of a Man*, 42.

50   indispensable to white companies: Booker T. Washington, *Up from Slavery* (New York: Doubleday, 1901), 60–61, 85–88, 107; Franklin and Moss, *From Slavery to Freedom*, 299–306.

50   "spend a dollar in an opera house": Washington, *Up from Slavery*, 218–25.

50   shop exclusively at Black businesses: Manning Marable, *W. E. B. Du Bois: Black Radical Democrat* (London: Routledge, 2016), 134–35; Manning Marable, *How Capitalism Underdeveloped Black America: Problems in Race, Political Economy, and Society* (Chicago: Haymarket Books, 2015), 129.

51   race massacre in 1921: Alfred L. Brophy, *Reconstructing the Dreamland: The Tulsa Riot of 1921, Race, Reparations, and Reconciliation* (New York: Oxford University Press, 2002); Tim Madigan, *The Burning: Massacre, Destruction, and the Tulsa Race Riot of 1921* (New York: Thomas Dunne Books, 2001).

51   banning discrimination in all war contracts: Rhonda Jones, "A. Philip Randolph, Early Pioneer: The Brotherhood of Sleeping Car Porters, National Negro Congress, and the March on Washington Movement," in *The Economic Civil Rights Movement: African Americans and the Struggle for Economic Power*, ed. Michael Ezra (New York: Routledge, 2013), 9–21.

51   "starvation wages or no wages at all": Michael Ezra, "Introduction: The Economic Dimensions of the Black Freedom Struggle," in *The Economic Civil Rights Movement: African Americans and the Struggle for Economic Power*, ed. Michael Ezra (New York: Routledge, 2013), 2.

51   leverage that economics gave them . . . "buy black" campaigns: Ezra, "Introduction," 1; J. Michael Butler, "Economic Civil Rights Activism in Pensacola, Florida," in *The Economic Civil Rights Movement: African Americans and the Struggle for Economic Power*, ed. Michael Ezra (New York: Routledge, 2013), 95–99; Meier and Rudwick, *CORE*, 170–71.

51   the bread to buy a burger?: Ned Cline, "Soul City Founder Is Mixing His Politics," *Greensboro Daily News*, August 24, 1972; McKissick interview with Robert Wright, 22.

51   for Black families it was $5,400: US Bureau of the Census and US Bureau of Labor Statistics, *The Social and Economic Status of Negroes in the United States, 1969* (Report P23-29), February 1970, vii, 22,

https://www2.census.gov/library/publications/1970/demographics/p23-029.pdf.

51   **double that of whites:** Franklin and Moss, *From Slavery to Freedom*, 545.

51   **"families are crowded into rat-infested slums":** Floyd McKissick, "A Nation Within a Nation," *New York Amsterdam News*, June 1, 1968, 15.

52   **still attended segregated schools:** Gary Orfield, "Public School Desegregation in the United States: 1968–1980," Joint Center for Political Studies, Washington, DC 1983, 4.

52   **From the perspective . . . strike by Black sanitation workers:** Laurent, *King and the Other America*; Goudsouzian, *Down to the Crossroads*, 256–58; Branch, *At Canaan's Edge*, 683–722; Timothy J. Minchin, *From Rights to Economics: The Ongoing Struggle for Black Equality in the U.S. South* (Gainesville: University Press of Florida, 2007), 11.

52   **But no Black leader . . . "black capitalism":** McKissick interview with Robert Wright, 11–13; McKissick, *Three-Fifths of a Man*.

52   **He preferred "black entrepreneurialism":** "McKissick Says Blacks Should Control Harlem," *New York Amsterdam News*, July 5, 1969, 10.

52   **whatever the label . . . leading proponent of Black capitalism:** Joshua D. Farrington, "'Build, Baby, Build': Conservative Black Nationalists, Free Enterprise, and the Nixon Administration," in *The Right Side of the Sixties: Reexamining Conservatism's Decade of Transformation*, edited by Laura Jane Gifford and Daniel K. Williams (New York: Palgrave Macmillan, 2012), 63–64; "Black Capitalism—What Is It?" *U.S. News & World Report*, September 30, 1968, 64; George Rood, "Franchising Called New Answer for Negro," *New York Times*, July 5, 1968, 36.

52   **Meanwhile, Black businesses . . . operated by a Black man:** Ibram H. Rogers, "Acquiring 'A Piece of the Action': The Rise and Fall of the Black Capitalism Movement," in *The Economic Civil Rights Movement: African Americans and the Struggle for Economic Power*, edited by Michael Ezra (New York: Routledge, 2013), 176; Robert E. Weems, *Business in Black and White: American Presidents and Black Entrepreneurs in the Twentieth Century* (New York: New York University Press, 2009), 79–89; Frazier, *Harambee City*, 191; Stephanie Dyer, "Progress Plaza: Leon Sullivan, Zion Investment Associates, and Black Power in a Philadelphia Shopping Center," in *The Economic Civil Rights Movement: African Americans and the Struggle for Economic Power*, edited by Michael Ezra (New York: Routledge, 2013), 137–53; Leon H. Sullivan, *Build, Brother, Build: From Poverty to Economic Power* (Philadelphia: Macrae Smith, 1969), 170–75.

53   **key to solving the urban crisis:** Weems, *Business in Black and White*, 122; Rogers, "Acquiring 'A Piece of the Action,'" 174.

53   **"virtue of attainability":** Rowland Evans and Robert Novak, "CORE's Reply to Poor People's March Offers Hope for Peaceful Solution," *Washington Post*, May 8, 1968, A17.

53   **"that often misapplied term":** Weems, *Business in Black and White*, 115; Davies, *Mainstreaming Black Power*, 83–84.

53   **accused Nixon of cribbing from CORE's press releases:** "Nixon Using CORE Material Charged," *Chicago Daily Defender*, July 2, 1968, 6; "Black Power and Private Enterprise," *Wall Street Journal*, May 21, 1968, 16.

53   **The meeting took place ... large margins in both houses:** Weems, *Business in Black and White*, 116; Farrington, "Build, Baby, Build," 65–66.

54   **not all Black leaders were on board:** Davies, *Mainstreaming Black Power*, 85–86.

54   **"a cruel hoax":** Andrew Brimmer, "The Trouble with Black Capitalism," *Nation's Business*, May 1969, 78; Weems, *Business in Black and White*, 147–50.

54   **called Black capitalism "simple nonsense":** Roy Wilkins, untitled contribution to "Symposium on Black Capitalism," *Bankers Magazine*, Spring 1969, 13.

54   **"the transfer of the oppressive apparatus":** Robert Allen as quoted in Weems, *Business in Black and White*, 152.

54   **acknowledged the historical racism of capitalism:** McKissick, *Three-Fifths of a Man*, 28; McKissick interview with Robert Wright, 12–13.

54   **But he believed ... "Black People can gain power":** Floyd McKissick, "Black Capitalism," *New York Amsterdam News*, December 21, 1968, 7.

55   **all commercial real estate on 125th Street:** Rogers, "Acquiring 'A Piece of the Action,'" 174.

55   **retaliation by white banks and businessmen:** "Memorandum from FM to North Carolina Leadership Conference on Economic Development," CORE Archives Addendum, Reel 6, undated; "What Is CORE Doing Now," undated memo, Papers of the Congress of Racial Equality, Reel 5; Rhee, "Visions, Illusions, and Perceptions," 6–8, 32.

55   **"new environment fit for men":** "Presentation by FM to Executive Reorganization Subcommittee of the Government Operations Committee," Papers of the Congress of Racial Equality, Reel 5, December 8, 1966, 10.

55   **"to be owned and controlled by Black People":** "A Black Manifesto," CORE Archives Addendum, Reel 5, July 31, 1967.

55   **"a black community from the ground up":** Val Adams, "Black Community Planned by CORE," *New York Times*, September 6, 1967, 38.

55   leave of absence to study the matter: Rhee, "Visions, Illusions, and Perceptions," 13.

55   CORE was in no position . . . describing its membership: Meier and Rudwick, *CORE*, 418–23; Frazier, *Harambee City*, 153–59.

56   "the direction that CORE is going": Earl Caldwell, "CORE Eliminates 'Multiracial' in Describing Its Membership," *New York Times*, July 6, 1967, 1.

56   in support of boycotting the Olympics: Frank Litsky, "Negro Olympic Boycott Group Demands Brundage Resign," *New York Times*, December 15, 1967, 69; Garrow, *Bearing the Cross*, 589.

56   "over the institutions in their own communities": Floyd McKissick, "Black Self-Determination," *New York Amsterdam News*, February 17, 1968, 4.

56   establishment of a separate school board: Floyd McKissick, "Harlem's Own School Board," *New York Amsterdam News*, March 30, 1968, 15.

56   And on April 4 . . . 3M stock to CORE's Cleveland chapter: Jerry M. Flint, "CORE Bids Business Set Up Plants for Negroes," *New York Times*, April 5, 1968, 22; Wilfred Ussery interview with the author, January 4, 2017.

57   "tolerate this killing of their males": "McKissick Says Nonviolence Has Become Dead Philosophy," *New York Times*, April 5, 1968, 26; "Did He Give Life in Vain," *Chicago Daily Defender*, April 8, 1968, 26.

57   "should be torn to bits by black people": Clay Risen, *A Nation on Fire: America in the Wake of the King Assassination* (Hoboken: John Wiley & Sons, 2009), 56.

57   refused to attend a meeting of civil rights leaders: Jean M. White, "McKissick Refused to Meet LBJ," *Washington Post*, April 11, 1968, A7; Risen, *Nation on Fire*, 90–91.

58   "Now that the drum major is gone": Claude Sitton, "After King, the Search Is On for a New 'Drum Major,'" *New York Times*, April 14, 1968, E2.

58   last two pieces of Great Society legislation: Nick Kotz, *Judgment Days: Lyndon Baines Johnson, Martin Luther King Jr., and the Laws That Changed America* (Boston: Houghton Mifflin Company, 2005), 388–421; Wendell E. Pritchett, *Robert Clifton Weaver and the American City: The Life and Times of an Urban Reformer* (Chicago: University of Chicago Press, 2008), 311–24.

59   the fractured civil rights community: Earl Caldwell, "Wilkins, in Talk to CORE, Seeks to Close Negro Rift," *New York Times*, July 6, 1968, 1.

59   "people who beg on moral grounds": "Young Calls for 'Open Society,'" *New York Amsterdam News*, July 13, 1968, 1; Jean M. White, "Militancy Voiced by Urban League," *Washington Post*, July 7, 1968, A1.

59   **"white people happy if I leave"**: Robert Horan, "CORE to Analyze Political Parties," *Columbus Evening Dispatch*, July 5, 1968, 1.

59   **the convention went downhill . . . electing a national director**: Earl Caldwell, "CORE Dissenters Quit Convention," *New York Times*, July 8, 1968, 1; "Internal Strife, Power Struggle Plague CORE Convention's End," *Columbus Dispatch*, July 8, 1968, 6B; "2 Rebel CORE Chapters Here Form a New Group," *New York Times*, July 9, 1968, 23.

59   **Two months later . . . separation as its goal**: Frazier, *Harambee City*, 208–9.

59   **"a Black Nationalist Organization"**: Meier and Rudwick, *CORE*, 424; Jean M. White, "CORE Turns the Corner to Black Nationalism," *Washington Post*, July 8, 1968, A1.

4: DREAMS INTO REALITY

61   **or run for a seat in Congress**: "Candidates for Powell's House Seat Still Lacking," *Chicago Daily Defender*, March 11, 1968, 19.

61   **he started his own business**: Clayton Willis, "McKissick Moves in New Direction," *New York Amsterdam News*, October 5, 1968, 1.

61   **With a fifty-thousand-dollar loan . . . "all its trimmings"**: "Floyd B. McKissick Announces a New Program for Economic Development," Press Release, October 3, 1968, McKissick Papers, folder 5135.

62   **bathrooms frequently out of service**: Letter from William Rutherford to William Harrington, April 29, 1969, McKissick Papers, folder 5524.

62   **carry out McKissick's expansive vision**: Gordon Carey interview with the author, April 23, 2015; email from Gordon Carey to author, November 14, 2017.

62   **held court in a corner booth**: Thomas A. Johnson, "Frank's: Harlem Place to See and Be Seen," *New York Times*, December 18, 1968, 65.

62   **three administrative assistants . . . "Dreams into Reality"**: Ball-Groom, *Salad Pickers*, 10, 61–71.

63   **During its first few months . . . African-style food and entertainment**: Floyd B. McKissick Enterprises brochure, McKissick Papers, folder 1043; Fergus, *Liberalism*, 199–200.

63   **shopping mall in Mount Vernon**: "A Proposal by Floyd B. McKissick Enterprises, Inc., for Development of a Shopping Center," October 4, 1968, McKissick Papers, folder 6507.

63   **profits to address community needs**: Clayton Knowles, "Harlemites Buy Woolworth Shop," *New York Times*, December 11, 1968, 32.

63   **new line of hot sauce**: Rhee, "Visions, Illusions, and Perceptions," 35.

63   **For many years . . . crime, illness, and delinquency**: R. Allen Hays, *The Federal Government and Urban Housing*, 3rd ed. (Albany: State University of New York Press, 2012), 87–138; Richard Rothstein, *The*

Color of Law: A Forgotten History of How Our Government Segregated America (New York: Liveright, 2017), 24–37; Pritchett, *Robert Clifton Weaver*, 246–61; *The Pruitt-Igoe Myth*, directed by Chad Freidrichs (Columbia, MO: Unicorn Stencil Documentary Films, 2011).

64   **"going berserk":** John C. Calhoun, "Population Density and Social Pathology," *Scientific American* 206, February 1962, 139.

64   **"Behavioral Sink":** Wolfe, *Pump House Gang* (New York: Bantam Books, 1969) 231.

65   **the vast majority would live in cities:** National Committee on Urban Growth Policy, *The New City* (New York: Frederick A. Praeger, 1969), 17.

65   **rise in the global death rate:** Paul Ehrlich, *The Population Bomb* (New York: Buccaneer Books, 1968) 1.

65   **Since becoming president . . . oversee the effort itself:** "Chronological History of the New Communities Act of 1968," Jack Underhill Papers, George Mason University, box 1, folder 1; John Landis, "Model Cities Program," in *The Encyclopedia of Housing*, 2nd ed., edited by Andrew T. Carswell (Los Angeles: Sage, 2012), 458–61.

65   **Seventy years earlier . . . cover rent and maintenance:** Ebenezer Howard, *To-morrow: A Peaceful Path to Real Reform* (London: Swan Sonnenschein & Co., 1902).

66   **Howard's proposal . . . over to local homeowners' groups:** Jane Jacobs, *The Death and Life of Great American Cities* (New York: Vintage, 1961), 17–25; Eric Mumford, *Designing the Modern City: Urbanism Since 1850* (New Haven: Yale University Press, 2018), 87–89, 130–36, 190–91; Rosemary Wakeman, *Practicing Utopia: An Intellectual History of the New Town Movement* (Chicago: University of Chicago Press, 2016), 30–43; Joseph L. Arnold, *The New Deal in the Suburbs: A History of the Greenbelt Town Program, 1935–1954* (Columbus: Ohio State University Press, 1971); Lewis Mumford, *The Culture of Cities* (New York: Harcourt Brace Jovanovich, 1938).

67   **The drive to build new cities . . . nine planned villages:** Carlos C. Campbell, *New Towns: Another Way to Live* (Reston, VA: Reston Publishing, 1976), 19–26; Ann Forsyth, *Reforming Suburbia: The Planned Communities of Irvine, Columbia, and The Woodlands* (Berkeley: University of California Press, 2005), 1–52, 107–60; Wakeman, *Practicing Utopia*, 47–101.

68   **Despite the success of Park Forest . . . "Little boxes":** Campbell, *New Towns*, 32–115, 223; Forsyth, *Reforming Suburbia*, 135–40; Robert B. Semple, "Johnson to Offer Financing Plan Protecting New Investors," *New York Times*, February 25, 1968, 33.

69   **To remedy this problem . . . water, sewerage, and electricity:** "Chronological History of the New Communities Act of 1968," Jack Underhill Papers; Landis, "Model Cities Program," 458–61.

70   Johnson incorporated these proposals . . . "freshly planned and built":
        Lyndon B. Johnson, Special Message to the Congress on Urban Prob-
        lems: "The Crisis of the Cities." Online by Gerhard Peters and John
        T. Woolley, The American Presidency Project, https://www.presidency
        .ucsb.edu/node/239033.

70   Congress was less certain. . . . New Communities Act into law:
        "Chronological History of the New Communities Act of 1968," Jack
        Underhill Papers; 114 Cong. Rec. 15121 (1968).

71   For Carey . . . to jail in a wheelchair: Gordon Carey interview with
        the author, August 21, 2015; email from Gordon Carey to author,
        May 28, 2017.

72   Los Angeles Times ran a front-page story: "Draft Objector Toted to
        Court by FBI Men," Los Angeles Times, August 22, 1953, A1.

72   Against the advice . . . as assistant to the national director: Gordon
        Carey interview with the author, August 21, 2015; email from Gor-
        don Carey to author, May 28, 2017.

73   "a younger, Blacker group": Gordon Carey interview with the author,
        August 21, 2015.

73   "doesn't mean the races can't live together": Gordon Carey interview
        with the author, April 23, 2015.

73   Over the next . . . "root causes of urban blight": "A Proposal for
        Developing a New Town," October 18, 1968, McKissick Papers,
        folder 6595.

74   The Kerner Commission . . . make a difference: Ervin Galantay, "Black
        New Towns: The Fourth Alternative," Progressive Architecture 49,
        no. 8, August 1968, 126.

75   Carey had not read . . . plan and develop his city: "A Proposal for
        Developing a New Town," October 18, 1968, McKissick Papers,
        folder 6595.

5: KLAN COUNTRY

81   Irvine in Orange County: Campbell, New Towns, 165, 227–28; For-
        syth, Reforming Suburbia, 53–106.

82   Less dependent on slavery: John Hope Franklin, The Free Negro in
        North Carolina, 1790–1860 (Chapel Hill: University of North Caro-
        lina Press, 1995), 3–13, 17; Jeffrey J. Crow, Paul D. Escott, and Flora
        J. Hatley Wadelington, A History of African Americans in North Car-
        olina (Raleigh: North Carolina Department of Cultural Resources,
        2002), 11, 56.

82   "relentless forward determination": V. O. Key, Southern Politics in
        State and Nation (New York: Alfred A. Knopf, 1949), 205–28.

82   "repressed beyond endurance": Key, Southern Politics, 205–6.

82   **"a living answer to the riddle of race":** Key, *Southern Politics*, 205–6; Fergus, *Liberalism*, 2–3, 14–15, 50–53.

82   **Not that racism . . . poor, uneducated whites:** Key, *Southern Politics*, 207–9; David S. Cecelski and Timothy B. Tyson, eds., *Democracy Betrayed: The Wilmington Race Riot of 1898 and Its Legacy* (Chapel Hill: University of North Carolina Press, 1998), 3–13; David Zucchino, *Wilmington's Lie: The Murderous Coup of 1898 and the Rise of White Supremacy* (New York: Atlantic Monthly Press, 2020); William Mabry, *The Negro in North Carolina Politics Since Reconstruction* (Durham, NC: Duke University Press, 1970), 30–70; Crow, *History of African Americans*, 11, 84–95.

83   **"dying gasp of a reign of terror":** Franklin and Moss, *From Slavery to Freedom*, 345.

83   **racism held a powerful grip:** Bass and DeVries, *The Transformation of Southern Politics: Social Change and Political Consequence Since 1945* (Athens: University of Georgia Press, 1995), 218–47; Christopher A. Cooper and H. Gibbs Knotts, "Traditionalism and Progressivism in North Carolina," in *The New Politics of North Carolina*, edited by Christopher A. Cooper and H. Gibbs Knotts (Chapel Hill: University of North Carolina Press, 2008), 1–10; Elizabeth A. Herbin-Triant, *Threatening Property: Race, Class, and Campaigns to Legislate Jim Crow Neighborhoods* (New York: Columbia University Press, 2019); Crystal R. Sanders, "North Carolina Justice on Display: Governor Bob Scott and the 1968 Benson Affair," *Journal of Southern History* 79, no. 3 (August 2013), 660–61; Karen Kruse Thomas, *Deluxe Jim Crow: Civil Rights and American Health Policy, 1935–54* (Athens: University of Georgia Press, 2011), 182–207, 229–49.

83   **Aycock was a white supremacist:** Key, *Southern Politics*, 208–9; Cecelski and Tyson, *Democracy Betrayed*, 3–13.

83   **"their prejudices as well as their allergies":** Paul R. Clancy, *Just a Country Lawyer: A Biography of Senator Sam Ervin* (Bloomington: Indiana University Press, 1974), 215; John Hope Franklin and Isidore Starr, eds., *The Negro in Twentieth Century America: A Reader on the Struggle for Civil Rights* (New York: Vintage Books, 1967), 34–35.

83   **"no picnic ground for its Negro citizens":** Key, *Southern Politics*, 209.

83   **strong tradition of Black activism . . . Malcolm X Liberation University:** Fergus, *Liberalism*, 1–12, 54–90; Timothy B. Tyson, *Radio Free Dixie: Robert F. Williams and the Roots of Black Power* (Chapel Hill: University of North Carolina Press, 1999), 121, 262–86, 295–302.

84   **fewer than 20 percent of Asheville's residents:** US Bureau of the Census, "Summary of General Characteristics: 1970," Table 16, in *Census of Population: 1970*, vol. I, *Characteristics of the Population*, part 35, North Carolina, 51.

85   **Theaoseus Theaboyd Clayton . . . North Carolina politics:** "Drake
and Clayton Announce for House," *Warren Record* (Warrenton, NC),
March 20, 1964, 1; T. T. Clayton interview with the author, March
6, 2015; Eva Clayton interview with Kathryn Nasstrom, July 18,
1989, Documenting the American South, University of North Carolina at Chapel Hill, 7–11; Luci Weldon, "Longtime Attorney Clayton
Dies at 88," *Warren Record* (Warrenton, NC), April 9, 2019; email
from Gordon Carey to author, July 4, 2017.

86   **As an attorney . . . nine miles west of Warrenton:** T. T. Clayton inter-
view with the author, March 6, 2015; "Report on Architectural and
Historical Evaluation with Proposal for Adaptive Reuse," McKissick
Papers, folder 2152, 1–3.

87   **designer of the original Confederate flag:** Rhee, "Visions, Illusions,
and Perceptions," 36.

87   **"Shocco Springs Hotel":** Amanda Shapiro, "Welcome to Soul City,"
Oxford American 80 (Spring 2013): 80; Lizzie Wilson Montgom-
ery, *Sketches of Old Warrenton: Traditions and Reminiscences of the
Town and People Who Made It* (Raleigh, NC: Edwards & Broughton
Printing Co., 1924), 40, 78.

87   **Horace Greeley . . . Annie Carter Lee:** Robert C. Williams, *Horace
Greeley: Champion of American Freedom* (New York: New York
University Press, 2006), 39; Manly Wade Wellman, *The County of
Warren, North Carolina, 1586–1917* (Chapel Hill: University of
North Carolina Press, 1959), 143–44, 156; Montgomery, *Sketches*,
146, 425–26.

87   **By 1968, though . . . "at least still a gamble":** Dwayne E. Walls, *The
Chickenbone Special* (New York: Harcourt Brace Jovanovich, 1971),
25–86; Nicholas Lemann, *Promised Land: The Great Black Migra-
tion and How It Changed America* (New York: Vintage Books, 1992);
Isabel Wilkerson, *The Warmth of Other Suns: The Epic Story of
America's Great Migration* (New York: Vintage Books, 2011).

87   **90 percent of all Black Americans:** Woodson, *Century of Negro
Migration*, 167–92.

87   **almost half of all Blacks lived outside the South:** Lemann, *Promised
Land*, 6; Campbell Gibson and Kay Jung, "Historical Census Statistics
on Population Totals by Race, 1790 to 1990, and by Hispanic Origin,
1970 to 1990, for the United States, Regions, Divisions, and States,"
US Census Bureau, 2002, Table 4.

88   **bottom 10 percent of counties nationwide:** Van Deburg, *New Day in
Babylon*, 135; Yvonne Baskin, "Skepticism, Fear of Soul City Abound
in Warren County," *Durham (NC) Morning Herald*, March 9, 1969.

88   **lacked a proper kitchen . . . lacked connection to a public sewer:** US
Bureau of the Census, "Income and Poverty Status in 1969 of the
Negro Population for Counties: 1970," Table 128, in *Census of*

Population: 1970, vol. I, *Characteristics of the Population*, part 35, North Carolina, 466; US Bureau of the Census, "Occupancy, Utilization, and Plumbing Characteristics of Housing Units with Negro Head of Household, for Counties: 1970," Table 64, in *Census of Housing: 1970*, vol. I, *Housing Characteristics of States, Cities, and Counties*, part 35, North Carolina, 246; US Bureau of the Census, "Structural, Plumbing, Equipment, and Financial Characteristics of Housing Units with Negro Head of Household, for Counties: 1970," Table 66, in *Census of Housing: 1970*, vol. I, *Housing Characteristics of States, Cities, and Counties*, part 35, North Carolina, 257.

88   **"You have to study each shack"**: Hank Burchard, "'Soul City' Stirs Its Future Neighbors," *Washington Post*, January 26, 1969, 35.

88   **The history of the Circle P Ranch . . . fall of 1968**: "Report on Architectural and Historical Evaluation with Proposal for Adaptive Reuse," 1–3; T. T. Clayton interview with the author, March 6, 2015; Gordon Carey interview with the author, April 23, 2015.

89   **The two men met . . . "a beautiful golf course"**: T. T. Clayton interview with the author, March 6, 2015.

90   **After viewing the property . . . "But you'll like it"**: T. T. Clayton interview with the author, March 6, 2015.

90   **And McKissick did . . . "people who owned slaves"**: T. T. Clayton interview with the author, March 6, 2015.

90   **only 178 residents . . . first Black officer**: US Bureau of the Census, 1970 Census of the Population, vol. I, Characteristics of the Population, North Carolina, Part 35, "Educational and Family Characteristics for Counties: 1970," Table 120, Issued March 1973 (http://www2.census .gov/prod2/decennial/documents/1970a_nc.zip); "Harvard University Study," 1969, McKissick Papers, folder 6573, 1; "Soul City, North Carolina: A Proposal Under Title IV of the 1968 Housing and Urban Development Act to Secure a Guarantee for This New Community," February 1, 1970, McKissick Papers, folder 6602, 8; Burchard, "'Soul City' Stirs Its Future Neighbors."

91   **fears of a Black uprising had swept the area**: Crow, *History of African Americans*, 44–47.

91   **compared to 1,270 whites**: Mabry, *The Negro in North Carolina*, 78.

91   **"You Are in the Heart of Klan Country"**: Strain, "Soul City," 61; Burchard, "'Soul City' Stirs Its Future Neighbors."

92   **$1,500 per acre paid by James Rouse**: Forsyth, *Reforming Suburbia*, 114.

92   **attractive to industry**: "Soul City: A Pioneering Experiment in New-Town Planning," Industrial Development and Site Selection Handbook, 1976, McKissick Papers, folder 1762.

92   **more than an hour . . . line to the entire Southeast**: "Soul City: A Pioneering Experiment in New-Town Planning," Industrial Development

and Site Selection Handbook, 1976, McKissick Papers, folder 1762; "A Factual Presentation Relating to Site Selection, Transportation," McKissick Papers, folder 2130, 4–6; Herbert Ray Burrows, *Norlina: Nothing Could Be Finer* (Norlina, NC: Burrows, 2005), 3–4, 14, 42.

93   **"fought integration like a tiger"**: Wooten, "Integrated City."

93   **and "Premble, Inc."**: Forsyth, *Reforming Suburbia*, 114; Charles Haar and Lance Liebman, *Property and Law*, Second Edition (Boston: Little Brown, 1985), 685.

94   **signed their names to the contract**: Documents Relating to Acquisition by McKissick Enterprises, Inc., October 11, 1973, McKissick Papers, folder 6589.

6: "INTEGRATION BLACKWARDS"

94   **acquired title to over fourteen thousand acres**: Forsyth, *Reforming Suburbia*, 132–33.

94   **Secretary of Agriculture Orville Freeman**: Rhee, "Visions, Illusions, and Perceptions," 45.

94   **cared deeply about issues of poverty . . . across rural America**: David Stout, "Orville Freeman, 84, Dies; 60's Agriculture Secretary," *New York Times*, February 22, 2003, B6; Wakeman, *Practicing Utopia*, 241.

95   **Monday, January 13, in Freeman's office**: "McKissick Enterprises to Build New Town," *New York Amsterdam News*, January 25, 1969, 3.

95   **McKissick dropped a bombshell . . . "decaying cities"**: "Text of Statement by Floyd McKissick," January 13, 1969, McKissick Papers, folder 5134.

96   **"adopt the white man's racism"**: "Negroes to Build Their Own 'New Town' in North Carolina," *New York Times*, January 14, 1969, 39.

96   **"determine their own futures"**: Roy Parker Jr., "Negroes to Build Town in Warren," *News & Observer* (Raleigh, NC), January 14, 1969, 1.

96   **"welcome white people as equals"**: Strain, "Soul City," 57–58.

96   **announcement made a splash**: Spencer Rich, "McKissick Is Planning 'Soul City,'" *Washington Post*, January 14, 1969, A1; "Negroes to Build Their Own 'New Town' in North Carolina," *New York Times*; "Negroes to Build 'Soul City,'" *Philadelphia Inquirer*, January 14, 1969, 6.

97   **"have looked reality straight in the eye"**: "The 'Soul City' Dream," *News & Observer* (Raleigh, NC), January 16, 1969, 4.

97   **against the longest of odds**: "'Soul City' Faces Formidable Odds," *Charlotte Observer*, January 15, 1969, 24.

98   **"All-Negro City Planned"**: "All-Negro City Planned for Warren County Site," *Warren Record* (Warrenton, NC), January 16, 1969, 1.

98   an "all-black settlement": "Black Cities / North Carolina / Alabama #2089," *ABC Evening News*, January 13, 1969, video, 5:50, Vanderbilt Television News Archive.

98   "hopes lie in an integrated society": "Black Town," *Greensboro Daily News*, reprinted in *Warren Record* (Warrenton, NC), January 23, 1969, 2.

98   A native of Georgia . . . Sitton's articles from beginning to end: Gene Roberts and Hank Klibanoff, *The Race Beat: The Press, the Civil Rights Struggle, and the Awakening of a Nation* (New York: Vintage, 2007), 186–98, 224–55, 259–69.

98   Slight of build . . . find the truth himself: Roberts and Klibanoff, *Race Beat*, 259–60.

98   A stickler for the facts . . . "duck-tail haircuts": Roberts and Klibanoff, *Race Beat*, 224; Dennis Hevesi, "Claude Sitton, 89, Acclaimed Civil Rights Reporter, Dies," *New York Times*, March 10, 2015, A22.

99   one of his most chilling reports . . . slashed with a knife: Roberts and Klibanoff, *Race Beat*, 263–66.

99   "interpreting the race story in the South": Roberts and Klibanoff, *Race Beat*, 367.

99   "more dissent on closer examination": "Among the Recent Letters to the Editor," *New York Times*, February 26, 1961, BR 52–53.

100   Burned out and tired . . . the *Raleigh Times*: Claude Sitton interview with Joseph Mosnier, July 12, 2007, 4-5; Roberts and Klibanoff, *Race Beat*, 367; "Claude Sitton, 89, Acclaimed Civil Rights Reporter, Dies," *New York Times*, March 10, 2015, A22; "A Long Career in Black and White," *News & Observer* (Raleigh, NC), October 28, 1990, 1J.

100   "Soul City's Plan or Wilkins' Way?": Claude Sitton, "Soul City's Plan or Wilkins' Way?" *News & Observer* (Raleigh, NC), January 19, 1969.

101   "same thing as the Chinese have done": "McKissick / Soul City #442314," *NBC Evening News*, January 13, 1969, video, 2:40, Vanderbilt Television News Archive.

101   "who years ago moved to the suburbs": "'Racism Semantics' Hit by McKissick," *Durham Morning Herald*, May 3, 1969.

102   "own, control, and develop this city": Tony Lentz, "Men Named to Guide Soul City Birth," *Durham Morning Herald*, January 19, 1969.

102   "intend to control the new town": Jim Smith, "McKissick Says Plans Due in 2 Weeks for New City," *News & Observer* (Raleigh, NC), January 19, 1969.

102   called it "black-inspired": Cornelia Olive, "N.C. College Aid Pledged to Soul City," *Durham Morning Herald*, February 5, 1969; Mike Wolff, "Black 'Soul City' Described," *Minneapolis Star*, April 24, 1969, 1B.

102   other times "black-built": Mixon, *Soul City*, McKissick Papers, folder 6574, 11.

102   **still others "black-oriented":** "A Proposal for Developing a New Town," October 18, 1968, McKissick Papers, folder 6595, 3.

102   **rejected the label "integrated":** Baskin, "Skepticism, Fear of Soul City Abound in Warren County," March 9, 1969.

102   **"neither integration nor segregation":** Wolff, "Black 'Soul City' Described," April 24, 1969.

102   **He made a similar point . . . "American as apple pie":** Conversations Between The Rouse Company and Floyd B. McKissick Enterprises, Chapter II, McKissick Papers, folder 6583, 19–23.

103   **"we black folks make the plans":** Henry H. Parker to FM, January 14, 1969, McKissick Papers, folder 5523.

103   **"do not intend to fail":** FM to Henry H. Parker, January 15, 1969, McKissick Papers, folder 5523.

103   **If the mainstream press . . . "different results in Soul City":** Elizabeth Tornquist, "Black Capitalism and Soul City, North Carolina," *North Carolina Anvil*, April 19, 1969.

103   **McKissick had an answer . . . "several companies show interest in this":** Roy Parker Jr., "McKissick Outlines Soul City Financing," *News & Observer* (Raleigh, NC), February 13, 1969; Jean M. White, "'Soul City' Backers Need $500,000," *Washington Post*, February 13, 1969, A3.

105   **"halfway between almost socialism":** Geoffrey Gould, "Soul City: Black Leader's 'Magnificent Obsession,'" *Charlotte Observer*, May 9, 1971.

105   **"may be known as McKissick's folly":** Elizabeth Tornquist, "Puppet Capital in the Black South," *Hard Times*, May 26–June 2, 1969.

105   **Black press covered the story closely:** "'Soul Town' Planned to Relieve Ghetto Dwellers," *Chicago Daily Defender*, January 14, 1969; "McKissick Enterprises to Build New Town," *Los Angeles Sentinel*, January 16, 1969; "Black Architects to Design Soul City," *Chicago Daily Defender*, January 20, 1969, 8; "Floyd B. McKissick Plans 'Soul City' in N. Carolina," *New Pittsburgh Courier*, January 25, 1969, 1; "McKissick Enterprises to Build New Town," *New York Amsterdam News*, January 25, 1969, 3; "'Soul City' Big Topic in N.C. Area," *Baltimore Afro-American*, January 25, 1969, 1; "4 Firms Interested in Soul City Plan," *Chicago Daily Defender*, February 1, 1969, 7; "Soul City Makes Go Go Boy of McKissick," *New York Amsterdam News*, February 1, 1969, 3; Guy Olson, "Soul City Foundation to Aid Black Equality," *Chicago Daily Defender*, February 6, 1969, 5.

105   **The editors of the *Carolina Times* . . . "set out to achieve":** "The Soul City Project of Warren County," *Carolina Times*, January 25, 1969, 2A.

106   **A few days after . . . longed to return home:** Rick Nichols, "Present at the Creation," *News & Observer* (Raleigh, NC), November 4, 1973, 1; Rhee, "Visions, Illusions, and Perceptions," 46–47.

106   **In cities throughout the North . . . the worst apartments:** Franklin

and Moss, *From Slavery to Freedom*, 524, 542–43; Walls, *Chicken-bone Special*, 22–23; Lemann, *Promised Land*, 225–306; Wilkerson, *Warmth of Other Suns*, 242–50.

106   **"ain't human up there"**: Walls, *Chickenbone Special*, 23.

106   **Many Black transplants were homesick … to return home**: Walls, *Chickenbone Special*, 113–14; Wilkerson, *Warmth of Other Suns*, 238–41.

107   **he was inundated with letters**: General Correspondence, 1967–1980 and undated, McKissick Papers, folders 5523–688; Contacts for Soul City: Letters of Inquiry, 1969–1973, McKissick Papers, folders 5806–9.

107   **Some, such as F. N. Kurtz … "take part in the overall planning"**: F. N. Kurtz to Orville Freeman, January 15, 1969, McKissick Papers, folder 5806; Robert E. Martin to FM, January 26, 1969, McKissick Papers, folder 5806.

107   **"gone to live in peace and harmonie"**: John Council and Tody Foster letters in "Soul City Contacts," January 21, 1969, McKissick Papers, folder 5806; Ronnie Collins to FM, received February 12, 1969, McKissick Papers, folder 5555.

107   **Not all the letters … grading work for the project**: Waved Ruffin to FM, January 14, 1969, McKissick Papers, folder 5806; Isaac B. Markham to FM, August 25, 1969, McKissick Papers, folder 5806.

108   **Could Turner pull some strings?**: Rhee, "Visions, Illusions, and Perceptions," 46.

108   **"on the basis of the letters we've received"**: Parker, "McKissick Outlines Soul City Financing," February 13, 1969.

108   **In early January … could "play a major part"**: FM to Whitney Young, January 8, 1969, Whitney M. Young Papers, Columbia University, Rare Book and Manuscript Library, box 21.

109   **"cannot get excited about starting another one"**: Whitney Young to FM, January 13, 1969, Whitney M. Young Papers, Columbia University, Rare Book and Manuscript Library, box 21.

109   **Young's letter raised … mistakes of the past**: FM to Whitney Young, January 27, 1969, Whitney M. Young Papers, Columbia University, Rare Book and Manuscript Library, box 21.

110   **"Heart Cities, Head Cities, Hand Cities"**: Gordon B. Hancock, "High Cost of Hand-Out," *Norfolk Journal and Guide*, February 22, 1969, 9A.

110   **"to disappoint and delude the ignorant"**: M. A. Farber, "Advocate of 'Black Education' Argues With Negro Moderate," *New York Times*, January 16, 1969, 28.

111   **"They've been trying to get integration"**: Parker, "Negroes to Build Town in Warren," January 14, 1969.

111   **five stages of grief**: Baskin, "Skepticism, Fear of Soul City Abound in Warren County," March 9, 1969.

111   "county tax structure would get a real boost": Jim Smith, "Warren Officials Surprised by Soul City," *News & Observer* (Raleigh, NC), January 15, 1969.

112   "hog maws and overcooked greens": Burchard, "'Soul City' Stirs Its Future Neighbors."

112   editor of the *Warren Record*: Bignall Jones, *Boyhood Days in Warrenton* (Warrenton, NC: Record Print Co., 1993).

112   "pull down the pillars of the temple": Bignall Jones as quoted in Tyson, *Radio Free Dixie*, 328 fn 36.

112   "I carry all the nigger weddings": Geoffrey Gould, "Waiting to Be Born: Soul City," *New Republic*, July 3, 1971, 10.

112   Jones was troubled ... "did not see any persons in rags": Bignall Jones, "Mostly Personal," *Warren Record*, January 30, 1969, 3.

113   "I'd hate to see it happen": Burchard, "'Soul City' Stirs Its Future Neighbors."

113   as strange as any foreign nation's: Nichols, "Present at the Creation," November 4, 1973.

114   "definitely not true": Jim Smith, "Soul City for 'All Citizens,'" *News & Observer* (Raleigh, NC), January 22, 1969, 5.

114   "When city rioters come": Tornquist, "Puppet Capital in the Black South."

114   "going to do something on it": Rhee, "Visions, Illusions, and Perceptions," 48; "Soul City's Need Is Green Power," *BusinessWeek*, January 17, 1970.

7: GREEN POWER

115   In the weeks ... industrial trade organization: "Architectural Firm Chosen for 'Soul City' in Carolina," *New York Times*, January 19, 1969, 76; Lentz, "Men Named to Guide Soul City Birth," January 19, 1969; "Soul City Group Sees Gov. Scott," *News & Observer* (Raleigh, NC), January 24, 1969; "Soul City Makes Go Go Boy of McKissick," February 1, 1969.

116   let alone cover a down payment: Internal Memorandum from W. H. Clanton to FM, November 29, 1968, McKissick Papers, folder 5523.

116   more than $25 million to build Columbia: Connecticut General Life Insurance Company, 1969, McKissick Papers, folder 6405; Forsyth, *Reforming Suburbia*, 113, 136.

116   Operating informally ... an ideal applicant: Leonard Sloane, "A Loan Criterion: Potential," *New York Times*, September 20, 1970, 160.

117   "Just work with me": T. T. Clayton interview with the author, March 6, 2015.

117   "keep the black man in his place": "Another Opinion: Why the Negro Must Rebel," *New York Times*, July 30, 1967, E9.

117   criticized Chase Manhattan . . . "are the enemy": McKissick, *Three-Fifths of a Man*, 39–41.

118   "They are the people with the influence": McKissick, *Three-Fifths of a Man*, 41.

118   "moral right to their remaining millions": McKissick, *Three-Fifths of a Man*, 40.

118   "You owe it": T. T. Clayton interview with the author, March 6, 2015.

118   The Chase team . . . "you'll do the title work": T. T. Clayton interview with the author, March 6, 2015.

119   needed cash immediately: Hammer, Green, Siler Associates, "Preliminary Economic Analysis," February 13, 1969, McKissick Papers, folder 2738e.

119   McKissick had scheduled . . . smoothly to a stop: Email from Gordon Carey to author, March 5, 2018.

120   Once on the ground . . . the missed deadline: Email from Gordon Carey to author, March 5, 2018.

120   stack of paperwork . . . two hundred years earlier: "Soul City Land Deal Is Delayed," *News & Observer* (Raleigh, NC), February 20. 1969; "Soul City Deal Said Closed," *News & Observer* (Raleigh, NC), February 21, 1969.

120   "good here for the whole country": "Soul City Deed Filed," *News & Observer* (Raleigh, NC), February 22, 1969.

120   spent several times that amount: Forsyth, *Reforming Suburbia*, 136.

121   "Need Is Green Power": "Soul City's Need Is Green Power," 106.

121   reservations about relying on government loans: Rhee, "Visions, Illusions, and Perceptions," 44.

121   most businesses prefer tax breaks and subsidies: "Harvard University Study," 1969, 37, McKissick Papers, folder 6573.

121   "get out of that bag": McKissick interview with Robert Wright, 14–15.

122   "into programs that have failed": "Transcripts of Acceptance Speeches by Nixon and Agnew to the GOP Convention," *New York Times*, August 9, 1968; Walter Rugaber, "Nixon to Retain Poverty Agency; Shifts 2 Projects," *New York Times*, February 20, 1969, 1.

122   appointed as its director Donald Rumsfeld: John Herbers, "Rumsfeld Hopes to Speak for Poor," *New York Times*, May 2, 1969, 21; Mehrsa Baradaran, *The Color of Money: Black Banks and the Racial Wealth Gap* (Cambridge: Harvard University Press, 2017), 167.

122   without yet allocating any funds: Baradaran, *Color of Money*, 180.

122   Born in High Point . . . "able to go home again": Robert Brown interview with the author, July 19, 2016.

123   After the election . . . accepted the job: Robert Brown interview with the author, July 19, 2016.

123   **He wasn't the only Black official . . . went straight to him:** Milton Viorst, "The Blacks Who Work for Nixon," *New York Times*, November 29, 1970, 260.

123   **McKissick lodged his first complaint . . . "certain agencies":** FM to Robert Brown, February 4, 1969, McKissick Papers, folder 6199.

124   **Six weeks later . . . "before the honeymoon ends":** FM to Robert Brown, April 4, 1969, McKissick Papers, folder 6199.

125   **lack of access to the president:** Frank C. Porter, "Black Coalition Claims Nixon Is Avoiding Talks," *Washington Post*, January 26, 1969, 6.

125   **cutting back on the SBA:** Wolff, "Black 'Soul City' Described," April 24, 1969.

125   **"the right to have Black-run factories":** "McKissick Says Blacks Should Control Harlem," *New York Amsterdam News*, July 5, 1969, 10.

125   **consider alternative sources of funding:** Rhee, "Visions, Illusions, and Perceptions," 44.

126   **insurance and hair products industries:** Franklin and Moss, *From Slavery to Freedom*, 521.

126   **"income producing properties and homes":** J. J. Henderson to FM, November 9, 1971, McKissick Papers, folder 6022.

127   **"until he admits that he is defeated":** FM to Edward Kennedy, July 25, 1969, McKissick Papers, folder 6198.

127   **Fitzgerald said he had never heard from Kennedy:** Gordon Carey interview with the author, April 23, 2015.

127   **those discussions went nowhere:** Gordon Carey interview with the author, July 19, 2016.

127   **he and McKissick were different races:** Gordon Carey interviews with the author, April 23, 2015, and July 19, 2016; email from Gordon Carey to author, May 25, 2017.

127   **"the deep rooted latent racism of white America":** FM to Louis Winnick, Ford Foundation, March 11, 1969, McKissick Papers, folder 5541 (filed in SC correspondence with Ford Foundation).

128   **"word to the wise":** Irving Fain to FM, January 22, 1969, McKissick Papers, folder 6408b.

129   **the beneficence of the federal government:** Rhee, "Visions, Illusions, and Perceptions," 44.

129   **Building on the proposal . . . "will surprise the skeptics":** "A Proposal to Develop Soul City," April 1, 1969, McKissick Papers, folder 6596.

129   **town of Jonathan, Minnesota:** "Table 4.1—Basic Data on Selected New Community Proposals Which Were Never Approved (Alphabetized), Key Dates and Final Disposition," Jack Underhill Papers, George Mason University, box 10, folder 12; "U.S. Backs Its First New City," *Washington Post*, February 14, 1970, A2.

130   **raised precisely this concern:** "Table 4.1—Basic Data on Selected New Community Proposals Which Were Never Approved (Alphabetized),

Key Dates and Final Disposition," Jack Underhill Papers, George Mason University, box 10, folder 12.

130 **if it were truly integrated:** Rhee, "Visions, Illusions, and Perceptions," 53; Fergus, *Liberalism*, 202.

131 **the addition of a white developer:** Rhee, "Visions, Illusions, and Perceptions," 54.

131 **had doubts about the project himself:** Rhee, "Visions, Illusions, and Perceptions," 55.

131 **"Manifestly, the taxpayers of the United States":** Rhee, "Visions, Illusions, and Perceptions," 55.

131 **assigned a young planner on his staff:** Carlos Campbell interview with the author, January 25, 2019.

131 **"cannot be treated as an ordinary case":** Rhee, "Visions, Illusions, and Perceptions," 53.

132 **"something we should be encouraging":** James Welsh, "McKissick's 'Soul City' Gets No Federal Help," *Evening Star* (Washington, DC), February 18, 1969.

132 **apply for a planning grant:** Memorandum from Gordon Carey to FM, May 28, 1969, McKissick Papers, folder 5527; Sam Jackson to FM, August 18, 1969, McKissick Papers, folder 6140.

132 **writing to Bob Brown:** FM to Robert Brown, October 9, 1969, McKissick Papers, folder 6201.

132 **"new life to a rural, depressed area":** FM to Spiro Agnew, July 24, 1969, McKissick Papers, folder 6199.

133 **"'We don't know'":** FM to Spiro Agnew, August 12, 1969, McKissick Papers, folder 6199.

133 **green light to Soul City:** FM to John Parker, October 8, 1969, personal papers of David Godschalk, copy on file with author; FM to Robert Brown, October 17, 1969, McKissick Papers, folder 6201; FM to Ray O'Keefe, October 9, 1969, McKissick Papers, folder 6392.

133 **good news from Sam Jackson:** Memorandum from Gordon Carey to T. T. Clayton, November 17, 1969, McKissick Papers, folder 5527; Memorandum from D. R. Godschalk, D. H. Moreau, and J. A. Parker to The Faculty, November 25, 1969, personal papers of David Godschalk, copy on file with author.

133 **"ready to move ahead":** Gordon Carey to David Godschalk, September 8, 1969, personal papers of David Godschalk, copy on file with author.

8: A FRESH START

135 **McKissick and his staff . . . a thriving community:** Mixon, *Soul City*, 20.

135 **Jack Parker . . . department like a fiefdom:** Edward J. Kaiser and Karla Rosenberg, *The School That Jack Built: City and Regional Planning at*

the University of North Carolina at Chapel Hill, 1945–2012 (Chapel Hill: Department of City and Regional Planning, University of North Carolina at Chapel Hill, 2013), xiv; 13, 88.

135 **dispatched a telegram to McKissick's office:** Telegram from John A. Parker to Leslie Roberts, January 10, 1969, personal papers of David Godschalk, copy on file with author; Memorandum from John A. Parker to the Faculty, January 13, 1969, personal papers of David Godschalk, copy on file with author.

136 **The meeting . . . effort to plan Soul City:** Rhee, "Visions, Illusions, and Perceptions," 40, 51; Kaiser and Rosenberg, *School That Jack Built*, 95; Memorandum from John A. Parker to the Faculty, January 16, 1969, personal papers of David Godschalk, copy on file with author.

136 **"yet another Soul City planning conference":** Memorandum from David H. Moreau and John D. Patton to the Faculty, March 18, 1969, personal papers of David Godschalk, copy on file with author.

137 **"Can Black folks do it?":** Harvard University Study, 1969, McKissick Papers, folder 6573, 4.

137 **"projected an air of total confidence":** David Godschalk interview with the author, August 19, 2015.

137 **"the belief that a thing can be done":** Floyd McKissick, "Will v. Reason," undated yearbook editorial, personal papers of Charmaine McKissick-Melton, copy on file with author.

138 **"land is ideal for a city":** Harvard University Study, 1969, McKissick Papers, folder 6573, 3, 19–20.

138 **the population projections grew:** Strain, "*Soul City*," 60; Report of Soul City Foundation, April 12, 1974, Bradley H. Patterson Jr. (White House Central Files: Staff Member and Office Files), box 64, Richard Nixon Presidential Library and Museum; "McKissick: Initial Plans Are Ready for Soul City," *News & Observer* (Raleigh, NC), January 15, 1970; "Soul City Hopefully Waits for Federal Bond Approval," *News & Observer* (Raleigh, NC), February 11, 1972.

138 **"the very boldness of this project":** Gould, "Soul City: Black Leader's 'Magnificent Obsession,'" May 9, 1971.

139 **The size of the project . . . in a new light:** Harvard University Study, 1969, McKissick Papers, folder 6573, 18–19; "A Proposal Under Title IV of the 1968 Housing and Urban Development Act to Secure a Guarantee for This New Community," February 1, 1970, McKissick Papers, folder 6603, 43.

140 **"The mutual needs for water":** "A Proposal Under Title IV," February 1, 1970, folder 6603, 43.

141 **"a fresh start":** "The First City in the World That's Built Around Your Family," Advertisement, *Black Enterprise*, June 1977, 22.

141   In pursuing this goal . . . conceived and built: Mumford, *Designing the Modern City*, 253–81; David Godschalk interview with the author, August 19, 2015.

141   challenged the prevailing consensus . . . the two as interchangeable: Jacobs, *Death and Life*.

142   Jacobs's book was groundbreaking . . . environmental sustainability: Mumford, *Designing the Modern City*, 295–304; Andres Duany, Elizabeth Plater-Zyberk, and Jeff Speck, *Suburban Nation: The Rise of Sprawl and the Decline of the American Dream* (New York: North Point Press, 2010).

143   "irresponsibility, and superficial values": Forsyth, *Reforming Suburbia*, 111.

143   He preferred small . . . not enough: Forsyth, *Reforming Suburbia*, 110–12; 114–19; William Severini Kowinski, "A Mall Covers the Waterfront," *New York Times*, December 13, 1981.

143   "dignity, beauty, growth!": James Rouse, "Cities That Work for Man—Victory Ahead" (speech, Lions International / University of Puerto Rico Symposium on "The City of the Future," San Juan, PR, October 18, 1967), http://ebot.gmu.edu/bitstream/handle/1920/2038 /638_05_03_01.pdf?sequence=1&isAllowed=y.

143   To mitigate . . . "garden for growing people": Forsyth, *Reforming Suburbia*, 114–19; Amanda Kolson Hurley, "Here's a Suburban Experiment Cities Can Learn From," *Washington Post*, July 13, 2017.

144   Columbia aimed . . . imitation Swiss chalets: Forsyth, *Reforming Suburbia*, 122–32; Hurley, "Here's a Suburban Experiment Cities Can Learn From."

144   followed a regular course of study: Memoranda from GC to FM, June 25 and June 30, 1969, McKissick Papers, folder 5527.

144   They learned . . . "more than they succeed": Conversations Between The Rouse Company and Floyd B. McKissick Enterprises, Inc., 1969–71, McKissick Papers, folders 6576–6587.

145   He found just the man . . . program at MIT: Harvey Gantt interview with the author, October 14, 2015.

145   seventy-two job categories: "Soul City Team of 20 to Move in Shortly," *News & Observer* (Raleigh, NC), November 12, 1969.

145   So McKissick invited . . . "a different story": Harvey Gantt interview with the author, October 14, 2015.

146   As for transportation . . . light-rail service: "A Proposal Under Title IV," February 1, 1970, folder 6603, 40.

148   recreation and animal habitats: "A Proposal Under Title IV of the 1968 Housing and Urban Development Act to Secure a Guarantee for This New Community," February 1, 1971, McKissick Papers, folder 6604, 27–52; Harvey Gantt interview with the author, October 14, 2015.

148   "in the social arena": "A Proposal Under Title IV," February 1, 1971, folder 6604, 73.

148   "live together in a community": Conversations Between The Rouse Company and Floyd B. McKissick Enterprises, Inc., 1969–71, McKissick Papers, folders 6576–6587.

149   seventy-five patients a day: Floyd McKissick Jr. interview with the author, October 12, 2015.

149   enough money to buy a station wagon: "Rural Fire Department Ends Ambulance Service," *Warren Record*, January 4, 1968, 1; "Ambulance Service for County Nearer," *Warren Record*, January 25, 1968, 1.

150   a blatant attempt to evade *Brown*: *Turner v. Warren County Board of Education*, 313 F. Supp. 380 (E.D. N.C.) (May 23, 1970).

150   little sense for the county to build new facilities: Harvard University Study, 1969, 20–21.

151   a long history of privately owned towns: Forsyth, *Reforming Suburbia*, 35, 153–55; Campbell, *New Towns*, 69.

151   governing body of the new community: "How Govern Soul City?" September 1971, McKissick Papers, folder 2043.

152   "the compromises from the ideal": Rhee, "Visions, Illusions, and Perceptions," 59 and fn. 105.

152   "project hinges on one single factor: "A Proposal Under Title IV," February 1, 1971, folder 6604, 15–16.

152   General Electric agreed to build a plant: Forsyth, *Reforming Suburbia*, 139.

152   McKissick couldn't offer . . . record on racial issues: Harvard University Study, 1969, 10.

153   "ultimately become an economic reality": Harvard University Study, 1969, 9.

153   "They both come first": Conversations Between The Rouse Company and Floyd B. McKissick Enterprises, Inc., 1969–71, McKissick Papers, folders 6576–6587.

9: "THE SALAD PICKERS"

154   "land with a tremendous potential": FM to Leon Perry, September 18, 1969, McKissick Papers, folder 2738e.

154   As 1969 . . . large and boisterous family: Gordon Carey interview with the author, August 21, 2015; Beverly McNeill interview with the author, April 25, 2015; FM to Duncan McNeill, December 19, 1969, McKissick Papers, folder 5537.

155   For Groom . . . a life in Soul City after all: Ball-Groom, *Salad Pickers*, 23–102.

158   Which is what . . . "dust of past generations": Ball-Groom, *Salad Pickers*, 103–29, 194–202.

159   **"getting the physical systems going"**: Rhee, "Visions, Illusions, and Perceptions," 88.
160   **dripping on cold winter nights**: Ball-Groom, *Salad Pickers*, 112–13.
160   **like a pair of suburban cowboys**: Gordon Garey interview with the author, July 19, 2016.
160   **At times . . . spuds upside down**: Ball-Groom, *Salad Pickers*, 138–41.
160   **But their inexperience . . . new neighbors**: Gordon Carey interview with the author, August 21, 2015.
161   **Nature presented . . . across the fields**: Ball-Groom, *Salad Pickers*, 145–46.
161   **It wasn't just the environment . . . on edge**: "Warrenton District Schools to Be Closed Indefinitely," *Warren Record*, November 12, 1970, 1; "Warren County Schools Resume Operations Wednesday Morning," *Warren Record*, November 19, 1970, 1; "Police and Firemen Called to John Graham High School," *Warren Record*, December 3, 1970, 1; "Black Students Return to John Graham High School," *Warren Record*, December 17, 1970, 1.
161   **Things were even worse . . . a ghost town**: Timothy B. Tyson, *Blood Done Sign My Name: A True Story* (New York: Broadway Books, 2005).
162   **"no crank calls, or letters"**: "A Proposal Under Title IV," February 1, 1971, folder 6604, 25.
162   **shrugged and played dumb**: Ball-Groom, *Salad Pickers*, 177–78.
162   **Writing a check for $8.70**: Letter from FM to Mammoth Mart, November 24, 1971, McKissick Papers, folder 5593.
163   **Despite the difficulties . . . camp run by the Quakers**: Ball-Groom, *Salad Pickers*, 110–78.
163   **The adults had joys . . . to reach by foot**: Ball-Groom, *Salad Pickers*, 110–78; Gordon Carey interview with the author, July 19, 2016; Harvey Gantt interview with the author, October 14, 2015.
164   **"about hay and chickens"**: Harvard University Study, 1969, McKissick Papers, folder 6573, 3.
164   **One reason for the delay . . . not existing ones**: "Table 4.1—Basic Data on Selected New Community Proposals Which Were Never Approved (Alphabetized), Key Dates and Final Disposition," Jack Underhill Papers, George Mason University, box 10, folder 12.
165   **McKissick had hired . . . by Lyndon Johnson**: J. Y. Smith, "Philip Gibbon Hammer, 85, Dies," *Washington Post*, January 23, 2000.
165   **Hammer's report on Soul City . . . "pre-condition will be met"**: "Economic Base Study," Hammer, Green, Siler, December 1969, McKissick Papers, folder 1701.
166   **hopeful it would allay doubts . . . more than a month**: F. S. Tolbert to T. T. Clayton, December 10, 1969, McKissick Papers, folder 5792; FM

to Raymond T. O'Keefe, January 6, 1970, McKissick Papers, folder 6394; FM to Sam Jackson, January 22, 1970, McKissick Papers, folder 5562; FM to Sam Jackson, February 11, 1970, McKissick Papers, folder 5562.

167   But he reserved . . . "move things right away": FM to Sam Jackson, February 11, 1970.

167   Elected in 1968 . . . disproportionate to the danger posed: Rob Christensen, *The Rise and Fall of the Branchhead Boys* (Chapel Hill: University of North Carolina Press, 2019), 118, 197–201; Sanders, "North Carolina Justice," 670–72.

168   state was endorsing the project: Campbell, *New Towns*, 123; Jim Lewis, "State Preparing Standards for 'Soul City' Project," *News & Observer* (Raleigh, NC), October 29, 1970, 2.

169   lend McKissick another $200,000: FM to Sam Jackson, April 15, 1970, McKissick Papers, folder 5561.

169   earmarked for the Warren Regional Planning Corporation: Lewis, "State Preparing Standards for 'Soul City' Project."

10: NAMING RIGHTS

170   more than twenty-five firms: Memorandum from Gordon Carey to William Nicoson, October 11, 1971, McKissick Papers, folder 5601.

171   ownership or profit sharing: Untitled clipping, *Boston After Dark*, April 25, 1972, McKissick Papers, folders 2929–3066.

171   "too poetic and fancy": Philip Sporn to FM, March 2, 1970, McKissick Papers, Folder 6593.

171   "gimmicry and cultural segregation": Harvard University Study, 1969, McKissick Papers, folder 6573.

171   sounded "hard edged": David Godschalk interview with the author, August 19, 2015.

171   "leading to a true multi-racial program": As quoted in Rhee, "Visions, Illusions, and Perceptions," 53.

171   "New City": Lewis, "State Preparing Standards for 'Soul City' Project," 2.

171   In a word, it needed "soul": Rhee, "Visions, Illusions, and Perceptions," 40.

172   "essence of cityhood": Toynbee, *Cities of Destiny*, 13.

172   "it was a unilateral decision": Gordon Carey interview with the author, June 23, 2018.

172   referred to Harlem as "Soul City": Junius Griffith, "The Last Word from Soul City," *New York Times*, August 23, 1964, SM 62.

172   "recommend that we get the city built first": Memorandum from Harold Brown to FM, December 31, 1968, McKissick Papers, folder 5527.

172   a letter to the Rockefeller Foundation: FM to George Harrar, president of the Rockefeller Foundation, January 8, 1969, McKissick Papers, folder 5554.

173   "my life for nothing": Gail Miller, "Floyd McKissick Is Planning a New City with Soul; Now All He Needs Is the Bread," CITY, October 1969, 38.

173   "no one thinks of it as all white": T. T. Clayton interview with the author, March 6, 2015.

173   Alex Haley's African ancestor in Roots: Alex Haley, Roots: The Saga of an American Family (Boston: Da Capo Press, 2014), 275–76.

174   perhaps even himself?: FM to Philip Hammer, April 24, 1970, McKissick Papers, folder 5866.

174   The answer came . . . "play it for all it's worth": Philip Hammer to FM, McKissick Papers, folder 5866.

175   told his client what he wanted to hear: Gordon Carey interview with the author, June 23, 2018.

175   In the summer . . . children in the house: "Odell Kearney Dies of Self-Inflicted Wound," Warren Record, June 18, 1970; Charmaine McKissick-Melton interview with the author, July 18, 2016.

176   "utmost importance to me": FM to Irving Fain, December 22, 1969, McKissick Papers, folder 6412.

176   when he planned to repay: Norman Fain to FM, October 7, 1970, McKissick Papers, folder 6408b.

176   By late 1970 . . . Radiant City: Campbell, New Towns, 245.

177   enthusiasm for new towns . . . remake the urban landscape: National Committee on Urban Growth, The New City, 19, 115; Wakeman, Practicing Utopia, 241–42; John Fischer, "Planning for the Second America," Harper's, November 1969, 21.

177   ten new towns each year: Forsyth, Reforming Suburbia, 168.

177   Congress wasn't prepared . . . legislative calendar: Forsyth, Reforming Suburbia, 168; Housing and Urban Development Act of 1970, PL91-609, 84 Stat. 1770 (1970).

177   With both HUD . . . until two o'clock: D. L. Waller to Carolyn Wakefield, February 22, 1971, McKissick Papers, folder 6145; "Preliminary Dry Run Presentation," February 23, 1971, McKissick Papers, folder 6145; D. L. Waller to Joyce Monroe, February 19, 1971, McKissick Papers, folder 6337.

178   The preparation . . . provide for the entire area: Campbell, New Towns, 124; "Questions Asked by HUD Officials," February 24, 1971, McKissick Papers, folder 6145.

179   "announcement of the offer of commitment": FM to William Nicoson, April 27, 1971, quoted in Rhee, "Visions, Illusions, and Perceptions," 61–62.

180   **"no closer to the guarantee":** FM to Sam Jackson, April 13, 1971, McKissick Papers, folder 6145.

180   **"we are broke again":** FM to Sam Jackson, April 30, 1971, McKissick Papers, folder 5588.

181   **to meet this final condition:** Notes of conversation between Mr. F. B. McKissick and Mr. Samuel Jackson, June 10, 1971, McKissick Papers, folder 7291a; Sam Jackson to FM, July 13, 1971, McKissick Papers, folder 6147.

181   **summer feeding program for impoverished children:** "Soul City Foundation to Sponsor Summer Feeding Program," *Warren Record*, June 24, 1971.

181   **students as summer counselors:** "Students Enjoy Soul City Project," *New York Amsterdam News*, July 24, 1971, A12.

181   **He and Evelyn moved down . . . left behind in New York:** Charmaine McKissick-Melton interviews with the author, March 14, 2015, August 22, 2015, July 18, 2016, and April 1, 2019.

182   **Also arriving . . . "'Warren County, North Cackalacky'":** Lewis Myers interviews with the author, May 14, 2015, August 20, 2015, and March 29, 2019.

183   **But Myers . . . kicked out of Spelman College:** Charmaine McKissick-Melton interview with the author, April 1, 2019.

183   **"come to a meeting and just cuss":** Jane Ball-Groom interview with the author, March 5, 2015.

183   **Myers was more affable . . . from Mars:** Lewis Myers interviews with the author, August 20, 2015, and March 29, 2019.

185   **"want to live with my people":** Walter R. Gordon, "Soul City: Try at Black Power," *Baltimore Sun*, August 11, 1971, A1.

185   **"not qualify for Title VII assistance":** Sam Jackson to FM, August 27, 1971, McKissick Papers, folder 6152.

185   **"The record speaks for itself":** FM to Sam Jackson, September 7, 1971, McKissick Papers, folder 6151.

186   **the promise of five hundred thousand dollars:** FM to Sam Jackson, September 14, 1971, McKissick Papers, folder 6147; FM to Harold Greenberg, March 14, 1972, McKissick Papers, folder 5638.

186   **a revised list of industrial prospects:** Sam Jackson to FM, September 28, 1971, McKissick Papers, folder 6147.

187   **"reason to lose faith":** Draft letter from FM to Sam Jackson, October 1, 1971, McKissick Papers, folder 6151.

187   **hoped to have better news:** Handwritten note on draft letter from FM to Sam Jackson, October 1, 1971, McKissick Papers, folder 6151.

187   **before the money was actually released:** George Romney to FM, October 15, 1971, McKissick Papers, folder 6147.

11: "THEORY OF THE SUGAR TIT"

189   **Bob Brown at the White House:** FM to Sam Jackson, November 8, 1971, McKissick Papers, folder 5592. This letter was sent to both Sam Jackson and Bob Brown, but only the copy sent to Jackson has been located.

189   **"special thrust":** FM to Robert Brown, October 14, 1971, McKissick Papers, folder 6201.

190   **centerpiece of their pitch:** Agenda for Washington, DC, Meeting, January 18, 1972, McKissick Papers, folder 6201; FM to Robert Brown, January 20, 1972, McKissick Papers, folder 6201.

190   **"large white corporations":** Floyd McKissick, "Nixon and Tax Incentives," *New York Amsterdam News*, December 28, 1968, 7.

190   **surveillance of radical groups:** Floyd McKissick, "Nixon's Law Enforcement," *New York Amsterdam News*, May 2, 1970, 17.

190   **"law and order—racist style":** Floyd McKissick, "'Law and Order' Candidates," *New York Amsterdam News*, July 18, 1969, 17.

190   **during the development phase:** Rhee, "Visions, Illusions, and Perceptions," 68.

190   **"He was being expedient":** Eva Clayton interview with the author, March 6, 2015.

190   **crafted a plan to reach Black voters:** Agenda for Washington, DC, Meeting, January 18, 1972; FM to Robert Brown, January 20, 1972; FM to Robert Brown, February 8, 1972, McKissick Papers, folder 6201; Telegram from Robert Brown, March 2, 1972, McKissick Papers, folder 6201.

191   **"power, action and economics":** FM to Robert Brown, March 3, 1972, McKissick Papers, folder 6201; FM to Robert Brown, May 30, 1972, McKissick Papers, folder 6201.

191   **wouldn't say anything more about it:** "'Organize Around Economics' McKissick Tells Pittsburgh," *New Pittsburgh Courier*, March 25, 1972, 28.

191   **"civil rights workhorse":** Joshua D. Farrington, *Black Republicans and the Transformation of the GOP* (Philadelphia: University of Pennsylvania Press, 2016), 59.

192   **"cannot long endure or merit support":** Farrington, *Black Republicans*, 59–60.

192   **"highest mandates of moral law":** Farrington, *Black Republicans*, 71.

192   **NAACP named him an honorary member:** Joseph, *Waiting 'Til the Midnight Hour*, 239.

192   **Nixon continued to court . . . close to matching since:** Branch, *Parting the Waters*, 356–78.

192   **support the Civil Rights Act of 1964:** Stephen E. Ambrose, *Nixon*, vol. 2, *The Triumph of a Politician, 1962–1972* (New York: Simon & Schuster, 1989), 89.

192   **to woo those voters himself:** Ambrose, *Nixon*, 89–90.

193   **tacit appeals to white racism:** Rick Perlstein, *Nixonland: The Rise of a President and the Fracturing of America* (New York: Scribner, 2009), 341–42, 464–67; Corey D. Fields, *Black Elephants in the Room: The Unexpected Politics of African American Republicans* (Oakland: University of California Press, 2016), 47–48.

193   **"burn-America-down type of leaders":** Ambrose, *Nixon*, 163.

193   **"we as Negroes are in serious trouble":** Weems, *Business in Black and White*, 125.

193   **4 percent of the Black vote:** Farrington, "Build, Baby, Build," 68.

193   **Once in the White House . . . his funeral:** Ambrose, *Nixon*, 474; Perlstein, *Nixonland*, 359–60, 515–16; Leah Wright Rigueur, *The Loneliness of the Black Republican* (Princeton: Princeton University Press, 2015), 136–76; Farrington, "Build, Baby, Build," 69–70.

193   **Minority Business Enterprise was severely underfunded:** Rogers, "Acquiring 'A Piece of the Action,'" 177–79.

193   **"benign neglect" on racial matters:** Perlstein, *Nixonland*, 459–60.

193   **At times, Nixon went beyond . . . busing as a means of integration:** Ambrose, *Nixon*, 523; Perlstein, *Nixonland*, 421–22, 459–62, 474–75.

194   **resigned less than two years into the job:** Meier and Rudwick, *CORE*, xii.

194   **the first "anti-Negro" administration:** Martin Arnold, "NAACP Decides It Has a New Enemy," *New York Times*, July 5, 1970, 91.

194   **"silent black majority":** Michael Javen Fortner, *Black Silent Majority: The Rockefeller Drug Laws and the Politics of Punishment* (Cambridge: Harvard University Press, 2015), 133.

194   **"will be key politically":** *Final Report of the Select Committee on Presidential Campaign Activities*, "Section III: The Responsiveness Program" (Washington, DC: US Government Printing Office, 1974), 375; Testimony of Robert Brown to United States Senate Select Committee on Presidential Activities, February 25, 1974, 35.

195   **"utilized as a source of contributions and volunteers":** *Final Report of the Senate Select Committee on Presidential Campaign Activities*, "Section III: The Responsiveness Program," 377.

195   **dependent on his support for the president:** *Final Report of the Senate Select Committee on Presidential Campaign Activities*, "Section V: Results of the Responsiveness Program and Other Related Activities," 405–9.

196   **never actually delivered on his promise:** *Final Report of the Senate Select Committee on Presidential Campaign Activities*, "Section III: The Responsiveness Program," 405.

196   **HealthCo, a comprehensive health-care center:** "Report of the Comptroller General of the United States: Information on the New Community of Soul City, North Carolina," December 18, 1975, GAO Audit, 21–25, available online at https://www.gao.gov/assets/120/113011.pdf.

196   **"Don't worry, Floyd":** T. T. Clayton interviews with the author, March 6, 2015, and March 22, 2019.

196   **no record of McKissick and Clayton meeting:** McKissick did meet with Nixon later in the year, but Clayton was not present. Presidential Daily Diary, October 6, 1972, Richard Nixon Presidential Library and Museum, https://www.nixonlibrary.gov/sites/default/files /virtuallibrary/documents/PDD/1972/085%20October%201-15%20 1972.pdf.

196   **mimicking Nixon's throaty growl:** Eva Clayton interviews with the author, March 6, 2015, and March 22, 2019.

196   **Charmaine also recalls her father:** Charmaine McKissick-Melton interview with the author, April 1, 2019.

197   **"no quid pro quo kind of deals made":** Testimony of Robert Brown to United States Senate Select Committee on Presidential Activities, February 25, 1974, 36–37.

197   **an offer of commitment:** "Meeting Minutes," December 14, 1971, New Community Development Corporation Records, Meeting and Activity Records, 1971–1982; Memorandum from Sam Jackson to Board of Directors, May 19, 1972, New Community Development Corporation Records, Meeting and Activity Records, 1971–1982.

197   **"a desire to give a black developer a chance":** "Allegations Regarding Soul City Project in News and Observer Series," Memorandum from D. Lee Rudd to Otto Stolz, March 12, 1975, New Community Development Corporation Records, Program Records Relating to Soul City, container 1.10.

198   **a fundraising gala for Black Nixon supporters:** FM to Willie C. Mason, May 17, 1972, McKissick Papers, Folder 7550.

198   **boisterous and star-studded affair . . . "America for all Americans":** Rigueur, *Loneliness*, 187; Ronald Taylor, "2,500 Blacks Meet to Plan Ways to Re-Elect President," *Washington Post*, June 11, 1972, A2; Ethel L Payne, "From Hair to Zaire and President Mobutu Too," *Chicago Daily Defender*, June 17, 1972, 10; Allen Howard, "Good Bye Sugar Tit," *Call and Post* (Cleveland), June 17, 1972, 2B.

199   **McKissick spoke last . . . "goodbye old sugar tit!":** McKissick, "The Theory of the Sugar Tit," June 10, 1972, personal papers of Charmaine McKissick-Melton, copy on file with author.

200   **couldn't repress a smile:** Payne, "From Hair to Zaire and President Mobutu Too."

200   **"because he's earned it":** "Black Leaders Hear McKissick at Washington D.C. Dinner," *Atlanta Daily World*, June 22, 1972.

200   **he received letters of appreciation:** Maurice Stans to FM, June 19, 1972; Paul Jones to FM, July 10, 1972; Robert Brown to FM, July 20, 1972, McKissick Papers, folder 7550.

200   **"up to $14,000,000":** Sam Jackson to FM, June 28, 1972, McKissick Papers, folder 6155.

12: BLACK ELEPHANTS

205   **"systematically executing that commitment":** FM to Robert Brown, May 30, 1972, McKissick Papers, folder 6201.

206   **couldn't spoil the positive vibes inside:** Perlstein, *Nixonland*, 686–99.

206   **on stage during the nominating concert:** "Minority Representation up at '72 GOP Convention," *Twin Cities Courier*, August 17, 1972; "Republican Convention: Blacks Will Have Role," *New Journal and Guide* (Norfolk, VA), August 19, 1972, 1.

206   **McKissick played a prominent . . . and a wigmaker:** "Minority Representation up at '72 GOP Convention," August 17, 1972; Leslie Wayne, "Soul City Exhibit Thrives," *News & Observer* (Raleigh, NC), August 24, 1972; Ned Cline, "Soul City Founder Is Mixing His Politics," *Greensboro Daily News*, August 24, 1972; "McKissick, Innis Bid Nonwhites to Join GOP," *Afro-American* (Baltimore), August 26, 1972, 9.

206   **A few weeks later . . . reelection efforts:** Farrington, *Black Republicans*, 213; "Floyd B. McKissick Forms Committee for National 2 Party System Politics," *Atlanta Daily World*, September 22, 1972, 1; Rudy Johnson, "McKissick Forms New Group to Help the Republican Party," *New York Times*, October 15, 1972, 52.

207   **But if McKissick was enjoying . . . riddled with bullets:** Paul Delaney, "Black Supporters of President Under Fire," *New York Times*, October 17, 1972, 29; "Stars for Nixon Camp Assailed," *Chicago Daily Defender*, October 23, 1972, 6.

207   **"they have sold out":** Paul Delaney, "Black Supporters of President Under Fire," *New York Times*, October 17, 1972, 29.

207   **"political prostitutes":** "Blacks for Nixon Sharply Rebuked," *New York Times*, August 3, 1972, 18.

207   **"their pieces of silver":** "Calls Soul City 30 pieces of silver," letter to the editor, *New York Amsterdam News*, September 9, 1972, A4.

207   **"happy hooker":** Kay Longscope, "McKissick Urges Blacks to Work for Self-Interest," *Boston Evening Globe*, October 6, 1972.

207   **He also fired back . . . "crow and humble pie":** Statement of Floyd McKissick, September 1, 1972, McKissick Papers, folder 7550.

208   **"That's Action":** Undated ad, McKissick Papers, folder 7555.

208   **"Blacks as political hostage":** "Minutes of Black Surrogate's Briefing Meeting," September 7, 1972, McKissick Papers, folder 7554.

208   **"able to change with the seasons"**: Longscope, "McKissick Urges Blacks to Work for Self-Interest," October 6, 1972; Robert Benjamin, "Blacks for Nixon Push Campaign," *New Journal and Guide* (Norfolk, VA), October 7, 1972, 1; Bill Lewis, "Former CORE Director Visits LR, Plugs for Re-election of Nixon," *Arkansas Gazette*, October 28, 1972, 11A; George M. Coleman, "McKissick Points Out Value of Two-Party Participation," *Atlanta Daily World*, October 31, 1972, 1.

208   **The message . . . in dozens of Black newspapers and magazines**: Farrington, "Build, Baby, Build," 73; Associated Press, "Baptist Leader Backs Nixon," *New York Times*, September 6, 1972, 32; "Boston NAACP President Switching to Republicans," *Washington Post*, September 8, 1972, A2; "Republicans Rally North and South," *New York Amsterdam News*, October 14, 1972, A1.

208   **It wasn't just . . . "Nixon is 'The Man' for us"**: "Young Negroes Say Nixon Is 'The Man' for Them," undated clipping, McKissick Papers, folder 7552.

209   **praise for the incumbent . . . "Ain't no Black cat ever got"**: Ernest M. Pharr, "Name of the Game Is Economics," *Atlanta Inquirer*, August 26, 1972; Jack Nelson, "Evers Expects Nixon to Get Big Black Vote," undated clipping, McKissick Papers, folder 7555.

209   **a sizable share of the Black vote**: "Nixon Goal 24 Per Cent of Black Vote," undated clipping, McKissick Papers, folder 7555.

209   **To thank those . . . "changing the tide"**: Presidential Daily Diary, October 6, 1972, Richard Nixon Presidential Library and Museum, https://www.nixonlibrary.gov/sites/default/files/2018-07/1972%20 Presidential%20Daily%20Diary.pdf; Nixon White House Tapes, October 6, 1972, Nixontapeaudio.org, http://nixontapeaudio.org /cab/rmn_e108a.mp3.

210   **his 1968 total**: Associated Press, "Survey Reports McGovern Got 87% of the Black Vote," *New York Times*, November 12, 1957, 57.

210   **six to five in the North**: C. Vann Woodward, *The Strange Career of Jim Crow* (New York: Oxford University Press, 1974), 214.

210   **Still, Nixon was grateful . . . state dinner at the White House**: Jeannette Smyth, "Inaugural Concert Chairmen," *Washington Post*, January 3, 1973, B3; Floyd McKissick Jr. interview with the author, April 22, 2019; Presidential Daily Diary, February 1, 1973, Richard Nixon Presidential Library and Museum, https://www.nixonlibrary.gov/sites /default/files/virtuallibrary/documents/PDD/1973/093%20February%201-15%201973.pdf.

210   **"greater image of an open door"**: George Bush to FM, April 12, 1973, McKissick Papers, folder 7703; Fergus, *Liberalism*, 212–13.

211   **"maker of presidents and breaker of senators"**: Ernest B. Furgurson, *Hard Right: The Rise of Jesse Helms* (New York: W.W. Norton, 1986), 8.

211   "six-foot, two-hundred-pound gorilla": Furgurson, *Hard Right*, 30.

211   Like McKissick ... for the candidate in his spare time: Furgurson, *Hard Right*, 30–55.

212   "White People, Wake Up": William A. Link, *Righteous Warrior: Jesse Helms and the Rise of Modern Conservatism* (New York: St. Martin's Press, 2008), 38.

212   Helms later denied ... "see and advise on": Furgurson, 53–54; Link, *Righteous Warrior*, 39–40.

212   Whatever Helms's involvement ... "The Nuisance and Disturber": Furgurson, *Hard Right*, 56–62.

213   editorial on the events of the day: Link, *Righteous Warrior*, 70.

214   "The name of the game is now survival": Osha Gray Davidson, *The Best of Enemies: Race and Redemption in the New South* (New York: Scribner, 1996), 3.

214   "reverts to the law of the jungle": Furgurson, *Hard Right*, 215.

214   "racial distinctions in group intellect": Furgurson, *Hard Right*, 217.

214   "single most dangerous piece of legislation": Link, *Righteous Warrior*, 80.

214   signed off each night by playing "Dixie": Link, *Righteous Warrior*, 70.

214   "the University of Negroes and Communists": Tyson, *Radio Free Dixie*, 67.

214   "mean for Jesus": Furgurson, *Hard Right*, 28.

214   Like nearly all ... margin of eight points: Link, *Righteous Warrior*, 120–29.

215   he was noncommittal: Wayne, "Soul City Exhibit Thrives," August 24, 1972.

216   "In spite of the fact no two men think alike": FM to Jesse Helms, November 10, 1972, McKissick Papers, folder 794.

216   "all things essential to mutual progress": Washington, *Up from Slavery*, 221–22.

216   viewed McKissick as a reckless agitator: Jesse Helms, editorial, *Viewpoint*, September 25, 1964, Raleigh, NC, television broadcast, transcript, North Carolina Collection, Wilson Library, UNC.

216   "nobody's Republican or anything else": Rob Christensen, *The Paradox of Tar Heel Politics: The Personalities, Elections, and Events that Shaped Modern North Carolina* (Chapel Hill: University of North Carolina Press, 2009), 63.

216   "I do not favor the expenditure of taxpayers' funds": Jesse Helms to FM, November 27, 1972, McKissick Papers, folder 794.

217   "my request for a conference with you": FM to Jesse Helms, November 30, 1972, McKissick Papers, folder 794.

217   Walking through the cavernous hall ... "I sure did": T. T. Clayton interview with the author, March 6, 2015.

13: PRESENT AT THE CREATION

218   "About $14 million": Nellie R. Dixon, "Soul City Converting Skeptics," *Charlotte Observer*, October 8, 1972.

218   editorials praising McKissick's plan: "'Soul City': A Vital Experiment," editorial, *Washington Post*, July 6, 1972, A16; "A Not Impossible Dream," editorial, *New York Times*, July 8, 1972, 24.

218   "No Scoffers Heard Now": Jack Scism, "Soul City: No Scoffers Heard Now," *Greensboro Daily News*, June 3, 1973, A1.

219   "monument to your belief and perseverance": Roy Wilkins to FM, November 5, 1973, White House Central Files: Staff Member and Office Files, Bradley H. Patterson Jr., box 64, Richard Nixon Presidential Library and Museum.

219   whatever help he needed: Ross Scott, "Warren Commissioners Endorse Black Project," *Durham Morning Herald*, October 7, 1972.

219   construction of a regional water system: FM to Leonard Garment, February 16, 1973, McKissick Papers, folder 6204.

219   "Sometimes in order to help yourself": Campbell, *New Towns*, 125.

219   they were now coming to see him: Joel Haswell, "Soul City Groundbreaking Is Planned in Two Months," *Durham Morning Herald*, July 20, 1973; FM to Albert F. Trevino Jr., October 11, 1973, White House Central Files: Staff Member and Office Files, Bradley H. Patterson Jr., box 64, Richard Nixon Presidential Library and Museum.

220   "high expectation for the future": Philip S. Morse to FM, January 3, 1973, McKissick Papers, folder 5469; Emil Kesselman to FM, November 22, 1972, McKissick Papers, folder 5469.

220   "Well prior to the completion of your plant": FM to Philip S. Morse, January 24, 1973, McKissick Papers, folder 5469.

220   As it turned out . . . holding Soul City up: Memo from Leonard Garment to Melvin Laird on June 21, 1973, White House Central Files: Staff Member and Office Files, Bradley H. Patterson Jr., box 64, Richard Nixon Presidential Library and Museum.

221   each month's delay was costing them: FM to Leonard Gordon, February 26, 1973, McKissick Papers, folder 6589.

221   "350 jobs from Morse Electro Products": GC to Edward Lamont, January 23, 1973, McKissick Papers, folder 6170.

221   at a New York law firm: Jeannette Smyth, "Tribute to a Policy-Maker," *Washington Post*, April 27, 1973, E3.

222   petition on Soul City's behalf: Eric Lichtblau, "Leonard Garment, Lawyer and Nixon Adviser During Watergate, Dies at 89," *New York Times*, July 15, 2013.

222   still owned only 2,200 acres: FM to James Lynn, October 23, 1973, White House Central Files: Staff Member and Office Files, Bradley

H. Patterson Jr., box 64, Richard Nixon Presidential Library and Museum.

222   **two to three times that amount:** Report from LV Associates, June 10, 1974; and FM to Robert Thompson, March 28, 1973, White House Central Files: Staff Member and Office Files, Bradley H. Patterson Jr., box 64, Richard Nixon Presidential Library and Museum.

222   **"pay through the nose":** Fergus, *Ordeal*, 326.

222   **requesting an update on Soul City:** Leonard Garment to James Lynn, February 5, 1973, White House Central Files: Staff Member and Office Files, Bradley H. Patterson Jr., box 64, Richard Nixon Presidential Library and Museum.

222   **"or a great deal goes down the tube":** Leonard Garment to James Lynn, March 27, 1973, White House Central Files: Staff Member and Office Files, Bradley H. Patterson Jr., box 64, Richard Nixon Presidential Library and Museum.

223   **reviewing several HUD initiatives:** James Lynn to Leonard Garment, April 10, 1973, White House Central Files: Staff Member and Office Files, Bradley H. Patterson Jr., box 64, Richard Nixon Presidential Library and Museum.

223   **"done him a real disservice":** Leonard Garment to Paul O'Neill, April 11, 1973, White House Central Files: Staff Member and Office Files, Bradley H. Patterson Jr., box 64, Richard Nixon Presidential Library and Museum.

223   **"should give Soul City the green light":** Memo from Leonard Garment to Melvin Laird on June 21, 1973.

223   **to promote the company's move:** FM to Philip S. Morse, March 7, 1973, McKissick Papers, folder 5469; FM to Philip S. Morse, March 22, 1973, McKissick Papers, folder 5469.

223   **decided to postpone the expansion:** FM to Al Trevino, October 11, 1973, White House Central Files: Staff Member and Office Files, Bradley H. Patterson Jr., box 64, Richard Nixon Presidential Library and Museum.

224   **Once shovels were in the earth:** Rhee, "Visions, Illusions, and Perceptions," 86.

224   **Nixon could fly down by helicopter:** FM to Leonard Garment, July 2, 1973, White House Central Files: Staff Member and Office Files, Bradley H. Patterson Jr., box 64, Richard Nixon Presidential Library and Museum.

224   **"a dramatic change of pace":** Schedule proposal from Leonard Garment, July 11, 1973, White House Central Files: Staff Member and Office Files, Bradley H. Patterson Jr., box 64, Richard Nixon Presidential Library and Museum.

224   **"To commit the President at this time personally":** Memorandum from Michael Raoul-Duval to David Parker, July 30, 1973, White

House Central Files: Staff Member and Office Files, Bradley H. Patterson Jr., box 64, Richard Nixon Presidential Library and Museum.

225 **As the groundbreaking neared ... in a time capsule:** Ball-Groom, *Salad Pickers*, 281–91.

225 **The groundbreaking took place ... "build you a city":** "First Shovels of Earth Turned at Soul City," *Warren Record*, November 15, 1973; Groundbreaking program, McKissick Papers, folder 1755; Ball-Groom, *Salad Pickers*, 292–95.

226 **"50 percent chance" of success:** Lewis, "State Preparing Standards for 'Soul City' Project," 2; Christensen, *Rise and Fall*, 206.

226 **The high point ... John F. Kennedy:** Rich Nichols, "Gov. Holshouser Hails Soul City," *News & Observer* (Raleigh, NC), November 10, 1973.

226 **"There are those ... have become believers":** Speech by Gov. Jim Holshouser, groundbreaking for Soul City, November 9, 1973, McKissick Papers, folder 5067.

228 **"people back to North Carolina":** "First Shovels of Earth Turned at Soul City," November 15, 1973.

228 **"let Soul City serve as a lesson":** Speech by Gov. Jim Holshouser, November 9, 1973.

228 **"it's becoming a reality":** Billy Rowe, "New Ideas an Old Life-Style," *New York Amsterdam News*, November 24, 1973.

228 **the celebration moved to Durham ... back to Soul City:** Groundbreaking Program, McKissick Papers, folder 1755; Ball-Groom, *Salad Pickers*, 293–95; "John Parker Wins Soul City Award," *News & Observer* (Raleigh, NC), November 16, 1973.

229 **"I had no doubt in my mind":** Rhee, "Visions, Illusions, and Perceptions," 74.

229 **"this weekend to celebrate, to laugh":** Ball-Groom, *Salad Pickers*, 295–96.

14: CREAM OF THE CROP

230 **could proceed to closing:** "Minutes of Meeting," December 17, 1973, New Community Development Corporation Records, Meeting and Activity Records, 1971–1982.

230 **snapped up by Liberty National Life Insurance:** "From a Dream to a Reality: Soul City Gets Bread," press release, March 7, 1974, McKissick Papers, folder 1752.

230 **"Nobody is giving Soul City any five million dollars":** Strain, "Soul City," 67.

230 **the *New York Times* sent a reporter down:** Wayne King, "Soul City, N.C., Is Moving from Dream Stage to Reality," *New York Times*, January 4, 1974, 34.

230   **Both reports were glowing ... and health care:** Hattie Bell to FM, February 4, 1974, McKissick Papers, folder 543.

231   **as far away as Colorado and California:** Visitors registers, McKissick Papers, folders 5145–50.

231   **a tour of local landmarks:** Memorandum from John Edwards to Charmaine McKissick, June 7, 1975, McKissick Papers, folder 5142b.

231   **electrical wires and streetlights:** "Report of the Comptroller General of the United States: Information on the New Community of Soul City, North Carolina," December 18, 1975, 3, 10.

232   **"What is needed here is an infusion":** Rhee, "Visions, Illusions, and Perceptions," 134 fn 14.

233   **quarter of the employees at Soul City were white:** Rhee, "Visions, Illusions, and Perceptions," 96.

233   **A graduate of Vassar ... "considered crazy":** Dorothy Webb interview with the author, June 4, 2019.

233   **There were no trailers ... herd of pigs:** Dorothy Webb interview with the author, June 4, 2019.

233   **"Everybody waves at everybody":** Residents Handbook, McKissick Papers, folder 5059.

234   **showed a lack of respect:** Beverly McNeill interview with the author, April 25, 2015.

234   **"He could be himself":** Gordon Carey interview with the author, July 19, 2016.

235   **"not exactly a fan of Gordon Carey":** Charmaine McKissick-Melton interview with the author, April 1, 2019.

235   **Not that Carey ... nothing had happened:** Harvey Gantt interview with the author, October 14, 2015; Gordon Carey interview with the author, June 23, 2018.

235   **"Floyd's was deep purple":** Jane Ball-Groom interview with the author, October 15, 2015.

236   **While the residents ... the job anyway:** Ball-Groom, *Salad Pickers*, 159–60, 166–67, 216–17.

236   **Local whites ... "the more business":** Rick Nichols, "Present at the Creation," *News & Observer* (Raleigh, NC), November 4, 1973.

236   **this being Klan Country ... "fear":** Ball-Groom, *Salad Pickers*, 188–91.

237   **"all the niggers should move in there":** Nichols, "Present at the Creation," November 4, 1973.

237   **As the wife ... head of the Sanitary District:** Ball-Groom, *Salad Pickers*, 148; Floyd McKissick Jr. interview with the author, October 12, 2015; Charmaine McKissick-Melton interview with the author, March 4, 2015.

238   **"I can't solve your problems":** Ball-Groom, *Salad Pickers*, 155.

238   **Not long after ... everyone was safe:** Ball-Groom, *Salad Pickers*, 180–81.

239   **Gordon Carey's wife . . . baby born in Soul City:** Gordon Carey interviews with the author, April 23, 2015, and July 19, 2016.

239   **Soul City made progress . . . storm drainage lines:** "Report of the Comptroller General of the United States: Information on the New Community of Soul City, North Carolina," December 18, 1975, GAO Audit, 51; "A Paper on Soul City, Prepared for William J. White," January 3, 1978, McKissick Papers, folder 1750.

240   **The recession hit . . . put it up for sale:** Thomas W. Lippman, "Some Near Financial Collapse: New Towns Face Crisis," *Washington Post*, November 15, 1974, A1.

241   **At the same time . . . fast-growing urban areas:** Lippman, "Some Near Financial Collapse: New Towns Face Crisis."

241   **Soul City wasn't mentioned . . . achieve Black autonomy:** Pamela Hollie, "Search for 'Soul': Black Separatists Get New Followers, Create New Towns," *Wall Street Journal*, July 31, 1974, 1.

243   **"babies ritually mutilated":** FM to Frederick Taylor, August 2, 1974, McKissick Papers, folder 845.

243   **All made the same point:** Eva Clayton to Frederick Taylor, August 2, 1974; Charles Allen to Frederick Taylor, August 2, 1974; Gordon Carey to Frederick Taylor, August 2, 1974; S. J. Velaj to Editor, *Wall Street Journal*, August 5, 1974; Philip Hammer to Frederick Taylor, August 15, 1974. McKissick Papers, folder 845.

243   **"how you came to misinterpret so drastically":** Dorothy Webb to Pam Hollie, August 2, 1974, McKissick Papers, folder 845.

244   **"presenting the true facts to the readers":** Steven Thal to Frederick Taylor, August 5, 1974, McKissick Papers, folder 845.

244   **"rectify this injury":** Steven Thal to Edward Cony, August 15, 1974, McKissick Papers, folder 845.

244   **"long been excluded because of prejudice":** "Letters to the Editor," *Wall Street Journal*, August 19, 1974, 9.

245   **McKissick moved quickly . . . since the 1972 election:** FM to Gerald Ford, August 27, 1974, McKissick Papers, folder 7269.

245   **to attend his first budget message:** Stanley Scott to FM, September 6, 1974, McKissick Papers, folder 7269; Telegram from FM to William J. Baroody, Assistant to the President for Public Liaison, January 19, 1975, McKissick Papers, folder 7269.

245   **getting out of the new town business:** Thomas W. Lippman, "HUD Ends New Town Programs," *Washington Post*, January 11, 1975, A1.

15: BLINDSIDED

246   **One day . . . pressing for an answer:** Rhee, "Visions, Illusions, and Perceptions," 94–95.

246   The result . . . smattering of trailers: Pat Stith, "Private Roads Get Public Funds at Soul City," *News & Observer* (Raleigh, NC), November 3, 1974, A1.

247   "profit prospects in which he shares": "Soul City Gets Special Treatment," *News & Observer* (Raleigh, NC), editorial, November 9, 1974, 8.

248   "one hundred thousand ignorant Negro voters": Mabry, *The Negro in North Carolina*, 29–72; Lee A. Craig, *Josephus Daniels: His Life and Times* (Chapel Hill: University of North Carolina Press, 2013), xiii–xiv, 111–22, 178–91; Franklin, *Negro in Twentieth Century America*, 30.

248   against the social mixing of whites and Blacks: Craig, *Josephus Daniels*, 188, 414.

248   "than to give up their prejudices": Charles W. Eagles, "Two 'Double V's': Jonathan Daniels, FDR, and Race Relations During World War II," *North Carolina Historical Review* 59, no. 3 (July 1982), 255.

249   "secession from civilization": Roberts and Klibanoff, *Race Beat*, 23, 118, 172.

249   discrimination in the workplace: Gene Roberts interview with Joseph Mosnier, *News & Observer*, 1945–1995, Oral History Series, February 7, 2008, Southern Oral History Program Collection, University of North Carolina at Chapel Hill, 12–15.

249   "so irascible and unreliable": Madison, "Objections Sustained," 34.

249   Although Carey . . . taking it out on Soul City: Gordon Carey interview with the author, April 23, 2015.

250   "I was an integrationist": Claude Sitton interview with Joseph Mosnier, *News & Observer*, 1945–1995, Oral History Series, July 12, 2007, Southern Oral History Program Collection, University of North Carolina at Chapel Hill, 20.

251   "without going back to Abe Lincoln?": Wayne King, "A Long Career in Black and White," *News & Observer* (Raleigh, NC), October 28, 1990, 1J.

251   "recognized limits in his virtues": King, "A Long Career in Black and White."

251   A dogged reporter . . . suburb outside Raleigh: Pat Stith, "Goodbye Charlotte," *Final Edition* (blog), January 28–30, 2019, http://patstith.com/index.php/2019/01; Pat Stith interview with the author, August 26, 2019.

252   He outed the state highway commission: Pat Stith, "Stone from Commissioner's Quarry Purchased by State Highway Unit," *News & Observer* (Raleigh, NC), February 29, 1972, 1.

252   phone calls on the state's dime: Pat Stith, "Cohoon's Calls Billed to N.C.," *News & Observer* (Raleigh, NC), November 17, 1972, 1.

252   more frequently than members of the public: Pat Stith, "Legislators

Slip Through Traffic Law Loophole," *News & Observer* (Raleigh, NC), November 4, 1973, 7.

252   **thirteen Japanese maples:** Pat Stith, "Short Trees . . . Tall Price Tag," *News & Observer* (Raleigh, NC), April 8, 1972, 30.

252   **cosponsor a professional golf tournament:** Pat Stith, "C&D Buys 'Spot' in Golf Tourney," *News & Observer* (Raleigh, NC), August 27, 1971, 1.

252   **Stith's fixation . . . help pay the bills:** Pat Stith, *Final Edition* (blog), http://patstith.com/index.php/about/. See "A Taste of Poor," August 12, 2019; "The Sweat Shop," July 5, 2019; "Motivating With Money," December 1, 2017; "How Can I Help You?" October 2, 2017; "Mmmmm, Good Lettuce," October 13, 2017; and "Payback," April 10, 2017.

253   **He thought he was just as good . . . Pulitzer Prize:** Pat Stith interview with the author, August 26, 2019.

253   **"He wasn't listening":** Eva Clayton interview with the author, March 6, 2015.

253   **The bomb went off . . . "no Soul City":** Pat Stith, "Soul City: A Tangled Web," *News & Observer* (Raleigh, NC), March 2, 1975, 1.

254   **"applications for $5 million more":** Stith, "Soul City: A Tangled Web."

254   **"still no homes, no shops":** Pat Stith, "Soul City: Empty Fields and a Mass Transit Bid," *News & Observer* (Raleigh, NC), March 9, 1975.

254   **"mobile homes standing like sheep":** Charles Craven, "A Beautiful Location to Build a New City," *News & Observer* (Raleigh, NC), March 3, 1975.

255   **faulted Soul City for lacking:** "Report of the Comptroller General of the United States: Information on the New Community of Soul City, North Carolina," December 18, 1975, GAO Audit, 1.

255   **"a single British new town":** Biles, "The Rise and Fall of Soul City," 65.

255   **grant to help McKissick's for-profit company:** Stith, "Soul City: A Tangled Web."

256   **the one to reap the profits:** Pat Stith, "McKissick: U.S. OKd His Interlocking Roles," *News & Observer* (Raleigh, NC), March 2, 1975, 4.

256   **the paper printed a diagram:** Stith, "McKissick: U.S. OKd His Interlocking Roles."

257   **a huge profit on the deal:** Stith, "Soul City: A Tangled Web."

257   **took a bath on the deal:** "Report of the Comptroller General of the United States: Information on the New Community of Soul City, North Carolina," December 18, 1975, 64.

257   **failed to recruit any industry:** Stith, "Soul City: A Tangled Web."

257   **geared strictly toward planning:** "Report of the Comptroller General," December 18, 1975, 68.

257   **self-perpetuating cash machine:** Stith, "Soul City: A Tangled Web."

257   **objectives that Stith did not mention:** "Report of the Comptroller General," December 18, 1975, 71–72.

257   **allegations were all correct:** "Report of the Comptroller General," December 18, 1975, 3–8, 66–69.

258   **would soon double again:** "Report of the Comptroller General," December 18, 1975, 67–68.

16: THE BATTLE OF SOUL CITY

259   **motivated by racism:** Rick Nichols, "Delay Defended by McKissick," *News & Observer* (Raleigh, NC), March 21, 1975, 1; Floyd McKissick Jr. interview with the author, October 12, 2015.

259   **"this harassment of Soul City":** Pat Stith, "Soul City Articles Attacked," *News & Observer* (Raleigh, NC), Feb. 10, 1976.

260   **"whites who have castigated him so hard":** J. B. Harren, "Field Day Against Blacks," *Carolinian*, March 15, 1975, 7.

260   **"a black in control and command":** Emsar Bradford Jr. to FM, April 25, 1975, McKissick Papers, folder 1806.

260   **embraced the cause of racial equality:** Claude Sitton, "Soul City Issue Stirs Up News Critics," *News & Observer* (Raleigh, NC), February 15, 1976.

260   **simply as "the way it was":** Pat Stith, "More Growing Up Country," *Final Edition* (blog), Aug. 24, 2018, http://patstith.com/index.php /2018/08/page/2/.

260   **"social mixing" of the races:** Pat Stith, "The Racist," *Final Edition* (blog), July 30, 2018, http://patstith.com/index.php/2018/07/.

260   **"fight for it in Viet Nam":** Pat Stith, "The Peacenik Band," *Final Edition* (blog), November 26, 2018, http://patstith.com/index.php/2018 /11/.

260   **When I interviewed . . . "believe right down to my toenails":** Pat Stith interview with the author, August 26, 2019.

261   **exaggeratedly large lips:** Dwane Powell, editorial cartoon, *News & Observer* (Raleigh, NC), March 7, 1975, 4.

262   **"I can't control them":** Pat Stith interview with the author, August 26, 2019; email from Pat Stith to author, August 27, 2019.

262   **referring all questions to his lawyer:** "Soul City Audits Are Welcome, Official Asserts," *News & Observer* (Raleigh, NC), March 8, 1975, 1.

262   **nearly a dozen allies:** Press conference package, March 20, 1975, McKissick Papers, folder 1601b.

262   **He began . . . "we are succeeding":** Statement of Floyd McKissick, March 20, 1975, McKissick Papers, folder 1601b.

264   **In addition . . . articles never appeared:** Gordon Carey interview with the author, April 23, 2015.

265   **"independent audit that can trace all the sources":** "Soul City Needs Thorough Audit," *News & Observer* (Raleigh, NC), editorial, March 5, 1975.

265   **a full audit of Soul City:** Steve Berg, "Fountain, Helms Ask Audit of Soul City," *News & Observer* (Raleigh, NC), March 6, 1975, 1.

265   **mismanaged state funds:** Daniel C. Hoover, "Aid Cutoff Plan Decried," *News & Observer* (Raleigh, NC), April 9, 1975.

265   **"A $19 million rip-off":** *National Enquirer*, August 24, 1975, cited in Madison, "Objections Sustained," 35.

265   **until the audit was complete:** Associated Press, "Conflict of Interest Investigation Holds Up Funds for Soul City," *New York Times*, April 12, 1975, 12.

265   **"questions being raised":** Charles C. Allen to David C. Robinson, Director of Mass Transit, Department of Transportation and Highway Safety, State of North Carolina, April 15, 1972, McKissick Papers, folder 767.

266   **"more balanced attitude, investigation, and report":** Melvin Margolies, letter published as "Text of Official's Letter," *News & Observer* (Raleigh, NC), May 6, 1975, 6.

266   **the full text of Margolies's letter:** "HUD Official Criticizes N&O's Soul City Series," *News & Observer* (Raleigh, NC), May 6, 1975, 6.

267   **"who that 'somebody' is":** 121 Cong. Rec. 25133–25135 (July 26, 1975).

267   **vanishing liberal wing:** Fields, *Black Elephants*, 49.

267   **"a nation of laws, not of men":** 121 Cong. Rec. 25135–25136 (July 26, 1975).

267   **"confidence in your important work":** Edward Brooke to FM, July 31, 1975, McKissick Papers, folder 791.

268   **financing for the project:** "Report of the Comptroller General of the United States: Information on the New Community of Soul City, North Carolina," December 18, 1975, GAO Audit, 1.

268   **wouldn't so much as accept a cup of coffee:** Gordon Carey interview with the author, July 19, 2016.

268   **Reynolds would not be expanding its operations:** Robert Thompson to FM, April 8, 1975, McKissick Papers, folder 5500.

268   **"clear up some questions in your mind":** FM to Robert Thompson, May 12, 1975, McKissick Papers, folder 5500.

269   **"need not speak defensively":** Devin Fergus, "The Ordeal of Liberalism and Black Nationalism in an American Southern State, 1965–1980," PhD diss., Columbia University, 2002, 336.

269   **"had the education and experience":** "Report of the Comptroller

General of the United States: Information on the New Community of Soul City, North Carolina," 6, 11, 60–65.

269   **"evidenced by more basic amenities"**: "Report of the Comptroller General," 11, 65.

270   **forty-four dollars per patient**: "Report of the Comptroller General," 45, 66–68.

270   **"moral obligation" to fund the water system**: "Report of the Comptroller General," 4.

270   **"unallowable expenditures in the future"**: "Report of the Comptroller General," 8–12, 75–83.

271   **poor bookkeeping practices**: Pat Stith, "McKissick Lauds GAO Report," *News & Observer* (Raleigh, NC), December 18, 1975, 1.

271   **"welcome Christmas present"**: Statement of Floyd McKissick, December 15, 1975, McKissick Papers, folder 890.

271   **buried deep in the article**: Pat Stith, "GAO Hits Handling of Soul City Funds," *News & Observer* (Raleigh, NC), December 17, 1975, 1.

272   **"make their enemies more effective"**: "Soul City Blunders Are Costly," *News & Observer* (Raleigh, NC), editorial, December 18, 1975.

272   **"GAO Audit Clears Soul City Project"**: *Carolina Times*, January 17, 1976, 1.

272   **"Man Enough to Apologize?"**: *Carolina Times*, editorial, January 17, 1976, 2.

272   **"greatest single waste of public money"**: Gary Pearce, "Review of Audit Urged by Helms," *News & Observer* (Raleigh, NC), Dec. 17, 1975.

272   **"no further prosecutive consideration"**: FBI memorandum, May 3, 1976, received by author in response to Freedom of Information Act request.

17: GOOD PLACE TO LIVE

275   **"would justify a health facility"**: Pat Stith, "HEW Dries Up Funds for Soul City Clinic," *News & Observer* (Raleigh, NC), December 16, 1975; Pat Stith, "Two Agencies Drop Soul City Funding," *News & Observer* (Raleigh, NC), December 22, 1975.

276   **"already at minimum levels"**: Pat Stith, "Governor Makes Plea for Soul City Clinic," *News & Observer* (Raleigh, NC), January 31, 1976, 19.

276   **continue to fund HealthCo**: "Clinic Stand Is Reversed," *Durham Morning Herald*, February 4, 1976.

276   **McKissick also received . . . Founders' Day Banquet**: FM to Charles S. Hope, February 6, 1976, McKissick Papers, folder 5469.

276   **Soul Tech I . . . reenergize a beleaguered workforce**: Pat Stith, "Two New Firms Plan to Locate at Soul City," *News & Observer* (Raleigh, NC), April 2, 1976; Ball-Groom, *Salad Pickers*, 304–5.

276   Elsewhere . . . engraved on both sides: Chet Fuller, "Soul City: Will It Make It?" *Atlanta Journal*, June 13, 1976, 1.

277   city's first subdivision: "A Paper on Soul City, Prepared for William J. White by The Soul City Company," January 3, 1978, 4, McKissick Papers, folder 1750; "Home Parade Ready to Roll," *Durham Morning Herald*, November 24, 1976.

277   "report what actually exists here": Memorandum from Floyd B. McKissick Jr. to FM, April 5, 1976, McKissick Papers, folder 321.

278   While the staff . . . lined with dogwoods: FM to William Hoffman, December 1, 1975, McKissick Papers, folder 738m; FM to Albert F. Trevino, April 3, 1974, McKissick Papers, folder 738m.

279   a dream had been fulfilled: Ball-Groom, *Salad Pickers*, 287, 319–25.

279   scene out of *Brigadoon*: Voyette Perkins-Brown, interview with the author, August 22, 2015.

279   The benefits . . . "whole doggone country": Minchin, "Brand New Shining City," 135, 151; Howard Covington, "Soul City Beholds Its Dream Deferred," *Charlotte Observer*, June 30, 1979.

280   "Good Place to Live": *Soul City Sounder*, November 1975.

280   While Soul City . . . given another chance: Alan S. Oser, "U.S. Reevaluating 'New Towns' Program," *New York Times*, July 23, 1976; "Soul City Is Proving Out, While Other 'New Towns' Hit Skids," *Ledger-Star* (Norfolk, VA), November 23, 1976.

281   But he had . . . the project agreement: Fergus, *Liberalism*, 217; FM to John V. Hunter, April 1, 1976, McKissick Papers, folder 1807.

282   Ronald Reagan's announcement . . . convention that summer: Fergus, *Liberalism*, 218–25; Rick Perlstein, *The Invisible Bridge: The Fall of Nixon and the Rise of Reagan* (New York: Simon & Schuster, 2015), 645–48; Ferrel Guillory interview with the author, April 20, 2020; "Petition to Nominate Senator Ed. Brooke Vice President of the United States," McKissick Papers, folder 7730.

283   "vigorous, adverse reaction": Fergus, *Liberalism*, 224.

284   HealthCo for another year: Ann Pelham "U.S. Agency Extends Funding for Soul City Health Clinic," *News & Observer* (Raleigh, NC), November 19, 1976.

284   "wizard at shaking undeserved money": "Soul City Hits Taxpayers Again," *News & Observer* (Raleigh, NC), editorial, November 22, 1976.

284   HUD received more than two dozen letters: Letters of support for Soul City, 1976, McKissick Papers, folder 1808.

284   "lies and innuendoes": Linda Nesbitt to Carla Hills, December 14, 1976, McKissick Papers, folder 1808.

284   "unwarranted": Mary Richardson to Carla Hills, December 9, 1976, McKissick Papers, folder 1808.

284   "rejoice in your decision": Melvin C. Holmes to Carla Hills, December 6, 1976, McKissick Papers, folder 1808.

18: PRIDE OR PREJUDICE

285   The election . . . benefit Soul City: Timothy J. Minchin and John A. Salmond, *After the Dream: Black and White Southerners Since 1965* (Lexington: University Press of Kentucky, 2011), 168–87; B. Drummond Ayres Jr., "1976 Surprise: Carter Is Running Well," *New York Times*, December 26, 1975, 1; "Black Campaign Perspectives: Carter Involves Many Blacks," *Afro-American* (Baltimore), October 23, 1976; Charles Mohr, "Carter, with a Long List of Campaign Promises, Now Faces the Problem of Making Good on Them," *New York Times*, November 15, 1976.

285   with Ford posters: Memorandum from Larnie Horton to Members of the Executive Board of the National Black Republican Council, August 24, 1976, McKissick Papers, folder 7698a; Martin Dinkins to FM, September 28, 1976, McKissick Papers, folder 7698a.

286   influence with a Democratic administration: Minchin, "Brand New Shining City," 148.

286   existing loan programs and interest subsidies: Strain, "*Soul City*," 68; Marable, *Race, Reform, and Rebellion*, 170.

286   first Black woman nominated to a cabinet position: Eric Pianin, "Patricia Harris: A Life of Striving to Be a Champion," *Washington Post*, September 7, 1982; Juan Williams, "Patricia R. Harris Dies at 60," *Washington Post*, March 24, 1985.

287   "problems of the poor": Hearing Before the Committee on Banking, Housing, and Urban Affairs, January 10, 1977 (Washington, DC: US Government Printing Office, 1977), 1–4.

287   "If you think that I have forgotten that": "Hearing Before the Committee on Banking," January 10, 1977, 41.

287   While Proxmire . . . young Joe Biden: "Hearing Before the Committee on Banking," January 10, 1977, 25–29.

288   McKissick was left in limbo: Rhee, "Visions, Illusions, and Perceptions," 114.

288   Then, once the board . . . in January: "Minutes of Meeting," October 17, 1977, New Community Development Corporation Records, Meeting and Activity Records, 1971–1982, container 12, 5-6; Jesse Helms to Patricia Harris, June 20, 1977, and July 14, 1977, New Community Development Corporation Records, Program Records Relating to Soul City, container 1.3.

289   When McKissick . . . naturally into place: "A Paper on Soul City, Prepared for William J. White," January 3, 1978, McKissick Papers, folder 1750.

290   **When White submitted ... federal bureaucracy:** "Soul City, North Carolina, Report to the NCDC Board," January 1978, New Community Development Corporation Records, Meeting and Activity Records, 1971–1982, container 12.

290   **At its January meeting ... "harder each day to get out":** "Transcript of Proceedings," Board of Directors Meeting, January 18, 1978, New Community Development Corporation Records, Meeting and Activity Records, 1971–1982, Container 12, 45–48.

290   **Much of the debate ... "not even going to answer it":** "Transcript of Proceedings," Board of Directors Meeting, January 18, 1978, New Community Development Corporation Records, Meeting and Activity Records, 1971–1982, Container 12, 50–51, 58–59.

291   **The most logical ... "gear up for the cutoff":** "Transcript of Proceedings," Board of Directors Meeting, January 18, 1978, New Community Development Corporation Records, Meeting and Activity Records, 1971–1982, Container 12, 48, 51, 60; FM to William White, December 14, 1977, New Community Development Corporation Records, Program Records Relating to Soul City, container 1.3.

291   **and Soul City:** "History of New Communities Program," *HUD News*, January 18, 1978, Jack Underhill Papers, box 13, folder 8.

291   **In announcing ... "make Soul City viable":** Warren Brown, "HUD Trims Role in 'New Communities' Program," *Washington Post*, January 19, 1978, C10; Ferrel Guillory, "Soul City's on HUD's List of New Towns to 'Salvage,'" *News & Observer* (Raleigh, NC), January 19, 1978.

292   **In an editorial ... "zip by on I-85":** "Fresh Dollars for Soul City," *News & Observer* (Raleigh, NC), editorial, January 22, 1978.

292   **At fifty-one, Sorg ... own consulting firm:** Walter Larke Sorg résumé, McKissick Papers, folder 6130.

293   **"exceptionally well-managed":** Walter Larke Sorg to Walter J. Schularick, January 24, 1978, McKissick Papers, folder 847.

293   **Without the money ... shares in the Soul City Company:** Walter Larke Sorg to Gerald Campbell, July 18, 1978, McKissick Papers, folder 1274.

293   **"getting that first commitment":** Walter Larke Sorg to Ray J. Graham, March 7, 1978, McKissick Papers, folder 5501b.

294   **one-eighth of its water supply:** "Projected Statement of Sources and Uses of Cash," December 15, 1972, McKissick Papers, folder 1297; Lewis Myers interview with the author, August 20, 2015.

294   **Miller went elsewhere:** Dan Pleasant to Gordon Carey, November 7, 1975; Gordon Carey to Robert Stewart, October 21, 1975, McKissick Papers, folder 5467a; Lewis Myers interview with the author, August 20, 2015.

294   **"pissing and shitting in"**: Lewis Myers interview with the author, August 20, 2015.

294   **The obvious solution . . . the sewer system**: Gordon Carey interview with the author, July 19, 2016.

295   **"Without sewerage, you're nothing"**: Gordon Carey interview with the author, April 23, 2015.

295   **"not be having this conversation"**: Lewis Myers interview with the author, August 20, 2015.

295   **"potentially volatile situation"**: Walter Larke Sorg to Walter J. Schularick, January 24, 1978, McKissick Papers, folder 847.

296   **"becoming more of a disadvantage"**: Memorandum from John P. Stewart Jr. to FM, January 23, 1978, McKissick Papers, folder 528.

296   **"dramatize to the public the true concept"**: "Recommendations on Changing the Name of Soul City," Carmichael and Company, January 24, 1978, McKissick Papers, folder 528.

296   **"not one has been bought by a white homeowner"**: Memorandum from Gordon Carey to FM, February 14, 1978, McKissick Papers, folder 528.

297   **"a good excuse for people's inability"**: Floyd McKissick, "Reasons Why We Should Not Change the Name," February 17, 1978, McKissick Papers, folder 528.

297   **a truly fresh start**: "Recommendations on Changing the Name of Soul City," Carmichael and Company, February 28, 1978, McKissick Papers, folder 528.

297   **proposed "Kerr Lake"**: Julian C. Madison to FM, February 23, 1978, McKissick Papers, folder 528.

298   **"switch horses in midstream"**: Harvey Gantt to FM, March 7, 1978, McKissick Papers, folder 528.

298   **"must not falter from its original goal"**: Irving L. McCaine to FM, March 2, 1978, McKissick Papers, folder 528.

298   **"there was no turning back"**: Gordon Carey interview with the author, April 23, 2015.

299   **"black accomplishment:"** Harvard University Study, 1969, McKissick Papers, folder 6573, 5.

299   **annual payroll of more than $2 million**: "Soul City Gets First Industry," *New Pittsburgh Courier*, April 22, 1978, 24.

299   **personally visit Soul City**: Phillip Drotning to FM, April 26, 1978; and John E. Swearingen to FM, July 24, 1978, McKissick Papers, folder 5504; Floyd McKissick, "The Economics of Being Black" (speech, Red Crown Lodge, Arbor Vitae, WI, June 23, 1978), McKissick Papers, folder 7481b, and in personal papers of Charmaine McKissick-Melton, copy on file with author.

300   **"popping in the next couple of months"**: Walter Larke Sorg to FM, December 19, 1978, McKissick Papers, folder 5521.

19: MASERATIS AND MICROWAVES

301   **oak, sweet gum, and cedar:** Memorandum from FM to Residents of Green Duke Village, November 22, 1978, McKissick Papers, folder 548b.

302   **completion date in the spring of 1981:** "Timeline of Accomplishments," McKissick Papers, folder 1811; "Highlight Report on Soul City Prepared for the HUD Task Force," February 22, 1979, McKissick Papers, folder 258.

302   **"alive and kicking and beautiful":** Walter Larke Sorg to FM, November 6, 1978, McKissick Papers, folder 2575.

302   **General Motors had ruled out Soul City:** Lewis Myers to Stuart R. Hochman, November 3, 1978, McKissick Papers, folder 5429.

302   **"cloud over an otherwise unblemished record":** FM to Thomas A. Murphy draft letter, undated, McKissick Papers, folder 5429.

303   **revised budget in January:** Gordon Carey to William J. White, December 29, 1978, McKissick Papers, folder 1970.

303   **final $4 million in bonds:** Memorandum from William White to Patricia Harris, December 29, 1978, New Community Development Corporation Records, Program Records Relating to Soul City, container 1.3.

303   **no longer a financially acceptable risk:** Edward Cachine to FM, January 16, 1979, McKissick Papers, folder 258; Memorandum to file from Kathy Gibbons, January 5, 1979, New Community Development Corporation Records, Program Records Relating to Soul City, container 1.12; *Soul City Company v. United States*, Complaint, August 17, 1979, McKissick Papers, folder 1831, 12.

304   **"to make Soul City a success":** "Task Force Named on Soul City, N.C.," *HUD News*, February 17, 1979; Memorandum from Patricia Harris to William White and Sterling Tucker, February 5, 1979, New Community Development Corporation Records, Program Records Relating to Soul City, container, 1.3.

304   **into combat once more:** Jacqueline Trescott, "Sitting in for Civil-Rights Veteran James Farmer," *Washington Post*, March 5, 1979, B7; Thomas A. Johnson, "CORE's Founder and Ex-Members Planning a New Civil Rights Group," *New York Times*, March 5, 1979, A14.

304   **After spending . . . check on his condition:** Charmaine McKissick-Melton interview with the author, March 4, 2015; "McKissick Badly Hurt in Wreck," *News & Observer* (Raleigh, NC), March 7, 1979, 27.

306   **"headed in the wrong direction":** Floyd McKissick Jr. interview with the author, October 12, 2015.

306   **"Come Out Better Than Segregationists":** Neil Maxwell, "Mixed Fortunes: Black Leaders of the 1960s Have Come Out Better Than Segregationists," *Wall Street Journal*, March 12, 1979, 1.

307   **give them a fair shake:** Charmaine McKissick-Melton interview with the author, April 1, 2019.

307   **"Sustained by Federal Money":** Susan Harrigan, "An Old 'New Town' Hangs On, Sustained by Federal Money," *Wall Street Journal*, April 19, 1979.

309   **"and to make a profit":** FM to The Editor, *Wall Street Journal*, April 23, 1979, McKissick Papers, folder 1810.

309   **"alive in the minds of readers":** John V. Hunter III to FM, April 25, 1979, McKissick Papers, folder 1810.

309   **"concrete evidence of progress":** FM to William J. White, April 25, 1979, McKissick Papers, folder 261.

310   **massive infusions of cash to survive:** Pat Stith, "Progress Lags at Soul City as Costs Soar," *News & Observer* (Raleigh, NC), May 13, 1979.

310   **"treated Soul City like a favorite nephew":** Pat Stith, "Red Tape, Federal Laws No Problem When Soul City Seeks New Funds," *News & Observer* (Raleigh, NC), May 13, 1979.

310   **McKissick's salary had increased:** Pat Stith, "Family Finds the Good Life at Soul City," *News & Observer* (Raleigh, NC), May 13, 1979.

310   **"McKissick's money spigot":** "Hard Reality Hits Soul City," *News & Observer* (Raleigh, NC), editorial, May 17, 1979.

310   **"Another couple-a-million?":** Dwane Powell, editorial cartoon, *News & Observer* (Raleigh, NC), May 15, 1979, 4.

310   **"accomplished for the state of North Carolina":** Pat Stith, "Soul City Founder Expecting More Aid," *News & Observer* (Raleigh, NC), May 29, 1979.

311   **praising Soul City's efforts:** Daniel Pollitt to President Carter, May 31, 1979, New Community Development Corporation Records, Program Records Relating to Soul City, container 1.3.

311   **"rally around the project":** "Soul City: Attacked Again," *Carolina Times*, editorial, May 26, 1979, 5.

311   **"hold a cocktail glass the same":** Harrigan, "An Old 'New Town' Hangs on, Sustained by Federal Money."

311   **"more in the years to come":** "Without Soul City's Help," *Warren Record*, editorial, undated clipping circa May 1979.

311   **"understanding of the Soul City situation":** Claude Sitton to Lewis Myers, May 29, 1979, McKissick Papers, folder 1810.

311   **"such use of the taxpayers' money":** 125 Cong. Rec. 9235 (May 1, 1979).

312   **"a way around it":** Pat Stith, "Helms to Seek Funding Cutoff," *News & Observer* (Raleigh, NC), May 17, 1979.

312   **weren't being welcomed properly:** Memorandum from Dorothy L. Waller to FM, May 4, 1979, McKissick Papers, folder 262.

312   **at 8:35 a.m. on a recent morning:** Memorandum from Gordon Carey to Lewis Myers, May 11, 1979, McKissick Papers, folder 262.

312   **new plant on the East Coast:** Memorandum from Gordon Carey to Lewis Myers, March 19, 1979, McKissick Papers, folder 260.

312   **marketed as a retirement community:** Gordon Carey to HUD, McKissick Papers, folder 262.

312   **"The future is there":** Thomas A. Johnson, "Soul City Seeks to Get Recruits from the North," *New York Times*, June 16, 1979, 6.

313   **three thousand dollars in annual premiums:** Dorothy L. Waller to the Paul Revere Company, May 24, 1979, McKissick Papers, folder 1270.

313   **"It won't help":** Gordon Carey interview with the author, July 19, 2016.

313   **"tried and convicted in the press":** FM to Birch Bayh, June 5, 1979, McKissick Papers, folder 264.

313   **with a similar request:** FM to Robert Morgan, June 8, 1979, McKissick Papers, folder 1810; FM to L. H. Fountain, June 11, 1979, McKissick Papers, folder 1811.

313   **"Dear Senator Helms":** FM to Jesse Helms, June 12, 1979, McKissick Papers, folder 1811.

314   **ever visit Soul City:** Gordon Carey interview with the author, July 19, 2016.

314   **improve the town's public image:** "The Status and Future of the Soul City Community, Prepared by the Soul City Company," April 12, 1979, McKissick Papers, folder 1825.

314   **decided against foreclosure:** "Task Force Report," June 27, 1979, 6, McKissick Papers, folder 1824; *Soul City v. United States*, Complaint, August 17, 1979, McKissick Papers, folder 1831, 15.

315   **"an alien atmosphere":** "Analysis of Financial Viability of Soul City and Cost Ramifications of Alternative Proposals," Avco Community Developers, June 21, 1979, 4, McKissick Papers, folder 1827; Minchin, "Brand New Shining City,"147.

315   **further assistance from HUD:** "Task Force Report," June 27, 1979.

315   **Although McKissick . . . "like the entire staff had died":** Rhee, "Visions, Illusions, and Perceptions," 127–28.

315   **For Floyd Jr. . . . that it wasn't:** Floyd McKissick Jr. interview with the author, October 12, 2015.

316   **"We're just beginning":** Ball-Groom, *Salad Pickers*, 303–8; Jane Ball-Groom interview with the author, June 3, 2014.

316   **"a rural, isolated area":** Associated Press, "HUD Cuts Financing; Dream of Soul City Dies in N. Carolina," *Washington Post*, June 29, 1979, A7.

316   **William White . . . "a friendly foreclosure":** A. O. Sulzberger Jr., "H.U.D. to Foreclose on Soul City, Troubled 'New Town' in Carolina," *New York Times*, June 29, 1979, A12.

316   **Soul City was not in default:** Statement by F. B. McKissick Sr., June 28, 1979, McKissick Papers, folder 1810.

316   **"got to fight this"**: Joanne Omang, "Fighting Still: Founder Won't Surrender His Hopes for Soul City," *Washington Post*, July 2, 1979, A1.

317   **"until we couldn't continue anymore"**: Rhee, "Visions, Illusions, and Perceptions," 128.

20: "SORROW'S KITCHEN"

318   **circulating a petition**: Save Soul City, signed petitions, McKissick Papers, folders 1814, 1815a, 1815b.

318   **hosting a picnic at Soul City**: Thomas A. Johnson, "Blacks in Carolina Battle to Save Soul City," *New York Times*, July 3, 1979, A6; Thomas A. Johnson, "North Carolina Blacks Support Troubled New Town," *New York Times*, August 27, 1979, A12.

318   **hundreds of letters from ministers**: Letters of support for Soul City, 1979, McKissick Papers, folders 1816–1823.

318   **"threatened with a cut-off"**: William Feyer to FM, July 10, 1979, McKissick Papers, folder 1820.

319   **"stem this tide"**: Malvin Goode to FM, July 9, 1979, McKissick Papers, folder 1819.

319   **"start an organic vegetable farm"**: Katherine Heaton Daye to FM, July 1, 1979, McKissick Papers, folder 1819.

319   **Walter Sorg ... "support your logic"**: Walter Larke Sorg to Jesse Helms, July 26, 1979, McKissick Papers, folder 1818.

320   **"arrogance with which they spend the money"**: Eric Chandler, letter to the editor, *News & Observer* (Raleigh, NC), July 11, 1979.

320   **"paying for foolish dreams"**: 125 Cong. Rec. S9377 (daily ed. July 13, 1979) (statement of Sen. Helms).

320   **prosecutor named John Kerry**: Stacy Jolna, "Brooke Divorce Perjury Probe Begins in Mass.," *Washington Post*, June 17, 1978, A1.

320   **approved his proposal by a voice vote**: Richard Whittle, "Senate Opposes Soul City Loans," *News & Observer* (Raleigh, NC), July 14, 1979, 1.

321   **"profited enough from this venture"**: Whittle, "Senate Opposes Soul City Loans."

321   **support from his allies in Congress**: Memorandum from Gordon Carey to FM, July 14, 1979, McKissick Papers, folder 261.

321   **"and the right to be a successful entrepreneur"**: Telegram from FM to Members of Congressional Black Caucus, July 16, 1979, McKissick Papers, folder 885; Steve Levin, "'Vendetta' by Helms Spurring Soul City Cutoff, Director Says," *News & Observer* (Raleigh, NC), July 15, 1979, 1.

321   **At the same time ... new sewage treatment plant**: Pat Stith, "Official Says McKissick Hinted at Negotiations," *News & Observer* (Raleigh, NC), 21; Richard Whittle, "Warren Will Still Get Sewage

Plant Grant," *News & Observer* (Raleigh, NC) 14; Cole C. Campbell, "Smaller Soul City Facility Backed," *News & Observer* (Raleigh,
NC), July 27, 1979, 15; *Soul City v. United States*, Complaint, August
17, 1979, McKissick Papers, folder 1831, 20–21; Press Release, The
Soul City Company, August 17, 1979, folder 892, 2.

321   **final $4 million in bonds:** *Soul City v. United States*, Complaint,
August 17, 1979, McKissick Papers, folder 1831; Associated Press,
"Developer of Soul City Files Suit Saying U.S. Has Hindered Project,"
New York Times, August 19, 1979, 16.

322   **push the project into default:** *Soul City Company v. United States*,
Temporary Restraining Order, August 17, 1979, McKissick Papers,
folder 1839.

322   **"it is only the personalities that change":** FM to David Stith, August
3, 1979, McKissick Papers, folder 1819.

322   **"please feel free to call":** FM to Gordon Carey, July 12, 1979, personal papers of Gordon Carey, copy on file with author.

323   **"walked in and been cordial":** Gordon Carey interview with the
author, July 19, 2016.

323   **"disagreed with the thrust of his letter":** Email from Gordon Carey to
the author, February 14, 2019.

323   **"had to go on with our lives somehow":** Gordon Carey interview
with the author, July 19, 2016.

324   **to negotiate a settlement:** Rhee, "Visions, Illusions, and Perceptions,"
130–32.

324   **Perdue Foods agreed to buy:** "Perdue Inc. Purchases Land from Soul
City," *Wall Street Journal*, January 3, 1980, 4.

324   **a private homeowners' association:** "U.S. to Acquire Soul City in
Jan.," *News & Observer* (Raleigh, NC), June 27, 1980; Minchin,
"Brand New Shining City," 151–52.

324   **"Everything that I owned was in hock":** Rhee, "Visions, Illusions, and
Perceptions," 129.

324   **"can't ask for more than that":** Rhee, "Visions, Illusions, and Perceptions," 129.

325   **"no taps or tears":** "No Taps for McKissick," *News & Observer*
(Raleigh, NC), editorial, June 30, 1980, 4.

325   **"it all goes down the drain":** Rhee, "Visions, Illusions, and Perceptions," 132.

325   **"I have been in Sorrow's kitchen":** Zora Neale Hurston, *Dust Tracks
on a Road: An Autobiography* (Urbana: University of Illinois Press,
1984), 280.

325   **"gavel had been slammed down":** Ball-Groom, *Salad Pickers*, 326–27.

326   **$1.5 million was quickly accepted:** Associated Press, "Failed Soul City
Auctioned Off, with U.S. as the Only Bidder," *Washington Post*, January 31, 1981, A7.

326   "there was no such place": "Group Wants Road Signs for Soul City Back Up," *News & Observer* (Raleigh, NC), February 12, 1982, 17A.

EPILOGUE: MIXED BLESSINGS

327   terminating the program: Andre Shashaty, "HUD Closing New Towns Program," *Washington Post*, January 15, 1983, E1.

328   party had changed . . . "senile turncoat": Marable, *Race, Reform, and Rebellion*, 180; Fields, *Black Elephants*, 49–55.

328   rejoined the Democratic Party: Hunter James, "Hope Still Lingers for Soul City," *Greensboro News & Record*, December 26, 1984.

328   rented a storefront office: Rhee, "Visions, Illusions, and Perceptions," 147.

329   "I was talking with God": Pat Bryant, "McKissick Preaches Trial Sermon," *Carolina Times*, August 11, 1979, 1.

329   "Tell it like it is": Bryant, "McKissick Preaches Trial Sermon"; Bob Sherrill, "Politics of 1980 Thread Bible-Thumper Sermon," *Durham Morning Herald*, August 6, 1979, 1A.

330   "lost a lot of his fire": Robert Brown interview with the author, July 19, 2016.

330   charged him with impeding traffic: Ken Allen, "7 Arrested Protesting PCB Site," *Charlotte Observer*, September 17, 1982, 31; United Press International, "100 Arrested in PCB Protest," *Afro-American* (Baltimore), September 25, 1982, 1.

330   "I will never leave, period": Minchin, "Brand New Shining City," 155.

331   "I am my brother's keeper": Charmaine McKissick-Melton interview with the author, August 22, 2015.

331   "need dedicated social engineers": McKissick, *Three-Fifths of a Man*, 86–90.

332   "took a deep breath, and that was it": Charmaine McKissick-Melton interview with the author, August 22, 2015.

332   "civil rights maverick": Glenn Fowler, "Floyd McKissick, Civil Rights Maverick, Dies at 69," *New York Times*, April 30, 1991, D19.

332   "giants of the civil rights struggle": Claudia Levy, "CORE Director, N.C. Judge Floyd B. McKissick Dies," *Washington Post*, April 30, 1991, B6.

332   Printed inside the program: "A Celebration of Life," Floyd B. McKissick Sr., May 2, 1991, Daniel H. Pollitt Papers, folder 131.

333   "I didn't really": Gordon Carey interview with the author, July 19, 2016.

334   Helms's profile . . . nuclear deterrence: Furgurson, *Hard Right*.

335   "Harvey Gantt says it is": Rob Christensen, "Racial Themes Arise in Senate Campaign," *News & Observer* (Raleigh, NC), November 1, 1990.

335   **After that campaign ... "wonders for the psyche":** Harvey Gantt interview with the author, October 14, 2015.

336   **Helms served ... "better have a bodyguard":** Link, *Righteous Warrior*, 407, 414, 428.

336   **"for Senator Helms":** Sherrill, "Politics of 1980 Thread Bible-Thumper Sermon."

336   **Sitton won the Pulitzer Prize:** Richard Hart, "Sitton Wins Pulitzer for Commentary," *News & Observer* (Raleigh, NC), April 19, 1983, 1.

337   **By the time he retired ... recovery of $2.4 million:** James T. Hamilton, *Democracy's Detectives: The Economics of Investigative Journalism* (Cambridge: Harvard University Press, 2016), 208–78.

337   **When I interviewed ... "I didn't care":** Pat Stith interview with the author, August 26, 2019.

338   **a hundred acres of former Soul City land:** "1,300 Jobs, 85 Homes Forecast at Soul City by New Investors," *Durham Morning Herald*, February 15, 1989; Minchin, "Brand New Shining City," 151–52.

338   **a prison would provide jobs:** Thurletta M. Brown, "Dissatisfaction Expressed By Some Over Proposed Location of Prison," *Warren Record*, January 5, 1994.

340   **$6.5 million in yearly revenue:** Karen Brown interview with the author, October 15, 2015.

342   **Voyette tells me ... "what everyone's looking for":** Voyette Perkins-Brown interview with the author, August 22, 2015.

342   **"beautiful place to live":** Jane Ball-Groom interview with the author, August 22, 2015.

344   **"it was a blessing":** Jane Ball-Groom interview with the author, June 3, 2014.

BIBLIOGRAPHY

MANUSCRIPT COLLECTIONS

Ralph Bunche Oral History Collection, Moorland-Spingarn Research Center, Howard University.

Floyd B. McKissick Papers #4930, Southern Historical Collection of the University of North Carolina at Chapel Hill and the African American Resources Collection of North Carolina Central University.

The Papers of the Congress of Racial Equality: Addendum, 1944–1968, Martin Luther King Jr. Center for Nonviolent Social Change, Atlanta.

Daniel H. Pollitt Papers #5498, Southern Historical Collection, the Wilson Library, University of North Carolina at Chapel Hill.

Richard Nixon Presidential Library and Museum, US National Archives and Records Administration, Yorba Linda, CA.

North Carolina Collection, the Wilson Library, University of North Carolina at Chapel Hill.

Records of the New Community Development Corporation, Record Group 207.7.8, National Archives and Records Administration, College Park, MD.

Stanley S. Scott Papers, Gerald R. Ford Presidential Library, Ann Arbor, MI.

Jack Underhill Papers, Collection #C0134, Special Collections Research Center, George Mason University Libraries.

BOOKS AND ARTICLES

Adler, Renata. *After the Tall Timber*. New York: New York Review Books, 2015.

Ambrose, Stephen E. *Nixon*. Vol. 2, *The Triumph of a Politician, 1962–1972*. New York: Simon & Schuster, 1989.

Arnold, Joseph L. *The New Deal in the Suburbs: A History of the Greenbelt Town Program, 1935–1954*. Columbus: Ohio State University Press, 1971.

Ball-Groom, E. Jane. *The Salad Pickers: Journey South*. Morrisville, NC: Lulu, 2012.

Baradaran, Mehrsa. *The Color of Money: Black Banks and the Racial Wealth Gap*. Cambridge: Harvard University Press, 2017.

Bass, Jack, and Walter DeVries. *The Transformation of Southern Politics: Social Change and Political Consequence Since 1945*. Athens: University of Georgia Press, 1995.

Biles, Roger. "The Rise and Fall of Soul City: Planning, Politics, and Race in Recent America." *Journal of Planning History* 4, no. 1 (February 2005): 52–72.

Branch, Taylor. *Parting the Waters: America in the King Years, 1954–1963*. New York: Simon & Schuster, 1988.

———. *Pillar of Fire: America in the King Years, 1963–65*. New York: Simon & Schuster, 1998.

———. *At Canaan's Edge: America in the King Years, 1963–68*. New York: Simon & Schuster, 2006.

Brophy, Alfred L. *Reconstructing the Dreamland: The Tulsa Riot of 1921, Race, Reparations, and Reconciliation*. New York: Oxford University Press, 2002.

Brown-Nagin, Tomiko. *Courage to Dissent: Atlanta and the Long History of the Civil Rights Movement*. New York: Oxford University Press, 2011.

Burby, Raymond J., Thomas G. Donnelly, and Shirley F. Weiss. *New Communities USA*. Lexington, MA: Lexington Books, 1976.

Burrows, Herbert Ray. *Norlina: Nothing Could Be Finer*. Norlina, NC: Burrows, 2005.

Campbell, Carlos C. *New Towns: Another Way to Live*. Reston, VA: Reston Publishing, 1976.

Carson, Clayborne. *In Struggle: SNCC and the Black Awakening of the 1960s*. Cambridge: Harvard University Press, 1995.

Chafe, William H. *Civilities and Civil Rights: Greensboro, North Carolina, and the Black Struggle for Freedom*. New York: Oxford University Press, 1981.

Christensen, Rob. *The Rise and Fall of the Branchhead Boys*. Chapel Hill: University of North Carolina Press, 2019.

Coates, Ta-Nehisi. "The Case for Reparations." *Atlantic*, June 2014.

Cooper, Christopher A., and H. Gibbs Knotts. "Traditionalism and Progressivism in North Carolina." In *The New Politics of North Carolina*, edited by Christopher A. Cooper and H. Gibbs Knotts, 1–10. Chapel Hill: University of North Carolina Press, 2008.

Craig, Lee A. *Josephus Daniels: His Life and Times*. Chapel Hill: University of North Carolina Press, 2013.

Crockett, Norman L. *The Black Towns*. Lawrence: Regents Press of Kansas, 1979.

Crow, Jeffery J., Paul D. Escott, and Flora J. Hatley Wadelington. *A History of African Americans in North Carolina*. Raleigh: North Carolina Department of Cultural Resources, 2002.

Davidson, Osha Gray. *The Best of Enemies: Race and Redemption in the New South*. New York: Scribner, 1996.

Davies, Tom Adam. *Mainstreaming Black Power*. Oakland: University of California Press, 2017.

Duany, Andres, Elizabeth Plater-Zyberk, and Jeff Speck. *Suburban Nation: The Rise of Sprawl and the Decline of the American Dream*. New York: North Point Press, 2010.

Du Bois, W. E. B. *The Souls of Black Folk*. Chicago: A.C. McClurg & Co., 1907.

Dyer, Stephanie. "Progress Plaza: Leon Sullivan, Zion Investment Associates, and Black Power in a Philadelphia Shopping Center." In *The Economic Civil Rights Movement: African Americans and the Struggle for Economic Power*, edited by Michael Ezra, 137–53. New York: Routledge, 2013.

Ezra, Michael, ed. *The Economic Civil Rights Movement: African Americans and the Struggle for Economic Power*. New York: Routledge, 2013.

Farrington, Joshua D. "'Build, Baby, Build': Conservative Black Nationalists, Free Enterprise, and the Nixon Administration." In *The Right Side of the Sixties: Reexamining Conservatism's Decade of Transformation*, edited by Laura Jane Gifford and Daniel K. Williams, 61–80. New York: Palgrave Macmillan, 2012.

———. *Black Republicans and the Transformation of the GOP*. Philadelphia: University of Pennsylvania Press, 2016.

Fergus, Devin. "The Ordeal of Liberalism and Black Nationalism in an American Southern State, 1965–1980." PhD diss., Columbia University, 2002.

———. *Liberalism, Black Power, and the Making of American Politics, 1965–1980*. Athens: University of Georgia Press, 2009.

Fields, Corey D. *Black Elephants in the Room: The Unexpected Politics of African American Republicans*. Oakland: University of California Press, 2016.

Forsyth, Ann. *Reforming Suburbia: The Planned Communities of Irvine, Columbia, and The Woodlands*. Berkeley: University of California Press, 2005.

Franke, Katherine. *Repair: Redeeming the Promise of Abolition.* Chicago: Haymarket Books, 2019.

Franklin, John Hope. *The Free Negro in North Carolina, 1790–1860.* Chapel Hill: University of North Carolina Press, 1995.

Franklin, John Hope, and Alfred A. Moss Jr. *From Slavery to Freedom: A History of African Americans,* 8th ed. Boston: McGraw Hill, 2000.

Franklin, John Hope, and Isidore Starr, eds. *The Negro in Twentieth Century America: A Reader on the Struggle for Civil Rights.* New York: Vintage Books, 1967.

Frazier, Nishani. *Harambee City: The Congress of Racial Equality in Cleveland and the Rise of Black Power Populism.* Fayetteville: University of Arkansas Press, 2017.

Furgurson, Ernest B. *Hard Right: The Rise of Jesse Helms.* New York: W.W. Norton, 1986.

Galantay, Ervin. "Black New Towns: The Fourth Alternative." *Progressive Architecture* 49, no. 8 (August 1969): 126–31.

Garrow, David J. *Bearing the Cross: Martin Luther King, Jr., and the Southern Christian Leadership Conference.* London: Jonathan Cape, 1988.

Gifford, Laura Jane, and Daniel K. Williams, eds. *The Right Side of the Sixties: Reexamining Conservatism's Decade of Transformation.* New York: Palgrave Macmillan, 2012.

Gillan, Zachary. "Black Is Beautiful But So Is Green: Capitalism, Black Power, and Politics in Floyd McKissick's Soul City." In *The New Black History: Revisiting the Second Reconstruction,* edited by Manning Marable and Elizabeth Kai Hinton, 267–86. New York: Palgrave Macmillan, 2011.

Goudsouzian, Aram. *Down to the Crossroads: Civil Rights, Black Power, and the Meredith March Against Fear.* New York: Farrar, Straus and Giroux, 2014.

Haley, Alex. *Roots: The Saga of an American Family.* Boston: Da Capo Press, 2014.

Hamilton, Kenneth Marvin. *Black Towns and Profit: Promotion and Development in the Trans-Appalachian West, 1877–1915.* Urbana: University of Illinois Press, 1991.

Hays, R. Allen. *The Federal Government and Urban Housing,* 3rd ed. Albany: State University of New York Press, 2012.

Herbin-Triant, Elizabeth A. *Threatening Property: Race, Class, and Campaigns to Legislate Jim Crow Neighborhoods.* New York: Columbia University Press, 2019.

Hermann, Janet Sharp. *The Pursuit of a Dream.* Banner Books. New York: Oxford University Press, 1981.

Hill, Lance. *The Deacons for Defense: Armed Resistance and the Civil Rights Movement.* Chapel Hill: University of North Carolina Press, 2004.

Howard, Chris D. "Keep Your Eyes on the Prize: The Black Struggle for Civic Equality in Durham, North Carolina, 1954–63." Undergraduate honors thesis, Duke University, 1983.

Howard, Ebenezer. *To-morrow: A Peaceful Path to Real Reform*. London: Swan Sonnenschein & Co., 1902.

Hurston, Zora Neale. *Dust Tracks on a Road: An Autobiography*. Urbana: University of Illinois Press, 1984.

———. *Their Eyes Were Watching God*. New York: Harper Perennial Modern Classics, 2013.

Jacobs, Jane. *The Death and Life of Great American Cities*. New York: Vintage, 1961.

Jennings, Chris. *Paradise Now: The Story of American Utopianism*. New York: Random House, 2016.

Johnson, Hannibal. *Acres of Aspiration: The All-Black Towns in Oklahoma*. Austin, TX: Eakin Press, 2007.

Jones, Bignall. *Boyhood Days in Warrenton*. Warrenton, NC: Record Print Co., 1993.

Jones, Rhonda. "A. Philip Randolph, Early Pioneer: The Brotherhood of Sleeping Car Porters, National Negro Congress, and the March on Washington Movement," in *The Economic Civil Rights Movement: African Americans and the Struggle for Economic Power*, edited by Michael Ezra, 9–21. New York: Routledge, 2013.

Joseph, Peniel E. *Waiting 'Til the Midnight Hour: A Narrative History of Black Power in America*. New York: Henry Holt, 2006.

Key, V. O. *Southern Politics in State and Nation*. New York: Alfred A. Knopf, 1949.

Killens, John Oliver. *Black Man's Burden*. New York: Trident, 1965.

Kotz, Nick. *Judgment Days: Lyndon Baines Johnson, Martin Luther King Jr., and the Laws That Changed America*. Boston: Houghton Mifflin Company, 2005.

Landis, John. "Model Cities Program," in *The Encyclopedia of Housing*, 2nd ed., edited by Andrew T. Carswell, 458–61. Los Angeles: Sage, 2012.

Laurent, Sylvie. *King and the Other America: The Poor People's Campaign and the Quest for Racial Equality*. Oakland: University of California Press, 2018.

Lemann, Nicholas. *The Promised Land: The Great Black Migration and How It Changed America*. New York: Vintage Books, 1992.

Lester, Julius. *Look Out, Whitey! Black Power's Gon' Get Your Mama!* New York: Grove Press, 1969.

Levy, Peter B. "The Dream Deferred: The Assassination of Martin Luther King Jr., and the Holy Week Uprisings of 1968." In *Baltimore '68: Riots and Rebirth in an American City*, ed. Jessica Elfenbein, Elizabeth Nix, and Thomas Hollowak. Philadelphia: Temple University Press, 2011.

————. *The Great Uprising: Race Riots in Urban America during the 1960s.* Cambridge, UK: Cambridge University Press, 2018.

Link, William A. *Righteous Warrior: Jesse Helms and the Rise of Modern Conservatism.* New York: St. Martin's Press, 2008.

Mabry, William. *The Negro in North Carolina Politics Since Reconstruction.* Durham, NC: Duke University Press, 1970.

Madigan, Tim. *The Burning: Massacre, Destruction, and the Tulsa Race Riot of 1921.* New York: Thomas Dunne Books, 2001.

Madison, Emily Webster. "Objections Sustained: The Conception and Demise of Soul City, North Carolina." Essay submitted for Honors in History, University of North Carolina at Chapel Hill, April 1995.

Marable, Manning. *Race, Reform, and Rebellion: The Second Reconstruction in Black America, 1945–2006,* 3rd ed. Jackson: University Press of Mississippi, 2007.

————. *How Capitalism Underdeveloped Black America: Problems in Race, Political Economy, and Society.* Chicago: Haymarket Books, 2015.

————. *W. E. B. Du Bois: Black Radical Democrat.* London: Routledge, 2016.

McKissick, Floyd B. *Three-Fifths of a Man.* New York: Macmillan, 1969.

Meier, August, and Elliot Rudwick. *CORE: A Study in the Civil Rights Movement, 1942–1968.* Urbana: University of Illinois Press, 1975.

Minchin, Timothy J. "'A Brand New Shining City': Floyd B. McKissick Sr. and the Struggle to Build Soul City, North Carolina." *North Carolina Historical Review* 82, no. 2 (April 2005): 125–55.

————. *From Rights to Economics: The Ongoing Struggle for Black Equality in the U.S. South.* Gainesville: University Press of Florida, 2007.

Mixon, Herman, Jr. *Soul City: The Initial Stages, the Genesis and First Two Years of the Soul City Project, with Questions for the Future.* Chapel Hill: Center for Urban and Regional Studies, University of North Carolina, 1971.

Montgomery, Lizzie Wilson. *Sketches of Old Warrenton: Traditions and Reminiscences of the Town and People Who Made It.* Raleigh, NC: Edwards & Broughton Printing Co., 1924.

Morris, Aldon D. *The Origins of the Civil Rights Movement: Black Communities Organizing for Change.* New York: The Free Press, 1986.

Mumford, Eric. *Designing the Modern City: Urbanism Since 1850.* New Haven: Yale University Press, 2018.

Mumford, Lewis. *The Culture of Cities.* New York: Harcourt Brace Jovanovich, 1938.

National Committee on Urban Growth Policy. *The New City.* New York: Frederick A. Praeger, 1969.

Painter, Nell Irvin. *Exodusters: Black Migration to Kansas after Reconstruction.* New York: W.W. Norton, 1986.

Perlstein, Rick. *Nixonland: The Rise of a President and the Fracturing of America.* New York: Scribner, 2009.

————. *The Invisible Bridge: The Fall of Nixon and the Rise of Reagan*. New York: Simon & Schuster, 2015.

Pritchett, Wendell E. *Robert Clifton Weaver and the American City: The Life and Times of an Urban Reformer*. Chicago: University of Chicago Press, 2008.

Purnell, Brian. *Fighting Jim Crow in the County of Kings: The Congress of Racial Equality in Brooklyn*. Lexington: University Press of Kentucky, 2013.

Rhee, Foon. "Visions, Illusions, and Perceptions: The Story of Soul City." Thesis in fulfillment of Honors in History, Duke University, 1984.

Risen, Clay. *A Nation on Fire: America in the Wake of the King Assassination*. Hoboken: John Wiley & Sons, 2009.

Roberts, Gene, and Hank Klibanoff. *The Race Beat: The Press, the Civil Rights Struggle, and the Awakening of a Nation*. New York: Vintage, 2007.

Rogers, Ibram H. "Acquiring 'A Piece of the Action': The Rise and Fall of the Black Capitalism Movement." In *The Economic Civil Rights Movement: African Americans and the Struggle for Economic Power*, edited by Michael Ezra, 172–87. New York: Routledge, 2013.

Rothstein, Richard. *The Color of Law: A Forgotten History of How Our Government Segregated America*. New York: Liveright, 2017.

Sanders, Crystal R. "North Carolina Justice on Display: Governor Bob Scott and the 1968 Benson Affair." *Journal of Southern History* 79, no. 3 (August 2013): 659–80.

Shapiro, Amanda. "Welcome to Soul City: Exploring the Remains of a Black Power Utopia." *Oxford American* 80 (Spring 2013).

Strain, Christopher. "Soul City, North Carolina: Black Power, Utopia, and the African American Dream." *Journal of African American History* 89, no. 1 (Winter 2004): 57–74.

Sugrue, Thomas J. *Sweet Land of Liberty: The Forgotten Struggle for Civil Rights in the North*. New York: Random House, 2009.

Sullivan, Leon H. *Build, Brother, Build: From Poverty to Economic Power*. Philadelphia: Macrae Smith, 1969.

Thomas, Karen Kruse. *Deluxe Jim Crow: Civil Rights and American Health Policy, 1935–54*. Athens: University of Georgia Press, 2011.

Turner, Morris. *America's Black Towns and Settlements: A Historical Reference Guide*. Rohnert Park, CA: Missing Pages Production, 1998.

Tyson, Timothy B. *Radio Free Dixie: Robert F. Williams and the Roots of Black Power*. Chapel Hill: University of North Carolina Press, 1999.

————. *Blood Done Sign My Name: A True Story*. New York: Broadway Books, 2005.

Van Deburg, William L. *New Day in Babylon: The Black Power Movement and American Culture, 1965–1975*. Chicago: University of Chicago Press, 1993.

Wakeman, Rosemary. *Practicing Utopia: An Intellectual History of the New Town Movement*. Chicago: University of Chicago Press, 2016.

Walls, Dwayne E. *The Chickenbone Special*. New York: Harcourt Brace Jova-
    novich, 1971.

Washington, Booker T. *Up from Slavery*. New York: Doubleday, 1901.

Weems, Robert E. *Business in Black and White: American Presidents and Black
    Entrepreneurs in the Twentieth Century*. New York: New York University
    Press, 2009.

Wilkerson, Isabel. *The Warmth of Other Suns: The Epic Story of America's
    Great Migration*. New York: Vintage Books, 2011.

Woodard, Harold. "Floyd McKissick: Portrait of a Leader." Master's thesis,
    University of North Carolina at Chapel Hill, 1981.

Woodson, Carter G. *A Century of Negro Migration*. Washington, DC: Associ-
    ation for the Study of Negro Life and History, 1918.

Woodward, C. Vann. *The Strange Career of Jim Crow*. New York: Oxford
    University Press, 1974.

ACKNOWLEDGMENTS

In writing this book, I relied heavily on the memory of those who played a part in Soul City's history and on the archives where the documentary record is stored. I owe a huge debt to both sources.

For sharing their thoughts and recollections with me, I am grateful to Ihsan Abdin, Jane Ball-Groom, Robert Brown, Carlos Campbell, Gordon Carey, Karen Carey, Eva Clayton, T. T. Clayton, Arthur Evans, Danny Gant, Harvey Gantt, David Godschalk, Ferrel Guillory, Magnolia Jackson, Floyd McKissick Jr., Charmaine McKissick-Melton, Beverly McNeill, Lew Myers, Voyette Perkins-Brown, Ruth Perot, Glenn Powell, Pat Stith, Wilfred Ussery, Kristina Vetter, Dorothy Webb, Stu Wechsler, and Linda Worth. Although all these individuals gave generously of their time, I am especially indebted to Jane Ball-Groom, Gordon Carey, and Charmaine McKissick-Melton, each of whom met with me on numerous occasions and answered countless follow-up questions. I also had conversations with many people who were not involved in Soul City but who offered valuable assistance and information, including Monica Berra, Karen Brown, SheRea DelSol, Forest Fesperman, Carla Norwood, Foon Rhee, Gini Richards, and Harold Woodard.

For helping me navigate the documentary record, I am grateful foremost to Maja Basioli, whose expertise and resourcefulness aided me every step of the way. And for making Maja's help possible—and providing additional support—I am grateful to the entire staff of the Rodino Library at Seton Hall Law School, including Kristina Anderson, Dierdre Freamon, Karlyne Merant, Barbara Mol, Dianne Oster, Brittany Persson, and Elaine Poplaski.

The most important archival resource for Soul City are the Floyd B. McKissick Papers, which are held jointly by the Southern Historical Collection of the University of North Carolina at Chapel Hill and the African American Resources Collection of North Carolina Central University. Housed in UNC's Wilson Library, the McKissick Papers are vast and comprehensive, filling nearly eight thousand folders. Going through these folders reminds one of the incredible amount of work required to organize and maintain a collection like this, and I am grateful to both UNC and NCCU for taking on the task. I am also indebted to the many staff members and administrators at Wilson Library who welcomed me and guided me through the collection, including Sarah Carrier, Bryan Giemza, Tim Hodgdon, and Matthew Turi.

In addition to the Floyd McKissick Papers, I relied upon collections at many other institutions. For help in accessing these collections, I thank the following: Atlanta University Center's Robert W. Woodruff Library; Margaret Gers at the Enoch Pratt Free Library; Zoe Rhine at the Buncombe County Public Library; Columbia University's Rare Books and Manuscripts Library; the Columbus Metropolitan Library; Duke University's David M. Rubinstein Rare Book & Manuscript Library; the Gerald R. Ford Presidential Library and Museum; Howard University's Moorland-Spingarn Research Center; Indiana University's Archives of African American Music and Culture; the Lyndon Baines Johnson Library and Museum; the Library of Congress Manuscript Division; Michigan State University's G. Robert Vincent Voice Library; Jana L. Hill at Mississippi State University's Special Collections Department; the National Archives at College Park, Maryland; the New York Public Library's General

Research Division and Schomburg Center for Research in Black Culture; the Newark Public Library; the Richard M. Nixon Presidential Library and Museum; the State Library of North Carolina; the North Carolina Legislative Library; Michael Wallace at North Carolina State University's D. H. Hill Jr. Library; Saundra R. Cropps at the Olivia Raney Local History Library; Mabel Wong at Seton Hall University's Walsh Library; the Sophia Smith Collection at Smith College; Cheryl B. Martin at the US Army Corps of Engineers Mobile District Library; the US Army Heritage and Education Center; the Center for Legislative Archives at the US National Archives and Records Administration; Deborah Chiarella at University at Buffalo Libraries; Allison Benedetti and Simon Elliot at UCLA's Charles E. Young Research Library; the Mansfield Library at the University of Montana; the North Carolina Digital Heritage Center; the Vanderbilt Television News Archive; David Spence at the Warren County Memorial Library; and the Wisconsin Historical Society Library.

The writing of this book was supported by a number of grants and fellowships, including a Guggenheim Fellowship; a Public Scholars Grant from the National Endowment for the Humanities; a summer research grant from the Documenting Social Change Library Fund at the University of North Carolina; and the Sheila Biddle Ford Foundation Fellowship from the Hutchins Center for African and African American Research at Harvard University. In addition to financial support, the Hutchins Center provided me with an academic home for a semester and the companionship of an amazing group of fellows. For making my semester in Cambridge so memorable and productive, I thank Henry Louis Gates Jr., Krishna Lewis, my co-fellows, and the entire staff of the Hutchins Center. Thanks also to Trevor Morrison and New York University Law School for welcoming me as a visiting scholar and to Kendall Thomas and the Center for the Study of Law and Culture at Columbia Law School for doing the same. The hospitality and intellectual stimulation of both institutions was immensely helpful to me.

In researching this book, I was lucky to have the help of some terrific student assistants. For their hard work and dedication, I thank

Ryan Allen, Brenden Carol, Angelica Halat, Seton Hartnett, Elizabeth Kaminski, Levi Klinger-Christiansen, and Lauren McNamara. For supporting me and my research assistants and for taking on the monumental task of organizing the archival documents I collected, I thank Silvia Cardoso, whose good cheer and commitment to excellence make her a pleasure to work with.

Numerous people read all or part of this manuscript. For their generosity and insightful comments, I thank Michelle Adams, Arlene Chow, Carl Coleman, Tristin Green, Tom Hackett, Olatunde Johnson, Krishna Lewis, Solangel Maldonado, and Najarian Peters. I am also grateful to the many colleagues, friends, and mentors who provided support, encouragement, and advice, including Jake Barnes, Robert Beatty, Vincent Blasi, Kristen Boon, Kathleen Boozang, Kip Cornwell, Michael Dorf, Deborah Edwards, Tim Glynn, Gregg Hecimovich, John Jacobi, Maggie Lewis, Andrea McDowell, Andrew Moore, Todd Richissin, Michael Risinger, Brenda Saunders-Hampden, Brian Sheppard, Cameron Smith, Charles Sullivan, and Richard Winchester. One friend and mentor whose help was especially important, Robert Ferguson, did not live to see this book completed. I was fortunate to have known him and to have had his support.

I am grateful to Seton Hall Law School for providing research funding and a yearlong sabbatical to work on this project, and to workshop participants at Seton Hall, Columbia Law School, the Hutchins Center at Harvard University, Rutgers Law School, and the University of North Carolina.

Thanks to my agent Ryan Harbage for his guidance and enthusiasm and to my editors Grigory Tovbis and Sara Bershtel for once again shepherding me through the editorial process with superb skill and judgment. Thanks also to Molly Pisani for excellent copy editing.

Finally, thanks to my entire family—sisters, brothers, nieces, and nephews—for their love and support, to Adele and Juliet for filling my days with laughter and joy, and most of all to Arlene for sustaining me in so many ways during the course of this project—and long before—with her wit, warmth, and wisdom.

INDEX

Page numbers in *italics* refer to illustrations.

ABOUT THE AUTHOR

THOMAS HEALY is the author of *The Great Dissent*, which won the Robert F. Kennedy Book Award. He is a professor at Seton Hall Law School and has received fellowships from the Guggenheim Foundation and the Hutchins Center for African & African American Research at Harvard University. A native of North Carolina, he lives in New York City with his wife and two daughters.